Contract Law

Contract Law is an engaging and accessible new textbook aimed at students on core LLB and GDL courses. Combining comprehensive coverage of the curriculum with carefully developed pedagogical tools, the authors help students learn, gain an enhanced understanding of how the law works, and develop their ability to apply this newfound knowledge and understanding in assessment situations.

To be successful in assessments, students must be able to analyse and solve legal problems, while accurately and appropriately applying legal authority. The *Spotlights* series models these core skills alongside a full and thorough exposition of the substantive law.

Tracey Hough is an Associate Professor and the LLB Programme Director at Birmingham City University.

Ewan Kirk is Senior Lecturer in Law at Birmingham City University, where he has previously led the CPE/GDL Programme, as well as the LLB Programme and associated pathways.

SP●TLIGHTS

SHEDDING LIGHT ON THE LAW

Routledge Spotlights Series

*A new textbook series designed to help you translate
your knowledge of the law to assessment success.*

AVAILABLE NOW:

EU Law, Gerard Conway
Equity & Trusts 2nd edition, Scott Atkins
Public Law, Michael Doherty

FORTHCOMING TITLES:

English Legal System, Ryan Murphy

WWW.ROUTLEDGE.COM/CW/SPOTLIGHTS

SP☀TLIGHTS
SHEDDING LIGHT ON THE LAW

Contract Law

TRACEY HOUGH
EWAN KIRK

Routledge
Taylor & Francis Group

LONDON AND NEW YORK

First published 2019
by Routledge
2 Park Square, Milton Park, Abingdon, Oxon OX14 4RN

and by Routledge
711 Third Avenue, New York, NY 10017

Routledge is an imprint of the Taylor & Francis Group, an informa business

British Library Cataloguing-in-Publication Data
A catalogue record for this book is available from the British Library

Library of Congress Cataloging-in-Publication Data
Names: Hough, Tracey, author. | Kirk, Ewan, author.
Title: Contract law / by Tracey Hough and Ewan Kirk.
Description: Abingdon, Oxon [UK] ; New York, NY : Routledge, 2018. | Includes
    bibliographical references and index.
Identifiers: LCCN 2018003997 | ISBN 9781138933958 (hbk) | ISBN 9781138933972 (pbk) |
    ISBN 9781317390718 (epub) | ISBN 9781317390701 (mobipocket)
Subjects: LCSH: Contracts—Great Britain. | LCGFT: Textbooks.
Classification: LCC KD1554 .H675 2018 | DDC 346.4102/2—dc23
LC record available at https://lccn.loc.gov/2018003997

ISBN: 978-1-138-93395-8 (hbk)
ISBN: 978-1-138-93397-2 (pbk)
ISBN: 978-1-315-67828-3 (ebk)

Typeset in Bembo, Bell Gothic and Avenir
by Apex CoVantage, LLC

Printed by CPI Group (UK) Ltd, Croydon CR0 4YY

Visit the companion website: www.routledge.com/cw/spotlights

The dog on the front cover is Branko, a former street dog rescued by Balkan Underdogs, Charity no. SC045210 www.balkanunderdogs.com

OUTLINE CONTENTS

DETAILED CONTENTS

5 TERMS OF A CONTRACT

GUIDE TO THE SPOTLIGHTS SERIES

The Routledge Spotlights series is an exciting new textbook series that has been carefully developed to help give you a head start in your assessments. We've listened to lecturers and examiners to identify what it takes to succeed as a law student and we've used that to develop a brand new series of textbooks that combines detailed coverage of the law together with carefully-selected features designed to help you translate that knowledge into assessment success.

AS YOU READ

sections at the start of each chapter introduce you to the key questions and concepts that will be covered within the chapter to help you to focus your reading.

AS YOU REA

The focus of th

■ Identify th

KEY LEARNING POINTS

throughout each chapter highlight important principles and definitions to aid understanding and consolidate your learning.

KEY LEARN

■ Collective
  confider
  respo

EXPLAINING THE LAW

brings the subject to life through the use of practical examples to provide valuable context to your learning.

EXPLAININ

Only one as
dismissal w
Parliam

ANALYSING THE LAW

invites you to consider your own response to legal dilemmas and debates. Critical thinking is key to assessment success and, with this feature, our authors invite you to critique the law or evaluate conflicting arguments in a debate.

ANALYSIN

Take a mom
distinction.
Health S

APPLYING THE LAW

Problem questions will form a large part of your
assessment and **Applying the Law** allows you to
develop your problem-solving skills by showing how
the law can be applied to a given situation. Learn
how to interpret the law and apply it to any problem
question.

APPLYING

Imagine that
national cha
office tha

MAKING CONNECTIONS

will help you impress examiners, showing you how a
topic fits into the bigger picture, not just of the wider
subject but also across the legal curriculum.

MAKING CC
+ + + + + + + +
When you lo
of law, judic
operatic

POINTS TO REVIEW

bring together all of the principles and themes for the
chapter, helping to reinforce your learning.

POINTS TO

■ Tribunals car
■ Their merits
◀ The Le

TAKING IT FURTHER

Reading widely impresses examiners! **Taking it
Further** provides annotated lists of journal articles,
book chapters and useful websites for further reading
which have been carefully selected to help you to
demonstrate an enhanced understanding of the topic.

TAKING IT F

K McMillan and
not a law book
underpin mu
ook an

GUIDE TO THE WEBSITE

LEGAL EXERCISES
to test knowledge and promote critical thinking,
including exam/coursework questions and thinking
points for further study and reflection.

MULTIPLE-CHOICE QUESTIONS
for self-testing, helping you to diagnose where you
might feel less confident about your knowledge so you
can direct your revision time in the right direction.

REVISION ADVICE AND STUDY
TIP PODCASTS
will help you to improve your performance and raise
your grades.

KEY CASE FLASHCARDS
will help you to revise and remember the key cases
and the legal principle they illustrate.

UPDATES
on cases and legislation will help you to stay on top
of all the most important recent legal developments in
the subject area.

TABLE OF CASES

ALL REFERENCES ARE TO PAGE NUMBER

TABLE OF STATUTES

ALL REFERENCES ARE TO PAGE NUMBER

TABLE OF STATUTORY INSTRUMENTS

ALL REFERENCES ARE TO PAGE NUMBER

TABLE OF EUROPEAN LEGISLATION

ALL REFERENCES ARE TO PAGE NUMBER

1

CHAPTER 1
INTRODUCTION TO THE LAW OF CONTRACT

1.1 INTRODUCTION

Contract law plays an important function for us both in our roles as individuals and consumers; in commercial contracts, corporate and domestic conveyancing, employment law and many other areas of legal practice. It governs the rights and obligations of those entering into legally binding agreements.

Contract law falls under the umbrella of private law, which is part of the civil law legal system. It defines, governs and enforces relationships among individuals, associations and corporations in contrast to public law which focuses on the role of the law between citizens and the state. The main distinction between public and private law lies in those affected by its jurisdiction. Public law affects society as a whole, whereas private law affects individuals or small groups, businesses and families. Private law encompasses both property rights (rights in rem) and personal obligations (rights in personam). Let us look at an example to aid our understanding of the distinction between public and private law:

EXPLAINING THE LAW

If you saw a man run from a superstore with some stolen groceries under his arm, he is violating **public law**. He has committed the crime of theft, and that can be said to affect everyone. If the wedding caterer fails to turn up to your wedding to provide the catering services that they have agreed to then they have committed a breach of contract; this will affect you personally and not society at large. This falls under the umbrella of **private law**.

The law of obligations is one branch of private law and is the body of rules that organises and regulates the rights and duties arising between individuals. Obligations can be separated into two categories:

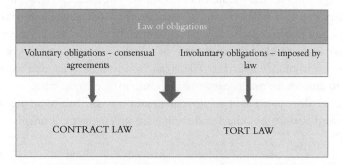

Figure 1.1 Categories of obligation

As illustrated in Figure 1.1, the law of tort and contract law are two important categories falling under the law of obligations. Consider the examples below to conceptualise the difference between the two bodies of law:

1) An agreement between two parties, where A agrees to sell a car to B for £10,000 to be delivered on 30 August, has arisen as a result of consent between two parties. The actions were voluntary and a contract has been created.

On the other hand, some obligations do not arise as a result of voluntary consent:

2) A restaurant owner will owe a duty of care to his clients to take care in food preparation to ensure that no harm can be caused to individuals from consuming contaminated food. The restaurant owner will have chosen to prepare your food, but will not have chosen to take care in its preparation. This duty has been imposed by law and is governed under the rules of tort; it is an involuntary obligation.

Whilst contract law is involved with voluntary obligations, it is important to mention that even where a voluntary contractual agreement has been made, in most instances there are involuntary obligations implied into the agreement and these involuntary obligations will bind the parties. These obligations originate as a result of common law and statute which impact upon the freedom of the respective parties to agree whatever terms they wish. The underlying concept of freedom of contract will be discussed a little later on, but it is appropriate to mention here that the law plays a significant role in the regulation of consumer contracts, mainly to ensure an equilibrium between traders and consumers where an imbalance in bargaining power frequently exists. The Consumer Rights Act 2015 is a recent example of statutory intervention in contract law in the regulation of consumer contracts.

1.2 WHAT IS A CONTRACT?

Both consumers and businesses enter into contracts on a very frequent basis. Contracts can be formed orally, by conduct, or in writing. Most organisations will wish to have a written contract so that all terms and conditions can be documented, but the method of creation will very much depend upon the nature of the contract. For instance, we would not expect to receive a written contract when buying a magazine from the newsagent or from a street vendor for a bunch of flowers. As far as legal requirements are concerned, it is not necessary to have a written contract unless the contract is of a particular nature, such as a contract for the sale of land or an insurance contract. There can, however, be evidential issues when a party is seeking to enforce an oral contract in demonstrating exactly what has been agreed. One party may deny the existence of an agreement and it is difficult to adjudicate cases where it is one party's word against the others and there is no independent confirmation of the agreement.

A contract can range from the very formal to the informal and some contracts are immediate whereas others are ongoing. Handing over a chocolate bar in the local shop for payment, purchasing a coffee from a vending machine, or downloading a song from the internet are all examples of immediate or instantaneous contracts. A more formal contract may involve booking a holiday, buying a car; or maybe purchasing something online, some flowers for your mother, a copy of Hough and Kirk *Contract Law* textbook from Amazon. Or you may wish to acquire something for use in your business; a builder may enter into a contract to purchase or hire a cement mixer, or order a weekly supply of concrete etc. Ordering a meal in a restaurant, having your hair cut, having a manicure or jumping on a bus are further examples of contracts, but for the provision of a service rather than actual goods. Then there are the more formal agreements, such as an agreement to purchase a piece of land, the lease of a flat, the acquisition of some shares in a company etc.

Examples of an ongoing service would be an agreement between a university and a catering services company to provide food and beverages in its cafeteria outlets or a delivery of milk three times a week to your home. Indeed, whether it be formal or informal, it is rare that a day will go past where you do not enter into some form of contract. Most of the time you will not really give much thought to the simple agreements; in purchasing a coffee in a local fast food restaurant your interest will focus more on how good the drink will taste rather than the fact that you have entered into a contract. That is, until something goes wrong. What if there are lumps in the coffee because the milk was sour? Or you were given tea instead of coffee. At this point you may stop to think of your rights and the rules of contract law will come into play.

Right at the outset, it is important to acknowledge that in order to have rights or to seek remedies under a contract, the first hurdle that needs to be overcome is to show that a valid contract exists. We will be looking at the components of a valid contract in the early chapters of this book, but it is pertinent to mention at this point that not all agreements will be enforceable under contract law. We first have to ascertain whether a promise made by one party to another is contractual. An obligation may not always be enforceable as a contract, for example the promise of a gift is not a 'contractual' obligation. A contractual obligation arises where a party has agreed to provide something in return for something of value given by the other party and in both cases the obligation must be voluntary in nature. So, in essence, the parties must not only show that there is an agreement; they must demonstrate that there is a 'bargain'. There must be no duress or undue influence. Provided that there is voluntary consent and a meeting of the minds, and indeed an intention to create legal relations, a contract will be formed and can be enforced. Once correctly formulated, if something does go wrong with the deal, it is open to either of the parties to prove the existence of a vitiating factor or to show a breach in order to pursue a contractual remedy.

Thus far, our contractual examples have involved commodities or services, but contracts span into many areas of life and commerce such as contracts of employment, land purchase, lease agreements, commercial contracts and many other areas that are far wider than the scope of this book and in many cases have their own special rules.

1.3 ORIGINS OF CONTRACT LAW

Contract law dates back to the middle ages at a time when the court system was made up of local and manorial courts. Whilst the history of dispute resolution from this time onwards is of historical interest, it is considered to be of limited importance to the system that we have today, which can be seen to have its roots in the nineteenth century at the time of the industrial revolution; so that is where we will begin.

Often referred to as the golden age of contract, the nineteenth century is where the classical or will theory prevailed. The classical theory advocates the notion of freedom of contract; an ideology that contractual terms should be left to the parties to agree between themselves. This ideology is underpinned by the concept of *laissez faire*, which translated roughly means that individuals should be left alone to make their own agreements with minimal or no external interference

The theory respects the sanctity of contract and relies upon the courts to respect the will of the parties (the Will Theory) and only to become involved where a dispute arises within a contract. The court should not involve itself in whether or not the terms were fair or whether there was an equilibrium in bargaining power; moreover, the approach should be that the parties have an inalienable right to regulate their own affairs and the courts should only be there to enforce agreements. Under the classical theory, courts were wary of interfering in agreements, whoever the parties were. This was specifically emphasised by Sir George Jessel MR in *Printing and Numerical Registering Co v Sampson*[1] where he declared:

> if there is one thing which more than another public policy requires it is that men of full age and competent understanding shall have the utmost liberty of contracting, and that their contracts when entered into freely and voluntarily shall be held sacred and shall be enforced by Courts of justice.

Thus, in essence, under the classical approach, a party to a contract should expect a contract to be enforced according to its terms even if the terms are unfair.

A popular area of debate in contract law and a common topic of assessment often revolves around whether the concept of freedom of contract really does exist and whether the classical or will theory is still a valid foundation upon which the rules of contract are based. Perhaps as a starting point we could draw upon many examples to show that the parties are still free to pursue their interests with minimal interference. For example, under the doctrine of consideration, the fact that the law will not protect us from a bad bargain still holds strong. One of the key principles of consideration in contract law is that 'consideration must be of some value but need not be adequate'.[2] So if I am silly enough to agree to sell my Porsche to you for £2,000, when it is really worth £60,000, the law will not protect me from this

---

1   19 Eq 462 (1875).
2   *Chappell v Nestle* [1960] AC 87.

bad bargain (unless of course some form of duress had been involved). On the other hand, particularly in more modern times, there are significant examples of intervention by the judiciary and the state that indicate a significant shift away from the classical approach. The main area of intervention involves areas where inequality in bargaining power exists between the parties. Intervention has been particularly prominent with regards to the terms of a contract, misrepresentation, duress and undue influence. As you work through the chapters of this text you will come across many areas where precedent has developed or statute has been passed, in the main to aid the consumer, although intervention can also be seen at play, but to a lesser extent, in commercial contracts.

Following the industrial revolution and over the twentieth century, legislative interventions and changes in judicial attitude led to a shift away from the strict *laissez faire* approach prevalent up to this time. As mentioned above, the most significant changes can be observed in non-commercial contracts, where freedom of contract appeared to be skewed far more to the advantage of large business, who traded using standard form contracts, over which the consumer had little, if any, input at all. Consumer contracts came to be regarded as 'contracts of adhesion' where there was no real negotiation and the attitude of the trader was that the buyer could either take it or leave it. There was little, if any, room for deviation from the standard terms. Contracts of adhesion were introduced as a means of saving time and prevent duplication in areas where large numbers of contracts are entered into and where it would not be practical to negotiate each agreement separately. Imagine if every time a mobile phone was sold, the trader had to draw up a specific contract for every deal.

Important pieces of legislation such as the Sale of Goods Act 1979, Unfair Contract Terms Act 1977 and the Misrepresentation Act 1967 are examples of just a few Acts that were passed with the aim of redressing the imbalance in power between large businesses and consumers. More recently, the Consumer Rights Act 2015 has been enacted, which provides significant rights for consumers in the sale of goods and services and the provisions for unfair terms to be struck down if they create a significant imbalance between the parties.

Indeed, today there are many types of contract that are regulated in some form or another, be it a contract of employment or a leasehold contract governed by various statutory protection. Whilst the principle of caveat emptor (let the buyer beware) does still exist today, it can be said to subsist in a much watered down form than existed a few hundred years ago. It is also true to say that the level of protectionism currently experienced in the commercial world is far more prolific in contracts with consumers than it is in business-to-business commercial contracts.

Overall, it can be seen that contract law has substantially evolved over the last century and up to the current time. Freedom of contract does still exist but has been substantially eroded as a result of the paternalistic approach of Parliament, which has intervened in many areas to prevent the abuse of power by those who enjoy superior economic control. It is recognised that a level of freedom must exist in the market to ensure competition and entrepreneurship, but at the same time this needs to be balanced with an acknowledgement that the more vulnerable elements of society, which generally speaking is the consumer, need a standard level of protection. The challenge for the law maker lies in balancing these two competing perspectives.

1.3.1 THE IMPACT OF EUROPEAN LAW

At the time of writing, Article 50 of the EC Treaty has recently been triggered following the UK's referendum vote to leave the EU. Consumer law in the UK is heavily influenced by EU law and, in the light of the fact that consumer protection law in the UK has recently undergone significant change with the implementation of the EU Consumer Rights Directive into UK law via the Consumer Rights Act 2015, many may wonder how the UK exit (hereafter referred to as Brexit) will impact on the law in this area.

Nothing will change in the short term, as we are obliged to follow EU law until we leave. In the medium term, the European Communities Act 1972 will be repealed and Parliament will enact legislation incorporating all current EU law into domestic law. In the longer term, any changes will very much depend upon how our future relationship with the EU evolves. Clearly the EU is a substantial trading party and it will be in the interests of all parties to pursue a relationship of mutual benefit. In future trade deals with EU members, the UK will have to comply with EU law, so it goes without saying that any changes in our domestic law will need to be compatible and not in conflict with our European counterparts.

Consumer law in the UK is mainly governed by statutes such as the Consumer Rights Act 2015 and, as such, the status quo should not be greatly affected by our departure from the EU. Much of the EU law will also survive, since EU directives require a member state to draft their own domestic legislation in order to implement their provisions and, as such, directive-derived UK statutes would require specific repeal to remove their provisions from domestic law. EU regulations, on the other hand, will need to be enacted by domestic law if we wish their status to be retained in UK law.

At the present time, there has been no consent on what sort of Brexit the UK will settle upon and the outcome may not contain everything that is sought, and an element of compromise may prove to be the way forward. A soft 'Brexit' is likely to entail an agreement wherein the UK retain a level of, or full access to, the European Single Market and European Economic Area (EEA) membership. Whilst EEA membership would allow full access to the Single Market, it is likely that, in return, the UK would have to contribute to the EU budget, permit freedom of movement and be subject to EU law without being able to contribute to it. A 'hard' Brexit on the other hand could possibly lead to no agreement being reached resulting in the UK having to conduct trade with the EU under the terms of the World Trade Organisation rules.

TAKING IT FURTHER

Atiyah, *The Rise and Fall of the Freedom of Contract* Oxford University Press, 1979

2

CHAPTER 2
FORMATION OF A CONTRACT

AS YOU READ

At the end of this chapter you should be able to:

- Identify the crucial components of an agreement
- Identify and appreciate the differences between bilateral and unilateral contracts
- Distinguish between an offer and an invitation to treat
- Distinguish between an acceptance and a counter-offer
- Identify the ways that an offer can be revoked
- Distinguish the various rules on acceptance

2.1 THE FACT OF AGREEMENT

A contract is a legally binding agreement consisting of enforceable obligations that have been voluntarily agreed between the parties. It is crucial to focus on the voluntary nature of an agreement as there are certain areas of law where obligations are not negotiated but are imposed by legal rules, such as tort law and criminal law.

In order for an agreement to be enforceable it must be possible to demonstrate that there has been a meeting of the minds, often referred to as a *consensus ad idem*.

In order to determine the *consensus ad idem*, the courts adopt an **objective approach** when assessing the intentions of the parties.

> **ESSENTIAL** DEFINITION: OBJECTIVE APPROACH
>
> The court will not necessarily be swayed by the interpretation placed upon the words and actions of the parties by themselves, nor can they reach into the minds of the parties at the time that the agreement took place (a subjective approach). Moreover, a conclusion will be drawn from the interpretation that a reasonable person, observing the behaviour of the parties, would place upon their exchanges. This is known as the 'objective' approach.

Perhaps the most cited case in this area is *Smith v Hughes* (1871),[1] in which Blackburn J famously stated:

> If, whatever a man's real intention may be, he so conducts himself that a reasonable man would believe that he was assenting to the terms proposed by the other party, and that other party upon that belief enters into the contract with him, the man thus conducting himself would be equally bound as if he had intended to agree to the other party's terms.

Many years later in *Storer v Manchester City Council*[2] Lord Denning succinctly summarised the position when he said: 'you do not look into the actual intent in a man's mind. You look at what he said and did. A contract is formed when there is, to all outward appearances, a contract.'

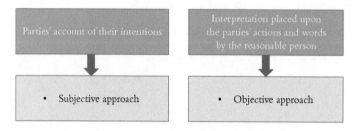

Figure 2.1 Objective v subjective

In *Investors Compensation Scheme Ltd v West Bromwich Building Society*[3] on interpreting a written document, Lord Hoffmann said:

> Interpretation is the ascertainment of the meaning which the document would convey to a reasonable person having all the background knowledge which would reasonably have been available to the parties in the situation in which they were at the time of the contract.

The case referred to above will be discussed in greater details in the later chapter on terms of a contract.

Recent cases provide us with evidence that the objective approach still holds strong. Focusing on the Supreme Court case of *Rainy Sky SA v Kookmin Bank*,[4] a clear reinforcement of the objective approach can be observed when Lord Clarke expresses the ultimate aim of interpreting a contractual provision 'is to determine what the parties meant by the language used, which involves ascertaining what a reasonable person would have understood the parties to have meant'.

1   *Smith v Hughes* (1871) LR 6 QB 597.
2   [1974] 1 WLR 1404.
3   [1998] 1 WLR 896.
4   [2011] UKSC50, [2011] 1 WLR 2900.

> ## KEY LEARNING POINT
> ....
>
> Certainty of law is extremely important in commercial transactions and permits individuals and companies to regulate their behaviours with a set of specific rules. If the subjective approach were favoured in contract law, the trading world would be rendered a rather uncertain place. If a subjective approach were followed, a party to a contract would no doubt express his intentions as being those that favour him at the time of disagreement rather than what the intention at the time of the contract truly was. Transactions must be certain, a function that would be severely undermined if, for example, one party were able to argue that when he agreed to sell a necklace for £5, he meant £500. An objective approach should ascribe a reasonable interpretation to the actions of the parties, based on the agreement at the time that it was concluded and is more likely to result in a consistent approach and uphold certainty within the market place.

This leads us on to question who the reasonable person might be. Historically referred to as the reasonable man, this person has been described as 'an ordinary person of either sex, not exceptionally excitable or pugnacious, but possessed of such powers of self-control as everyone is entitled to expect that his fellow citizens will exercise in society as it is today'.[5] In essence, the reasonable person is an individual from whose point of view the behaviour of a defendant can be judged. There is no technical definition, but it is fair to summarise from cases that have been before the courts that the reasonable person will be a fair-minded and informed observer[6] with a reasonable level of education.[7]

Having established a meeting of the minds, it is crucial to remember that the agreement must fall within the definition of a bargain. In the absence of a bargain there will be no binding obligation between the parties and the agreement will not be enforceable. The agreement will constitute a bargain if it is supported by consideration or made by deed. In addition, the law will not enforce social agreements, so the ability to establish an intention to create legal relationships is crucial. These concepts will be fully covered in later chapters.

The objective approach requires external evidence of an agreement. The traditional method of ascertaining this is through the identification of clear and unambiguous offer made by one of the parties and a full and unequivocal acceptance by the other party. Sometimes it is not quite as straightforward as the definition suggests and there is evidence within the law of other evidence being factored into decisions where the traditional, somewhat mechanical approach is unable to provide an answer. That said, instances where the traditional offer method of contractual analysis has not been followed tend to be exceptions rather than the norm.[8] *G Percy Trentham Ltd v Archital Luxfer Ltd* provides judicial recognition that the

....

5   *DPP v Camplin* [1978] UKHL 2.

6   *Healthcare at Home Ltd v The Common Services Agency* [2014] UKSC 49.

7   *Hall v Brooklands Auto-Racing Club* (1933) 1 KB 205.

8   *Tekdata Interconnections Ltd v Amphenol Ltd* [2009] EWCA Civ 1209, [2010] 2 All ER (Comm) 302, [2009] 2 CLC 866.

traditional approach will apply in the vast majority of cases,[9] maintaining relative certainty and consistency within contract formation.

It must, however, be acknowledged that alongside the traditional method there exists an alternative 'subjective' philosophy on the determination of an agreement. There is evidence to suggest that Lord Denning favoured a *laissez faire* (subjective) approach in determining whether or not an agreement had been reached. In *Butler Machine Tool Co Ltd v Ex-Cell-O Corpn (England) Ltd*,[10] Denning opined that traditional analysis of offer and acceptance is outdated, arguing that a better way would be to consider the totality of communications that have taken place between the parties and evaluate the outcome of whether an agreement has been reached based upon their conduct. Whilst Denning's view was rejected in favour of the traditional approach, the approach has found favour in cases where it has not been possible to break the agreement into distinct categories for interpretation. The subjective approach can be clearly observed in the judgment of *G Percy Trentham Ltd v Archital Luxfer* mentioned above, where Steyn LJ stressed the importance of not losing sight of the commercial nature of the transaction. His conclusion was reached following an analysis of the actions and statements of the parties during the contractual negotiations. Notwithstanding the approach taken in this case, Steyn conceded that a contract could also have been established using the traditional method.

Whilst the subjective approach certainly has a place in the modern–day analysis and reflects the commercial reality of some agreements, the traditional classical method, based on an objective approach, still holds strong within the foundations of contractual agreement. In most instances the courts will strive to analyse the agreement in line with the classical approach, seeking out the distinct components of an offer, acceptance, consideration and legal intention to contract.

APPLYING THE LAW

Mohammed owned two antique swords that had been in his family for over 100 years. He had been advised by an antique dealer that the swords were worth about £10,000 each and that he should not accept any less than £9,000 for each piece. Mohammed emailed Iqbal offering to sell him a sword for £8,000 (his finger slipped on the keyboard when typing his message; he meant to ask £9,000 for the sword). Iqbal read the email one hour later and replied immediately, agreeing to pay the £8,000 asked by Mohammed. Mohammed emailed back and apologised, saying that he had intended to ask for £9,000 as that is what the sword had been valued at.

Using the objective test of agreement, do you think that Mohammed will be compelled to sell the sword to Iqbal and, if so, what price must he sell the sword for?

---

9 [1993] 1 Lloyd's Rep 25.
10 [1979] 1 All ER 965.

Whilst it is clear that Mohammed intended to sell the sword for £9,000, the price that he offered in the email was £8,000. The offer was clear and unequivocal and so would constitute a valid offer. What would a reasonable person believe was being offered? A reasonable person would believe that the asking price was £8,000. Indeed, Iqbal believed Mohammed was offering to sell the sword for £8,000. It is irrelevant what Mohammed's intentions were (subjective); the picture that was portrayed to any reasonable person looking at the activity between the parties was that there was an offer of a sale for £8,000.

2.1.1 OFFER

In order for an agreement to constitute an enforceable contract, the offeror (that is the person making the offer), must make an offer that is capable of being accepted by the other party, known as the offeree. An offer has been defined by Professor Treitel as 'an expression of willingness to contract on certain terms, made with the intention that it shall become binding as soon as it is accepted by the person to whom it is addressed'.[11]

The expression of willingness to contract may be oral or in writing. The most usual methods are by letter, advertisement, email and even by conduct provided that it is possible to identify a definite promise to be bound by specified terms. The intention will be determined by an objective assessment of what was intended and not what was going on in the actual minds of the parties at the time of the agreement, or indeed what the parties claim to have been their intention at the time. The objective approach can be clearly identified in the statement of law approved by Goff LJ in *Allied Marine Transport v Vale do Rio Doce Navegacao SA (The Leonidas)*:[12] 'If the offeror so acts that his conduct, objectively considered, constitutes an offer and the offeree, believing that the conduct of the offeror represents his actual intention, accepts the offer, a contract will come into existence.' An offer can be made to an individual, a group of persons and to the world at large.[13]

2.1.2 OFFER VS INVITATION TO TREAT

Fundamental to the process of determining an agreement is being able to pinpoint exactly when an offer has occurred. An offer must be distinguished from all other negotiations that take place leading up to the agreement. Referring back to Treitel's definition, you will note that an offer must be capable of acceptance in its unaltered format. Any statement falling short of this definition or inviting further negotiation is known as an invitation to treat. For example, 'Would you be interested in buying my iPad?' would be classed as an invitation to treat as it is an attempt to start a negotiation process. It is not always easy to determine when a statement constitutes and offer and when it will be an invitation to treat; the lines are sometimes blurred.

....

11 Treitel, *The Law of Contract*, 13th edn, p. 8.

12 [1985] 1 WLR 925.

13 *Carlill v Carbolic Smoke Ball Co* [1893] 1 QB 256.

By way of illustration, take a look at the case of *Harvey v Facey*,[14] which involved the sale of a piece of land:

HARVEY V FACEY [1893] AC 552

A telegram was sent to the respondent which said 'Will you sell us Bumper Hall Pen? Telegraph lowest cash price.' The respondent replied saying 'Lowest price for Bumper Hall Pen, £900.' The appellants replied by telegram stating 'We agree to buy Bumper Hall Pen for £900 asked by you.' The appellant, having received no response, brought an action for **specific performance** against the respondent.

Held: the statement 'Lowest price for Bumper Hall Penn, £900' was simply a response to a request for information, i.e. a minimum price that the respondent required if he decided to sell. The final telegram was deemed to be an offer that was never accepted.

Contrast this decision to *Bigg v Boyd Gibbons Ltd*,[15] where a different conclusion was reached on the sale of a piece of land. Here, the court was of the view that the parties had gone far enough in their negotiations for a binding agreement to have been reached. This case is also significant as it confirms that even where the word 'offer' has been used in negotiations, it will not necessarily mean that there is an offer in law.

ESSENTIAL DEFINITION: SPECIFIC PERFORMANCE

An equitable remedy awarded by a court requiring a party to perform a specific contractual act. It is an alternative to awarding damages, and is frequently used in actions concerning land

---

APPLYING THE LAW

Look at the following two statements and see if you can determine which statement will constitute an offer and which will be an invitation to treat:

'I am thinking of selling my Rolex watch. I have been advised that £4,000 would be a fair asking price. Would you be interested in buying it?'

---

14 [1893] AC 552.
15 [1971] 2 All ER 183.

Does this statement fulfil the criteria of an offer? Is it a definite promise to be bound by specified terms?

'I will sell you my Rolex watch for £4,000.'

Is this statement a definite promise to be bound by specified terms?

The first statement is the invitation to treat. It would not amount to an offer as the very words 'I am thinking' do not show the requisite commitment to selling the watch at a specified price. The statement is simply inviting negotiation. The second statement is far more clear and specific and would fulfil the requirements of an offer.

In considering the distinction between an offer and invitation to treat it is helpful to look at and contrast two cases from the 1970s, *Gibson v Manchester City Council*[16] *and Storer v Manchester City Council.*[17]

In *Gibson*, the dialogue between the parties was analysed to determine whether an intention to be bound could be established:

GIBSON V MANCHESTER CITY COUNCIL [1979] 1 WLR 294

The case arose at a time when the council permitted tenants to purchase their council homes. Mr Gibson requested details on purchasing his home and received a letter from the council stating that it 'may be prepared to sell the house to you'. Mr Gibson was invited to complete an application if he wished to pursue the sale. The form was completed, but in the period between making the initial enquiry and the submission of the completed form the council changed its policy on house sales. The issue before the court was whether or not a contract for sale had been concluded when Mr Gibson submitted his form.

Held: the agreement was not upheld. The House of Lords found no clear indication in the letter from the council that it intended to make a binding promise. The letter was no more than an invitation to treat and Mr Gibson's completed form was an offer which had never been accepted by the council.

Storer v Manchester City Council differed somewhat in its facts. The tenant received a communication from the council which stated 'If you will sign the Agreement and return it to

---

16 [1979] 1 WLR 294.
17 [1974] 1 WLR 1403.

me, I will send you the Agreement signed on behalf of the Council in exchange'. The words of the communication were deemed to fulfil the formalities required to constitute a valid offer. At the point in time that the tenant accepted this offer a binding agreement was concluded.

As illustrated, the courts will look at the facts of each case in reaching a decision on the distinction between an offer and an invitation to treat. However, due to the sheer volume of transactions that take place on a daily basis, it is fortunate that some principles are well established in law and ably assist us in drawing the distinction between the two categories. We shall now consider these areas.

2.1.3 ADVERTISEMENTS

In most instances, advertisements will be classified as invitations to treat, with the exception of unilateral contracts (discussed further below). The case of *Partridge v Crittenden*[18] provides reliable authority that a newspaper advertisement is an invitation to treat.

PARTRIDGE V CRITTENDEN [1968] 1 WLR 1204

The defendant was charged with the offence of offering for sale a live wild bird, contrary to s. 6(1) Protection of Birds Act 1954. The advertisement read:

'Bramble finch cocks, bramble finch hens 25s each.'

Held: the defendant was not guilty of the offence as the advertisement was an invitation to treat. The offer would come later, when a person offered to buy a bird at the stated price.

If advertisements falling into this category were regarded as offers, the result could be irrational. A contract would be formed every time a customer requested the advertised goods. This could lead to problems if the seller ran out of the advertised product, a conundrum often referred to as 'the limited stocks argument'.[19] If a product were suddenly in high demand and ran out, imagine the impact upon the seller who could be sued for breach of contract by potentially hundreds of people!

An exception to the rule is where a unilateral contract exists. A unilateral contract is an agreement where one party promises to perform a specified act subject to performance of a reciprocal act by the other party. Such contracts are often referred to as 'if' contracts or 'reward' contracts and are generally open to the whole world. In the main, contracts will be bilateral, which means that they involve a promise in exchange for a promise. The contract will only be unilateral if it is not possible to provide a promise in response to the promise made by the offeror. A unilateral offer can only be accepted by performance of the specified

---

18 [1968] 1 WLR 1204.

19 *Grainger and Sons v Gough* [1896] AC 325.

act. An example is an advertisement promising a reward to a person who finds the missing dog of Dr Kirk (illustrated on the cover of this text) and returns him safely to Dr Kirk. In such instances, you could not claim the reward by promising to find and return the dog; you would need to actually present the dog to its owner! So, to summarise, where it is only possible to accept an offer by performing the stated act, the contract will be unilateral.

The leading case on unilateral contracts is set out below:

CARLILL V CARBOLIC SMOKE BALL COMPANY [1893] 1 QB 256

This very well-known case involved the sale of a flu prevention medicine called 'the Carbolic Smoke Ball'. The advertisement for the smoke ball included a promise by the defendants that they would pay £100 to any person who contracted influenza after using the smoke ball correctly for a specified period of time. The defendants also stated that they had deposited a sum of £1,000 with a named bank as a gesture of their sincerity in their offer. Mrs Carlill purchased a smoke ball and used it in the prescribed manner but contracted influenza. She claimed the £100 but the defendants refused to pay. The main defences raised by the Smoke Ball Company were:

1   the advertisement was a 'mere puff' – nothing more than advertising hype, and
2   the offer had not been directed to a specific person and that Mrs Carlill had not accepted the offer.

Held: in considering the 'mere puff' argument, the House of Lords determined that a reasonable person in the shoes of the defendant would have taken the offer seriously and, in particular, would have been influenced by the cash that had been deposited to settle claims.

Nor did the House of Lords yield to the contention that the advertisement failed to be an offer because it had not been directed to a specific person. On the contrary, the Lords were satisfied that an offer had been made to any person who fulfilled the condition stated in the advertisement. Since this case, it is now accepted that an offer can be made to the world at large. On the argument put forward that Mrs Carlill had not accepted the offer, the House of Lords was satisfied that the nature of the offer had had the effect of waiving the need to communicate acceptance. It was inconceivable that every person who purchased the smoke ball would contact the company; moreover the reality of the situation dictated that only purchasers who contracted influenza after using the smoke ball were likely to communicate with the company.

Another case that provides a proficient illustration of a unilateral contract is *O'Brien v MGN Ltd*.[20] Here an advertisement in the *Daily Mirror* for a scratch card game with a high cash

---

20 [2001] EWCA Civ 1279, [2002] CLC 33.

prize was held to be an offer. Acceptance came when anyone with a winning scratch card telephoned the company to claim their prize.

As mentioned earlier, reward cases are further examples of unilateral contracts. If Dr Kirk placed his advertisement in the local shop window offering a £100 reward for the safe return of his dog, it would be a nonsense to say that the person returning the dog was only making an offer at that stage. It would put Dr Kirk in the advantageous position of having not to pay the reward to the person who returned the dog! There are two leading cases on rewards that illustrate the position well[21] and these are discussed later in this chapter under communication of an offer.

2.1.4 GOODS ON DISPLAY

The general rule is that goods on display in a shop will constitute an invitation to treat. The rule is well established and can be illustrated from an analysis of many cases. One of the best-known cases on shop window displays is *Fisher v Bell*:[22]

FISHER V BELL [1961] 1 QB 394

The case involved the sale of a flick-knife displayed with a price in a shop window. A prosecution was taken against the shopkeeper under the Restriction of Offensive Weapons Act 1961, a statute that made it an offence to offer for sale items of this nature.

Held: the shopkeeper was found not guilty of the offence on the basis that Lord Parker determined that the display of a priced article in a shop window was an invitation to treat and not an offer for sale.

The law on goods for sale on a self-service display is also well established. The case of *Pharmaceutical Society of Great Britain v Boots Cash Chemists (Southern) Ltd*[23] provides the authority for the fact that goods for sale on shelves constitute an invitation to treat.

PHARMACEUTICAL SOCIETY OF GREAT BRITAIN V BOOTS CASH CHEMISTS (SOUTHERN) LTD [1952] 2 ALL ER 456; [1953] 1 ALL ER 482

Customers were able to take certain medicines from the shelf in a self-service store. The products would then be taken to the till and paid for. However, the Pharmacy and Poisons Act 1933 made it an offence to sell certain medicines unless they were under

---

21 *Williams v Carwardine* (1833) 5 C & P 566, 172 ER 1101, *R v Clarke* (1927) 40 CLR 227.
22 [1961] 1 QB 394.
23 [1952] 2 All ER 456, [1953] 1 All ER 482.

the supervision of a registered pharmacist, and Boots Cash Chemists were charged under this offence. The prosecution argued that the sale took place when the customer put the item(s) in their basket, whereas the defendants argued that the sale took place at the cash counter.

Held: the sale was completed at the cash desk, where the customer made an offer to the cashier to buy. At this point a registered pharmacist would supervise the sale and could either accept or reject the offer, thus meeting the requirements of the statute.

ANALYSING THE LAW

Imagine the position if goods on display were held to be an offer. A customer would be regarded as accepting that offer as soon as s/he selected the goods and put them in the trolley. The contract would come into place at this point and the customer would not be able to put the goods back. Such a rule would lead to absurd consequences. Imagine if you were to put a net of oranges into your basket and later decide that you would prefer a punnet of plums. If the display was an offer, it would be too late for you to change your plums for oranges as the contract would have been complete when you put the oranges into your basket. What other consequences could you envisage in such circumstances? Think about electronic transactions; imagine if once you clicked on an item and placed it in your basket you were obliged to buy – what if you were purchasing some new shoes and you had clicked on the wrong size or colour?

Fortunately, the law has followed a pragmatic approach in this area and we can freely add or remove items for our basket up until the time that we have checked them out with the cashier or self-service checkout area, i.e. when the shop takes payment for the goods. There are also specific rules for goods purchased on the internet which will be discussed later in this chapter.

There are some limited circumstances in which a display of goods may amount to an offer, but this is the exception rather than the norm. An example might be where there are goods being promoted in a special sale. The American case of *Lefkowitz v Great Minneapolis Surplus Store*,[24] is a good illustration of this point:

LEFKOWITZ V GREAT MINNEAPOLIS SURPLUS STORE, 86 NW 2D689 (1957)

A newspaper advertisement placed by GMSS read: 'Saturday 9 a.m. sharp: 3 brand new fur coats, worth $100. First come first served. $1 each.' The plaintiff, who was a

24 86 NW 2d689 (1957).

man, arrived at the defendant's store wishing to buy one of the coats. The defendant refused to sell to him on the grounds that the coats were for women.

Held: the advertisement was an offer. It was clear and unambiguous and left nothing at all for negotiation.

KEY LEARNING POINT

The act of determining between an invitation to treat and a unilateral offer often creates uncertainty. That is because it is not always as clear cut as we would like it to be. Let us offer some further clarification on this point.

Consider where a promise is made in response to another promise, for example: Would you like to purchase one of my puppies when they have reached 3 weeks old for £200? If you provide an affirmative response, there will be a bilateral contract. The promise to buy at the stated price is sufficient to create an agreement that is legally enforceable.

On the other hand, a unilateral contract will only exist when a requested act has been performed. Hence, if I place an advert in the local newspaper stating that I will give a puppy to the first person coming to my home and paying £200, the conditions are very clear and unequivocal and the only way that acceptance can occur is by performance of the stated act. The defining point is that a unilateral contract will only exist if the method of response is by performance of an act. In the example above, that would be for a person to come to the house and pay £200 for a puppy. On the other hand, the bilateral contract can come into existence via an exchange of promises and it does not matter that the transfer of the goods will take place in the future. Thus, in the example above the promise to purchase the puppy when it reaches three weeks old is sufficient to cement the agreement.

2.1.5 AUCTIONS

A notice advertising an auction will constitute an invitation to treat only,[25] even if the notice states that lots will be offered for sale.[26] With regard to bids, the rule that a call for bids is an invitation to treat and the resulting bids amount to offers was established long ago in the case of *Payne v Cave*[27] and has since been embodied into s. 57(2) Sale of Goods Act 1979. The auctioneer can then accept or reject these bids. The sale is completed on the fall of the auctioneer's hammer, before which either party can withdraw.

25 *Harris v Nickerson* (1873) LR 8 QB 286.
26 *British Gas Auctions Ltd v Wright* [1972] 1 WLR 1519.
27 (1789) 3 Term Rep 148.

SECTION 57 SALE OF GOODS ACT 1979

(1) Where goods are put up for sale by auction in lots, each lot is prima facie deemed to be the subject of a separate contract of sale.
(2) A sale by auction is complete when the auctioneer announces its completion by the fall of the hammer, or in other customary manner; and until the announcement is made any bidder may retract his bid.
(3) A sale by auction may be notified to be subject to a reserve or upset price, and a right to bid may also be reserved expressly by or on behalf of the seller.

Where goods are sold at auction with a reserve price, no contract will exist if the auctioneer attempts to accept a bid lower than the stated reserve price. However, where no reserve has been stipulated, the lot itself will constitute a unilateral offer and a contract will be formed between the property owner and the highest bidder, even if the auctioneer fails for whatever reason to accept the highest bid. This rule can leave the owner of property in a position of having to sell their goods at a value much lower than their worth.[28] So what is the relationship between the auctioneer and the highest bidder? In *Warlow v Harrison*[29] it was held that a **collateral contract** exists between the auctioneer and the person making the highest bid. The collateral contract is formulated in the sense that the auctioneer, in making a call for bids, is making an offer to accept the highest bid. This offer is accepted by the making of bids. If the auctioneer then refuses to sell to the highest bidder he will be in breach of his contract with that person, as illustrated in the following case:

BARRY V HEATHCOTE BALL & CO (COMMERCIAL AUCTIONS) LTD (2000), THE TIMES, 31 AUGUST (CA)

Two machines were placed for auction without a reserve. When it became apparent that the highest bid would fall nowhere near the value of the machines, the auctioneer withdrew them from sale. The claimant contended that, as the highest bidder, he was entitled to the machines for a price of £200 each regardless of the fact that their value was £14,251 each.

Held: following the precedent in *Warlow v Harrison*, the court confirmed that there was a **collateral contract** between the auctioneer and the claimant and the damages awarded to the claimant were calculated based upon the difference between the market value and his highest bid.

28 *Barry v Heathcote Ball & Co (Commercial Auctions) Ltd* (2000) The Times, 31 August (CA).
29 (1859) 1 E & E 309.

ESSENTIAL DEFINITION: COLLATERAL CONTRACT

A collateral contract will exist where the parties to one contract enter into or promise to enter into another contract. Thus, the two contracts are connected and the secondary contract may be enforced even though it forms no constructive part of the original contract.

2.1.6 TENDERS

It is commonplace for businesses to outsource certain functions or ancillary responsibilities relating to their business. Some examples would be the cleaning of an office building, or the provision of catering services within a large organisation like a factory or university. Local authorities usually contract out the provision of refuse collection services and housing maintenance services. Where a business wishes to outsource a service, they will call for the submission of tenders for the work. A request to tender will generally constitute an invitation to treat and the tenders will be offers. The business is then free to accept the tender that it considers to be most appropriate to their needs. Care must be taken when drafting a tender, however, as in certain instances a call for tenders has amounted to an offer. Once such instance occurred in *Harvela Investments Ltd v Royal Trust Company of Canada Ltd*,[30] where two parties were invited to tender for the shares of another individual in the company. The telex inviting tenders stated that the company would accept the highest offer. When a dispute arose, the House of Lords ruled that the telexes were offers of a unilateral contract to sell to the highest bidder, which would be accepted by the person having met the condition.

The issue was also considered in the following case:

BLACKPOOL & FYLDE AERO CLUB LTD V BLACKPOOL BOROUGH COUNCIL [1990] 1 WLR 1195, CA

The local authority sent invitations to tender to the claimant and several other interested parties for concessions to operate pleasure flights from Blackpool airport. The invitation specified a date and time by which all tenders had to be received. The aero club posted its tender in the town hall letter box ahead of the deadline. The letter box should have been emptied at noon on the deadline date, but due to an oversight it was not opened until later. Consequently, the aero club's tender was not considered.

Held: the Court of Appeal found there to be an implied promise by the council that they would consider tenders submitted in accordance with the invitation. Tenders

---

30 [1986] AC 207, HL.

had been invited from a small number of specific parties connected with the airport and the invitation had laid down a clear and familiar procedure, which would foster a reasonable expectation by tenderers that, if their tender had been submitted in accordance with the instructions, it would be considered. As well as a bilateral contract with the party from whom the council had accepted the tender, the council also had a separate unilateral contract with the aero club. Since the aero club had met the specified criteria of the offer, they had the right to have their tender considered and, in not considering their tender, the council was liable for damages to compensate the aero club for loss of opportunity.

2.2 COMMUNICATION OF OFFERS

An offeree must be aware of an offer in order to accept it.[31] Thus the timing of an offer can be critical.

EXPLAINING THE LAW

Let us consider the example of a poster in a shop window advertising a £100 reward to anyone who finds and returns the advertiser's Persian cat. If Simon, who has not seen the advertisement, returns the cat, he cannot claim the reward. However, if Sam sees the advertisement and returns the cat because it is making a nuisance of itself in his garden but also with a view to claiming the reward, there will be a contract and he can claim the reward. Whereas if Ellie saw the poster, but has forgotten about it by the time she returns the cat, there will be no contract and she cannot claim the reward.

The two reward cases mentioned earlier illustrate this principle:

Williams v Carwardine[32] concerned the provision of information that led to the conviction of a murderer. It was ascertained that the reason for giving the information was not specifically in relation to claiming the reward. The court held that, although the provision of information by the claimant was induced by other motives, and not the offer of a reward, she still knew about the offer and thus could claim the reward. Her reasons for giving the information were irrelevant. Alternatively, in the Australian case of *R v Clarke*[33] a claim for a reward, which also

31 *Taylor v Laird* (1856) 1 H & N 266, 25LJ Ex 329.
32 (1833) 5 C & P 566, 172 ER 1101.
33 (1927) 40 CLR 227.

involved a request for information that led to the conviction of a murderer, was not upheld. Clarke had provided the required information, but his motive had been to clear himself of the conviction. In this instance, it was found that a contract had not come into existence. It was unclear whether Clarke had the reward in mind or not when he provided information that led to the conviction of a murderer, as explained by Higgins J:

> Clarke had seen the offer ... but it was not present in his mind – he had forgotten it and gave no consideration to it in his intense excitement as to his own danger. There cannot be assent without knowledge of the offer; and ignorance of the other is the same thing, whether it is due to never hearing of it or to forgetting it after hearing.

2.2.1 TERMINATION OF OFFER

2.2.1.1 REVOCATION

An offer can be revoked at any time before acceptance, but cannot be revoked after acceptance has taken place.[34] But what is the position where an offeror has agreed to keep an offer open for a specified period of time? Clearly, the offer cannot be accepted after the time period has elapsed, but the position needs to be considered more carefully when the offeror states a wish to withdraw the offer before the time limit has elapsed. By way of illustration, if Bill offers to sell his collection of toy soldiers and agrees to keep the offer open for a week, can he can change his mind and revoke the offer after three days? The answer is yes, he can do this. Authority descends from the case of *Routledge v Grant*,[35] where the defendant agreed to keep an offer in relation to a leasehold agreement open for six weeks. After three weeks the defendant changed his mind and revoked his offer. This led to a dispute when the plaintiff attempted to accept the offer at the six-week stage. Since there was no consideration to support the promise to keep the offer open for a specified period the court determined that the offer could be withdrawn at any time, notwithstanding the fact that the withdrawal occurred before the expiry of the time limit.

Conversely, if consideration (i.e. something of value) is given for a promise to keep an offer open, revocation cannot be made before the time limit expires. For example, the payment of £1 for an option to keep an offer open in *Mountford v Scott*[36] for a specified period of time prevented revocation prior to the expiry of the time limit. The fact that a payment had been made specifically for this benefit meant that a contract had come into place. It did not matter that the consideration for the promise was only a nominal amount.

In order for revocation to be effective, it must be communicated and it will be effective when communication is received. Any later reference to the postal rule (discussed later in this chapter) for acceptances is not relevant to revocation of offer.

---

34 *Payne v Cave* (1789) 3 Term Rep 148.
35 (1828) 4 Bing 654.
36 [1975] 1 All ER 198.

The rules for communication of a revocation and acceptance by post are distinct from each other and should not be confused.

In *Byrne & Co v Van Tienhoven & Co*[37] withdrawal of an offer was valid upon receipt of a fax.

BYRNE & CO V VAN TIENHOVEN & CO (1880) 5 CPD 344

A letter of revocation was posted in Cardiff on 8 October to an address in New York. Acceptance of the offer was telegraphed on 11 October from New York to Cardiff. At this time the letter of revocation had not arrived at the New York address.

Held: there was a valid contract as the acceptance had taken place before the revocation had been received. This was the case even though the revocation was 'physically sent' before the acceptance.

EXPLAINING THE LAW

The law on revocation of offer is clearly established. Revocation is valid not when it is 'sent' but when it is communicated. On the other hand, caution must be exerted when considering an acceptance. As mentioned earlier, an acceptance by post is valid upon posting, something that will be discussed later in this chapter under the 'postal rule'. It is thus crucial to recognise that a **revocation** by post will be treated differently to an **acceptance** by post. It is possible for a revocation to be instigated before acceptance has taken place, but due to the special postal rules for acceptance, it could practically mean that an acceptance can take place even after a revocation has been attempted. Let us look at an example: Anil wrote to Beatrice offering for sale a consignment of wine for £200 on 15 June, but changed his mind the following day and posted a letter by second class post on 16 June revoking the offer. On the morning of 17 June, Beatrice wrote a letter of acceptance. The letter of revocation was received on the morning of 18 June. There will be a valid contract for the sale of the wine, even though the revocation was instigated before the acceptance. This is because revocation is effective upon communication – in this example, revocation was communicated on the morning of 18 June. The acceptance had been made before the revocation, because, as you have learned, postal acceptances are valid at the point of deposit with the post

---

37 (1880) 5 CPD 344.

office establishment, which in our example was the morning of 17 June. If you are thinking that may be unfair and possibly lead to harsh results, you are probably right, but that is the law!

Nowadays, it is acknowledged that many of our communications are instantaneous or electronic, which can in itself give rise to further issues regarding the time that a communication is effective.

2.2.1.2 INSTANTANEOUS COMMUNICATIONS

Where instantaneous communications are concerned, such as an agreement made on the telephone, it is deemed that a contract is formed when the words are clearly heard by both of the parties, so the acceptance must be within the hearing radius of the offeror. The case of *Entores Ltd v Miles Far East Corpn*[38] offers useful insight into this area of agreement formation. This case will be considered later when we look at acceptance of an offer.

What then is the position when a communication is received but is not read? Again, this is an area that has been the subject of litigation over the years. If Xavier sends a fax at 3pm from his office in London revoking an offer to Yogi at his business address in Cambridge, will the revocation be effective immediately? What if the same fax was sent at 11pm in the evening? Would the revocation take effect immediately, even though Yogi's office is closed at that time and does not re-open until 8am the next day?

The case of *Brinkibon Ltd v Stahag Stahl und Stahlwarenhandelsgesellschaft Gmbh*[39] is authority for the fact that the communication is effective when it arrives on the fax machine of the recipient. The fax in this case arrived during normal working hours. In *The Brimnes*,[40] a revocation notice sent during office hours but not seen by staff until the following Monday was held to be effective when it was received. This decision has been confirmed in the later case of *Mondial Shipping and Chartering BV v Astarte Shipping Ltd*.[41]

MONDIAL SHIPPING AND CHARTERING BV V ASTARTE SHIPPING LTD
[1995] CLC 10

A telex message withdrawing a ship from charter due to non-payment of the hire charge was sent just before midnight on a Friday. The time of revocation was crucial in relation to the agreement as the charterers were not in breach of their payment terms

---

38 [1955] 2 QB 327.
39 [1983] 2 AC 34, [1982] 2 WLR 264.
40 [1975] QB 929, [1974] 3 WLR 613.
41 [1995] CLC 1011.

until after midnight and if the revocation did take place before midnight, the notice would have been premature and invalid.

Held: the notice was effective at the commencement of business on the next working day, in this case that was the following Monday. Gatehouse J summarised the position in saying 'what matters is not when the notice is given/sent/dispatched/issued by the owners but when its content reaches the mind of the charterers'.

ANALYSING THE LAW

In *Mondial*, Gatehouse J placed a high level of significance upon when the content of a notice 'reaches the mind' of the other party. We have seen that the outcome in this case was that the revocation was effective on the next working day. This outcome is consistent with the decision and reasoning adopted in *The Brimnes*, where the notice was effective upon receipt because it was received during normal office hours, albeit not seen until the next working day. If we focus on when the notice would have 'reached the mind' of the other party, this would have been when it was received, which in this case was during working hours. Lord Wilberforce in *Brinkibon* focused on an analysis of the 'intentions of the parties' and stated that 'No universal rule can cover all such cases; they must be resolved by reference to the intention of the parties, by sound business practice and in some cases by judgment where the risks should lie.'

Henceforth, whilst the conclusion on effective revocation is not completely straightforward, case law does provide strong guidance to assist in reaching a reasoned conclusion in this area. We need to ask:

1 When was the revocation communicated?
2 Was that within normal office hours?
3 If out of normal office hours, when did business re-commence?
4 What is the normal practice followed by the parties in contractual communications in this line of business?

Since these cases were determined, there has been a radical shift in the way that we communicate within modern society. Nowadays, communications by fax and post are far less frequent than instantaneous modems of exchange. Internet, email, telephone and texting are all popular ways of conducting transactions. These areas will be covered later in this chapter when considering forms of acceptance.

So far, we have looked at revocation in the context of a bilateral offer. But what if the offer is unilateral? Remember a unilateral offer is one made to the world at large. Where an offer is unilateral, it would in many cases be impossible to communicate the revocation to the offerees, since in most cases the offerees will not be known to the offeror. Remember, a unilateral offer can be made to the world at large.[42] Guidance on revocations in this area can be taken from the American case of *Shuey v United States*,[43] where the court accepted that an offer can be revoked by using the same method of communication and same degree of publication as the initial offer.

ANALYSING THE LAW

In considering a unilateral contract, it has been established that acceptance takes place when the requisite condition is completed, i.e. the lost dog is returned to its owner. However, such a principle could lead to unjust results where an individual has almost completed the required conditions.

For example, let us consider the position if the Cornish Cycling Society were to offer a reward to anyone who cycled from Lands' End to John O'Groats and arrived before 5pm on 15 September. If Winston was three miles from the finishing post on the morning of 15 September, and the cycling society revoked their offer, the usual rule on revocation of unilateral contracts could mean that Winston had wasted much time, effort and expenditure only for the offer to be revoked just before completion. Whilst the behaviour of the offeror would be unethical, and would result in grave injustices, would such an action be upheld in law?

As a general rule, the courts will not permit an offer to be revoked once the offeree has commenced performance. This is supported by the judgment in *Errington v Errington and Woods*,[44] where a father permitted his son and daughter-in-law to live in a house that he had purchased on the condition that they paid the mortgage instalments. In compliance with a promise made by the father that the house would be theirs once the mortgage was paid off, the couple diligently made all payments. However, when the father died, his widow claimed possession of the house. The court held there to be a contract in place that could not be revoked whilst the couple continued to pay the mortgage instalments. Thus, following the approach of the court, it would seem, in our example, that the cycling society would be unable to revoke the unilateral offer made in respect of the cycle venture on the basis that Winston (and indeed many other competitors) has commenced and indeed almost completed performance.

2.2.1.3 LAPSE OF TIME

When an offer has no specified time limit stated for acceptance, it will come to an end when it is no longer possible for acceptance to take place. If an offer is open for a specified period of time, it will lapse at the end of the time period. Where a time period is not specified, the

42 *Carlill v Carbolic Smoke Ball Co* [1893] 1 QB 256.
43 92 US 73 (1875).
44 [1952] 1 KB 290.

general rule is that an offer will lapse after a reasonable period of time. The problem that then arises is what period of time can be regarded as a reasonable period of time? The outcome of any dispute will vary depending upon the subject nature of the contract. In *Ramsgate Victoria Hotel Co Ltd v Montefiore*[45] a purported acceptance in November of an offer made in June was deemed to be too late for an allocation of shares. It was deemed that the offer would have lapsed by the time that acceptance was attempted. Thus, in practical terms it could be said with some degree of certainty that an offer to sell a consignment of fresh fish is likely to lapse far more quickly than an offer to sell a consignment of tinned fruit.

2.2.1.4 DEATH

The death of the offeror will have the effect of terminating the contract if it relates to personal services that s/he had agreed to provide. Thus, if a celebrity had offered to take part in a reality TV show for a sum of £250,000, the offer would certainly lapse if he died.

If the offer was for non-personal services, the personal representatives may have to ensure completion of the services promised by the offeror. Much will depend on whether the death was notified to the offeree before acceptance was communicated. If the offeree was notified of the death before acceptance then the estate will not be bound by the contract. Whilst no authority exists relating to death of the offeree, it is generally accepted that death of an offeree will terminate the offer.

Figure 2.2 summarises the methods by which an offer can be terminated.

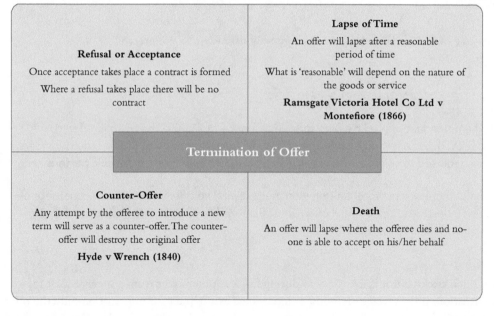

Figure 2.2 Termination of offer

---

45 *Ramsgate Victoria Hotel Co Ltd v Montefiore* (1866) LR 1 Ex 109.

2.2.1.5 ACCEPTANCE

For an acceptance to be valid, it must match the terms of the offer exactly. The acceptance must be clear and unequivocal and contain no conditions. Once again, the test is an objective one (see earlier). The famously cited words of Professor Treitel provide a succinct summary of the necessities of a valid acceptance: 'a final unqualified expression of assent to all the terms of an offer'.

As well as the acceptance having to 'mirror' the offer, it must also be communicated to the offeror and this can be by statement or conduct.

2.2.1.6 COUNTER-OFFERS

It is clear from Treitel's definition that an acceptance must be unqualified. This means that the acceptance must correspond exactly to the terms of the offer. If the offeree suggests different terms in response to an offer, it cannot constitute a valid acceptance. So, if George offers to sell his iPad for £250 and Poppy says that she will give him £225, Poppy's statement can never constitute acceptance. In fact, Poppy's statement will amount to a **counter-offer** which will destroy the offer for £250. Poppy cannot later come back to George and insist that he sells to her for £250.

ESSENTIAL DEFINITION: COUNTER-OFFER

A counter-offer will arise where the offeree responds to an offer and changes the terms of the offer. It will be an implied rejection of the initial offer and can in itself constitute a fresh offer. Once a counter-offer has been made the initial offer cannot be revived.

The case of *Hyde v Wrench*[46] provides a good illustration of a counter-offer:

HYDE V WRENCH (1840) 3 BEAV 334

The defendant offered his farm for sale at a price of £1,000. The plaintiff offered to pay £950, but a few days later agreed to pay the asking price of £1,000. The defendant then refused to sell to him and the plaintiff brought an action for **specific performance**.

Held: there was no contract between the parties. The offer of £950 was a counter-offer which destroyed the original offer. Thus, the initial offer of £1,000 was no longer open to the plaintiff to accept.

It is often tricky, but it is necessary to distinguish a counter-offer from a mere request for information. If the offeree's response is interpreted as a request for information only, the offer will remain open and available for acceptance, as illustrated in the case below.[47]

---

46 (1840) 3 Beav 334.
47 *Stevenson, Jacques and Co v McLean* (1880) 5 QBD 346.

STEVENSON, JACQUES AND CO V MCLEAN (1880) 5 QBD 346

The defendant offered to sell iron for a specified price per ton. The plaintiffs had responded and asked whether the defendant would accept the stated price for delivery over two months, or, if not, the longest limit that could be permitted.

Held: the plaintiff's statement was not a counter-offer but a mere request for information in relation to the offer terms. Thus, the offer remained open for acceptance after the plaintiffs request for information.

ASSESSMENT TIP

Provided that none of the terms have been altered by the offeree, there is a good chance that the offeree's response can be categorised as a request for information. The key questions to ask in distinguishing between a counter-offer and a request for information are:

1   Is the statement an attempt to clarify the terms and determine any flexibility? If yes, it is likely to constitute a request for information only and the offer will remain intact and capable of acceptance.
2   Does the statement go beyond a request for information and change the terms of the offer in any way? If yes, it is likely to constitute a counter-offer.

2.3 STANDARD FORM CONTRACTS

Nowadays many contracts are agreed using standard terms of business. Both parties will have their own trading provisions and will attempt to contract using their standard documentation to ensure that the contract is agreed on their particular terms. Confusion can often occur when both parties are seeking to secure a deal based on their own terms of business. The problem was illustrated in the following case which is often associated with the expression 'battle of the forms'.[48]

BUTLER MACHINE TOOL CO LTD V EX-CELL-O CORPN (ENGLAND) LTD [1979] 1 WLR 401

Ex-Cell-O had expressed an interest in purchasing a machine from Butler. Butler sent out a quotation for £75,535 accompanied with a copy of their standard terms of sale.

---

48 *Butler Machine Tool Co Ltd v Ex-Cell-O Corpn (England) Ltd* [1979] 1 WLR 401.

The terms included a price variation clause and a term that the seller's terms would prevail over any terms submitted by the purchaser. The machine was to be delivered at a later date. Ex-Cell-O placed an order for the machine at the stated price and sent their order along with a set of their own terms. Their terms did not include the price variation clause. The order contained an acknowledgement slip, which required a signature from Butler and a requirement to return the slip to Ex-Cell-O. The slip stated that the contract would be subject to the terms stated overleaf. Butler signed and returned the slip. Later, when the machines were delivered, Butler sought to enforce the price variation clause contained in their trading terms, and demanded an extra £2,892. Ex-Cell-O refused to pay, arguing that the contract had been agreed on their terms, which did not include a price variation clause.

Held: the offer to sell the machine on terms provided by Butler (which included the price variation clause) was destroyed by the counter-offer made by Ex-Cell-O. The contract was concluded on Ex-Cell-O's terms since Butler signed the acknowledgement slip accepting those terms.

From this case, it can be established that where there is a 'battle of the forms' with each party submitting their own terms, the 'last shot' rule will apply. This means a contract is concluded on the terms submitted by the party who is the last to communicate those terms before performance of the contract commences.

The decision in *Butler* is clearly consistent with the classical approach in determining an agreement, and also falls into line with the approach adopted in the earlier case of *Trollope and Colls Ltd v Atomic Power Constructions Ltd*[49] when Megaw J stated that 'the counter-offer kills the original offer'. That said, whilst the majority decision in *Butler* was underpinned by the classical approach, it is useful to look at the judgment of Lord Denning who did express his doubts on whether the classical approach was out-of-date in the modern commercial world:

In many of these cases our traditional analysis of offer, counter-offer, rejection, acceptance and so forth is out of date. The better way is to look at all the documents passing between the parties, and glean from them, or from the conduct of the parties, whether they have reached agreement on all material points – even though there may be differences between the forms and conditions printed on the back of them.[50]

It is clear from studying Denning's judgment that he took a more subjective approach in his analysis of the communications between the parties, showing preference for an analysis of the documentation and terms with a view to determining whether an agreement has been created based upon the material terms.

---

49 [1962] 3 All ER 1035.
50 Per Lord Denning in *Butler Machine Tool Co Ltd v Ex-Cell-O Corpn (England) Ltd* [1979] 1 WLR 401.

Whilst the traditional analysis still prevails in assessing whether an agreement has come into force, it appears nowadays that the courts will look both at the conduct of the parties and the formalities that have been exchanged when making a decision upon whether or not a binding contract has come into existence. And it is apparent from cases such as *Transformers & Rectifiers Ltd v Needs Ltd*[51] that where work has been done by the parties, it is more likely than not that a binding contract will exist.

2.4 COMMUNICATION OF ACCEPTANCE

The general rule is that in order to be effective, acceptance must be communicated[52] and received by the offeror.[53] Communication of acceptance can be made either by the offeror or an authorised agent. In some instances, it is possible for the offeror to waive the need for communication of acceptance. Unilateral contracts are a good example as in these types of contract it is generally accepted that the offeror has impliedly waived the need for communication. You will recall that a unilateral contract exists when the offeror makes a promise and the offeree performs the required act. In *Carlill*,[54] there was no requirement for acceptance to be communicated; the Court of Appeal determined that using the smoke ball in the specified manner was an act of acceptance.

The issue on the timing of communication arose in the following case concerning a bilateral contract.

ENTORES V MILES FAR EAST CORPN [1955] 2 QB 327

Entores, a London-based company, sent an offer by telex to purchase some goods from a company based in Amsterdam. The Dutch company sent an acceptance by telex but then failed to perform their obligations. Entores attempted to sue the owner of the Dutch company for damages. The controlling company, Miles Far East Corp, was based in the UK and under English law Entores could only bring the action in the UK if it could prove that the contract was formed in London rather than Amsterdam.

Held: the parties were in the same position as they would have been in if the discussion had taken place in each other's presence. Thus, acceptance took place when the acceptance was received by the plaintiffs, in London.

---

51 [2015] EWHC 269 (TCC), [2015] BLR 336.
52 *Powell v Lee* (1908) 99 LT 284.
53 *Entores v Miles Far East Corpn* [1955] 2 QB 327.
54 *Carlill v Carbolic Smoke Ball Co* [1893] QB 256, CA.

ANALYSING THE LAW

Ascertaining when an acceptance has been communicated is not always straightforward. The telex may arrive on a machine in an office but will not necessarily be read straight away. A message may be left on an answerphone but may not be listened to for some time after. So, when will acceptance be effective? These issues were considered earlier in the context of revocation of an offer. You will recall that there is no simple answer to the dilemma and considerations made in cases such as *The Brimnes*[55] and *Brinkibon Ltd v Stahag Stahl und Stahlwarenhandelsgesellschaft Gmbh*[56] are equally applicable to deciphering when acceptance is communicated. Indeed, you will recall from our earlier analysis on communication of a revocation that Lord Wilberforce summed up the position in *Brinkibon* when he mentioned the fact that no universal rule can cover such cases and the matters must be resolved by looking at business practice and an assessment of where the risks should lie.

2.4.1 SILENCE

A contract cannot be imposed upon an offeree by inserting a provision into the offer that the offeree's silence or inaction will amount to an acceptance. Imagine if you were telephoned by the owner of an expensive car garage who offered to sell you a Porsche for £50,000 and he stipulated that, if he heard nothing by the end of the week, he would assume you wanted the car and it was delivered to you the following day. This would constitute a somewhat ridiculous state of affairs! Thus, the rule exists to protect an unwilling offeree from being pulled into agreements where no consent has been given. The imposition of silence as a valid acceptance was considered in the following case.

FELTHOUSE V BRINDLEY (1862) 11 CB NS 869

An uncle offered to buy a horse from his nephew for a specified amount. He said that if he heard nothing further from the nephew he would consider the horse to be his for that sum of money. The nephew did not reply, but since he had previously agreed to sell the horse at auction, he asked the auctioneer to withdraw the horse from sale. The auctioneer erroneously sold the horse at the auction. The courts had to decide whether or not a contract existed between the uncle and the nephew for the sale of the horse

Held: the court determined that silence could not be imposed upon an offeree for the sale of an item. In this case, it was apparent that the nephew did want to sell to his uncle, but on the basis of the fact that this intention had not been communicated, there would be no contract of sale.

55 [1975] QB 929, [1974] 3 WLR 613.
56 [1983] 2 AC 34, [1982] 2 WLR 264.

2.5 POSTAL ACCEPTANCE

We have already established that the general rule on acceptance is that it must be communicated. We have noted that the unilateral contract is an exception to this rule. A further exception to the rule applies to acceptances that are made by post.

The rule on postal acceptances is that a contract will be formed at the time a letter is posted. This rule derives from the case of *Adams v Lindsell*.[57]

ADAMS V LINDSELL (1818) 1 B & ALD 681

The defendant wool-dealers wrote to the plaintiffs on 2 September 1817 offering to sell them a quantity of wool on certain terms. They requested an answer 'in the course of post'. Due to the fact that the defendants had incorrectly addressed the letter, it arrived two days later than would normally have been expected. On the same day of receipt of the offer letter (5 September), the plaintiffs posted a letter of acceptance. The defendant received the letter of acceptance on 9 September. However, on 8 September, having not received an acceptance to his offer posted on 2 September, the defendant treated the offer as having lapsed, and sold the wool to a third party.

Held: the offer was accepted as soon as the plaintiff's posted the letter of acceptance (5 September). This meant that the contract had been formed before the sale of the wool to the third party on 8 September and the defendant was in breach of contract.

The case was decided many years ago at a time when the rule that acceptance must be communicated had not been established. It was later confirmed in *Byrne v Van Tienhoven*,[58] when Lindley J stated that 'the contract is completed the moment the letter accepting the offer is posted, even though it never reaches its destination'.

On the point of the letter reaching its destination, the case of *Re London and Northern Bank, ex parte Jones*[59] provides authority that the letter must be properly stamped and addressed. Where accurately addressed, an acceptance will be valid even when it does not reach its destination. This was confirmed in *Household Fire and Carriage Accident Insurance Co v Grant*.[60]

---

57 1 B & Ald 681.
58 (1880) 5 CPD 344 at 348.
59 *Re London and Northern Bank, ex parte Jones* [1900] 1 Ch 220.
60 (1879) 4 Ex D 216.

HOUSEHOLD FIRE AND CARRIAGE ACCIDENT INSURANCE CO V GRANT
(1879) 4 EX D 216

The case concerned an allotment of shares. The defendant argued that he had never received the letter of allotment that had been posted out to him in response to his offer to purchase the shares.

Held: the court determined that a contract had been formed when the letter of allotment was posted, irrespective of the fact that the defendant did not receive the communication.

Brinkibon[61] is authority for the fact that acceptance is finalised when it is placed in the control of the Post Office, and this can occur either when the letter is placed into a post box, or when it is handed to an officer of the post who is authorised to handle postal communications.

It is possible for the postal rule to be ousted, or circumvented. *Henthorn v Fraser*[62] provides clarification that the postal rule will only apply where it is reasonable for the offeree to use the post as a method of communication. Thus in *Quenerduaine v Cole*,[63] where an offer was made by telegram, an acceptance by post was not valid, owing to the ruling of the court that an equally expedient mode of acceptance was required as that which had been used to communicate the offer. In the later case of *Holwell Securities Ltd v Hughes*,[64] the postal rule was ousted by the words 'by notice in writing' having been included in the offer terms. This meant that a letter of acceptance that had been posted by the offeree but not received by the offeror did not constitute valid acceptance as they had not had 'notice' in writing.

Thus, it is quite clear from established precedent that, in the event that a specific mode of communication is requested by the offeror, it must be complied with by the offeree to ensure that the acceptance is valid.[65]

ASSESSMENT TIP

When analysing an acceptance, the following sequence of questions should enable you to reach an accurate conclusion as to the validity and timing of an acceptance:

1   Does the offeror stipulate a specific method of acceptance and state that this is the only acceptable method? If yes, that method must be followed,

---

61 *Brinkibon Ltd v Stahag Stahl und Stahlwarenhandelsgesellschaft Gmbh* [1983] 2 AC 34, [1982] 2 WLR 264.
62 [1892] 2 Ch 27.
63 (1883) 32 WR 185.
64 [1974] 1 WLR 155.
65 *Manchester Diocesan Council for Education v Commercial and General Investments Ltd* [1969] 3 All ER 159.

> 2 Does the offeror stipulate a specific method and say nothing else? An acceptance will be valid by a different mode provided that the mode of acceptance is more expeditious than or equally as expeditious as the mode of acceptance requested. So, for example, where an offer has been made by telephone and the offeror has specified that the response should be by a return call, it would not be reasonable to post a reply and rely on the postal rule as providing an acceptable method of acceptance.

The postal rule does not apply to instantaneous communications such as fax and email.[66] Earlier in the chapter, we touched upon instantaneous forms of communication when we considered *Entores v Miles Far East Corpn*[67] and other similar cases[68] and concluded that what is really meant by something being communicated is when it 'reaches the mind' of the other party.[69] Whilst this is a useful guideline, there is no definitive definition available on when a communication will reach the mind of a contracting party. Indeed, Lord Wilberforce in *Brinkibon*,[70] recognised the issue, but did not provide any specific solution when he stated that no universal rule can cover all such cases.

Of course, where the parties are *inter praesentes* (within each other's presence), communication of acceptance is usually immediate. Any communication failure in such instances would be fairly obvious and could be rectified immediately. For example, using Lord Denning's example in *Entores*,[71] of acceptance being drowned out by a noisy aircraft: such an instance would require the acceptance to be repeated once the noise had subsided; or where a telephone line goes dead, the offeree must call back and complete the acceptance. But if it is the offeror's fault that the acceptance is not communicated, for example s/he does not hear the words, but fails to inform the other party, s/he cannot escape a contract on the basis that acceptance has not been communicated, since the offeree would be ignorant of the fact that the acceptance had not reached the mind of the offeror.

Where instantaneous communications are not simultaneous, once again the offeror cannot escape liability for a contract if it is his/her own fault that s/he does not receive a communication – for example, if the paper has run out in the fax machine, or if there is a fault on the telephone answerphone, or maybe his/her smartphone or email account has developed a fault and has lost his messages. However, if the offeree had been made aware that his communication has not been received by the offeror, there would be no binding contract.

---

66 *David Baxter Edward Thomas and Peter Sandford Gander v BPE Solicitors (a firm)* [2010] EWHC 306.
67 [1955] 2 QB 327.
68 *Brinkibon Ltd v Stahag Stahl und Stahlwarenhandelsgesellschaft Gmbh* [1983] 2 AC 34, [1982] 2 WLR 264, *The Brimnes* [1975] QB 929, [1974] 3 WLR 613, *Mondial Shipping and Chartering BV v Astarte Shipping Ltd* [1995] CLC 10.
69 Ibid.
70 *Brinkibon Ltd v Stahag Stahl und Stahlwarenhandelsgesellschaft Gmbh* [1983] 2 AC 34.
71 *Entores v Miles Far East Corpn* [1955] 2 QB 327.

In the current world of rapidly evolving technology, it would be helpful if we could provide more succinct guidance or specific criteria to follow when analysing transactions using the traditional methods of determining when an offer and acceptance has occurred. Sadly, such definitive guidance does not yet exist. We must work with the current, somewhat outdated, rules that we have, in the absence of modern precedent in this area.

APPLYING THE LAW

What then is the position if Jeff sends an email to Anna accepting an offer for the sale of a consignment of books that was made earlier that day by email but, due to a server failure, which is the fault of neither party, Anna does not receive Jeff's email. Will there be a contact?

The general rule for acceptances (not postal) is that the acceptance is effective when it ought reasonably to have come to the attention of the offeror.

A pertinent question to ask is which of the parties has greater control to avoid any risks?

What did Lord Wilberforce say generally on such matters in *Brinkibon*?

Emails are processed through servers, routers and internet service providers. Is an email an instantaneous form of communication? What rule should apply?

There are some statutory requirements in place for online purchases. Sellers must acknowledge receipt of payment under reg. 11 of the Electronic Commerce (EC Directive) Regulations 2002, but these regulations do not govern contracts created through email exchanges. The relevant regulation is set out below:

---

11. – (1) Unless parties who are not consumers have agreed otherwise, where the recipient of the service places his order through technological means, a service provider shall –
    (a) acknowledge receipt of the order to the recipient of the service without undue delay and by electronic means; and
    (b) make available to the recipient of the service appropriate, effective and accessible technical means allowing him to identify and correct input errors prior to the placing of the order.
(2) For the purposes of paragraph (1) (a) above –
    (a) the order and the acknowledgement of receipt will be deemed to be received when the parties to whom they are addressed are able to access them; and

(b) the acknowledgement of receipt may take the form of the provision of the service paid for where that service is an information society service.

(3) The requirements of paragraph (1) above shall not apply to contracts concluded exclusively by exchange of electronic mail or by equivalent individual communications.

Having now completed our study of the fundamental components of an agreement, we can look at Figure 2.3 to provide a brief summary of the key characteristics of an acceptance:

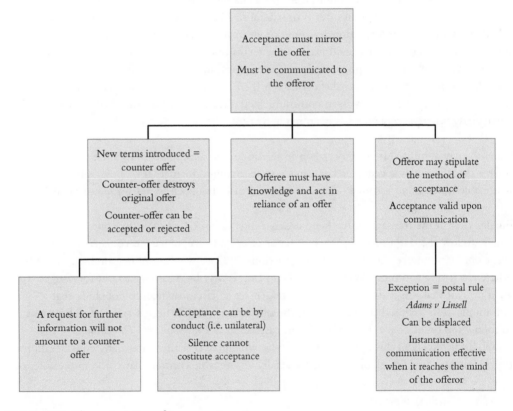

Figure 2.3 Characteristics of an acceptance

2.6 BRINGING IT ALL TOGETHER

You should now have a good understanding of the elements required to establish an agreement. We have looked at the various types of offer that can exist and the distinction between an offer and an invitation to treat. It is vital to establish the various stages of a contract following the traditional approach as far as possible to establish a valid agreement. It can often be the case later on, where a party seeking to avoid a contract may argue that there is no legally enforceable agreement in place. In such instances, the ability to identify each of the formal stages is paramount.

It is often not simply a case of pinpointing an offer and acceptance. The lines of categorisation are frequently blurred. For example, it may sometimes be difficult to establish whether a communication is an offer or an invitation to treat. Was the correspondence clear and unequivocal? Did the wording appear to be the start of a discussion over the terms, or was the wording very clear and final? A good way of deciding is to look at whether the communication can be accepted in its exact current form or whether further negotiation is required. Further factors that often need to be analysed are factors such as whether an offer was certain, or whether an offer is unilateral or bilateral. Maybe it is necessary to assess whether a request for information is simply to glean information or whether it can be interpreted as an attempted amendment to the terms upon which the offer has been made (usually the price). If so, the purported acceptance may amount to a counter-offer. Maybe there has been an attempt to revoke a contract. If so, it is necessary to establish whether the revocation has successfully been communicated ahead of any purported acceptance, particularly where acceptance has been made by post.

Careful analysis must also be undertaken in relation to an acceptance. Does the acceptance mirror the offer? Has acceptance been made in its required format? If by post, is the post a reasonable mode of acceptance to use? Maybe the offer has been by telephone or email?

Finally, what if the transaction has been entered into online? The rules for contracting online largely follow the traditional approach as far as offer and acceptance are concerned. The Electronic Commerce (EC Directive) Regulations 2002 assist with online purchases. However, where electronic communications have taken place, it may be necessary to put forward an argument that it is reasonable in the particular set of circumstances to conclude that a communication has reached the mind of the other party. Will it necessarily always be correct to follow the traditional rules established in cases such as *Brinkibon* and *The Brimnes*? No doubt, having worked through this chapter you will agree that there are many considerations to take into account in establishing that a legally enforceable contract has come into existence.

KEY LEARNING POINTS

- The key elements required for establishing a contractual agreement are offer and acceptance. A contract can be oral or in writing (some contracts must be in writing)
- An offer can be bilateral or unilateral. It must be clear and unequivocal
- It is important to understand the distinction between an offer and invitation to treat
- Important criteria of an offer – must be communicated, must be clear, can lapse after a reasonable period of time
- An offer can be terminated by acceptance, revocation, rejection, lapse of time, a counter-offer or death. Revocation must be communicated

- Acceptance must 'mirror' the offer. It must not be conditional. A conditional acceptance will amount to a counter-offer and destroy the original offer
- A mere request for information will not constitute a counter-offer
- Acceptance must be communicated. Unilateral offers can be accepted by conduct
- Where a specific method of acceptance is required, it must be followed
- An acceptance by post is valid as soon as it is posted, provided the post is an acceptable method by which to communicate
- The postal rule can be ousted by specific wording
- Instantaneous acceptances and electronic acceptances take place when they are communicated

TAKING IT FURTHER

Atiyah, *The Rise and Fall of Freedom of Contract* Oxford University Press, 1979

De Moor, 'Intention in the law of contract: elusive or illusory?' (1990) 106 LQR 632–655

Gower, 'Auction Sales of Goods Without Reserve' (1952) 68 LQR 457

Mik, 'The unimportance of Being "Electronic" or Popular Misconceptions about "Internet Contracting" ' (2011) 19(4) International Journal of Law and Information Technology 324

Morgan, 'Battle of the Forms: Restating the Orthodox' (2010) 69 Cambridge Law Review 230

Treitel, *The Law of Contract*, 13th edn, Sweet & Maxwell, 2011

3

CHAPTER 3
CONSIDERATION

3.1 INTRODUCTION

As we have seen from the last chapter, in order to establish the existence of a legally binding contract, it is necessary to identify certain essential elements. Without those elements, a contract simply cannot exist.

However, although a promise or an agreement can exist in fact, it may not be enforceable in law. The law does not enforce all promises, and even where there is a two-way relationship which results in agreement, there are still occasions when the law will not enforce them. This is where the element of consideration is important. Without consideration, there can be no legally enforceable contract in UK law. Therefore, unless supported by some form of consideration, an agreement will be viewed as a gratuitous promise, and will be unenforceable.

Consideration is a requirement in contract laws of all common law systems, including the UK and the US. However, it is not a requirement of Roman-law based systems and civil law systems, such as those found in continental Europe. This difference can result in questions asked about the relevance of consideration as part of contract; however, we will tackle this particular issue later in the chapter.

AS YOU READ

At the end of this chapter you should be able to:

- Understand the definition of consideration and its place in the requirements for a valid contract

- Identify the elements required for consideration to exist in a contract

- Understand the application of the rule of promissory estoppel as an alternative to the strict rule of consideration

- Apply the relevant legal tests to decide whether consideration exists in a given scenario

---

3.2 DEFINITION OF CONSIDERATION

For now, we need to consider the meaning of the word '**consideration**'. Unfortunately, this is a word which, when used in legal terminology, does not mean the same thing as it would do in everyday language, and so you need to ensure you are familiar with its meaning in a legal context.

ESSENTIAL DEFINITION: CONSIDERATION

'Some right, interest, profit or benefit accruing to the one party, or some forbearance, detriment, loss or responsibility, given, suffered, or undertaken by the other'[1] or 'the price for which the promise of the other is bought'.[2]

This is the key to the meaning of the word within its legal context. Consideration is the thing of value that forms the substance of the agreement itself. A key feature of this value is that there must be something of value moving in each direction. This goes to the heart of what consideration is there to regulate; there must be economic exchange taking place in the contract, 'something for something'. An everyday example would be when you buy something from a shop. You are exchanging something for something – your money for whatever you are buying.

This points to the essential role that consideration is there to play: to ensure that economic exchange between two or more parties is taking place within the contract. This is because contract law is there to regulate economic exchange, and this requires there to be a two-way transaction. It does not matter what value that exchange has – this is also a key element when thinking about consideration. As we see in section 5 below, the law is only there to ensure that this economic exchange has taken place, and not whether there is a bad bargain.

3.3 BENEFIT AND DETRIMENT

Within this definition it is probably quite easy to see where the benefit in a contract can come from – entering an agreement where you receive goods, services or monetary payment demonstrates clear benefit. There have been discussions regarding the amount of value involved, which will be discussed later. However, it can sometimes be more difficult to see where the 'detriment' in consideration can be found. Although it is possible to see how it acts as the mirror image of benefit, that where one party receives something of value it is because the other party is providing it, sometimes showing a detriment (or maybe showing how someone has avoided a detriment) as part of consideration can be more difficult. These issues were dealt with in the modern context in the case of *Williams v Roffey Bros and Nichols (Contractors) Ltd*,[3] which will be discussed later in this chapter.

---

1   *Currie v Misa* (1875) LR 10 Exch 153.
2   *Dunlop Pneumatic Tyre Co Ltd v Selfridge & Co Ltd* [1915] AC 79.
3   [1991] 1 QB 1.

APPLYING THE LAW

Think about how this works in practice with any contract you may have entered into recently. The rule of consideration requires that any contract, in order to be enforceable in law, has to have a benefit or detriment in it. Think of a few examples of where you have entered into agreements as part of everyday life – can you identify the 'thing of value' in the agreement? This has to be a two-way thing, with some identifiable thing of value passing in each direction. Not every 'agreement' you enter into will have that, but every contract must have that.

3.4 WHERE CONSIDERATION MOVES FROM AND TO

Another key element of consideration is the direction in which it is moving. In certain situations, it can be straightforward to identify the 'value' in a contract, but to show there is some value there is not enough. A contract is an exchange between two (or in more complex situations, more than two) persons, and therefore the economic exchange is moving between the parties themselves. So, another key element is that the value that is shown as consideration must also be seen to be moving between the parties. If a party is not involved in the exchange of consideration, there is an argument that they are not able to rely on the contract.[4] As Wightman J said in *Tweddle v Atkinson*,[5] 'no stranger to the consideration can take advantage of a contract'. This is illustrated in the case below.

DUNLOP PNEUMATIC TYRE CO LTD V SELFRIDGE & CO LTD [1915] AC 847

This case concerned a supply contract for tyres. The contract was part of a chain of contracts that linked the manufacturer with the retailer via the wholesaler as shown below:

The situation arose because of a minimum price agreement that Dunlop had entered into with the wholesaler. The wholesaler agreed not to sell tyres below this price when selling retail (to ultimate consumers) and also agreed that they would require the same

---

4   This relates to the doctrine of privity, which we will discuss in Chapter 15.
5   *Tweddle v Atkinson* (1861) 1 B & S 393.

of any companies that they sold the tyres onto by inserting the same terms into their contract. Selfridge sold the tyres below the minimum price, in defiance of the agreement, and Dunlop attempted to sue them to enforce this requirement.

Held: Dunlop were not able to sue Selfridge because the consideration had not moved from them. They were linked to this contract, but only indirectly, and the correct party to sue Selfridge in this situation would have been the wholesaler. Because Dunlop were not a party to Selfridge's contract, they were not privy to the contract.

This reinforces what Wightman J said about being a party to the consideration giving a person the right to sue. Therefore, in the majority of contracts, it is the direction that the consideration moves in that is also important in deciding whether there is valid consideration or not.

One major exception to this is with regard to the Contracts (Rights of Third Parties) Act 1999. To enforce the above rule would prevent third parties with claims under this Act from enforcing them. Therefore, the Act provides that third parties do not need to demonstrate consideration moving from them. However, this is an exception and, generally, a promisee will need to show that the consideration supporting the promise moves from them.

3.4.1 EXECUTED AND EXECUTORY CONSIDERATION

Consideration, as we have seen with regard to the definition at the beginning of this chapter, is often thought of as a promise to do something or a promise to provide something as part of an exchange where there is a corresponding promise in return. In reality the existence of an actual statement with the phrase 'I promise' is sometimes misleading. This is because you cannot always identify such a thing, similar to that which we have seen in the previous chapter regarding statements of 'I offer' or 'I accept'. People will often not make statements with precise language in that they promise to complete an action, but it will be clear from the language used that this is the case.

With regard to consideration, it will come in one of two forms, **executed** or **executory**, and the distinction will be a matter of timing.

ESSENTIAL DEFINITION: EXECUTED CONSIDERATION

Providing the consideration (e.g. the goods/services or money) at the same time as entering the legally binding agreement to provide that obligation.

For example, shopping tends mostly to involve executed consideration, as when entering an agreement to buy goods in a shop, the goods and the money exchange hands at the time of agreement.

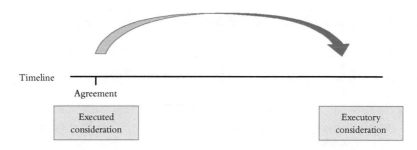

Figure 3.1 Executed v executory consideration

ESSENTIAL DEFINITION: EXECUTORY CONSIDERATION

This is a promise to perform an act in the future. The promise to perform is made at the time of the agreement, but the performance follows at a later date. This is still legally binding as the promise to perform (e.g. supply goods, perform services, etc.) has a value, but the timing is different from executed consideration.

For example, when you buy a brand new car from a car dealer, you enter into a binding contract to buy that car. If the car needs to be made to your specific order by the manufacturer, you do not receive it at the time you agree the contract, but there is an obligation under the contract to provide you with the car. As it will be supplied to you in the future, the car is executory consideration.

Once executory consideration has been performed, it becomes executed.

3.4.2 PAST CONSIDERATION

Past consideration differs from the two previously discussed forms of consideration because it is not a valid form of consideration. The nature of a contract is to encourage exchange between the parties, and therefore, if the consideration has already been provided, it deprives the contract of its purpose. A contract to bind someone to an action they have already performed is pointless. This has therefore provided us with the principle that consideration, whether executory or executed, has to coincide with the agreement itself. (See Figure 3.2.)

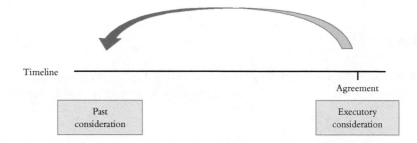

Figure 3.2 Past consideration

A number of cases illustrate this position and demonstrate the reasoning behind it.

ROSCORLA V THOMAS (1842) 3 QB 234, 114 ER 496

This was a case involving the sale of a horse. The claimant sold the horse to the defendant, with a warranty as to the condition of that horse – it was said to be sound and free from vice. When the horse did not match the description, the issue in this case was about the enforceability of the warranty that had been given.

Held: it was established that the warranty had been given after the agreement had been concluded. The warranty was a promise, an assurance, of the condition of the horse, and therefore could be considered to be something 'of value'; however, because it was made after the contract was agreed, and was not supported by any fresh consideration from the other party, it was merely a gratuitous promise and non-enforceable.

Another good example of the existence of past consideration was also shown in the case of *Re McArdle*.[6] This demonstrates that promises to carry out duties need to coincide with agreements to pay for those duties.

RE MCARDLE [1951] CH 669, [1951] 1 ALL ER 905

This case involved a house which was inherited by several children when their mother died. While the mother was still alive and living in the house, some repairs were carried out on the house by the wife of one of the children, living in the house at the time with the mother. An agreement was made after the completion of the repairs, that £488 would be paid to the wife from the mother's estate upon her death, which would cover the cost of those repairs. This agreement was made with all the children entitled to inherit the house.

Held: this agreement was unenforceable as the agreement to pay was made after the repairs were carried out. The promise to pay the £488 was not supported by consideration from the wife because the act of carrying out the repairs was past consideration.

ASSESSMENT TIP

There is an important distinction here between executed consideration and past consideration. It is vital not to confuse these two concepts – one is valid consideration

---

6   [1951] Ch 669, [1951] 1 All ER 905.

because it happens at the time of the agreement (executed consideration). This therefore makes it important to be able to identify when the agreement is made, as discussed in the previous chapter. The work that was the subject of the agreement in *Re McArdle* had already been completed at the point that the agreement was signed by the parties.

There is sometimes the temptation to think that both elements of consideration have to be performed at the same time, otherwise one of them is past. Do not fall into that trap – as long as there is an agreement that includes both elements of consideration, one of them can be executed and the other executory, and the contract will be valid. Past consideration is something that has been performed *before the contract is agreed* and is not valid consideration.

However, in the distinction between past and executed consideration, drawing precise lines between the two concepts can be difficult, particularly in the light of the point made earlier in this chapter, that precise language of 'offer' and 'acceptance' is often not used, and therefore the courts are left with the job of inferring intention from the actions and the language of the parties.

One case, which attempted to provide some illumination of the distinction between these two concepts, was *Lampleigh v Braithwait*,[7] an early example of courts resolving this issue in situations where it is clear from the intention of the parties that there should be a valid contract in existence even where the issue of consideration does not appear to have been conclusively dealt with.

In this case, at the time the agreement was made, there was no discussion of an amount to be paid in return for the promise made, and therefore, on a strict application of the rule of consideration, it would appear that the contract would not be enforceable. However, the court in this case said that because a service was requested, there is included an implication that the service is going to be paid for once performed.

LAMPLEIGH V BRAITHWAIT (1615) HOB 105

This case concerned a man who had been convicted of murder and had asked Lampleigh to obtain a pardon from the King for him in regard to this crime. Lampleigh successfully managed to do this and, as a result, Braithwait promised to pay him £100. On the face of it, it appears that the consideration for the £100 is past, as it was promised after the agreement. However the act of obtaining the pardon involved no small amount of effort and travelling on Lampleigh's part.

7   (1615) Hob 105.

Held: the court felt that the effort that had been gone to in obtaining the pardon should therefore be coupled to the payment that was promised. They therefore decided that, alongside the instruction to secure the pardon, there was an inference that a payment would be made for the service, regardless of the fact that the amount had not been explicitly agreed.

APPLYING THE LAW

Imagine how this might apply to everyday transactions. For example, if you have a burst pipe at home, you might telephone a plumber to come and fix it. Because it is an emergency, the plumber would probably start work on the problem immediately, even if you have not had the time to confirm with him exactly how much the repair will cost. However, does that mean that he is unable to charge you anything? A strict reading of the rule of consideration might suggest so, but the *Lampleigh v Braithwait* case shows that, if you have requested the service, you do so in the knowledge that you will be charged, even if it is uncertain what that charge would be.

The key point to remember here is that the reason the consideration is not thought of as past is because it was at the request of the other party. This is what distinguishes it from situations of mere past consideration as seen in the *Re McArdle* case. Along with the request to carry out work comes the corresponding expectation of payment.

The law was further discussed in *Re Casey's Patents, Stewart v Casey*,[8] a case that dealt with a promise to transfer one-third ownership of a patent in consideration of services that had already been performed. The court held that this was not past consideration as was claimed by the other party in this case. The point here was that there was an expectation that the services would be paid for in some way, at some point, but that the means and the amount had not yet been dealt with by the parties. In this way the court was seeing the transaction through the intentions of the parties involved.

The rule regarding this exception to past consideration was summarised by Lord Scarman in *Pao On v Lau Yiu Long*:[9]

An act done before the giving of a promise to make a payment or to confer some other benefit can sometimes be consideration for that promise. The act must have been done at the promisor's request, the parties must have understood that the act was to be remunerated further by a payment or the conferment of some other benefit, and payment, or the conferment of a benefit must have been legally enforceable had it been promised in advance.

8 [1892] 1 Ch 104.
9 [1980] AC 614 at 629.

ANALYSING THE LAW

Through these cases, it can be seen that the courts are distinguishing between situations where the consideration really was past, and other situations, particularly commercial ones, where although not expressed or given evidential certainty, the consideration for a promise can be read into the actions and intentions of the parties involved. It should therefore be possible to see a difference between the domestic situation in *Re McArdle* where it truly was a gratuitous offer of payment for an action carried out without any expectation of payment, and most commercial situations where a tradesman may be employed to carry out work on a house without any prior agreement as to amount of payment. You would still expect to pay the tradesman, and arguments as to past consideration would logically be defeated by the argument that, at the very least, a reasonable payment would be due for the work carried out. This would reflect the commercial reality of everyday situations.

3.4.3 VALUE OF CONSIDERATION: SUFFICIENCY VS ADEQUACY

Where the law has been somewhat illogical with its approach however, has been with regard to consideration itself. Traditionally the courts have avoided getting involved in determining what might be considered to be a 'fair' payment in the circumstances and, although this is the right thing to do, it has led to the principle on contract law that consideration must be sufficient, but need not be adequate.

Earlier we saw that consideration has to have some form of value. How much, or how little that value is, is no concern of the courts, and this is where the difference between sufficiency and adequacy comes in. All that is required is that there is some value, no matter how small. This means that the law will not protect you from a bad bargain – and it is down to your own freedom to enter into the contract regarding whether you get a good deal or not. So, for example, if I sell my Lotus sports car on eBay for 50p, it does not matter if its true economic value is £25,000.[10] See Figure 3.3.

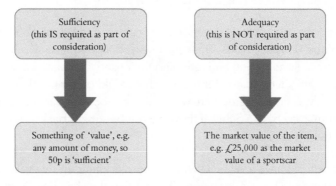

Figure 3.3 Sufficiency v adequacy

----

10 For an example of where this really happened, have a look at the following news story: http://news.bbc.co.uk/1/hi/england/west_midlands/4122842.stm.

THOMAS V THOMAS (1842) 2 QB 851, 114 ER 330

This case discussed the concept of 'peppercorn rent', a small payment as consideration which is far below market value, but nevertheless something with a monetary value to it.

A widow was trying to enforce her entitlement to live in one of her dead husband's properties, on the basis that it was part of his wishes for her to do so. The executors of his will agreed for her to do so, on the basis that she was responsible for any repairs and also paid £1 per year in rent. However, the executors refused to complete the transaction and claimed that it was not enforceable due to lack of consideration.

Held: the £1 rent was sufficient. It was consideration because it had a value, and it was immaterial what that value was. Patteson J was of the opinion that, although respecting the dead husband's wishes was not valid consideration here, the rent and the agreement to repair had real value and therefore were valid consideration.

The principle is therefore that whatever is offered as consideration must have some value in the eyes of the law, no matter how small. Money, as was seen in *Thomas v Thomas*, is very easy to assess in terms of its value. However there have been a number of cases on other forms of consideration which also have value.

3.5 PROVIDING GOODS AS CONSIDERATION

Money is usually easiest to quantify in terms of value. However, that does not mean that other objects cannot also be valued like this.

CHAPPEL & CO LTD V NESTLÉ CO LTD [1960] AC 87

In this case, used chocolate bar wrappers were considered to be valid consideration by a majority of the House of Lords. This case involved a promotion which involved members of the public collecting and returning their used chocolate bar wrappers, along with a small fee, in exchange for records that would be sent to them by Nestlé. The problem that was encountered here was that the chocolate bar wrappers would have been thrown away by the public if they had not been sent back to the company, and appeared to be worthless.

Held: the wrappers did have a value. No matter how insignificant that value might be, they could therefore be consideration. The fact that they had been requested by Nestlé, whatever their motivation for doing so, was enough for the majority of the court to consider them to have some value.

This reinforces the point from *Thomas v Thomas* about the need for some value, although not the amount. The value to Nestlé was probably in the sales generated by their marketing of this promotion, but the court did not question that motivation. The mere finding of some value was enough.

3.6 SERVICES AS CONSIDERATION

Similar findings have been found with regard to services performed, as value can be found in services in the same way as goods.

COLLINS V GODEFROY (1831) 1 B & AD 950

In this case, the claimant attempted to enforce payment for his services as an expert witness by claiming that such services constituted consideration, therefore making the contract enforceable. It is clear in such a situation that performance of a service would be considered to be 'of value'. However, in this situation the expert in question was already subpoenaed to appear in court.

Held: in the circumstances, it was not valid consideration.[11] Although a service provided could be shown to have value, in this case there was already an obligation to perform that service.

ANALYSING THE LAW

WHAT ARE THE LIMITS OF CONSIDERATION?

One question that the law has had to deal with is where the limits are regarding what is valid consideration. The notion of something 'of value' can at times be rather subjective, and therefore what might be of value to one party might be considered completely worthless by another. *Chappel v Nestlé* is a good example of where this may be seen in a particular situation – the used chocolate bar wrappers would be seen as rubbish by anyone else apart from Nestlé themselves.

In dealing with this issue, the courts have examined the nature of the transaction in the case at hand, and also the necessity for exchange required in the underlying purpose of contract law. This has led to some decisions that may at face appear to be illogical, but when examined more closely the underlying principle of exchange in the decision can be seen.

11 See discussion later in this chapter regarding legal obligations as consideration to a contract.

3.7 'BENEFIT' AS CONSIDERATION

Ward v Byham[12] is an example that might at first be considered to be rather marginal.

WARD V BYHAM [1956] 1 WLR 496

A maintenance agreement was made between a mother and father of a child. In exchange for the payment of the father, the mother agreed to keep the child 'well looked after and happy', and also to allow the child to decide whether it wanted to live with the mother or the father.

Held: there was consideration in this agreement. The first of these is an existing legal duty (the duty of a parent to look after their children), which will be dealt with later in this chapter; but the requirement to keep the child happy, along with agreeing that the child should be able to decide where it should live, were enough in the view of the court, to be valid consideration. There was a benefit to the father in these parts of the agreement, and therefore it was seen as valid consideration.

The notion of 'benefit' as value for consideration was also considered in *Williams v Roffey Bros and Nichols (Contractors) Ltd*[13] as it was seen to be of benefit to the main contractors to avoid a penalty clause in their own contract as being consideration for the agreement in question.

The concept of practical benefit was also discussed in *MWB Business Exchange Centres Ltd v Rock Advertising Ltd*,[14] where the case concerned the re-arrangement of payments under a licence agreement by the licensee. The issue of practical benefit was discussed, and it was decided that the licensor was getting a benefit beyond the mere payment of the original licence payments, which he was now getting predominantly later in the licence period due to the re-arrangement. The court said he was getting the benefit of the premises being occupied by the licensee and continued payment of the licence fees, which he would not have had if the licence had been defaulted upon. In addition, he did not have to find an alternative licensee to occupy the premises.

White v Bluett[15] is an example of something which has no value in law even though, subjectively, it may provide something of use to one of the parties to an agreement.

---

12 [1956] 1 WLR 496.
13 [1991] 1 QB 1. This case is discussed in more detail later in this chapter.
14 [2016] EWCA Civ 553, [2016] 3 WLR 1519.
15 (1853) 23 LJ Ex 36.

WHITE V BLUETT (1853) 23 LJ EX 36

Mr Bluett loaned a sum of money to his son, and told him he was not required to pay it back if he stopped complaining about the way his father's estate was to be distributed in his will. The son was required to repay the loan by his father's estate after his death, and he attempted to argue that his agreement to stop complaining was valid consideration.

Held: although the agreement might have given some peace to the father, this was not valid consideration: 'The son had no right to complain, for the father might make what distribution of his property he liked; and the son's abstaining from doing what he had no right to do can be no consideration.'[16]

ASSESSMENT TIP

Evaluating whether something is valid consideration therefore appears to be based upon a combination of issues of fact and law. The legal aspect focuses upon the finding of some form of value, whilst the facts of the situation determine whether that which is thought of as consideration has value in the situation (and not necessarily whether it has value to only one of the parties).

So, consideration can be found by a combination of the legal definition and the factual context – *Ward v Byham* and *Chappel v Nestlé* both demonstrate that there is some subjective element to the idea of what is of value in a given situation.

Think about how this might affect how you evaluate whether something is consideration or not – for example in a problem-based scenario in an assessment. How does what we have discussed here help you to make a decision?

3.7.1 CONSIDERATION AND EXISTING DUTIES

The general principle is that if you are already obliged in some way to perform a duty, you cannot then also provide that as consideration under a binding contract. The logic behind this is that if in some way you are already obliged to do something, you cannot duplicate your promise as part of a binding contract.

The main problem with this principle is that you cannot universally apply this as is – different types of obligation have been dealt with differently, and sometimes the solution has not been

---

16 Per Pollock CB in *White v Bluett* (1853) 23 LJ Ex 36.

about whether the duty is already owed, but about whether duplicating your promise changes someone's legal position. Generally, existing obligations in law will fall under one of three categories: existing legal obligations, existing contractual duties already owed to the other party, and existing obligations owed to a third party.

3.7.1.1 EXISTING LEGAL DUTIES

The approach towards existing legal duties is that they are not considered to be valid consideration in a contract. This is an approach grounded in logic – if you are already legally required to carry out an action or to provide something of value, how can a promise to do exactly that thing have any value to it? You are required to do it anyway, so gaining something from the other party in exchange for performing that obligation appears to be akin to 'money for nothing'.

FOAKES V BEER [1884] UKHL 1

In this case, there was a legal obligation by one party to pay the other an award of money from a previous court case. In order to pay this debt, an agreement was made whereby Dr Foakes would pay the amount of the court judgment to Mrs Beer over a period of time, in six-monthly installments, until the amount was completely repaid. In return, Mrs Beer agreed not to sue Dr Foakes for the outstanding amount owed.

Once the full amount was repaid, Mrs Beer sued Dr Foakes for interest on the money paid. No mention of interest to be added to the original amount had been made, and so effectively the money had been repaid essentially 'interest-free' over the time period.

Held: the court found in favour of Mrs Beer and ordered that interest be paid on the amount repaid. The question here was whether the agreement was legally binding or not. An agreement not to sue was clearly consideration on the part of one party;[17] however Dr Foakes was doing no more than he was legally obliged to do, as the amount owed was ordered by a court.

Clearly in this situation Dr Foakes was literally doing no more than he was already legally required to do. But also consider that the court was acknowledging that where money is paid over a period of time, there was an implication that there will be interest charged on it by default. Even though the parties had not considered this as part of their agreement, it was considered to be a commercial norm and therefore payable.

Legal duties do not have to be those imposed by a court. This category can cover a wide spectrum of situations. For example, in *Ward v Byham* (discussed above) a mother's obligation to look after her child was considered to be an existing legal obligation.

---

17 See *Alliance Bank v Broom* (1864) 2 Dr & Sm 289.

There are also a number of public duties that can be considered to be legal obligations which, although 'of value', cannot be valid consideration for a contract. For example, an organised police presence at an event or incident could be considered to be a service, which has value to the organisation that is receiving it, as usually such police presence is required to maintain order or to prevent unrest in a given situation. However, the local police authority has a legal duty in most situations to provide such a presence.

GLASBROOK BROS LTD V GLAMORGAN COUNTY COUNCIL [1925] AC 270

This case concerned a situation in which a police presence was provided at a mine in order to guard it against a strike by miners that was taking place. The dispute arose when Glamorgan County Council attempted to charge Glasbrook Brothers for the policing presence that had been provided. Glasbrook Brothers argued that as the police have a legal duty to keep law and order, such a police presence cannot be consideration under a commercial agreement.

Held: the court agreed with this on principle. However, in this situation Glasbrook Brothers had requested a higher level of police presence than the chief constable had deemed necessary. This was therefore a situation where the police presence could be consideration, as the legal obligation on the police was only for the level of presence deemed necessary under their legal obligation. The extra police could therefore be charged for.

This principle was also carried forward by the case of *Harris v Sheffield United Football Club*,[18] which reinforced this principle with a different example of where the police's legal obligation did not extend to the service provided.

HARRIS V SHEFFIELD UNITED FOOTBALL CLUB LTD [1988] QB 77, [1987] 2 ALL ER 838

This case involved the provision of a police presence at a football match. As with the *Glasbrook Brothers* case, the football club were invoiced for the policing presence required at football matches by the football club, despite the police's overarching obligation to keep law and order. Again, the argument from the football club was that the police were doing no more than they were legally obliged to do, and so there was a lack of consideration.

Held: the court disagreed, on the basis that the football club held an event at a time when it was obvious to the club that large numbers of opposing fans would attend,

---

18 [1988] QB 77, [1987] 2 All ER 838.

and the nature of the event itself was such that the possibility of public disorder meant a large police presence would be necessary inside as well as outside the ground. Because the club had created this situation voluntarily by organising the match, it was implied within this that there was an understanding that a certain level of policing would be necessary and therefore obvious to the organisers. The policing requirement was therefore above and beyond the normal duties of the police and could be consideration for a contractual agreement. The court argued in particular that policing inside the football ground was something that was the responsibility of the football club.

When looking at existing legal duties, it is therefore important to consider that there will be a limit on the extent of those duties. This means that anything above and beyond that limit will be something of value that could be consideration in a contract.

3.7.1.2 EXISTING CONTRACTUAL DUTIES

The law regarding existing contractual duties is clearer and appears more logical than other types of existing duty. The law in this area dates back to a nineteenth century case, *Stilk v Myrick*,[19] which demonstrated a strict approach to this area. The rule here is that if you are already bound by a contractual agreement to perform a duty, you cannot make a second agreement with that same person and use the same duty as the consideration for that agreement. An attempt to do so would result in the second agreement being unenforceable for lack of consideration.

STILK V MYRICK (1809) 2 CAMP 317, (1809) 6 ESP 129

In this case, a number of crew members were engaged to sail on a voyage. Stilk was one of the crew members, and the wage for the voyage was £5 per month. All crew members had agreed as part of the contract to carry out all necessary duties including dealing with emergencies. During the voyage, two of the crew deserted and left with a ship to sail back to the UK. The captain agreed to share the wages of the deserters amongst the remaining crew if they agreed to sail the ship two men short.

When the ship arrived safely in the UK, the crew (including Stilk) attempted to claim the extra wage. The captain refused, claiming that they had done no more than they were required to do by their original contracts.

Held: applying a strict interpretation of the definition of consideration, the court found in favour of the ship owner, as the original contract required them to 'do all that was necessary in an emergency'. Because of this, it was felt that there was a lack of consideration for the extra money to be paid.

---

19 (1809) 2 Camp 317, (1809) 6 Esp 129.

This case demonstrates a strict approach to the issue of existing contractual duties. The court's decision appears to be based upon whether the crew were doing anything extra as a way of identifying whether there was consideration or not. This approach, therefore, only looks at the factual issue of the actions carried out by the claimant. It can result in a clear and certain approach, but may appear to be rather harsh towards the crew members in this particular situation.

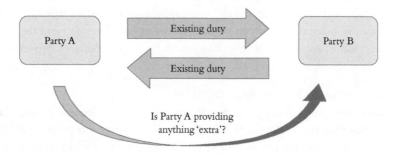

Figure 3.4 Consideration in a situation of existing contractual duty

There is also an important policy consideration, which influenced the case here. The decision in this case would have had important ramifications for other situations similar to this one, and in particular the possibility of the crew of ships sailing to remote destinations being able to effectively blackmail the captain in order to get extra money for the voyage. Although this was not what was happening in this case, it would be easier for agreements made hastily while in remote destinations to be enforced by the courts if they were not required to show some extra duties performed in return for the money promised.

However, what this decision mainly shows is a strict adherence to the requirement of consideration, and therefore a simple rule to follow – there must be something that is above and beyond that which was already agreed as part of the contract. If there is not, if the only thing being promised is something they are already contractually bound to do, there is no consideration.

A case that provides a useful contrast with *Stilk v Myrick* is *Hartley v Ponsonby*.[20] The facts are similar to *Stilk v Myrick*, with the exception that the number of crew that deserted was much higher, and there was nothing in the crew's contracts to say that

20 [1857] 26 LJ QB 322.

they agreed to deal with all emergencies. In this case, the court considered that the crew were putting themselves under a significant additional risk by entering into the agreement to perform the additional duties, and held that they had provided some consideration for the extra amount. They therefore found in their favour. This case, as a useful contrast with the *Stilk* decision, can assist in demonstrating the limits of the principle in *Stilk v Myrick*.

On the matter of policy, this also stepped outside the boundary of the original decision by the court in *Stilk*, as the sailors in *Hartley* were agreeing to do extra in a situation that was significantly more dangerous to them than the original voyage, and therefore was unlikely to result in any abuse of the situation by the crew of other ships in similar situations.

3.7.1.2.1 THE LINK WITH ECONOMIC DURESS

Had the two cases mentioned above been decided today, the policy issue regarding duress would probably not have been relevant. The doctrine of economic duress[21] would most likely mean that such a public policy would be unnecessary as there are safeguards in the law elsewhere. One example of this is the case of *The Atlantic Baron*.[22]

NORTH OCEAN SHIPPING V HYUNDAI CONSTRUCTION (THE ATLANTIC BARON) [1979] QB 705

This case was one where part way through a contract for the construction of a ship, the shipbuilders demanded an extra 10% on top of the agreed contract price. The implication here was that there was a possibility that the ship would either be delayed or not completed at all without the extra payment. Not wishing to upset a company that were building a ship for them, in a situation where they had already begun to schedule work for that ship once completed, North Ocean Shipping agreed to pay the extra price in order to 'preserve amicable relations'. They sued once the ship had been completed and delivered.

Held: the court held that this was not adequate consideration for the extra payment. Because 'amicable relations' cannot constitute valid consideration, this was a situation where there was no extra consideration for the extra 10% – the shipbuilder was merely doing what had already been agreed in the contract. The case was dealt with by way of duress and the contract was voidable because of this.

---

21 See Chapter 10.
22 *North Ocean Shipping v Hyundai Construction (The Atlantic Baron)* [1979] QB 705.

3.7.1.2.2 MODERN DEVELOPMENT OF CONSIDERATION

The strict approach that was introduced by *Stilk v Myrick* at the beginning of the nineteenth century had the advantage of being straightforward and certain; however, it provided little flexibility for anyone wishing to show that something of value had been conferred by the agreement. The rule remained until the case of *Williams v Roffey Bros & Nichols (Contractors) Ltd*,[23] which caused the courts to re-examine the nature of consideration, as well as whether the rule in *Stilk v Myrick* was too harsh, resulting in unfair consequences in some situations.

WILLIAMS V ROFFEY BROS & NICHOLS (CONTRACTORS) LTD [1991] 1 QB 1

This case involved a building contractor (Roffey Bros) who had entered into an agreement to refurbish a block of flats. This contract included a time penalty clause. The nature of such clauses meant that there would be a financial penalty if the contract was not completed by the deadline date stated in the agreement.

Roffey Bros subcontracted out some of the work in the contract, and one such subcontract was with Williams, who was engaged to carry out carpentry on the refurbishment, for the contract price of £20,000. However, part way through the contract it became obvious that Williams was not going to complete the work on time; this was therefore a threat to the time penalty clause in the main contract. Roffey Bros therefore offered Williams an additional sum of £575 per flat; in return Williams promised to complete the work on time. Williams completed eight of the flats but was only given £1,500 of the extra payment promised. So he sued for the remaining amount.

The argument from Roffey Bros was that Williams had done nothing extra for the additional sums of money and, in line with the principle from *Stilk v Myrick*, he had therefore provided no consideration in exchange for the extra money. This meant that the agreement to pay this was not legally binding and they were not obliged to pay.

Held: in deciding this case, the court identified that careful treatment of the rule of consideration was needed. The court identified in this case that there was benefit that had been provided by Williams in return for the money he was offered, and this related to the avoidance of the penalty from the time penalty clause in the main contract. It was of benefit to Roffey Bros to avoid this penalty, and therefore it could be consideration.

In deciding that something was 'of value' and therefore consideration, the court took a broad approach to the idea of a benefit provided by one party to the other. Glidewell LJ looked at three cases – *Ward v Byham*, *Williams v Williams* and *Pao On v Lau Yiu Long* – in defining

---

23 *Williams v Roffey Bros & Nichols (Contractors) Ltd* [1991] 1 QB 1.

the concept of benefit. In each of these cases, the court had seen fit to identify something which, although at first did not appear to involve one party providing something that could be consideration, it was established that there was something that was a benefit to the other party and therefore this could be classed as something 'of value' that could therefore be consideration under the contract.

This undoubtedly involved the court taking a different approach towards the question of consideration from the strict one in *Stilk v Myrick*, although none of the judges in the case expressed any reservation or problem with the principle that came from *Stilk v Myrick*. The key here was about the way in which value was found in the contract. Russell LJ commented that he felt that consideration should be found in situations where the parties had shown a clear intention to enter into a legally binding contract together.[24] This was, therefore, not a decision that suggested that consideration was unimportant, but was one where there needed to be flexibility in its approach in order to give effect to the commercial realities of agreements between parties.

The court in *Williams v Roffey Bros* also recognised that there were other factors in this particular case. The reason for Williams' difficulties related to the fact that the original contract price was too low – Roffey Bros had taken advantage of the fact that there was a recession on at that time in the building trade and therefore they were in a stronger bargaining position than Williams due to the scarcity of work. Consequently, Williams was unable to employ anyone to work with him and he had to complete the work alone. This was not a situation where Williams had exerted any duress on Roffey Bros in order to extract extra payment – in fact it was Roffey Bros who were in the stronger bargaining position, and this undoubtedly had an influence upon the reasoning of the judges in this case.

3.7.1.3 EXISTING OBLIGATIONS OWED TO A THIRD PARTY

Existing duties owed to a third party can be valid consideration in a contract. This again relates to the issue of obtaining a benefit from the agreement. Bearing in mind what has been said before about promising performance of a duty that you are already obliged to perform (whether that be contractually or legally), it might seem somewhat illogical that this is the case. However, it has been established that if you promise to perform a duty that you have already promised to a third party, this is good consideration in contract. In *The Eurymedon*,[25] Lord Wilberforce stated:

> An agreement to do an act which the promisor is under an existing obligation to a third party to do, may well amount to valid consideration and does so in the present case: the promisee obtains the benefit of a direct obligation which he can enforce.[26]

This is the essence of the principle. By entering into a contract, a person therefore has acquired grounds to be able to sue if that promised duty is not performed. If a person is not

24 [1991] 1 QB 1 at 18.
25 *New Zealand Shipping Co Ltd v AM Satterthwaite & Co Ltd (The Eurymedon)* [1975] AC 154.
26 Ibid, at 168.

party to that contract (or any other contract) where that duty is promised, the rules of privity prevent them from being able to enforce performance of that obligation. Entering into a contract to acquire such rights, even if those duties are already owed to someone else, provides you with a benefit, therefore consideration.

SHADWELL V SHADWELL (1860) 9 CB (NS) 159

This case is an example of where a benefit was given as a result of a promise that was already binding. This was an agreement between a nephew and uncle, whereby the uncle agreed to pay an annual income to his nephew in return for a promise that the nephew would marry his fiancée. At that time, getting engaged meant that you were contractually obliged to get married, and therefore this was an existing contractual duty. It might be argued that the benefit that the uncle gained from this arrangement might be a bit tenuous. However, the court agreed that this was a benefit to the uncle, although it might be considered to be somewhat subjective and sentimental.

Held: the existing legal obligation to marry could be valid consideration in the contract between the uncle and his nephew.

The case of *Pao On v Lau Yiu Long*[27] also involved an existing obligation owed to a third party. The contract included a promise to perform an existing obligation under an agreement with a third party. As with *Shadwell*, the court held that it was the promise itself that could be consideration for the contract, rather than the performance of the action itself. The principle is very similar to that in *The Eurymedon*, however, that there is a benefit being acquired under the contract (in the case of *Pao On* it was the promise itself) and therefore the contract had sufficient consideration.

3.7.1.3.1 PART PAYMENT OF A DEBT

Attempts have been made to use part payment of a debt as a way of settling an existing obligation owed. This has been done in situations where there is an existing debt owed under a contract, where one party has attempted to discharge that debt by making a fresh contract, binding the other party into a situation where they agree not to take action to enforce the legal obligation they are owed. That promise not to sue is argued to be consideration under that new contract, in exchange for partial payment of that existing debt. The issue here is with partial payment being valid consideration in that second agreement.

The main problem with these arrangements is that if an existing legal duty to the other party cannot be consideration in a fresh contract, logically partial performance of that existing obligation cannot be consideration either. Such agreements are therefore not legally enforceable.

---

27 [1980] AC 614.

> *D&C BUILDERS V REES* [1966] 2 QB 617
>
> There was an existing debt owed by Rees to D&C Builders for work done to their shop. The defendants had not paid this debt, and when the claimants were in financial dire straits, they had again gone to the defendant to request payment of the debt. The defendant's wife offered part payment of the debt on the condition that it was agreed as the full and final settlement. The claimants had no choice but to agree, due to their financial position. Therefore a cheque for the part payment was sent by the defendant. When D&C Builders sued for the remaining amount, the defendants argued that there was a binding contract for the lesser amount.
>
> Held: there was no consideration for the agreement to accept a lesser amount. Accepting either cash or a cheque for the lesser amount as full settlement of the debt was not binding in law.

ANALYSING THE LAW

The important principle here was that neither factually or as a legal principle was there anything that could be seen as 'of value' (above and beyond what was already owed) and therefore seen as consideration. The agreement to accept a lesser amount was not of benefit to the creditor because they were not choosing to settle the debt at that point rather than go through legal proceedings – the facts of the situation showed that the claimant had no choice in the matter due to their perilous financial situation.

This case was an important application of the rule from the seventeenth century *Pinnel's Case*.[28] This case established the principle that where the debtor is providing something additional to the part payment of the debt, it will be valid consideration for the agreement not to insist on the full amount owed. This is in line with the principle that consideration needs to be something of value, but it is immaterial how much that value is. Therefore, some benefit, no matter how small, will suffice. In this case, the court said that:

> payment of a lesser sum on the day in satisfaction of a greater, cannot be any satisfaction for the whole … but the gift of a horse, hawk, or robe, &c. in satisfaction is good. For it shall be intended that a horse, hawk, or robe, &c. might be more beneficial to the plaintiff than the money, in respect of some circumstance, or otherwise the plaintiff would not have accepted of it in satisfaction.

For example, payment in a more convenient form, or payment ahead of the due date, might be good consideration. The *D&C Builders* case involved a debt that was already overdue, and

---

28 [1602] 5 Co Rep 117a.

therefore payment of part of the debt was not considered to be good consideration. Nothing 'extra' was being provided.

The focus with this area is therefore not that you are only providing part payment of an existing obligation, but that you are providing something extra on top of that which you already promised, even though you are not completely fulfilling your existing obligation. Another important *caveat* to this rule is that the 'something extra' needs to have been provided at the request of the creditor, not at the suggestion of the debtor. To allow otherwise might result in debtors in such situations attempting to escape their obligations by foisting an additional benefit on the creditor in exchange for a promise that they were not going to pursue the extra amount.

Some useful examples of where this has applied have included:

1) *payment in a different form*. The case of *Sibree v Tripp*[29] was decided on the basis that a promissory note was of sufficient novelty to be considered 'a hawk, a horse or a robe' as indicated in *Pinnel's Case*. It was different to the original method of payment and therefore would count as payment in a different form.
2) *payment by a third party*. *Welby v Drake*[30] and *Hirachand Punamchand v Temple*[31] are both examples of where payment by a third party was also regarded as different under the rule in *Pinnel's Case*. In both these cases, the father of the debtor paid an amount to the creditor to clear his son's debts and, as a third party, not part of the original agreement, his payment of part of the debt in full satisfaction was held in both these cases as discharging the debt. This therefore satisfies the rule in *Pinnel's Case*.

There are three important exceptions to the rule in *Pinnel's Case*; they are the doctrine of promissory estoppel (discussed below), cheques, and compositions with creditors.

1) *cheques*. It was originally considered that paying by cheque would satisfy the requirement in *Pinnel's Case* for a different form of payment; however this is no longer the case. A cheque is an instruction to the bank to provide payment of the amount on the cheque, and therefore Denning's opinion in the *D&C Builders v Rees* case was that a cheque should be considered the same as cash.[32]
2) *compositions with creditors*. These are situations where a debtor may make an agreement with multiple creditors to accept a lesser amount than they are legally entitled to. The agreement is that each of the creditors will accept a lesser amount. This appears to contradict what we discussed earlier regarding partial payments and accepting lesser amounts, but this type of agreement is not individually between the debtor and the creditors, but one between the creditors that they each will accept a certain percentage of their debt from the debtor. Often the agreement is seen in

---

29 (1846) 153 ER 745.
30 (1825) 171 ER 1315.
31 [1911] 2 KB 330.
32 [1966] 2 QB 617 at 623.

terms of the consideration from the debtor being the agreement to pay, whilst the consideration from the creditors would be to agree not to file in bankruptcy for the full amounts they are entitled to. There was an attempt to extend this in the case of *Collier v P & M J Wright (Holdings) Ltd.*[33] However this attempt to divide up an existing debt that was jointly owed was unsuccessful.

COLLIER V P & M J WRIGHT (HOLDINGS) LTD [2007] EWCA CIV 1329

In this case, there were three debtors who were jointly liable for a debt to Wright Holdings. Collier was one of the debtors and secured an agreement to discharge their liability in exchange for payment of one-third of the debt. Normally all parties would be considered to be jointly liable for the whole debt. Collier paid one-third of the debt, claiming that this was his share of the obligation, despite the fact that the debt was jointly owed and not sub-divided. The other two debtors went bankrupt and Wright pursued all three debtors for the remaining debt. There was an attempt by Collier to argue that the agreement to discharge him from his obligations after paying the one-third share was binding.

Held: the court however disagreed, and decided that this did not further extend the exceptions in *Pinnel's Case.*

---

3) *promissory estoppel.* This is discussed in section 8 below. Promissory estoppel provides an important exception to the rule in *Pinnel's Case* purely because promissory estoppel does not depend upon the existence of valid consideration in order for a promise to be enforceable.

3.7.2 CONSIDERATION AND ALTERATION OF CONTRACT

Consideration is not only important when forming a contract, it is also a necessity when it comes to alteration of an existing contract. The usual rule is that for an alteration of contract to be legally binding, this must also be supported by consideration. In fact, this is treated as a separate agreement in itself in this regard. The rule in *Stilk v Myrick* regarding the existence of consideration is as important here as with formation of a contract.

3.7.2.1 PAYING MORE

Where a party attempts to make an agreement to be paid more under the contract, this has to be supported by fresh consideration in order to be binding. This was exactly the situation in *Stilk v Myrick*, discussed above. In order for the extra payment to be legally binding, it is necessary to show where that party has gone beyond the original contract and provided 'something extra'. It was this element that was missing in the *Stilk* case, but was present in *Hartley v Ponsonby*. It was also missing in *The Atlantic Baron* case, as the rules of consideration are identical to those for formation of contract – the 'something extra' has to be something of value.

---

33 [2007] EWCA Civ 1329.

3.7.2.2 PAYING LESS

Situations of paying less are as discussed in the previous section, regarding attempting to discharge the original contract by paying a lesser amount. Such an agreement would be seen as a variation or alteration of the original contract, and as such would require some further consideration in the form again of 'something extra'. This is what was missing in the *D&C Builders* case, and any situation which showed the 'something extra' would most likely be one that fell under the rule in *Pinnel's Case*. There would need to be 'a hawk, a horse or a robe', as discussed in that case.

Each agreement requires good consideration from *both* parties (see Figure 3.5).

Figure 3.5 Consideration in variation of contract

3.7.3 PROMISSORY ESTOPPEL

One important exception to the requirement that all promises have to be supported by consideration comes in the form of **estoppel**. Promissory estoppel is cited as an exception to the rule in *Pinnel's Case*, and is part of a more general doctrine of estoppel, which can be used in certain narrow circumstances to give justice to a situation. Estoppel is an equitable principle, intended to give justice and consistency to a situation.

> **ESSENTIAL** DEFINITION: ESTOPPEL
>
> Estoppel generally is the principle of preventing someone from going back upon their previous actions or statements, by judgment of a court. It is used in situations where the requirements of justice mean that the application of this equitable principle are seen by the court as appropriate.

Promissory estoppel is therefore intended to prevent someone from going back on a promise where it would be unjust to allow them to do so. This is different from contractual promises, which would be enforceable because they are supported by consideration – in this situation the promises in question would be 'gratuitous' and therefore not normally enforceable in contract law. This has developed out of a more general idea of *equitable* estoppel from the case of *Hughes v Metropolitan Railway*.

HUGHES V METROPOLITAN RAILWAY [1877] 2 APP CAS 439

This case involved a lease on a group of houses. This lease had a repair clause in it – the landlord could serve notice upon the tenant to repair the property if it was in need of repairs being carried out. The tenant would then have six months to carry out the repairs, or the lease would be forfeited.

In this case, the six-month repair notice was served but, shortly after this happened, rather than carry out the repairs, the tenant entered into negotiations to surrender the lease. However, while the negotiations were ongoing, the six-month notice had passed, and the landlord served notice to eject the tenant. The tenant argued that this was unfair as the six-month period included the time during which the negotiations were being carried out.

Held: the House of Lords (now the Supreme Court) in this case said that the notice period was suspended during the time of the negotiations, because it would be inequitable to do otherwise. In doing so, they found that in the letter from the landlord agreeing to the negotiations, there was an *implied* promise that the notice period would be suspended. Lord Cairns stated that with regard to the six-month notice, 'the person who otherwise might have enforced those rights will not be allowed to enforce them where it would be inequitable having regard to the dealings which have thus taken place between the parties'.[34] They were therefore *estopped* from going back on this implied undertaking.

It is from this judgment that Lord Denning developed the concept of *promissory* estoppel in the case of *Central London Property Trust Ltd v High Trees House*.[35] Denning took the concept of an implied promise in *Hughes* and applied it to express promises made by a party during the performance of a contract. Ordinarily, promises made without any supporting consideration would be unenforceable and, therefore, regardless of how the parties had treated such promises, the strict rule of consideration prevented them from being given the force of law. What Denning was attempting to do was to make such promises enforceable in situations where it was deemed that it would be *inequitable* to do otherwise, and so the doctrine of promissory estoppel was established.

CENTRAL LONDON PROPERTY TRUST V HIGH TREES HOUSE [1947] KB 130

This was a case involving a block of flats in central London. The block was leased to a company in 1937, who then sub-let individual flats to tenants. The case concerned the period covering World War II, at a time that the block of flats was only partially

---

34 Ibid, at 448.
35 [1947] KB 130.

occupied. This was because of the risks of living in central London during the war, due to the risk of being bombed during air raids carried out by the Luftwaffe (the German air force). The owner of the block made an agreement with the leasing company to accept half of the rent due to the circumstances, a situation which continued until 1945 when the war ended. At that point the block of flats slowly filled back up again until it was completely occupied. Once the block was fully occupied, a case was brought against the leasing company for the payment of full rent again.

Held: the Court of Appeal upheld the application for the other half of the rent for the second half of 1945, and Lord Denning made comments in *obiter* regarding any possible application to backdate the claim into the period of the war. He was of the opinion that the nature of the circumstances during the war years were such that the owner of the block of flats should be estopped from going back on their promise to accept less, as it was relied upon by the company leasing the entire block. An important factor was that the promise made was acted upon, and it was known by the party making the promise that this was the case.

This case was quite significant in what Denning was proposing – that in certain circumstances, the requirement for consideration would be bypassed, and a promise could be enforced without the need for this to be present.

ANALYSING THE LAW

The main thing to bear in mind is that very specific circumstances must be fulfilled in order for the principle of promissory estoppel to be upheld, and therefore this was not something that could generally replace the requirement for consideration, but instead be a specific exception applied to particular circumstances. It may seem strange that alongside the doctrine of consideration we also have a principle that appears to negate the doctrine, but it is important to maintain some perspective regarding this. As was pointed out by Lord Toulson in the Privy Council in *Prime Sight Ltd v Lavarello*:[36] 'consideration remains a fundamental principle of the law of contract and is not to be reduced out of existence by the law of estoppel'. The doctrine has very strict limits.

The three criteria needed to apply this doctrine are:

1) a promise – usually to do something or to forego a legal right
2) reliance upon that promise
3) a situation where it would be inequitable for that party to go back upon that promise.

---

36 [2014] AC 436 at 446.

3.7.3.1 THE CLEAR AND UNEQUIVOCAL PROMISE

One thing that was certain from the *High Trees* case was the existence of a promise by the owner of the block of flats. This was core to Denning's development of equitable estoppel into promissory estoppel, and what distinguishes it from the *Hughes* case. That case had been based upon an implied agreement to suspend the time limit, whereas there had been a clear promise not to insist upon the full rent in *High Trees*. However, the implied agreement was, in the eyes of the court, clear and unequivocal enough to satisfy the requirements for estoppel in that case. So, whether it is a promise, representation or agreement, it must satisfy this requirement. This is further supported by subsequent case authority. For example, in *Woodhouse Israel Cocoa SA v Nigerian Produce Marketing Co Ltd*,[37] Lord Hailsham focussed upon what would reasonably be understood from the representation being made. In a more recent case, that of *Baird Textile Holdings Ltd v Marks and Spencer plc*,[38] the lack of this sufficient certainty was enough for the representation made not to be considered enough to be a clear and unequivocal promise.

3.7.3.2 RELIANCE

The fact of a promise or representation made is not enough for the application of promissory estoppel. There must also be reliance upon that promise by the other party. This might lead us to believe that there had been some form of action by the other party to their detriment, but this is not the case. In the case of *WJ Alan Co Ltd v El Nasr Export & Import Co*[39] Denning stated that there was no need to show that the promisee had acted in detriment in response to the promise made. There was only the requirement that he had acted in reliance. Detriment however, could be evidence of having acted in reliance. In *The Post Chaser*[40] the court said that it was possible that the promisee could have benefitted from the other party going back on his promise, but it could still be shown to be inequitable for this to happen based on the fact that he had acted in reliance.

3.7.3.3 INEQUITABLE TO GO BACK ON PROMISE MADE

The above comments therefore link into the third requirement – that of inequity if the other party is able to go back on their promise. This was shown in the *High Trees* case on the basis that the letting company had not been too concerned to let the entire block of flats because of what they had been promised about the rent (which would have been extremely difficult bearing in mind it was in London at the time of the Blitz during World War II). They had therefore been able to let out enough flats to be able to pay half of the rent to the owner of the block, but to require them to then go back and find the other half of the rent in retrospect would have been unduly harsh. This might lead one to think that this therefore comes around to the idea of detriment but, as mentioned above, there is no requirement of detriment *per se*; however, where an individual has acted to their detriment, it may be that this is the easiest way to establish that inequity would result from the ability to go back on a promise. See Figure 3.6.

---

37 [1972] AC 741 at 756.
38 [2001] EWCA Civ 274.
39 [1972] 2 QB 189.
40 *Société Italo-Belge pour le Commerce et l'Industrie SA v Palm and Vegetable Oils (Malaysia) Sdn Bhd, The Post Chaser* [1982] 1 All ER 19.

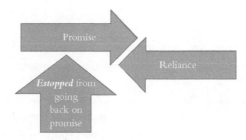

Figure 3.6 The elements of promissory estoppel

3.7.4 OTHER REQUIREMENTS FOR PROMISSORY ESTOPPEL

3.7.4.1 PROMISSORY ESTOPPEL ONLY SUSPENDS RIGHTS

The other significant point about this doctrine was that it was intended to suspend a legal right only, and not to extinguish it altogether. This is crucial when considering the practical application of this principle. In *Hughes v Metropolitan Railway*, estoppel merely suspended the six-month time limit for repair of the property. The time limit was to continue in the event of the negotiations to end the lease being unsuccessful.

Where it is not pre-determined when the ability to enforce the legal right once again arises, a concept of reasonable notice has been applied.

TOOL METAL MANUFACTURING CO LTD V TUNGSTEN ELECTRIC CO LTD [1955] 1 WLR 761

A right to receive a royalty under a patented invention was suspended by a promise that the royalty would not be payable as World War II had broken out. The owners of the patent attempted to revoke this promise in 1945 at the end of the war, but were unsuccessful as the court said that they had not given reasonable notice. A second case was brought, claiming again to enforce the contract.

Held: bringing the case itself was said to be reasonable notice, and therefore the first case involving the parties was reasonable notice. As this had now been served, the promise not to insist on payment of the royalty was no longer enforceable.

ANALYSING THE LAW

The rule that the right is suspended is straightforward when it comes to single obligations (as seen in the *Hughes* case); however, the effect of promissory estoppel on repeating obligations has been seen as somewhat more complicated. There is an argument to say that they have had the effect of extinguishing rights to individual repeating obligations, although not to the obligation as a whole.

For example, the payments on the lease in *High Trees* were reduced by half during the war, but once the war had ended the action to recover the other half of the money owed under the lease for the second half of 1945 was successful. The right to full rent was merely suspended whilst the situation of inequity (the difficulty caused by the war) was still in existence. However, Denning indicated in *obiter* comments in his judgment that had there been an action to recover back-payments dating back into the period of the war, this would have been unsuccessful. The effect therefore is that the right to the other half of the rent was lost, permanently. The same could be said of the royalty payments in the *Tool Metal* case. He repeated such comments in the *D&C Builders* case, and it is important to distinguish between individual payments as part of a series and the overall right to the payment.

3.7.4.2 PROMISSORY ESTOPPEL CANNOT BE RAISED AS AN ACTION IN ITSELF

The equitable maxim 'equity is to be used as a shield, not a sword' is applicable here – essentially it can be used as a defence to an action being brought against you and not as an action to sue another party. Denning's comments in *Combe v Combe*[41] confirm this approach:

Much as I am inclined to favour the principle stated in the *High Trees* case, it is important that it should not be stretched too far, lest it should be endangered. That principle does not create new causes of action where none existed before. It only prevents a party from insisting upon his strict legal rights, when it would be unjust to allow him to enforce them, having regard to the dealings which have taken place between the parties.

The wife's attempt to 'enforce' the promissory estoppel against her husband in this case was therefore unsuccessful. It is possible to see its correct operation in other cases already discussed here – *High Trees*, *Tool Metal* and other cases have all involved actions being brought against parties in an attempt to enforce a legal right where promissory estoppel was therefore a defence against the enforcement of this legal right.

3.8 CONTRACTS MADE BY DEED

There is one final exception to the requirement of consideration in English law, and that is where a contract is executed by deed. The requirements for a deed are contained within s. 1 of the Law of Property (Miscellaneous Provisions) Act 1989, and are discussed in more detail in Chapter 4.

41 *Combe v Combe* [1951] 2 KB 215 at 219.

The only thing we shall mention here is the effect that executing an agreement by way of deed has upon the consideration requirement. It is the only pure exception to the need for consideration. A deed is enforceable, as of itself, legally, without any need to show that consideration has moved in both directions. It can therefore be a useful device to make a gift enforceable in law. This has a number of applications, both in family matters (where someone promises to give money or goods to other family members) and also with regard to donations to charity, either by an individual or by a company or organisation, where such donations need to be established as legally binding (for example for tax purposes). It is often viewed as being fairly arcane and steeped in tradition; however the requirements have been modernised by the 1989 Act.

3.9 BRINGING IT ALL TOGETHER

Consideration is an important element of a **binding** contract. In order for a contractual agreement to be enforceable in law, it must be present. This strict requirement still remains as part of contract law today. The law does not regulate how much the consideration is, and so this still leaves plenty of scope for a wide range of agreements. Nevertheless, the existence of that consideration, something of value, still needs to be present.

As we have also seen, some promises can be enforced without the need for a binding contract – these exceptions are very specific and have been created to cover particular situations. Although they are important, you will still find that a binding contract will need consideration to be valid.

KEY LEARNING POINTS

Consideration provides the value in a contract. Remember that the following elements are important in assessing whether there is consideration in any one situation:

- It must be something of value in order to be valid consideration
- It must not be in the past
- It cannot be an obligation that is already owed to the other party
- It does not matter how big or small the value is

Consideration is necessary in all contracts, unless executed by deed, or where the criteria for promissory estoppel allow for equity to prevent one of the parties from going back on a promise that is not supported by consideration.

TAKING IT FURTHER

Austen-Baker, 'A strange sort of survival for *Pinnel's case: Collier v P & MJ Wright (Holdings) Ltd*' (2008) 71 MLR 611

Beatson & Burrows, *Anson's Law of Contract*, 29th edn, Oxford University Press, 2010

Chen-Wishart, 'A bird in the hand: consideration and contract modification', in Burrows & Peel (eds), *Contract Formation and Parties*, Oxford University Press, 2010

Chen-Wishart, 'In defence of consideration' (2013) 13 OUCLJ 209

Collins, 'Part-payment of debt: a variation on a theme?' (2017) 28 ICCLR 253

O'Sullivan, 'In defence of *Foakes v Beer*' (1996) CLJ 219

Peel, 'Part payment of debt is no consideration' (1994) 110 LQR 353

Peel, *Treitel on the Law of Contract*, 14th edn, Sweet & Maxwell, 2015

Trukhtanov, '*Foakes v Beer*: reform of common law at the expense of equity' (2008) 124 LQR 364

4

CHAPTER 4
INTENTION TO CREATE LEGAL RELATIONS, CAPACITY, AND FORM

4.1 INTRODUCTION

This chapter looks at several issues that have an effect upon the initial viability of a contract: intention, capacity and form. They each address different issues concerning validity of a contract, but the common thing they all share is that they point to a vital ingredient needed in a contractual agreement. They can each indicate a fatal flaw that might mean that a contract is not valid. Equally, they can each be irrelevant in particular contractual agreements.

The purpose of this chapter is to examine each of these concepts individually: to define them, show how they apply to particular contracts, and therefore to show you how you should consider them when applying contract law to specific agreements.

This chapter is therefore about validity of a contract, because of some defect that means that legally, the contract is not recognised in law. This affects the ability of an individual to enforce a contract, and also has a bearing on whether they are able to get a remedy if something goes wrong with that contract (see Chapters 13 and 14 on remedies for breach of contract).

You should also consider the difference between different forms of contractual invalidity. Some defects of a contract can render the agreement **void**, and therefore viewed in law as never having existed in the first place. Other defects can render the contract **voidable**, as we will also see in Chapter 10 regarding duress and undue influence. Voidable contracts are those that do exist in law, but can be voided at the discretion of one party. It is important to bear in mind the distinction between these two states, as the law treats them differently.

AS YOU READ

At the end of this chapter you should be able to:

- Understand the effect that intention, capacity and form have on the validity of a contract

- Appreciate the difference between a contract that is void from the very start, and one that becomes voidable at some point

- Identify the particular types of agreements that are likely to have issues with intention, capacity or form

- Apply the law regarding intention, capacity and form to situations in order to ascertain the validity of an agreement

4.2 INTENTION TO CREATE LEGAL RELATIONS

Because of the nature of a contractual agreement, we often refer to someone intending to bind themselves into a legally enforceable agreement. This is as important as the issue that we dealt with in Chapter 3, that of consideration. Although we would usually use the presence of consideration as the measure of the legally binding nature of a contract, it is also important to remember that the parties are at liberty to define the binding nature (or not) of any agreement that they enter into. This relates back to the will theory mentioned in Chapter 1 when considering the nature of a contract in the first place.

This means that parties expressing their intention to be legally bound, or even from inferences drawn from the nature of the agreement itself, can be a way of differentiating between situations that are intended to have the force of law, and those that are not.

The way this has been dealt with in law is not about the subjective intent in the mind of the parties to a contract, as that is very difficult to ascertain and is rather an unreliable way of measuring intention to be legally bound. Instead, the law has focussed upon the objective analysis of the expression of the parties, in other words how their statements in the contract look to the outside world. This was summarised in the case *RTS Flexible Systems Ltd v Molkerei Alois Müller GmbH & Co KG (UK Production)*[1] by Lord Clarke:

> Whether there is a binding contract between the parties and, if so, upon what terms depends upon what they have agreed. It depends not upon their subjective state of mind, but upon a consideration of what was communicated between them by words or conducts, and whether that leads objectively to a conclusion that they intended to create legal relations and had agreed upon all the terms which they regarded or the law requires as essential for the formation of legally binding relations.

Therefore, although it may at first appear simple, in reality this complicates the matter somewhat. The intention cannot be definitively said to be the true intention of the parties, only the objective assessment of this. Although the will theory indicates that a contract is about the expression of willingness to enter into a contract, this is not true – a contract is about the objective view of willingness to enter into a contract. Therefore, some contracts may have the relevant elements of a contract, but an objective assessment of those agreements would conclude that there is not the intention for the agreement to be legally bound. Domestic agreements are a good example of this.

1   [2010] 1 WLR 753 at 771.

APPLYING THE LAW

Examples of domestic or family arrangements can take many forms, but one common example would be that of a teenager's weekly pocket-money or allowance being dependent upon the completion of their weekly chores, e.g. tidying their room or emptying the dishwasher.

Although agreements such as this have the necessary elements for formation of a contract that we have discussed in Chapter 2, they lack the intention of the parties to give the agreement legally binding force. Neither party seriously expects to be able to take the other to court if the agreement is breached (although many teenagers may mischievously consider the prospect) and, if promises made under the agreement are broken, it is more likely to be an issue of parenting ethics than binding legal obligations.

The result is that such domestic agreements are not legally binding and therefore cannot be enforced by a court of law, because it is clear that this is not what the parties intend.

In reality, it would be very tiresome for the courts to have to specifically examine this issue with regard to every contract, particularly in the instance of those agreements where intention of the parties does not appear to have been at issue. Also, due to the breadth of situations involving agreements between two or more parties (from a teenager's allowance in exchange for chores to major multinational commercial agreements) it is necessary to have a starting point in every situation which can then be argued against in court if necessary.

Therefore, the law has evolved two presumptions regarding intention to create legal relations. In those agreements seen as commercial, the presumption is that, in the absence of contrary evidence, there is an intention to create a legally binding agreement. In those agreements seen as domestic, as with the example mentioned above, the presumption is that there is no intention to create legal relations. This is because normally we would not expect domestic or family arrangements to be subject to law, or for it to be appropriate to litigate disputes over them in court. Imagine being sued for not cleaning your room!

The nature of these as presumptions, however is somewhat different from where a presumption is used elsewhere in contract law. When a presumption is set up, it would normally be expected that this remains in place unless there is evidence to rebut that presumption. For example, the presumption set up in relation to undue influence (see Chapter 10) can be rebutted with contrary evidence regarding whether that person made a decision independently of the undue influence.

With the presumption regarding the intention to be legally bound, it is there to ensure that there is legal certainty regarding the enforceability of a contract, and therefore to allow it to be easily rebutted would damage the legal certainty that the presumption was supposed to establish in the first place. The comments of Lord Clarke in *RTS Flexible Systems* discussed above show that the requirement of intention to create legal relations is all about ensuring the certainty required to ensure that those contracts which should be legally enforceable are legally enforceable. In line with this, the presumptions here are rebuttable, but not easily.

4.3 PRESUMPTION OF AN INTENTION TO CREATE LEGAL RELATIONS

The existence of contract law is reliant upon an intention to create a legally binding contract (see Figure 4.1). The absence of this takes the agreement out of the law of contract, and therefore means that it is not enforceable using the law. For this reason, when beginning with a presumption, with commercial agreements the starting point is that there *is* an intention to create legal relations. Contract law was created to regulate commercial transactions, and this is therefore the logical conclusion to come to.

In line with the objective approach mentioned above, the law views agreements subject to this presumption to be those that a reasonable person would expect there to be legal consequences as a result of the agreement. As was discussed above, rebutting the presumption in commercial agreements would be very difficult, because of the underlying purpose of contracts to stimulate exchange. So, although this is stated as a presumption, there is difficulty in rebutting it because otherwise it would just be an unnecessary hurdle.

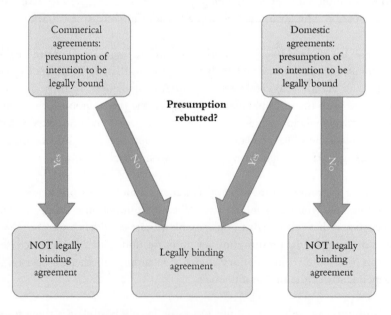

Figure 4.1 Has the presumption been rebutted?

> **ASSESSMENT** TIP
>
> Cases in this area therefore focus upon situations where a party is arguing that there is no intention to be legally bound, attempting to rebut the presumption. However, the cases below demonstrate the point made above: that it can be extremely difficult to rebut the presumption in commercial situations.
>
> This makes this one of those issues that therefore only needs to be addressed if it is clear that the status is in dispute. Otherwise, the presumption stands.

A written agreement between parties in commercial situations can often present no leeway in rebutting the idea that there is an intention for the parties to be legally bound. Cases have therefore looked at peripheral issues regarding relations between parties involved.

DHANANI V CRASNIANSKI [2011] 2 ALL ER (COMM) 799

There was an agreement between two parties regarding the setting up of a private equity fund. A signed letter had established a number of important aspects of the agreement, including the amount to be invested and various other details. However, it was not a complete agreement as other aspects were yet to be agreed upon. Before the fund could be set up, there was a breakdown in relations between the parties, and the fund was never set up. As a result, one party sued the other for breach of contract.

Held: this was merely an agreement to agree, rather than a binding contract from which legally binding obligations were to arise. An agreement to agree is not something that would be recognised by law as giving rise to enforceable obligations. Because there were a number of issues that a reasonable businessman would expect to be dealt with before the fund was set up, the agreement to agree was unenforceable.

The objective viewpoint of the binding nature of an agreement is therefore important, and the courts will use this as a guide in deciding whether there is an intention to create legal relations. The existence of a written agreement is not in itself conclusive of that, as we have seen in *Dhanani*, but there may be other factors that indicate that the presumption of intention to be bound should remain. For example, in *G Percy Trentham Ltd v Archital Luxfer*,[2] the intention to create a legally binding relationship was established at least partly by the conduct of the parties. The obligations under the contract had been performed in that work had been carried out and paid for and this, coupled with letters confirming that there was

---

2   [1993] 1 Lloyd's Rep 25, [1993] 63 BLR 44.

a contract in place, led the court to conclude that there was a legally binding agreement between the parties, which could be sued under.

Similarly, oral assurances have also been held to lead to a legally binding relationship. *J Evans & Son (Portsmouth) Ltd v Andrea Merzario Ltd*[3] involved an oral assurance that goods carried in a shipping container would be transported below deck. Previously goods had been carried in crates and stored below deck in order to protect them against the possibility of rust and, in switching to shipping containers, it was considered important to maintain this arrangement. Written terms and conditions contained no such assurances, but the court viewed the oral assurance as intending to create a legally binding relationship between the parties, even though this was contrary to the standard terms and conditions in the agreement.

EXPLAINING THE LAW

Cases like this demonstrate that although an objective standard is being applied, it does not result in a clear approach to how the issue of intention to create legal relations in commercial agreements should be dealt with. This was also demonstrated in the case of *Esso Petroleum v Customs and Excise Commissioners*,[4] which involved a 2–2 split between the Lords on the issue of intention to create a legally binding agreement. The case concerned whether World Cup commemorative coins were 'chargeable goods' for tax purposes. One of the arguments put forward in that case concerned a lack of intent to be legally bound by the agreement to give these away as part of a promotion to customers who bought fuel. Two of the Lords, Viscount Dilhorne and Lord Russell, argued that there was a lack of intent to be legally bound, but the other two Lords disagreed. Viscount Dilhorne argued[5] that the transaction could not be considered a matter of 'business relations', citing Megaw J in *Edwards v Skyways*,[6] whereas Lord Simon came to the opposite conclusion because, as a promotional exercise, it was designed to produce a 'commercial advantage'[7] for Esso in that it would increase sales of fuel to customers wishing to collect these coins. Conflicting opinion of judges on the application of the principle can also be seen in cases concerning advertising (see later in this chapter).

4.3.1 REBUTTING THE PRESUMPTION

The commercial nature of contracts sets up a presumption that is difficult to rebut; however, it is not impossible. It has been shown to be possible to rebut the presumption of an intention to create legal relations regarding commercial agreements, although this has to be done by express language to this effect in the contract.

3   [1976] 1 WLR 1078.
4   [1976] 1 WLR 1.
5   [1976] 1 WLR 1 at 5.
6   [1964] 1 WLR 349.
7   Ibid, [1976] 1 WLR 1 at 6.

JONES V VERNON'S POOLS [1938] 2 ALL ER 626

An example of this can be seen in the case of *Jones v Vernon's Pools*. This case concerned an individual who completed a coupon for football pools (a game involving selecting which of that week's football matches would result in a draw). It was sent off to the company running the game, but never received. There was an express statement at the bottom of the coupon stating that there was no intention for that coupon to give rise to a legally binding relationship, but that the conditions of the game would be binding in honour only. Jones sued over the lost pools coupon.

Held: because of the express language on the coupon, that intention to create a legally binding relationship was rebutted; it was therefore unenforceable in law.

This case followed the decision of the leading case on this issue, *Rose and Frank Co v JR Crompton & Bros Ltd*,[8] which also illustrated that express language was capable of rebutting the presumption of a legally binding relationship.

ROSE AND FRANK V JR CROMPTON & BROS LTD [1925] AC 445

This case involved an agreement between two UK tissue manufacturers, and a US company that became their sole distributor in the US. They made the agreement for the supply of the goods for exclusive distribution of their tissue products by the US company. The agreement was to last for three years and, under this agreement, the US distributor would place individual orders for the UK companies' tissue products which would be fulfilled as and when they were placed. It contained a clause, which read as follows:

> This arrangement is not entered into, nor is this memorandum written, as a formal or legal agreement, and shall not be subject to legal jurisdiction in the law courts either of the United States or England, but it is only a definite expression and record of the purpose and intention of the three parties concerned to which they each honourably pledge themselves with the fullest confidence – based on past business with each other – that it will be carried through by each of the three parties with mutual loyalty and friendly cooperation. This is hereinafter referred to as the 'honourable pledge' clause.

The relationship between these companies ran into difficulties, and the UK tissue manufacturers terminated the agreement without notice. At the time, there were orders that had been placed and accepted under the agreement, and the US distributor sued when these orders were not fulfilled.

---

8   [1925] AC 445.

Held: the exclusivity agreement was not legally enforceable because of the 'honourable pledge' clause. The clause was express language that rebutted the presumption of an intention to create legal relations. However, the individual orders placed under the agreement were legally enforceable, as they were separate legal agreements in their own right.

The nature of what can be used to prove that the presumption should be rebutted can be seen in the case of *Orion Insurance Co plc v Sphere Drake Insurance plc*.[9] This case involved an oral agreement in a meeting between the two parties which, when the agreement was later transposed in writing, did not contain a term that the agreement was not intended to be legally binding. The plaintiffs argued that, despite this, the agreement was not legally binding and should be treated as such.

In allowing the plaintiffs to establish this, it was permissible to admit parole evidence into the case. This was because, in arguing that the agreement was binding, that other party had introduced the meeting transcript as evidence that there *was* a legally binding agreement. To conclude otherwise would be unjustified.

Although, as we have discussed above, the presumption is not easily rebutted in commercial cases, the appropriate burden of proof still remained that of balance of probabilities.

4.3.2 BURDEN OF PROOF

Both *Jones v Vernon's Pools* and *Rose and Frank v Crompton* show that establishing express rebuttal of the presumption of legal relations in the contract is sufficient, but it raises the issue of who has the burden of proof in such matters. These cases suggest that any party wishing to rely upon a lack of intention to be legally bound has an obligation to prove this, and this is supported by the judgment in *Edwards v Skyways*.[10]

EDWARDS V SKYWAYS [1964] 1 WLR 349

This case involved an agreement to make *ex gratia* payments to pilots as part of a redundancy agreement. When Skyways failed to make the promised payments, they were sued by Edwards, one of the pilots made redundant. Skyways attempted to argue that the use of the term *ex gratia* meant that there was no intention to create a legally binding relationship.

The court in this instance looked at the ordinary meaning of the phrase *ex gratia*, and concluded that it did not rebut the presumption of a legally binding contract. The term

9   [1992] 1 Lloyd's Rep 239.
10 [1964] 1 WLR 349.

meant that payment was to be made without any admission of previous liability, rather than that the parties did not intend this to be a legally binding relationship.

The court's opinion was that the onus was on Skyways to establish there had been no intention to create a legally binding relationship, and that the company had not discharged that onus.

Held: the agreement for the payments was legally binding and enforceable against Skyways.

However, the outcome in *Kleinwort Benson Ltd v Malaysia Mining Corp*[11] took a different approach to the burden of proof. Rather than placing the responsibility for rebutting the presumption upon the party who did not wish to be bound by the agreement, they relied upon the way in which the terms used were construed in law.

KLEINWORT BENSON LTD V MALAYSIA MINING CORP [1989] 1 ALL ER 785, [1989] 1 WLR 379

This case concerned a loan facility given to 'M', subsidiary of the Malaysia Mining Corp (MMC) by Kleinwort Benson, the lender. Ordinarily such a loan would require some form of security in the event of the loan being defaulted upon, something that could be repossessed by the lender in this event. However this was not the case with this loan.

Instead, the lender relied upon a 'comfort letter' that they received from the parent company, MMC. The letter stated: 'it is our policy to ensure that the business of M is at all times in the position to meet its liabilities to you under the above arrangements'.

M ran into financial difficulties, and the company collapsed, leaving the lender with an outstanding loan amount that had not been paid. They attempted to recover the amount from MMC, treating the comfort letter as a guarantee. The MMC refused to pay.

Kleinwort Benson sued, claiming the letter of comfort was a contractual promise and demonstrated MMC's intention to honour a legal obligation to cover the debts of M in the event that they were unable to pay. MMC argued that the notion of a comfort letter was well known in the industry as merely being a way of reassuring the other party, 'by assuming, not a legal liability to ensure repayment of the liabilities of the subsidiary, but a moral responsibility only'.

Held: the Court of Appeal found in favour of MMC. Their approach to this situation was to look at the construction of the comfort letter, and regard how it was objectively

11 [1989] 1 All ER 785, [1989] 1 WLR 379.

viewed in the industry. It came to the conclusion that the letter was merely one giving comfort, and one assuming only a moral responsibility. They also argued that it was merely a statement of present intention, and not something that would bind them into a legal commitment of future conduct.

This appears to be at odds with the established approach of the burden of proof being with the party attempting to rebut the presumption of an intention to be legally bound. Instead it results in the other party implicitly being required to prove that the statement in question is not of a non-promissory nature, which was effectively the situation in the *Kleinwort Benson* case. The approach this case took, in focussing upon the promissory nature (or not) of statements made in deciding whether there is a binding legal obligation or not, has been criticised because it actually lessens the burden upon the party wishing to avoid legal liability. It has only been applied in one other case, *Bowerman v ABTA Ltd*, which is discussed in the context of advertisements, below. The court in that instance focussed upon the promissory nature of the advertisement in question in establishing an intention to be legally bound. However, such an approach should be used with caution because it flies in the face of the need to ensure that the majority of commercial agreements are governed by contract law. To make it too easy to rebut the presumption would cause problems with this.

4.3.3 ADVERTISING

Cases involving advertising have also involved arguments by the advertisers that their statements lack an intention to be legally binding. This can be traced back to the *Carlill v Carbolic Smoke Ball Co Ltd*[12] case that we discussed in Chapter 2 on formation of contract. This case involved the argument by the Carbolic Smoke Ball Co that the statements in their advertisements were 'mere puffs', and therefore demonstrated a lack of intention to be legally bound by them.

EXPLAINING THE LAW

A good example of a 'mere puff' comes in the form of advertising. Although there are now regulations guarding against misleading statements being made as part of advertising, 'mere puffs' are the type of comments that are made without any intention that they be taken literally. For example in a series of famous advertisements, it has been said that 'Red Bull™ gives you wings'. No-one has ever sued the makers of Red Bull because they have failed to grow wings after consuming their product, and they would probably argue that this is just a metaphor for the stimulant effect of their product. There are numerous other examples of throwaway comments made in advertising that are not intended to be taken literally, and these can be classified as 'mere puffs'. The key characteristic here is that they are not intended to have an effect upon the contractual relationship between the parties.

12 [1893] 1 QB 256.

The problem with the use of this argument in the *Carlill* case was that the court was unconvinced. This was because of statements in the advertisement regarding the deposit of funds in a particular bank (the Alliance Bank, Regent Street), to cover any potential claims from users of the Carbolic Smoke Ball who then contracted the 'flu. Ultimately appearing to guarantee the veracity of what they were saying meant that they were unable to argue that they did not intend their statements to have the force of law.

There is an argument here that such an approach is similar to that in the *Kleinwort Benson* case discussed above, as it relies upon objective interpretation of the statement rather than rebuttal of the presumption by the party wishing to escape liability.

A more modern example of an attempt to argue no intention to be bound in advertising can be seen in *Bowerman v ABTA*,[13] where an ABTA advertisement promised protection for holidaymakers in the event of an ABTA member travel agent going out of business. There was an attempt by ABTA to argue that there was no intention to create a legally binding relationship through this advertisement, and that this was intended to be a non-promissory assurance. However, the court concluded that customers would reasonably expect there to be a binding promise arising from this, and would act accordingly in booking their holiday with a member travel agent and expect to be able to enforce the protection. Again, this demonstrates the court's application of an objective interpretation of the relationship rather than relying upon whether there had been rebuttal of the presumption or not.

4.4 PRESUMPTION OF NO INTENTION TO CREATE LEGAL RELATIONS

In contrast to commercial agreements, there is a general presumption of a lack of intention to create a legally binding relationship in domestic agreements. This is driven by a policy against judicial intervention in domestic arrangements, and also relates back to a point made in the introduction to this section – that it would be unusual to use legal remedies against family members, and therefore it is not appropriate to use contract law in these circumstances.

However, as with the presumption in regard to commercial agreements, there is a presumption *against* intention to create a legally binding contract in domestic agreements. This means that it is possible to rebut it, and where evidence demonstrates that the parties intended to be legally bound, this will rebut the presumption. As a general guidance, trivial matters are unlikely to be expected to be legally enforceable, whereas those more significant matters are more likely to result in the presumption being rebutted. This is because, even in domestic situations, where a contract on a significant matter of high value is involved, it is more likely that the law of contract would be applicable. The court's willingness to find intention increases the more serious the promises made.

13 [1996] CLC 451.

In considering whether to rebut the presumption, the court must place itself in the parties' shoes at the time the contract was formed and ask whether it would be reasonable to expect legal obligations to be imposed where relationships had broken down.

The most common types of domestic arrangements are those involving family members, and the courts will generally view normal financial relationships between such family members as being a domestic matter only. For example, in *Gage v King*[14] the court ruled that the arrangement of having a joint bank account between husband and wife was not intended to mean that there were legal consequences between them regarding that account and how it was used.

APPLYING THE LAW

Therefore, the general presumption is that any agreements entered into between family members will not be subject to legal obligations. As with commercial agreements, this presumption can be rebutted, but the majority of situations involve agreements which, because they are domestic, are not intended to be subject to the force of law.

BALFOUR V BALFOUR [1919] 2 KB 571

This case involved an agreement between a husband and wife. The husband was a civil servant and they lived in Ceylon because of his job. He temporarily moved back to England with his wife, before returning to work in Ceylon, leaving his wife behind. The wife had to remain in England on medical advice. Before he left for Ceylon, the husband agreed to pay £30 per month maintenance to the wife so she could continue to live in England. This was to be paid until she was well enough to rejoin him in Ceylon.

However, this never happened, and the couple divorced. The wife took legal action to enforce the monthly maintenance payment from the husband as a legally enforceable contract.

Held: there was no intention to create legal relations, and should not be in the case of domestic arrangements. Domestic arrangements as part of a husband and wife relationship cannot be sued upon. The wife failed to enforce the maintenance payment.

14 [1960] 3 All ER 62.

This approach was followed in the case of *Spellman v Spellman*.[15] This case involved the purchase of a car by a husband for his wife. Relations between the two were not good, and the car was purchased by the husband as a way of trying to improve relations with his wife. The car was bought on hire purchase, so ownership remained with the hire purchase company while repayments were being made, but the registration document was in the wife's name. The husband made the repayments to the hire purchase company.

Relations between the husband and wife did not improve, and the husband left the wife, taking the car with him. The wife claimed that the car was a gift to her, and therefore she was legally entitled to it.

Applying *Balfour v Balfour*, the court held that, as a domestic arrangement, this could not be legally enforced. There was no intention to create a legally binding agreement, and it was considered to be merely a domestic matter.

Through these cases there is a clear principle that the law will not normally interfere with domestic arrangements. However, a distinction has been drawn between different types of arrangements in the case of *Merritt v Merritt*.[16]

MERRITT V MERRITT [1970] 2 ALL ER 760

This case involved an agreement between husband and wife at a point where they had separated. The husband had left the wife for another woman, while the wife remained in the matrimonial home. An agreement was made whereby the wife agreed to continue the mortgage payments on the house, and the husband would transfer the house to the wife's sole ownership once the wife had paid off the remainder of the mortgage. This was done by way of a written agreement, which the husband signed and dated.

Held: the agreement was intended to create a legally binding relationship between the parties and allowed it to be enforced.

KEY LEARNING POINT

What the court did here was to draw a distinction between different types of agreements between husbands and wives on the basis of their circumstances. *Balfour v Balfour* and *Spellman v Spellman* were both cases involving agreements made when the couples were considered to be 'together' in a domestic arrangement.

---

15 *Spellman v Spellman* [1961] 2 All ER 498.
16 [1970] 2 All ER 760.

Merritt v Merritt involved one where the parties were not. Regardless of the legal status of these couples, there is evidence to rebut the presumption against intention to be legally bound where the situation was no longer 'domestic'. Lord Denning quoted his own previous comments from *Gould v Gould* in his judgment in the *Merritt* case to support this:

> When ... husband and wife, at arm's length, decide to separate and the husband promises to pay a sum as maintenance to the wife during the separation, the court does, as a rule, impute to them an intention to create legal relations.[17]

In applying this to the *Merritt* case, Denning made reference to the need to evaluate the situation objectively, as is the case with commercial agreements: 'In all these cases the court does not try to discover the intention by looking into the minds of the parties. It looks at the situation in which they were placed and asks itself: would reasonable people regard this agreement as intended to be binding?'[18]

So far, we have referred to husband and wife relationships. However, the notion of 'domestic arrangements' is broader than this. *Jones v Padavatton*[19] is a case involving a mother and daughter that also raised issues of intention to be legally bound.

JONES V PADAVATTON [1969] 2 ALL ER 616, [1969] 1 WLR 328

This case involved a woman who, in 1962, left a well-paid job in Washington, DC to come to London to study for the Bar. She did this as a result of her mother promising to provide her with $200 a month in order to allow the daughter to support herself whilst studying. In 1964, the mother bought a house in London and the daughter lived there rent-free, and was allowed to rent out the other rooms in the house in order to generate income; this was *in lieu* of the maintenance payments.

After the daughter had failed to complete her studies after five years of studying, the mother attempted to gain repossession of the house she had bought, and the daughter claimed that she was unable to do so because of their agreement. The mother argued that, as a domestic arrangement, it lacked an intention to create a legally binding arrangement, and was therefore not enforceable.

Held: the mother was entitled to possession of the house, and the majority of the court (Dankwerts and Fenton-Atkinson LJJ) concluded that this was because it was a domestic arrangement that lacked an intention to be legally bound. Salmon LJ

---

17 [1969] 3 All ER 728 at 730.
18 [1970] 2 All ER 760 at 762.
19 [1969] 2 All ER 616, [1969] 1 WLR 328.

disagreed and concluded that the arrangement was of such a serious nature (giving up a well-paid job and moving to another country) that it would be wrong to consider it not legally binding. However, he came to the same conclusion as the rest of the court on the basis that the agreement should run for a 'reasonable' period of time. A reasonable period of time to complete the Bar course could not exceed five years.

The notion of seriousness of the agreement as a basis to rebut the presumption in domestic arrangements was also shown in the case of *Parker v Clark*.[20]

PARKER V CLARK [1960] 1 ALL ER 93, [1960] 1 WLR 286

This case involved two couples, the Clarks, who were elderly and lived in a large house, and the Parkers, who were related to the Clarks (Mrs Parker was Mrs Clark's niece).

The Clarks proposed to the Parkers that they should move in with them as they had a large house and could share living expenses. The Clarks also promised that the Parkers would therefore inherit the house upon the eventual death of the Clarks. The Parkers sold their own house and moved in with the Clarks. After a while, the arrangement went sour, and Mr Clark suggested to the Parkers that they should find somewhere else to live. The Parkers refused to do so. Life became so unpleasant that eventually the Parkers moved out, feeling that, if they did not do so, they would be evicted.

Held: the presumption against intention to create a legally binding agreement had been rebutted here due to the seriousness of the promises that had been made. The Parkers had taken quite a drastic step in selling their own house and moving in with the Clarks, such that an objective view of the situation would conclude that it was intended to be legally binding.

4.4.1 CONTEXTUAL APPROACH

One weakness of the system of presumptions discussed above is that it forces all contracts to be categorised either as domestic or commercial in order to establish which presumption should be the starting point. This creates problems in situations where it is not easy to do this, and in fact can lead to some rather artificial classifications just for the purposes of starting with a presumption. *Edmonds v Lawson*[21] is an example of this. The case was brought by a pupil barrister, who was attempting to argue that they

---

20 [1960] 1 All ER 93, [1960] 1 WLR 286.
21 [2000] EWCA Civ 69, [2000] QB 501.

should be entitled to be paid the minimum wage as per the Minimum Wage Act 1998, rather than being unpaid, as was the situation at the time. The court did not consider it to be a commercial situation, as they refused the argument to classify pupil barristers as apprentices, but similarly they did not consider it appropriate to classify an agreement for education as domestic either.

The court therefore decided upon a contextual approach and decided that, although the context was educational, there were significant implications for both parties as a result of the arrangement, and therefore on this basis there was no reason why the agreement could not be considered to be legally binding. The claim for minimum wage failed for other reasons; however, the court concluded that the arrangement had all the characteristics of a binding agreement.

ASSESSMENT TIP

The contextual approach is significant because of the fact that it points to a more flexible way of dealing with the intention issue; one which takes account of the fact that not every arrangement will fit neatly into one of the two categories for the purposes of setting up presumptions. Recognising the usefulness of this approach, and recognising where it could be applied, can demonstrate an ability to go beyond mere mechanical application of the presumptions and demonstrate an understanding of the challenges presented in this area.

4.5 CAPACITY

The law on capacity is something that does not affect the majority of contracts. This is because whether someone has the capacity to enter into a contract is only an issue in a number of minor, and rather specific, situations. The reason why this is an issue is because if someone is said to lack the capacity to enter into a legally binding contract, it calls into question the validity of the agreement made. This is therefore an issue for the person entering into a contract with that person, as they will be concerned with whether they are able to enforce the agreement against the individual who is said to lack capacity.

There are certain classes of persons who lack the capacity for one reason or another and therefore require protection from the *laissez faire* approach of the will theory mentioned in Chapter 1. The will theory assumes that we all have equal capacity and understanding to enter freely into contracts, and so we should be allowed the freedom to do so.

Contracts which have the potential for problems based on capacity are those shown in Figure 4.2:

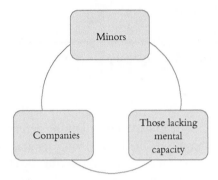

Figure 4.2 Parties to a contract who may lack capacity

These parties all have rules within contract law that govern their ability to enter into contracts. However, this does not mean that these parties can never enter into a contract; it just means that where normally the law does not interfere with the nature of a bargain, these are circumstances where the law can, if required. However, the aim is not to restrict, but to protect, those involved, on both sides of the contract, as we will see in this chapter.

The law in this area has a tricky job to perform. There is, on the one hand, the need to protect those in a position that may be exploited by others; but, on the other hand, a need to provide legal certainty to those who enter into contracts with anyone in the three categories mentioned above. See Figure 4.3.

Figure 4.3 The law on capacity balances between

4.5.1 NECESSARIES

'**Necessaries**' as a concept has an important role to play in the law regarding capacity. It is part of the 'legal certainty' side of the equation in the diagram above, as it allows certain contracts to go ahead on the grounds that otherwise, it may discourage people from entering into contracts where they believe there is a capacity issue. This is counter-productive to the need to encourage exchange and bargain that contract law is intended to promote, and therefore where a contract is for 'necessaries' then it will often be allowed to stand unless there are compelling reasons not to allow it.

> **ESSENTIAL** DEFINITION: NECESSARIES
>
> Sale of Goods Act 1979 s. 3(3):
>
> > In subsection (2) above 'necessaries' means goods suitable to the condition in life of the … person concerned and to his actual requirements at the time of the sale and delivery.

This concept is one that is not easily understood by just the definition in the Sale of Goods Act, and therefore has been subject to judicial discussion regarding what is meant by 'suitable to the condition in life'. This is very subjective, and therefore is reflected in the case law. We will examine this case law in the context of the categories of persons lacking capacity discussed below.

4.6 MENTAL CAPACITY

The first category is those who lack the mental capacity to enter into a contract. There is clear and logical reasoning as to why such persons should be protected: if they are unable to appreciate the nature of what they are doing when they enter a contract, their agreement to a contract is not an expression of their willingness to be bound by its terms.

The law in this area used to be complicated, and excluded certain persons permanently from the ability to enter into contracts. Anyone who was certified under Part IV of the Mental Health Act 1983 (commonly referred to as being 'sectioned') lacked the capacity to enter into a contract, and therefore was never bound by attempts to dispose of their own property by way of a contract.

However, the law was changed by the Mental Capacity Act 2005, with s. 2(1) defining those who lack capacity as follows:

> For the purposes of this Act, a person lacks capacity in relation to a matter if at the material time he is unable to make a decision for himself in relation to the matter because of an impairment of, or a disturbance in the functioning of, the mind or brain.

This demonstrates a much more flexible approach to the issue of mental capacity than previously, as those 'certified' under the Mental Health Act 1983 would never find themselves in a position to have the capacity to contract. This ignores the understanding of many mental health conditions that there may be times where an individual may lack capacity, and other times where they do not.

Section 2(2) goes on to add that the impairment can be temporary or permanent. This means that the definition of mental impairment can cover a wide range of conditions, as illustrated by the case of *Dunhill v Burgin*,[22] where the lack of capacity resulted from a head injury sustained in a road accident.

Section 3 provides further clarification on the nature of what needs to be understood, as explanation of the decision can be made to that person in a way that is appropriate to that person (s. 3(2), including visual aids, simplified language, etc.). It is also not relevant if the information relevant to the decision is quickly forgotten, as the focus is upon whether the person appreciated their decision at that point in time, rather than appreciation in the future. Section 3(1) states that:

> a person is unable to make a decision for himself if he is unable –
>
> (a) to understand the information relevant to the decision,
> (b) to retain that information,
> (c) to use or weigh that information as part of the process of making the decision, or
> (d) to communicate his decision.

4.6.1 TEMPORARY IMPAIRMENT: INTOXICATION

The advantage of the definition in the Mental Capacity Act 2005 is that it is deliberately broad in its scope. It can therefore cover a wide range of diagnosable medical conditions, but also other ways in which an individual can be impaired. This therefore also covers impairment through drink or drugs, as these can also result in a person's lack of ability to make a decision for themselves. This is a lot less rigid than the situation prior to the 2005 Act.

KEY LEARNING POINT

The law addresses the balance discussed above in the fact that intoxication only operates to negate mental capacity in a situation where it is evident to the other party at the time of making the agreement. This presents little problem in the majority of cases of persons intoxicated by alcohol, mainly because in the majority of situations the level of intoxication needing to be achieved to impair a person's abilities as per s. 2(1) of the Mental Capacity Act 2005 is high enough that the symptoms make it obvious that the person is impaired. However, if that impairment is not known to the other party, it may defeat an attempted argument of lack of capacity. This was illustrated by *Imperial Loan Co v Stone*.[23] Although this case concerned a mental disorder rather than drunkenness, the court established that it must be established that the mental impairment was known to the other party. This was also confirmed by the Supreme Court in *Dunhill v Burgin*.[24]

---

22 [2014] 1 WLR 933.
23 [1892] 1 QB 599.
24 [2014] 1 WLR 933.

The finding that a person lacks the mental capacity to enter into an agreement therefore results in a contract being voidable. This is because, particularly with temporary impairment, it is possible that a person may confirm the agreement at a later stage. If this later confirmation is made at a point that the individual is said to have contractual capacity, this results in the contract being considered validly consented to. *Matthews v Baxter*[25] illustrated this point.

MATTHEWS V BAXTER (1873) LR 8 EXCH 132, 42 LJ EX 73

A contract for the sale of land by auction was not signed by the party to the agreement, but by someone else on his behalf, because he was too drunk to sign himself.

Held: this made it a voidable agreement which could be later ratified by him once he had become sober.

4.6.2 NECESSARIES

As discussed above, those lacking mental capacity can still be required to pay for necessaries, by virtue of the Sale of Goods Act 1979 s. 3(2):

> Where necessaries are sold and delivered … to a person who by reason of mental incapacity or drunkenness is incompetent to contract, he must pay a reasonable price for them.

This therefore differentiates between executed and executory contracts because, even those agreements considered to be for necessaries will not be enforceable if the other party has not performed their duties under the contract. Only executed promises can be enforced. However, any agreement that falls outside the concept of 'necessaries' and where the contracting party lacks the capacity will be voidable and therefore, as this gives the impaired party the decision on whether the agreement should go ahead or not, makes it unenforceable unless there has been subsequent confirmation of the agreement (as discussed above in *Matthews v Baxter*).[26]

As pointed out above, this approach therefore addresses the need to strike a balance between protection of the mentally impaired and integrity of contracts where the other person was unaware of the mental state of the other party.

---

25 (1873) LR 8 Exch 132, 42 LJ Ex 73.

26 For further discussion on the application of the meaning of 'necessaries', please see the section on minors' contracts, below.

4.7 MINORS

A minor is anyone below the age of 18 in England and Wales.[27] All minors are treated equally regarding the issue of capacity: anyone under 18 is said to lack legal capacity to enter into a contract, and is therefore subject to special rules. Although this creates a situation whereby upon turning 18 a person instantly acquires the capacity that they did not possess a day earlier, the point here is to ensure that particularly young (and therefore most likely inexperienced) persons have the protection of the law, rather than it being thought of as a restriction.

4.7.1 NECESSARIES

As with those lacking mental capacity, minors are liable for 'necessaries' under s. 3(2) of the Sale of Goods Act 1979, but are required to pay a 'reasonable' price. The issue of what counts as a 'necessary' has been dealt with in a number of cases involving minors, mainly because it presents itself in the legislation as a rather vague term.

Several cases from the early twentieth century addressed this particular issue and established that it was very much a subjective issue based upon the individual concerned.

For example, in *Nash v Inman*[28] the case involved an order of clothing placed by a minor which had included, amongst other things, '11 fancy waistcoats'. The clothing had been sold and delivered to the minor, who had argued that the contract was not enforceable due to the fact that he was a minor. The court had to decide whether the one exception to this, that the goods were necessaries, was applicable here.

The definition of 'necessaries' from the Sale of Goods Act has three elements to it (see Figure 4.4).

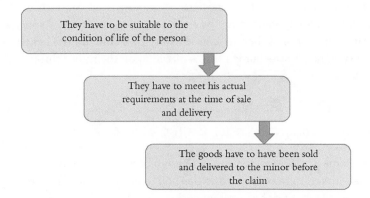

Figure 4.4 Contracts for 'necessaries' are enforceable when

---

27 In Scotland, the Age of Legal Capacity (Scotland) Act 1991 lowered the age of capacity in Scotland to 16.
28 [1908] 2 KB 1.

The first of these is the subjective part, and therefore in this case was based upon the position that the individual was in; what is 'necessary' for one person will not be 'necessary' for another. The second part requires the goods to meet the requirements of the individual, again somewhat subjective, but based upon the person's needs at the time.

ANALYSING THE LAW

In *Nash v Inman*, it was shown that the minor was already 'adequately clothed' at the time of sale and delivery. The seller was obliged to demonstrate that the minor fell within both parts of the definition in the Sale of Goods Act and, as he had not done so here, he was not able to establish that the goods were 'necessaries'. The minor in this case was not obliged to pay for them.

This does present a problem to anyone selling goods to a minor, in that they must be satisfied that the sale is for 'necessaries' if they wish to enforce the contract. It is arguably difficult for a salesperson to satisfy himself of this. Even more difficult is the salesperson possibly knowing whether the minor in question had already been adequately supplied with the items in question. The third part is the only one that the salesperson has any real control over, as the 1979 Act shows that the goods must have been sold and delivered. This does suggest that if the goods have not yet been supplied, the minor could repudiate the contract. It therefore follows that an executory contract is not enforceable, and in *Nash v Inman* it was the case that the goods had been supplied. *Roberts v Gray*[29] presents the alternative argument that an executory contract could be binding, but this was prior to the 1979 Act.

4.7.2 BENEFICIAL CONTRACTS OF SERVICE

One particular category of contracts for 'necessaries' are beneficial contracts of service. This includes contracts for apprenticeship or employment of the minor. As such they are enforceable against the minor as they are considered to be to the minor's benefit. However, if the benefit is outweighed by the burden that is placed upon the minor through the contract, they are not enforceable.

DE FRANCESCO V BARNUM (1890) 45 CH D 430, 60 LJ CH 63

This case concerned a contract for apprenticeship of a minor. The master who employed her agreed to teach her stage dancing, and to pay her for all engagements that she danced at as part of her apprenticeship. The minor agreed not to take any other professional work elsewhere, and not to marry during the time of the apprenticeship. However, the master had no obligation to find engagements for the minor, and no obligation to support her during periods of unemployment.

---

29 [1913] 1 KB 520.

The minor took an engagement to dance with someone else, and she and the person she worked for were sued by the master. He attempted to enforce the contract of apprenticeship against her.

Held: the terms of the contract were not reasonable, and would not enforce it against the minor.

However, not all minors' contracts will be approached in this way. The courts, because they are dealing with minors, will take a 'paternalistic' approach to such arrangements where it is seen as beneficial to the minor for them to adhere to the contract that they have agreed to.

DOYLE V WHITE CITY STADIUM [1935] 1 KB 110, [1934] ALL ER REP 252

This case concerned the terms of a minor's boxing licence. He agreed to adhere to the rules of the British Boxing Board (BBB). One of the rules concerned the money a boxer earned from a fight (the 'purse') being withheld in the event of the boxer 'committing a deliberate foul, for not trying, or retiring without sufficient cause, or if the referee gives a no contest decision'. The boxer engaged in a fight where he deliberately hit below the belt and was disqualified. As a result, his fee for the fight (£3,000, win, lose, or draw) was withheld and he challenged this.

Held: the agreement Doyle signed to abide by the BBB rules was enforceable against him, due to the fact that it was to his benefit to be required to stick to the rules of the sport. Although the boxer felt it was not to his benefit to forfeit the purse for the fight, it was decided that the contract as a whole was to his benefit.

A more recent example of a sports agreement with a minor concerned the footballer Wayne Rooney, in *Proform Sports Management Ltd v Proactive Sports Management Ltd.*[30]

PROFORM SPORTS MANAGEMENT LTD V PROACTIVE SPORTS MANAGEMENT LTD [2006] EWHC 2812 (CH), [2007] 1 ALL ER 542

This case concerned a management agreement entered into between the claimant and Rooney, then aged 15. It was a management contract for a two-year period, under which the claimant would act as Rooney's personal representative and negotiate all contracts on his behalf, in return for 5% plus VAT of all contract earnings and transfers. Rooney was prohibited from engaging anyone else in this capacity during the period of the contract.

30 [2006] EWHC 2812 (Ch), [2007] 1 All ER 542.

The defendant approached Rooney with a view to being his representative a few months prior to the end of the two-year period of the contract, and Rooney signed an agreement with him, sending a letter giving notice to the claimant repudiating the contract on the grounds that it was voidable at his option because he had signed it as a minor.

The claimant sued the defendant for procuring a breach of contract, and the defendant argued that, as the contract with Rooney was voidable, it was not possible to procure the breach of a voidable contract. The defendant claimed that the contract was not one for 'necessaries' because it was not one for training, education or instruction of the player, and so was not enforceable against Rooney as a minor.

Held: the management contract was not analogous to the type of agreement that was enforceable against a minor as being a contract for 'necessaries' and therefore, as it was voidable by Rooney, the defendants could not be liable for procuring a breach as it was a voidable contract. They therefore found in favour of the defendants.

4.7.3 CONTRACTS REPUDIATED BY AGE 18

Certain types of contract differ from the usual rule in that they can be enforced against a minor once that minor has attained the age of 18, unless they repudiate the agreement within a reasonable time of having done so. What counts as 'reasonable' is not completely clear. Contracts that are affected by this rule would include agreements for an interest in land or for shares in a company. The thing that these agreements have in common is that there is a continuing benefit that is acquired through such contracts, with corresponding obligations.

4.7.4 RESTITUTIONARY REMEDIES AGAINST MINORS

The consequence of the wording in s. 3(2) of the Sale of Goods Act 1979 implies that where goods have not been 'sold and delivered' (as discussed above), that the common law would prevent any party contracting with a minor from getting a remedy as the contract would be unenforceable.

This is an unfortunate position for anyone entering into contracts with minors and, were it allowed to stand, would most likely result in contracts entered into with a minor being only those of an executed nature. However, it is likely that the effect of this would be considered minimal, because for a minor to enter into an executory contract, it would involve the minor being able to purchase items on credit. Normal forms of consumer credit such as loans or credit cards are not available to the under 18s, which would affect this.

However, there is a resolution to this contained in s. 3(1) of the Minors' Contracts Act 1987, which allows the court to apply the equitable remedy of restitution in situations where the minor has acquired property under the contract. Section 3(1)(b) extends not only to the actual property acquired, but also to 'any property representing it'. This would prevent unjust enrichment by the minor in situations where the agreement cannot be enforced because of the age rule. Further information regarding restitution generally can be found in Chapter 14.

4.8 COMPANIES

The third category of persons affected by issues of capacity is companies. A company, being an incorporated entity registered with Companies House in the UK is considered to have legal personality. The consequence of this is that it is considered a separate legal entity from its members, shareholders, directors, etc.

This can be illustrated by the case of *Salomon v A Salomon & Co Ltd*,[31] which refers to the concept of the 'corporate veil' that exists between the company and its shareholders. This has the effect of protecting shareholders, for example, as their liability for the company is limited to the value of their shares. It also means, for the purposes of capacity, that any issue of capacity concerns the capacity of the company and not anyone connected with it through shareholding, directorship, etc.

The way in which the capacity to contract is judged is through the company's articles of association, which are its constitution. This sets out the purpose of the company and therefore effectively restricts its actions to only those purposes. Entering into a contract outside of the purpose set out in the constitution would be considered to be outside the capacity of the company to act. This is referred to as the company acting *ultra vires*.

Section 39 of the Companies Act 2006 removed this *ultra vires* rule for any agreement made between the company and any external person. It therefore meant that the rule concerning capacity was only of relevance when looking at agreements made between the company and its directors, shareholders etc. According to s. 40, any external person merely needs to demonstrate that they were acting in good faith in the contract they had entered into, regarding the purpose of the contract if it fell outside the company's constitution. The likelihood that someone external to the company would know the purpose of that company as set out in the constitution is much less than someone who worked for or in the company.

This concept of 'legal personality' attached to companies does not extend to all types of organisation. For example, limited liability partnerships are registered in the same way as companies and do have legal personality in the same way (except they have unlimited capacity, unlike companies). However unregistered organisations, like general partnerships, are not considered to be separate legal entities and therefore do not possess any particular status that gives them capacity beyond that of the partners in the organisation.

31 [1897] AC 22.

4.9 CONTRACTUAL FORM

The final element of contract law in this chapter that can have an effect upon validity is that of form. Generally, there are no formal requirements placed upon a contract: for the vast majority of agreements there is no obligation for a contract to be in writing. Depending upon the situation, it may be advisable for high value or complex agreements to be in writing, particularly those that are commercially very important. There is also the temptation to view contracts as needing to be in writing as this makes the job of the courts in enforcing them that much easier. This is usually the reason behind the above advice about high-value contracts.

However there has been a resistance to a universal rule requiring particular formalities because it assumes a 'one size fits all' approach. There are a number of everyday contracts that are entered into by the general public, which would be significantly inconvenienced by a requirement of a particular formality. Because of this, whether a contract is produced in writing or not will be by and large left to the parties concerned, and does not affect its enforceability. It is merely the convenience of having proof that is important.

ANALYSING THE LAW

The fact that there is no requirement for formalities in contract law demonstrates the need for it to be flexible in the light of practicalities. It would make the issue of formation of contract a lot more certain if there were certain requirements of form that made it clear when a contract was being entered into.

For example, the case of *Carlill v Carbolic Smoke Ball Co* that was discussed in Chapter 2 would have had a very different outcome if particular formalities were required as part of making the contractual agreement. If the contract had to be in writing, this would have prevented an agreement from existing, regardless of the intention of the parties involved.

Similarly in a contemporary context, many simple agreements like buying newspapers in a shop, or a drink in a pub, would be made either unnecessarily complicated or not legally binding. The law should be flexible enough to deal with everyday situations.

There are, however, certain categories of contract for which there are requirements of formality. They are in the minority, but where there is a requirement of formality, this will affect the validity of the contract. If the form is not followed, the agreement will be unenforceable. Those contracts that have a requirement of form can be broken down into the following categories (see Figure 4.5):

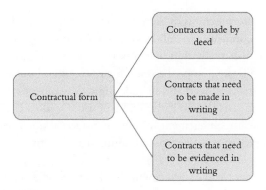

Figure 4.5 Contracts required to be in a certain form

4.9.1 CONTRACTS MADE BY DEED

Those contracts that fall into this category come from the common law rules regarding matters that need to be dealt with by way of a formal deed, under seal. This is a very old requirement, and one that is associated with some rather old traditions. However some of the more Victorian requirements have now been removed. For example, there is no longer a need to use a particular type of paper,[32] or to use a wax seal to execute a deed.[33]

Section 1 of the Law of Property (Miscellaneous Provisions) Act 1989 provides the guidance regarding what is necessary in order for an agreement to be executed as a deed (see Figure 4.6).

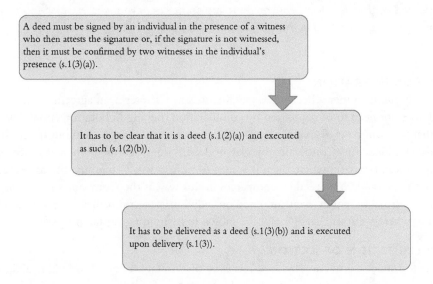

Figure 4.6 Requirements of a deed

---

32 See s. 1(1)(a) of the Law of Property (Miscellaneous Provisions) Act 1989.
33 See s. 1(1)(b) of the Law of Property (Miscellaneous Provisions) Act 1989.

Section 1(4) has a broad interpretation of 'signature' in relation to deeds, and includes the idea of 'making one's mark' as counting as a valid signature. The effect of this is therefore that a signature can be anything that fits within that very broad idea, and not restricted to merely signing one's name. There is the potential scope for this to extend out to digitally produced deeds, if the idea of an instrument can also include digital documents. Certainly if s. 1(1)(a) is read in conjunction with s. 1(4) then it should be possible to do so. It would also be in line with the move towards the encouragement to move contractual documents online with the Electronic Signatures Directive and Electronic Commerce Directive.[34]

The most commonly known form of agreement that has to be executed in this way is a contract for the sale of land, which is dealt with by ss. 52 and 54 of the Law of Property Act 1925. Anyone who has bought or sold a house will be familiar with the document involved here, although most people would not necessarily have recognised it as a deed, relying upon their solicitor to be concerned with such details.

EXPLAINING THE LAW

There are some contracts that are required to be made by deed, as we have discussed above. However, it is also worth pointing out at this stage that it is possible to execute any agreement by way of deed, following the requirements for a formal deed discussed earlier. In the main, where it is not required, most people will not bother with this method of executing a contract, mainly because the requirements are more of a hindrance than a help. However, there are some circumstances in which there are advantages to contracting in this way, as outlined below.

4.9.1.1 CONSIDERATION

Deeds are useful instruments because, as we discussed in Chapter 3, an agreement executed by deed does not need to be supported by consideration moving in both directions. This means that they can be used to make a gratuitous promise enforceable without the need for reciprocal consideration. Contracting by way of deed is not often used where it is not legally required, but can be useful where there is a need to make a legally binding gift, for example to charity. They can also be used by companies in this way, as the Companies Act 2006 extends the formality requirements imposed on individuals to companies.[35] This is useful to companies where a gift to charity has to be shown to be binding for tax purposes.

4.9.1.2 LIMITATION OF ACTION

One final feature of contracting by deed relates to the limitation period for taking action for breach of contract. As discussed in Chapter 11, any action for breach of contract has to be

---

34 See the Electronic Signatures Directive 1999/93/EC (to be replaced by Regulation 910/2014 on electronic identification and trust services for electronic transactions in the internal market) and the Electronic Commerce Directive 2000/31/EC, the combination of which pave the way for formalities in contracts to be done electronically.

35 See Part 4 of the Companies Act 2006, ss. 43–47 for further details.

commenced within six years. However, under s. 8(1) of the Limitation Act 1980, that period is extended to 12 years for contracts made by way of deed. The limitation period commences from the moment of breach; however contracting by deed may be helpful where it is possible that breach may not be discovered for a long period of time.[36]

4.9.2 CONTRACTS MADE IN WRITING

Some agreements have to be made in writing. These should be distinguished from the previous category because there is no need for them to be made using the formalities of a deed, but the contract itself must be a written document.

The following contracts have to be in writing (see Figure 4.7):

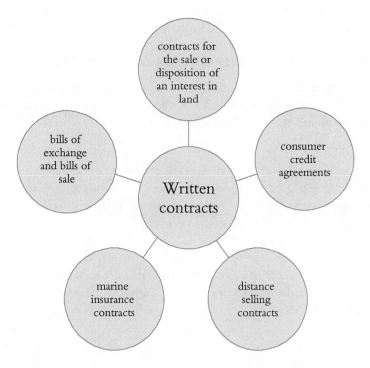

Figure 4.7 Contracts that must be in writing

4.9.3 CONSUMER CREDIT AGREEMENTS

One of the most important areas where contracts must be in writing is that regarding consumer credit agreements. The Consumer Credit Act 1974 (now amended by the Consumer Credit Act 2006) introduced this requirement, along with a number of formalities that needed to be part of the written agreement with the consumer. The provisions regarding

---

36 For example, where a piece of art is purchased and then several years later assessed to be a forgery, as was the case in *Leaf v International Galleries* [1950] 2 KB 86, [1950] 1 All ER 693 (see Chapter 8). Although it should be pointed out that this case was heard on the basis of misrepresentation and not breach.

the form required for a written contract for consumer credit are contained in s. 60 of the 1974 Act, and the prescribed form is described in regulations, most notably by the Consumer Credit (Agreements) Regulations 1983 and 2010.[37]

The regulations set out the form that must be used in an agreement, the fact that it has to be signed by the consumer, requirements of notice of rights to cancel and other information such as a clear indication of the interest rates charged, shown as an annual percentage rate (APR), and so on. The rationale behind this was to ensure that information that consumers were required to be given would ensure they were informed when they entered into such agreements.

Failure to comply with the regulations will not void the contract, but will make it unenforceable without a court order. Therefore, in the event of a default by the consumer on their credit or hire purchase agreement, the lender would not be able to recover the debt.

4.9.4 CONTRACTS FOR SALE/DISPOSITION OF AN INTEREST IN LAND

The largest area of contracts that are required to be in writing is with regard to the sale or disposition of an interest in land. This is dealt with in s. 2 of the Law of Property (Miscellaneous Provisions) Act 1989. Section 2(1) requires:

> A contract for the sale or other disposition of an interest in land can only be made in writing and only by incorporating all the terms which the parties have expressly agreed in one document or, where contracts are exchanged, in each.

This therefore requires that the contractual document incorporates all the terms to the agreement, or as set out in s. 2(2), it can be set out by reference to another document. However, if this is the case, the document containing the terms must be signed by each of the parties to the agreement.

RECORD V BELL [1991] 1 WLR 853

There was an attempt at incorporation of terms into a contract, where those terms were contained in a secondary document. On the date of exchange, the documents to be attached to the contract were not available in final form, and therefore exchange went ahead on condition that the documents were as they were expected to be. When the purchaser did not pay the contract price, there was an attempt to sue for

---

37 Form and content of consumer credit agreements is prescribed in regs. 2 and 3 of the Consumer Credit (Agreements) Regulations 1983 (S.I. 1983/1553) and supplemented by reg. 3 of the Consumer Credit (Agreements) Regulations 2010 (S.I. 2010/1014).

specific performance, but the vendor argued that the contract did not comply with s. 2 because of the absence of the secondary documents.

Held: where reference was made to further documents in the contract, that they needed to be attached in order for the sale to comply with the requirements of s. 2.

The other aspect of this is the requirement that the parties involved must have agreed to the terms. This would normally be done by signing the document. *Marlbray Ltd v Laditi*[38] involved a situation where a contract for the sale of land named both the husband and wife as the purchasers, but only the husband signed the relevant documents. As he had no authority to sign on his wife's behalf, the contract, although valid, was only binding upon him, and not his wife.

4.9.4.1 'IN WRITING' AND ELECTRONIC CONTRACTING

Formal requirements for contracts in writing were put in place before considerations of making contracts by electronic means became important. Even the 1989 Act came before email, and therefore this has posed a particular issue for dealing with parties who have dealt with each other in this way. The delivery of documents by electronic means is now widespread, and email in particular is full of terminology that invites people to consider it akin to dealing with people in writing by more traditional means. However, it does not automatically follow that contracts can automatically be considered to be 'in writing' where communication between the parties has been electronic.

The courts have accepted that email is capable of satisfying the requirement for something to be 'in writing' as a general principle. The case of *Green (Re Stealth Construction Ltd) v Ireland*[39] acknowledged that for the purposes of s. 2 of the Law of Property (Miscellaneous Provisions) Act 1989, email was capable of satisfying the need for a contract to be in writing. This was also the approach of Judge Pelling in the Chancery Division towards the definition of 'note or memorandum' under s. 4 of the Statute of Frauds 1677 in *J Pereira Fernandes SA v Mehta*.[40]

ANALYSING THE LAW

However, this does not mean that in every case a contract communicated by email will always be considered to satisfy this requirement. In *Re Stealth Construction*, the emails relied upon to satisfy the written requirement did not contain all the terms required in the contract, and did not suggest that they were to be considered to have a binding nature. The email in question also made reference to other documents that would

38 [2016] EWCA Civ 476, [2016] 1 WLR 5147.
39 [2011] EWHC 1305 (Ch).
40 [2006] EWHC 813 (Ch).

need to be drawn up and signed by the parties involved. For this reason, in that case the email was not said to be sufficient to satisfy the requirement of 'in writing'.

Similarly, in *J Pereira Fernandes SA*, the court concluded that the need for signature of an electronic document could be satisfied. However, the incidental inclusion of a name or email address into the message as part of the process of sending it was not enough. There had to be clear intention that the inclusion of the person's name was intended to be regarded as a signature for the purposes of the written requirement.

The Court of Appeal recognised an email contract to be considered to be 'in writing' in the absence of a physical signature (referred to as a 'wet ink' signature) in *Nicholas Prestige Homes v Neal*.[41] This case did not concern s. 2, but was for an agency agreement that was then breached by the owner of the property selling his house with a different agent. However, the court's view of the email agreement was that it was a valid agreement concluded 'in writing'.

The rules regarding electronic commerce should also be borne in mind here as directives concerning electronic signatures and contracting by electronic means will also provide the clarity required for courts to be able to establish that the required intention is present in an electronic communication.

4.9.4.2 EXCEPTIONS
Where a contract does not comply with the requirements of s. 2, it is without effect. However, it is possible to retrieve the situation through a number of possible solutions.

4.9.4.3 COLLATERAL CONTRACT
In *Record v Bell*, it was possible for the situation to be retrieved by the use of a collateral contract. Although the documents in question were not available at the time of exchange, their content was warranted by the solicitor of the vendor, and it was this that led to the court finding a collateral contract regarding the content of the other documents was in place and fell outside the requirements of s. 2 (because it was an agreement about the accuracy of the documents, not about an interest in land).

4.9.4.4 ANCILLARY AGREEMENTS
The difference between a contract for the sale or disposition of land and any other agreements that might surround that sale or disposition is that the ancillary agreements are not required to conform with the requirements of s. 2. *Nweze v Nwoko*[42] provides an example of this fine distinction.

----

41 [2010] EWCA Civ 1552.
42 [2004] EWCA Civ 379.

NWEZE V NWOKO [2004] EWCA CIV 379

In this case, there was an oral agreement to sell the property for £135,000, although the written contract that was signed stated the price at £105,000. This was paid by the purchaser in full. When the parties could not agree on a schedule for the payment of the extra £30,000, the two parties entered into a compromise agreement whereby the house would be re-sold, and the £30,000 would be paid out of the proceeds of the sale. Subsequently the house was not sold, and so the original seller took action to recover the £30,000 in dispute.

There were two ways in which the original seller tried to enforce the right to the £30,000:

1) Through an attempt to enforce the original oral agreement that the purchase price was £135,000. This failed because, as a contract for the sale of land, it did not meet the requirements of s. 2 Law of Property (Miscellaneous Provisions) Act 1989 as it was not in writing.
2) Through the enforcement of the compromise agreement. The court concluded that this was not subject to the requirements of s. 2 as, in itself, it was not a contract for the sale or disposition of an interest in land. It was an agreement to put the house on the market and, if a buyer was found, to enter into an agreement to sell.

Held: the original seller was therefore entitled to enforce the agreement in order to recover the £30,000.

4.9.4.5 PROPRIETARY ESTOPPEL

The doctrine of estoppel can be used in these circumstances where it can be shown that one party has acted to their detriment in reliance of a situation where they have been led to believe that they will acquire an interest in land. In this way, proprietary estoppel operates in a similar way to promissory estoppel, which was discussed in Chapter 3, in that it 'estops' the other party from enforcing rights.

The use of proprietary estoppel was successful in the case of *Yaxley v Gotts*.[43]

YAXLEY V GOTTS [2000] CH 162 (CA (CIV DIV))

This case concerned an agreement between Y and G that Y would renovate a property and act as managing agent. G would purchase the property, in exchange for which Y would be given ownership of the ground floor. Y did as stated in the agreement, but

---

43 [2000] Ch 162 (CA (Civ Div)).

the property was put into the name of G's son, and there was then a dispute where G denied promising Y the ground floor.

Held: proprietary estoppel was established in this case. On this basis, they therefore felt that this was sufficient basis for a constructive trust, and therefore Y was to be given ownership of the ground floor. This was challenged by G, on the basis of the written requirement of s. 2. However, because of a finding of a constructive trust, the court held that under s. 2(5)(c) the agreement was exempt from the requirements of s. 2.

The case of *Yeoman's Row Management Ltd v Cobbe*[44] is an example of an unsuccessful attempt to use proprietary estoppel in this way.

YEOMAN'S ROW MANAGEMENT LTD V COBBE [2008] UKHL 55, 1 WLR 1752

A property developer entered into an oral agreement that, if they successfully obtained planning permission for the redevelopment of a block of flats, they would be able to buy the block of flats at a set price. However, upon obtaining permission, the price was put up, and the developer argued that proprietary estoppel applied. The court however denied that this could be used, as proprietary estoppel would therefore go against the express requirements of s. 2.

Held: the developer would be entitled to a *quantum meruit* payment for the expenses he had incurred on the planning permission, but the oral agreement that would have given him an interest in the land was not enforceable.

4.9.4.6 DISTANCE SELLING CONTRACTS

The Consumer Contracts (Information, Cancellation and Additional Charges) Regulations 2013[45] replaced previous law on distance selling in the Consumer Protection (Distance Selling) Regulations 2000,[46] as well as the law on selling outside a normal place of business in the Cancellation of Contracts made in a Consumer's Home or Place of Work etc. Regulations 2008.[47] All of this was as a result of the Consumer Rights Directive's[48] repeal of previous EU law on the subject. It should be noted that, for any contracts entered into prior to 13 June 2014, the old law still applies.

---

44 [2008] UKHL 55, 1 WLR 1752.

45 Consumer Contracts (Information, Cancellation and Additional Charges) Regulations 2013 (S.I. 2013/3134).

46 Consumer Protection (Distance Selling) Regulations 2000 (S.I. 2000/2334).

47 Cancellation of Contracts made in a Consumer's Home or Place of Work etc. Regulations 2008 (S.I. 2008/1816).

48 Consumer Rights Directive 2011/83/EU.

This law covers two types of contract between a trader and a consumer:

1) those concluded at a distance (under the old Distance Selling Regulations)
2) those concluded away from the normal business premises of the trader.

There is a requirement under reg. 12 (off-premises contracts) and reg. 16 (distance selling contracts) for a copy of the signed agreement to be provided to the consumer within a reasonable time of the conclusion of the agreement. In the case of distance selling, the contract has to be provided in a 'durable medium', which can include email.

The regulations also stipulate the information that must be provided to the consumer as part of the written contract (regs 10 and 13) and, if these requirements are not met, the contract is rendered unenforceable.

The Regulations are also notable for bolstering consumer rights in this area, as the cooling-off period introduced by the Distance Selling Regulations has been extended from 7 to 14 days. Other information required (as stipulated in Sch. 2 of the Regulations) include supplier's identity, address, price, delivery costs and the trader's complaint handling policy.

4.9.5 CONTRACTS REQUIRED TO BE EVIDENCED IN WRITING

There is a difference between contracts that must be in writing and those that must merely be evidenced in writing. The requirements for the latter are less stringent, as we have seen from the above discussion, contracts in writing must contain all terms in the written document. Guarantees are contracts that must be evidenced in writing according to s. 4 of the Statute of Frauds 1677. A guarantee is defined in s. 4 as: 'any speciall promise to answere for the debt, default or miscarriages of another person'. According to s. 4, what is required is a 'Memorandum or Note' in writing and signed by the party concerned.

A guarantee is a situation where a party agrees to take on secondary liability in the event of the party with primary liability failing to meet his obligations. It can include agreeing to stand as guarantor for a loan: in the event of failure to pay, the guarantor has agreed to pay instead.

APPLYING THE LAW

An example of a guarantee is familiar to many students – when renting accommodation at university, a guarantor may be required, and therefore often parents will stand as guarantor for their child's rent payments. This type of contract will need to be evidenced in writing in order for it to be enforceable. It will need to be enforced if the student fails to pay their rent, and therefore the landlord can ask the parent to pay instead.

One famous example of a guarantee in commercial circumstances concerned the ITV Digital channel, which was owned by Carlton and Granada, and which collapsed when, after agreeing to pay a large amount in exchange for football broadcast rights, poor subscription sales left it unable to meet the cost of the broadcast rights. This resulted in the case of *Carlton Communications plc v The Football League*.[49] There was a dispute in this case concerning the existence of a guarantee by Carlton and Granada regarding the debts of ITV Digital to the Football League for the broadcast rights. However, the attempt by the Football League to recover the lost broadcast right payments failed because it was not able to establish a guarantee existed in the form that was required by s. 4 of the Statute of Frauds.

Discussion of the recognition of email communications as 'in writing' also extends to guarantees, as the judicial treatment of s. 4 Statute of Frauds is the same as has been discussed above. The case of *J Pereira Fernandes SA v Mehta* concerned a guarantee.

The case of *Actionstrength Ltd v International Glass Engineering SpA*[50] was an attempt at arguing that proprietary estoppel should be used in a situation where an oral guarantee had been made between the parties. The claimant attempted to argue that the use of estoppel should allow them to disregard the requirements of s. 4 Statute of Frauds. However, the House of Lords (now the Supreme Court) was unable to find a basis for estoppel, and therefore the requirements of s. 4 stood. These requirements were not met, and therefore the oral guarantee was not enforceable.

4.9.6 ELECTRONIC SIGNATURES AND ELECTRONIC COMMERCE

All the above discussion regarding the use of email to produce written agreements and show an intention to sign does not address the main hurdle to proper use of electronic communications such as email for entering into contracts. Reliable ways of concluding contracts and providing the proof that agreements have genuinely been entered into are needed for this to happen. In order to address this, the EU passed the Electronic Signatures Directive 1999/93/EC. This was implemented into UK law by the Electronic Communications Act 2000.

Although the *J Pereira Fernandes* case confirmed that a name added to an email in circumstances where it conveyed clear intention could be an electronic signature, business is more likely to rely upon some form of technological solution which will allow for the easy verification of signatures on electronic documentation. The legal regime has therefore been drafted in a deliberately broad fashion to accommodate whatever technology follows.

Section 7(1) of the 2000 Act allows admissibility of an electronic signature in legal proceedings as part of an electronic communication, and as part of this method of certification of that signature. This has been supplemented by s. 7A, which concerns the use of electronic seals and certificates as part of the verification process.[51] Section 15(2) explains

---

49 [2002] EWHC 1650 (Comm).

50 [2003] UKHL 17, [2003] 2 AC 541.

51 Inserted by the Electronic Identification and Trust Services for Electronic Transactions Regulations 2016 (S.I. 2016/696).

authenticity and refers to date and time, and whether the communication has been interfered with in any way.

Section 8 gives a general power to the Secretary of State to alter any law that interferes with the validity of electronic signatures. This power of 'authorising and facilitating the use of electronic communications' allows the law on formalities to be altered to allow use of electronic signatures and electronic means of contracting. This is aimed at preventing the traditional use of formalities from preventing electronic contracting, and therefore provides the potential for broadening the scope of the formalities themselves.

These rules on recognition of signatures should also be read in the light of a more general programme by the EU to ensure that member states' legal systems allow contracts to be concluded by electronic means, and that any legal requirements do not create obstacles to use of electronic means as opposed to traditional means. In particular, see Art.9 of the E-Commerce Directive 2000/31/EC.

4.10 BRINGING IT ALL TOGETHER

Issues of intention, capacity and form all have a bearing upon the enforceability of contracts because they each deal with important elements of the agreement that need to be satisfied at the time of making the agreement.

Although these elements may not each of themselves appear to be particularly significant (in fact, in many cases, these elements do not present any issues), and they are not as significant as the requirement for consideration (Chapter 3) or the need to show an agreement expressed as an offer and acceptance (Chapter 2), they still have a bearing upon how the law treats the agreement.

KEY LEARNING POINTS

Intention, capacity and form affect the validity and enforceability of a contract. This may affect the legal rights that a person is entitled to under an agreement. Consider the following points:

- Without the required intention to create a legally binding contract, an agreement does not demonstrate that it is enforceable
- Without the capacity to enter into an agreement, a person cannot demonstrate that they have shown the necessary agreement to be bound by its terms
- In situations where particular formalities are required, where they are not met, a contract will not be enforceable

Where these requirements present an issue, it therefore puts the legal remedies available under an agreement in jeopardy.

TAKING IT FURTHER

Beatson & Burrows, *Anson's Law of Contract*, 29th edn, Oxford University Press, 2010

Hedley, 'Keeping contract in its place: *Balfour v Balfour* and the enforceability of informal agreements' (1985) 5 OJLS 391

Peel, *Treitel on the Law of Contract*, 14th edn, Sweet & Maxwell, 2015

5

CHAPTER 5
TERMS OF A CONTRACT

5.1 INTRODUCTION

This chapter deals with the main issues of the content of a contractual agreement. So far in this book, we have concerned ourselves with the formation of the agreement, and the issues that might affect its initial validity. However, the content of the agreement is equally as important, as this will define the contractual relationship between the parties, and affect the way in which disputes will be resolved between them.

Not all of the issues are dealt with in this chapter. An agreement will often also contain exclusion clauses, a particular type of term that excludes or limits liability of one or other of the parties. These are dealt with in Chapter 6.

This chapter focusses upon the express and implied terms of the contract, how they can be identified, and how they are affected by both the common law, and also statute, for example the effect of the implied terms of the Consumer Rights Act 2015.

AS YOU READ

At the end of this chapter you should be able to:

- Understand the difference between terms, which are part of the contents of a contract, and other pre-contractual statements, which are not

- Be able to identify statements which are terms of a contract, whether they are express or implied

- Appreciate the different remedies applicable to a breach of a contractual term, in conjunction with Chapter 13 and 14 on remedies

- Understand the effect of the Consumer Rights Act 2015 on implied terms

---

5.2 TERMS

Contractual agreements are constituted of terms. This is the content of the agreement between the parties and will dictate the relationship between them. Because of this, terms are extremely important to the contract, and are the subject of many disputes when they are unclear. Therefore, as well as the existence of a contractual agreement, the next item of importance is the content of the agreement. This comes from a number of different sources (see Figure 5.1).

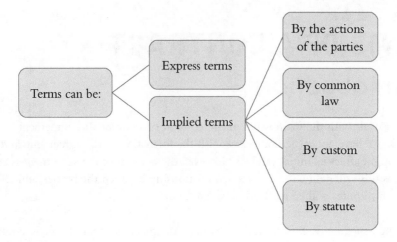

Figure 5.1 Different types of terms

The content of the agreement will also be important later on when considering any action to be taken for breach of contract. This is because it is important to establish that something was a term of the contract before it is possible to sue for breach on this basis. The purpose of this chapter is to consider how to determine what is part of the contractual agreement and what is not. This can be as simple as examining the written contractual document (if it exists) or as complicated as considering what must be part of the agreement because of legal or other requirements. Added to this is the additional complication that not every statement made, or everything discussed between the parties will subsequently form part of the contract, and this chapter will also consider what is part of the contract and what is not – the difference between:

- terms,
- representations, and
- mere puffs.

5.3 TERMS, REPRESENTATIONS, AND 'MERE PUFFS'

A contract, when negotiated between parties, will often be the result of discussions, negotiations and statements made by both parties. These negotiations will be full of **pre-contractual statements,** and this section is all about determining the status of those statements. Are they **mere puffs**, representations, or terms? The difficulty can sometimes be in interpreting what these pre-contractual statements mean. Parties will often place importance upon statements made by their counterparts in negotiations and, therefore, establishing what their status is, is an important part of establishing what forms part of the contents of a contract and what does not. This therefore leads us to the question: when do pre-contractual statements become part of the contract?

5.3.1 WHAT IS A 'MERE PUFF'?

ESSENTIAL DEFINITION: MERE PUFF

A 'mere puff' is a concept intended to demonstrate that something is a throwaway comment or something that contains no contractual significance.

EXPLAINING THE LAW

A good example of a 'mere puff' comes in the form of advertising. Although there are now regulations guarding against misleading statements being made as part of advertising, 'mere puffs' are the type of comments that are made without any intention that they be taken literally. For example in a series of famous advertisements, it has been said that 'Red Bull™ gives you wings'. No-one has ever sued the makers of Red Bull because they have failed to grow wings after consuming their product, and they would probably argue that this is just a metaphor for the stimulant effect of their product. There are numerous other examples of throwaway comments made in advertising that are not intended to be taken literally, and these can be classified as 'mere puffs'. The key characteristic here is that they are not intended to have an effect upon the contractual relationship between the parties.

The 'mere puff' argument was attempted in the case of *Carlill v Carbolic Smoke Ball Co*,[1] as one of the arguments of the Carbolic Smoke Ball Co was that the statements made in the advertisement were not intended to be taken literally or form part of the contractual agreement. However, some of the language in the advertisement, particularly that concerning the deposit of reward money in the Alliance Bank on Regent Street, meant that they were showing that they were serious about the claims they were making. 'Mere puffs' are not enforceable as they are not part of the contractual obligations.

5.4 TERMS

ESSENTIAL DEFINITION: TERM

A term of the contract is something that forms part of the contractual agreement. How it got to be a term is a matter that we shall discuss later in this chapter. However, at this stage we should emphasise that it is intended to be part of the agreement, and therefore an implied assurance as to its truth forms part of what it is.

---

1   [1892] EWCA Civ 1.

If a **term** is inaccurate, the mere fact that it is a term allows an action for breach of contract. This is what then leads to the argument that, because of this link to breach of contract, terms come with implied assurance that they are accurate. The implied assurance comes in the following form: 'if this is inaccurate, then you can take action by suing me for breach of contract'. No other type of statement made as part of the contractual process has the same level of significance: a false representation leads to an action for misrepresentation (see below), and 'mere puffs' are throwaway comments not intended to be legally binding upon the person that made the statement.

We will examine the different types of terms later in the chapter. For now, the importance is in distinguishing between what is a term and what is not a term for the purposes of the definition discussed in the box above.

5.5 REPRESENTATIONS

The key difference between a term and a **representation** is that representations, which are not considered to be part of the contractual agreement, therefore do not have that implied promise that they are true that we see with terms. There may be a number of statements made by the parties as part of negotiations, or in the run-up to finalising the agreement, but only those considered to be terms will form part of the contract. Representations are not part of the contract, and so even if they are breached, this cannot result in an action for breach of contract.

> **ESSENTIAL** DEFINITION: REPRESENTATION
>
> A representation is a pre-contractual statement which, although it may have induced a party to enter a contract, does not form part of that contract. It is therefore not actionable as a breach of contract, but instead there is liability for misrepresentation if it subsequently turns out to be false.

5.6 DISTINGUISHING TERMS AND REPRESENTATIONS

Because of the different legal consequences, it is therefore important to be able to distinguish between terms and representations. The liability that arises from each of these is different. When considering the reason behind why there is the difference between terms and representations, it again returns to the issue regarding whether there is an implied guarantee as to the truth of the statement. Was it the statement maker's intention to make a binding promise as to the truth of his or her statement, so that if the statement were inaccurate it would result in automatic breach of the contract?

The main problem with trying to take this approach with terms and representations is that proving such a thing may be difficult. It suggests that a degree of knowledge of the way in which the statement maker is thinking would be required, and this would mean a subjective element, which it would not be possible to ascertain.

In order to resolve the problems this will create, the intention of the statement maker has to be judged objectively. Whilst this may appear to be more difficult, it is actually more straightforward because you are not trying to read the mind of the individual making the statement. It can be done by looking at a number of factors that may indicate whether the statement was intended to be part of the contract or not. Case law has provided examples of what can be taken into account when considering whether something is a representation or a term. We therefore need to look at the number of these factors so that you can apply this to any situation in which you are attempting to judge whether something is a term or a representation.

EXPLAINING THE LAW

A representation is a pre-contractual statement that induces you to enter into a contract, but not a term of the contract itself. So, as a practical example, a prize raffle (which is a contract because you are entering into a contract for a game of chance) might have an advertisement that states 'thousands of pounds worth of prizes to be won' (a representation), and when purchasing your ticket, you may be told that 'the top prize is an Aston Martin car' (a term of the contract).

The representation may have induced you to enter the contract, but does not guarantee you a prize. However, if you enter into the contract and it turns out that the top prize is not an Aston Martin car, this would be a breach of contract because the guarantee implied in this is that, if you have the winning ticket, this is what you will get.

5.7 STARTING WITH A PRESUMPTION

As a helpful guide, it is possible to begin with a presumption regarding whether something was intended to be part of the contract or not. For example, where a contract has been turned into a written document, it is a common presumption that if the pre-contractual statement is in the written document, it is to be regarded as a term. Alternatively, in *Inntrepreneur Pub Co v East Crown Ltd*,[2] Lightman J suggested that the longer the interval between statement

---

2   [2000] 2 Lloyd's Rep 611.

and contract, the greater the presumption that the parties did not intend that the statement become a term. This therefore allows discussions at an early stage not to be given more emphasis than is appropriate when deciding what is a term or a representation.

However, such 'presumptions' are not completely decisive,[3] and may be rebutted by other factors that may affect whether in fact a statement is a term or a representation. They are as follows.

5.7.1 ACCEPTING RESPONSIBILITY FOR A STATEMENT OR NOT

Accepting responsibility for the truth of a statement you make can result in the statement being regarded as a term. This goes back to our earlier discussion concerning the statement maker guaranteeing the truth of their statements. The guarantee of truth makes this a term of the contract. For example, in *Schawel v Reade*,[4] where upon being informed that the horse that they wished to buy was sound, they stopped inspecting the horse, instead relying upon the statement that had been made. It was therefore made clear to the other party that they should realise that they are being held to a guarantee of the truth of the statement they are making.

However, there are also other situations where this implied guarantee of truth is not present in the statement. This is usually in situations where the statement maker advises the other party to check the reliability of the statement. They would normally do this by conducting a survey, or carrying out some other form of check. The effect that this has upon the situation is to dispel any idea that the statement is being impliedly guaranteed. If the other party is inviting you to carry out your own checks or inspection, rather than trying to guarantee the statement, they are giving you the opportunity to discover whether the statement is true or not. Where this is the case, the statement is a representation, as it clearly shows by his language that the statement was not intended to have a guarantee of its truth.

APPLYING THE LAW

Lauren is selling a watch and says it is a 'genuine Rolex Oyster in fabulous condition'. However, when Alec contacts her to buy the watch, she points out that she knows nothing about Rolex watches and only bought it because she liked the look of it. She gives Alec the opportunity to get it checked out professionally for condition and authenticity.

In this situation, Lauren is not accepting responsibility for the statement, but telling Alec to get it verified. This is therefore likely to be a representation rather than a term.

3 See *Heilbut, Symons and Co v Buckleton* [1913] AC 30, per Lord Moulton at pp. 50–51.
4 [1913] 2 IR 64, 46 ILT 281.

5.7.2 IMPORTANCE ATTACHED TEST

The importance that a party attaches to a statement can affect whether it is to be considered a term or a representation. Again, this must be dealt with objectively in order that it is possible to establish the intention of the party concerned. To do this, there are two elements:

1) The statement must be so important that the other party would not have contracted without it, and
2) It must be objectively clear that this is the case.

The application of this test therefore ensures that any unstated intentions cannot later be argued to have affected whether the statement is regarded as a term or not. Statements clearly shown to be important in the pre-contractual negotiations will therefore have an effect upon the way in which the contract is agreed.

An example of this can be seen in the case of *Bannerman v White*.[5]

BANNERMAN V WHITE (1861) 142 ER 685

This case concerned a contract for the purchase of hops to be used in brewing beer. As part of the pre-contractual discussion, the defendant in this case asked whether sulphur had been used in the production of the hops he was going to buy. He made it clear at that stage that, if it had, he would not be interested in proceeding any further with the contract. He was assured by the plaintiff that no sulphur had been used in the production of the hops. It was later discovered that a small proportion of the hops had been produced using sulphur, but that it was not possible to separate this out from the rest of the hops that did not contain sulphur.

On this basis, the defendant treated the contract as having been repudiated, on the basis that the stipulation about sulphur was a term that had been breached.

Held: the court had to decide whether this was a term, as the defendant argued, or whether it was merely a representation. Using the importance attached test, the court decided that because of the statement by the defendant that he was not interested in proceeding with the contract if sulphur had been used, this satisfied the two parts of the importance attached test. Without this stipulation, there was no contract, and the importance of it had been communicated to the other party clearly. The court therefore held that it was a term, and therefore a breach of contract.

Similarly, in *Eian Tauber Pritchard v Peter Cook & Red Ltd*,[6] the specification of a rally car bought by the plaintiff from the defendant was considered to be sufficiently important to be

---

5   (1861) 142 ER 685.
6   [1998] EWCA Civ 900.

a term of the contract, where the plaintiff had asked for the specification prior to agreeing the sale, and the defendant had copied it from the manufacturer's specifications onto their own headed paper. In addition to satisfying the requirements of the importance attached test, the presentation of the specification on their own paper suggested that the seller was assuming responsibility for its accuracy, and therefore it was considered to be a term of the contract.

Even where statements are made orally rather than in writing, it is possible for them to override written terms in a situation where they are considered to be so important to the other party that they are crucial to the contract.

COUCHMAN V HILL [1947] KB 554

An enquiry by a purchaser of two heifers at an auction prior to the sale concerned whether they were 'unserved' (i.e. there had never been an attempt to breed with them). The seller and the auctioneer both confirmed that they were in fact unserved, and it was subsequently discovered that this was not true.

Held: this was a condition of the contract due to the importance attached to it, and one which overrode written conditions in the catalogue exempting liability for inaccuracies of description in the catalogue.

5.7.3 STATEMENT MAKER'S SPECIAL KNOWLEDGE OF THE SUBJECT MATTER

Another method of assessing whether a statement is a term or representation is through a person possessing special knowledge or leading the other party to believe he has. Where this is the case, courts are more likely to hold that a statement is a term. This is because the implied guarantee required for establishing a term comes along with the expertise claimed in such situations. We expect experts to know what they are talking about, and therefore expertise is the required element for the guarantee of the truth of the statement.

What this also means is that where a person does not hold such expertise, we would not usually expect them to be held to such a standard – non-experts are not relied upon because we would not expect them to have such knowledge and therefore not rely upon the things that they say in negotiations for a contract.

OSCAR CHESS V WILLIAMS [1957] 1 WLR 370, [1957] 1 ALL ER 325

A private seller of a Morris Minor car represented it as being a 1948 model. It was in fact a 1939 model and, as it was nine years older, it was worth much less. In making a statement about the age of the car, the seller had relied upon the registration document that came with the car, because as a private seller he had no particular expertise in this area. Held: this statement was not regarded as a term. The seller had no special knowledge and had relied on the documentation available to him. In addition to this, the buyers were car dealers and would have had the knowledge and expertise to check the age of the car.

The *Oscar Chess* case is a good example of the opposite of what is needed regarding special expertise. This case should be contrasted with the one below.

DICK BENTLEY PRODUCTIONS LTD V HAROLD SMITH (MOTORS) LTD [1965] 1 WLR 623, [1965] 2 ALL ER 65

This case involved a sale by a car dealer. The claimant was sold a car by the defendant, who stated that the engine had done only 20,000 miles. There were a number of problems with the car after the sale, and eventually the claimant brought an action, claiming that the statement about mileage was a term of the contract. It turned out that the car had done closer to 100,000 miles.

Held: the statement should be treated as a term. It was treated by the court as a statement of fact, and had been made by the defendant in his capacity as a car dealer. Because of this, he had the special knowledge needed in order for the buyer to believe he could rely on the statement made.

There are two important points to note here from these cases, as discussed by Lord Denning, who was involved with both the *Oscar Chess* and *Dick Bentley* cases. Firstly, that expertise held by one party set up an important inference, that the person's statements should be relied upon as terms because of the position that they are held to be in, to know the truth of what they are saying (whether they have actually found out what they are saying is true or not). As such they therefore take responsibility for what they are saying through breach of contract if the statement is untrue.

Secondly, Denning was convinced of the role of fault in establishing that a statement was a term rather than a misrepresentation. Inferences could therefore be rebutted if it could be shown objectively that the statement was an innocent misrepresentation. In order to do this, it would be necessary to show on a standard of the intelligent bystander that he was innocent in the fault of making the statement, and it would not be reasonable in the circumstances for him to be bound by it. However, it would be extremely unlikely for someone with expertise in a particular field to be able to satisfy this test, based upon the inferences that come along with expertise, and hence Harold Smith Motors' attempts at arguing this failed.

The *Eian Tauber Pritchard* case mentioned above demonstrates the objective nature of this test, as the expertise point was also argued in this case. There was an attempt here to argue that the car dealer lacked the relevant expertise in rally car specifications, and therefore was making an innocent misrepresentation, as discussed by Denning in the *Dick Bentley* case. However, because they had copied the specification onto their own headed notepaper, to the intelligent bystander it appeared that they were accepting responsibility for the statement made. On this basis, their argument failed.

Any of the above points can affect whether something is considered a term or a representation, and therefore it is important to note that this is a matter to be decided objectively based upon the circumstances. We will return to some of these issues in the next section, as they are also grounds for considering whether a term has been incorporated or not. (See Figure 5.2.)

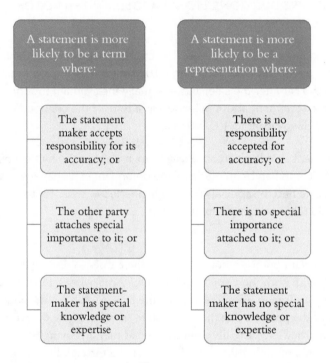

Figure 5.2 Is it a term, or a representation?

5.8 EXPRESS TERMS

ESSENTIAL DEFINITION: EXPRESS TERMS

Those items that have been specifically included by the parties at the time of their agreement.

Express terms are the most obvious and visible elements of a contract. They are the expressed promises of the parties to perform certain acts as part of the contractual agreement. They include exclusion clauses (see Chapter 6) as these are also promises to be bound by certain terms. As a result, express terms are therefore considered to be the most visible aspects of a contractual agreement.

5.8.1 INCORPORATION

Some disputes regarding the contract contents concern whether a term forms part of a contract or not. These issues are matters of incorporation, and this is important because, if a term is not incorporated, the other party is not bound by it. Matters of incorporation will therefore have a direct impact upon whether an action for breach of contract can be brought.

For a term to be considered part of a contractual agreement, it must be incorporated into the contract *before* the parties finally agree to contract with each other. Anything introduced after the agreement is not part of the contract. This is because the parties, in order to freely agree to enter a contract, must have reasonable opportunity to be aware of what they are contracting for. There are several different mechanisms by which a term can be incorporated into a contract – we will examine the following six examples (see Figure 5.3).

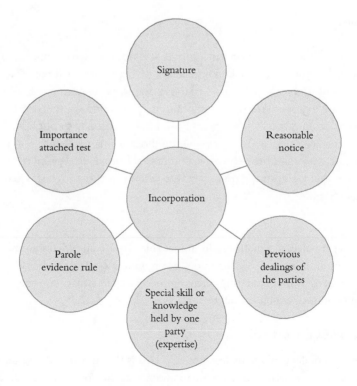

Figure 5.3 Methods of incorporation of terms

5.8.2 SIGNATURE

Contracts made by way of written documents will commonly be signed by both parties to indicate that they agree to the terms. In such situations, the document will constitute the entire contract, and all the terms will be listed. However, as such contracts will often be quite lengthy, it is not uncommon for parties to claim when a dispute arises that they were not aware of a particular term. However, if the contract has been signed by both parties, this is a method of ensuring that all terms in the contractual document are incorporated into the agreement. This principle comes from the case of *L'Estrange v Graucob*.[7]

In *L'Estrange v Graucob*, Scrutton LJ laid down the following principle:

> When a document containing contractual terms is signed, then, in the absence of fraud, or, I will add, misrepresentation, the party signing it is bound, and it is wholly immaterial whether he has read the document or not.

This deals with any claims by parties that attempt to escape liability by claiming they were unaware of terms. Scrutton's provisos in the above quote ensure that anyone who has not been given reasonable opportunity to read the terms is not bound by them, because otherwise there would be problems with parties using fraudulent methods to incorporate terms.

EXPLAINING THE LAW

When buying goods or services on the internet, it is necessary to either tick a checkbox or click a button (the online equivalent of 'signature' as it confirms the buyer's agreement to the terms) as part of the ordering process to indicate that you agree to the seller's general terms and conditions. This is necessary to ensure that an opportunity has been given to the buyer to read them – usually through an additional link that you can click on to go to a page where these terms are listed. The fact that very few of us actually read these terms is immaterial from a legal point of view – we click to indicate that we agree to them, and are bound by them, even if we do not bother to read them.

Not every contract involves a signature, and in fact this is quite an old-fashioned notion of contracting, bearing in mind that UK law does not require a contract to be written at all. Therefore, other means of incorporating terms are necessary in situations where there is not an entire written contract which lists all terms.

5.8.3 REASONABLE NOTICE

One example is the concept of 'reasonable notice'. This is the idea that the other party has been given adequate information to make them aware that the contract they are entering

---

7   [1934] 2 KB 394.

into is bound by certain terms. This can be done by way of documents, signs or even just discussing the terms with the other party prior to the agreement being made. There are numerous examples of where reasonable notice has been given in various different situations.

For example, where a contract is made verbally, there may be terms contained in some form of written document that the other party intends to form part of that agreement. Where this is the case, they must ensure that reasonable notice is given to the other contracting party by providing them with a copy of that document prior to the agreement being made between the parties.

CHAPELTON V BARRY UDC [1940] 1 KB 532

In this case there was a deckchair hire business on the seafront. Customers who wished to hire a deckchair would pay the deckchair attendant, who would provide them with a ticket, which could be used as proof that payment for hire had been made. The ticket contained an exclusion clause on the back, which the deckchair hirer attempted to rely upon in the event of certain liability as a result of hiring a deckchair.

Held: as the ticket was supplied only once payment had been made (and payment was the point at which the agreement was made), the ticket was a mere voucher or receipt after the contract was made so had not been successfully incorporated into the contract. As a result, it could not be relied upon.

There are a number of examples of where attempts have been made to incorporate terms into contracts by way of notices or signs. These are no different to documents in that they need to serve the purpose of bringing the term to the attention of the other party *before* they enter into the contract. As we saw with the *Chapelton* case above, if the term is introduced after the contract is made, it is not a valid part of the agreement.

OLLEY V MARLBOROUGH COURT HOTEL [1949] 1 KB 532

This case concerned a hotel that sought to exclude liability for loss of the personal possessions of guests staying in the hotel. They did this by way of displaying a notice in the hotel informing hotel guests of this term. However, the term was only displayed on the back of the door of each individual hotel room, and therefore was only visible to guests once they had entered their room and closed the door.

Held: the term was not incorporated into the contract because it was not available at the time of entering the contract.

The problem here was one of timing, as seen in *Chapelton*: the contract between the hotel and a guest staying at the hotel was made when checking into the hotel, which was done at the reception desk, and therefore before they were made aware of the exclusion clause on the back of their room door. This therefore meant that the term could not be incorporated as part of the contract, and the hotel could not rely upon it to exclude liability.

EXPLAINING THE LAW

Although the way in which we enter into agreements with hotels when staying in them has changed, the principle is still relevant. Often hotel bookings are now made online, and therefore the agreement is made on the internet prior to setting foot in the hotel itself. However, any terms still need to be incorporated before the agreement is made, and so terms and conditions such as the exclusion clause in the *Olley* case would need to be brought to the reasonable attention of the customer prior to them placing their booking.

THORNTON V SHOE LANE PARKING LTD [1971] 2 QB 163

Another case concerning the use of notices is *Thornton v Shoe Lane Parking Ltd*. This case involved a notice at the entrance of a car park, which indicated that parking on the premises was 'at the owner's risk'. However, entrance to the car park was by automatic barrier, and therefore a customer of the car park would have to gain entry to the car park before seeing the notice. The ticket dispensed by the machine was 'issued subject to conditions displayed on the premises'. A notice inside the car park contained several conditions, one of which excluded liability for personal injury to customers whilst on the premises. On returning to his car, the plaintiff was injured in an accident.

The Court of Appeal held: that the exemption clause excluding liability for personal injury was not incorporated into the contract. Lord Denning stated that the notice at the entrance of the car park was a standing offer, which the customer accepted through the taking of a ticket, and the contract is made at this point. This meant that the notice on the back of the ticket and the conditions displayed inside the car park were too late to be part of the contract.

It is worth noting in this case that there were two notices of relevance here. The one that was displayed at the car park entrance was in time to be incorporated by reasonable notice, because it was clearly displayed at a point before the contract between the car park and the customer was made. However, because it referred to the parking of the car being 'at the owner's risk', it was construed to be about potential damage to the car being parked, and not to include personal injury.

So far, all the discussion has been about timing of reasonable notice. However, it is also important to consider what might be considered 'reasonable' in terms of the content of the term being incorporated. The more onerous a term is, the more it must be brought specifically to the other party's attention.

A good example of this is *Interfoto Picture Library v Stiletto Visual Programmes Ltd.*[8]

INTERFOTO PICTURE LIBRARY V STILETTO VISUAL PROGRAMMES LTD [1988] QB 433

This case concerned the borrowing of photographs and video from a picture library, something that is sometimes done by television programme makers when they need standard pictures or video footage of a location, for example. Interfoto Picture Library's terms and conditions included a penalty fee of £5 per item, per day (plus VAT) for late return of photographic transparencies borrowed by a customer. Because of the number of transparencies and the number of days late, the total charge was £3,783.50. This was considered to be a rather steep penalty to be applied to the customer, and they argued that it was too onerous to have been incorporated into the contract.

The Court of Appeal held: that the clause was unusual and onerous, and therefore it would not be fairly regarded as being brought to the attention of the other party unless it was brought to their attention specifically. This, in their judgment, went beyond what had actually happened, which was that this term was one of four that had merely been provided as part of written terms. The court held that a more appropriate late charge should be applied (which they judged to be £3.50 per item per week).

It is important to note that where a term is considered to be unusual or excessively onerous, there is an obligation on the party wishing to rely upon it to bring it to the attention of the other party more specifically rather than just to include it with all the other terms of the agreement. Lord Denning, in *J Spurling Ltd v Bradshaw*[9] stated: 'Some clauses which I have seen would need to be printed in red ink on the face of the document with a red hand pointing to it before the notice could be held to be sufficient.' The application of this principle can be seen in operation in the judgment of Evans LJ in *Ocean Chemical Transport v Exnor Craggs.*[10] In dismissing the claim that the term in question was not incorporated because it was not sufficiently brought to the attention of the other party. Evans indicated that whether a term was of the type discussed by Denning in the quote above must be based upon the individual circumstances and type of term in question:

It seems to me that the question of incorporation must always depend upon the meaning and effect of the clause in question. It may be that the type of clause is relevant. It may be that the effect of the particular clause in the particular case is relevant.

---

8 [1988] QB 433.
9 [1956] 1 WLR 461 at 466.
10 [2000] 1 All ER 519.

This therefore leaves it to the judge in each case to ascertain whether the term in dispute needed Denning's red writing and red hand, or whether it can be incorporated through inclusion in a normal contractual document.

EXPLAINING THE LAW

The idea of an unusual or onerous term can be seen in everyday life. On example that you may have encountered can be seen on the high street when shops reduce the price of items in a sale. Many shops have a policy that items reduced in a sale cannot be returned for a refund when the purchaser has merely changed their mind, whereas normally they would be happy to do so for non-sale items (although they are not legally obliged to do so – legislation only requires refunds where items are faulty).

When buying an item in the sale, you might have noticed the shop assistant pointing out the 'no refunds' policy to you when buying the item, or a sign next to the till that points this out. The unusual nature of this term means that the shop is ensuring that it can rely upon this term in their contract with the consumer by pointing it out particularly, in a situation where you would not expect every term with the shop to be displayed at the till.

5.8.4 CONSISTENT COURSE OF DEALINGS

A term may be regarded as incorporated into the contract where there have been a number of occasions in the past where the two parties have dealt with each other *consistently*. The consistency of dealings is important, because it implies an established practice between the two parties. This therefore allows the term to be impliedly incorporated into the agreement if it is not mentioned in a contract made between them subsequent to this consistent course of dealings.

It works by making the assumption that the parties consistency of dealings implies that the term has only been left out accidentally. In this way, it can be seen to operate in a similar way to the officious bystander test in implied terms (see later in this chapter) discussed by MacKinnon LJ in *Southern Foundries (1926) Ltd v Shirlaw*.[11] Some examples of the way this can operate are below.

One key issue is that the previous course of dealings has to be consistent in order for it to be relied upon to incorporate a term. Lack of consistency will prevent the court from being able to make the assumption that the parties would have intended this to be part of their agreement, but it is missing this time because of oversight. *McCutchen v MacBrayne*[12] illustrates this particular point well.

....

11 [1940] AC 701.
12 [1964] 1 WLR 125.

MCCUTCHEON V DAVID MCBRAYNE LTD [1964] 1 WLR 125

The plaintiff had used the defendant's ferry service in the past to transport vehicles. There was a document containing an exclusion clause, which excluded the liability of the ferry operator for loss or damage to the vehicle being transported. Sometimes the plaintiff had signed the document excluding liability, sometimes not, and therefore there was not the sort of consistency in their dealings that is required here. On this particular occasion, the document was not signed by the plaintiff, and therefore when the ferry sank, taking all the vehicles onboard with it, there was an attempt by the plaintiff to claim for his losses. The defendant ferry operator attempted to rely upon the exclusion clause as the basis for escaping liability. He argued that the exclusion clause should be incorporated through the previous dealings with the plaintiff.

Held: because there was not a *consistent* course of dealings, the term was not incorporated.

As well as consistency, frequency of dealings is also important.

HOLLIER V RAMBLER MOTORS (AMC) LTD [1972] 1 ALL ER 399

This case is an example of where the infrequent nature of the dealings prevented the argument of a consistent course of dealings. In this case, the customer had used a garage to carry out work on their car on three or four occasions during a five-year period. On each occasion, the car had been taken to the garage by the customer, and a waiver had been signed concerning the garage's liability for damage to the vehicle by negligence whilst it was there. On the final occasion, the car was towed into the garage, and no waiver was signed. The garage was destroyed by fire, as was the customer's car, and there was an attempt to argue that the waiver was incorporated.

Held: there were not enough instances of previous dealings, and therefore the term was not incorporated through a consistent course of dealings.

5.8.5 OTHER WAYS OF BRINGING TERMS INTO WRITTEN AGREEMENTS

There are a few other general mechanisms by which terms can be argued to be part of a contract. This is not implying terms into the contract, which we will deal with later in this chapter, but rules used to bring some statements into the agreement.

For example, the **parole evidence rule**. This rule came from the case of *Goss v Lord Nugent*,[13] and was demonstrated in the case of *Henderson v Arthur*.[14]

---

13 (1833) 110 ER 713.
14 [1907] 1 KB 10.

ESSENTIAL DEFINITION: PAROLE EVIDENCE RULE

A written contract is to be treated as the whole contract, and nothing else can be subsequently added to this, whether it be other written documentation or oral evidence, to suggest that there was more content in the agreement.

Part of the reason for this is to protect the integrity of the agreement; where a contract is a written document, it is in the parties' interests for this to be considered the entire agreement, rather than the possibility that further, usually oral, evidence can be introduced. It means that a contractual document can therefore be trusted to be the only document of relevance to the contract.

However, there are issues with this rule. Firstly, it only applies to express terms in an agreement, and does not preclude the possibility of terms being implied into the contract. It only prevents there being further express terms in further written documentation. Secondly, it does not prevent there being any other alterations or additions to the contract because of mistake or misrepresentation.

However, there are exceptions to the parole evidence rule. These exceptions are important to ensure that this rule is not applied too rigidly. The effects of these exceptions may be to reduce or nullify the effect of the parole evidence rule in certain circumstances. The three main exemptions are as follows (see Figure 5.4).

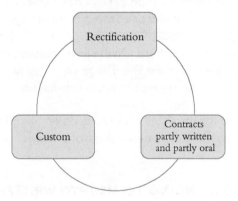

Figure 5.4 Other issues affecting incorporation

5.8.5.1 RECTIFICATION

Rectification is an equitable remedy. It allows a document to be revised where there has been a mistake made in the transcription of it. This may be relevant in situations where the agreement was finalised orally between the parties, and then has been subsequently reduced to a written document for the purposes of preserving evidence of the agreement itself. However, it is entirely possible that errors may be made in that transcription, for example a typographical error or an error in transcription from the original oral discussions.

In such a situation, if there is evidence to demonstrate that an error has been made in the contractual document, this may be introduced to show the error and how it needs to be corrected. This may take the form of notes made at meetings where the terms of the contract have been discussed and agreed, which may provide evidence of what the parties actually agreed. In this situation, it would be open to the court to order a rectification of the contractual document – but in all other ways, the contractual document still remains the single source of the content of the agreement between the parties.

5.8.5.2 CONTRACTS PARTLY WRITTEN AND PARTLY ORAL

Where a contract is claimed to be partly written and partly oral, it is possible to argue that the written document should not be considered as the entire contract. The types of situations where this would be a factor include contracts where an element of the agreement is not in the written contract, but instead was orally agreed, or in another written document separate to the contractual document.

For example, here are two cases where the courts were satisfied that the written contractual document was not the entire agreement.

COUCHMAN V HILL [1947] KB 554, [1947] 1 ALL ER 103

In this case the contract came about as a result of an auction for the sale of a heifer. There was an auction sale catalogue that described the heifer as 'unserved' (meaning that there had never been an attempt to use it for breeding), and when the auctioneer and the seller were asked whether this was accurate or not, they confirmed that it was. However, the auction catalogue also contained a disclaimer excluding liability for any errors in the descriptions.

It later turned out that the heifer was in calf, and died whilst giving birth. As a result, there was an action for breach of contract, which involved the court having to decide whether the oral assurance was part of the contract or not.

Held: the written document did not form the whole of the contract, and therefore the oral statement about the heifer being 'unserved' was part of the agreement, and the parole evidence rule was bypassed.

SS ARDENNES (CARGO OWNERS) V ARDENNES (OWNERS) [1947] 1 KB 55, [1950] 2 ALL ER 517

This case concerned a contract for the shipment of oranges from Spain to London. The standard terms allowed for the cargo ship to make stops on the route between Spain and London, but the exporters wanted their cargo to go directly to London. They obtained a verbal agreement from the ship owners that this would happen, but the ship travelled via Antwerp, causing a delay in the delivery of the oranges.

Held: the oral agreement was a binding part of the contract. The bill of lading was not exclusive evidence of the agreement, and therefore the parole evidence rule was not applicable.

The problem with examples such as these means that it can be exceptionally easy for one party to emasculate the parole evidence rule by the introduction of some evidence to show that the agreement was not contained exclusively in the written contract. It does therefore introduce the question about what the point is about the parole evidence rule. However, it remains the starting point, and it is still up to the other party to demonstrate that there is evidence of other elements of the contract that need to be taken into account.

5.8.5.3 CUSTOM

One other important exception to the parole evidence rule is the use of custom. Custom is an important factor that can affect the operation of contracts more generally (which will be discussed later in this chapter with regard to implied terms). When it comes to the parole evidence rule, custom sets this rule aside in the face of evidence of the claimed custom.

HUTTON V WARREN (1836) 150 ER 517

This case concerned a tenancy agreement between a tenant farmer and the landlord who owned the farm. The tenancy agreement contained provisions regarding what a tenant was entitled to take with him and what he was required to leave at the end of his tenancy. This was contrary to a local custom, which stipulated that a tenant was entitled to receive a reasonable allowance for seeds and labour used in the final year of tenancy, and a reasonable amount for leaving behind any manure for the landlord.

Held: the contract had to be construed in the light of the local custom, and therefore it was not the entirety of the contract in line with the parole evidence rule.

5.9 INTERPRETATION OF TERMS

Once the content of the contract has been established, the other task is the interpretation of the terms of the contract. This is because once it has been agreed what is in the contract, for the purposes of ascertaining what rights and duties the contract provides, it is then important to work out what those terms actually mean. This may, on the face of it, appear to be a simple proposition. However, as the case law has shown, it is not.

Firstly, this is because interpretation of the contract cannot be an interpretation of what the parties actually mean, as this results in the subjective views of the parties who, if the matter has got to court, are in dispute over the contract anyway. Instead, the courts are to ascertain the objective meaning of the contractual terms. This is much more desirable as it results in a great deal more legal certainty and avoidance of problems inherent in taking the alternative approach.

The traditional approach was to take the objective approach to such an extent that only the ordinary everyday meaning of words would be used in interpretation, and this has resulted in a strict and narrow approach taken, particularly when it came to exclusion clauses.[15]

The modern approach to interpretation of all types of terms has taken a different approach, with the recognition of a broader interpretation which is also based in the background knowledge of the parties in the circumstances. This was explained by Lord Hoffmann in the following case:

INVESTORS COMPENSATION SCHEME LTD V WEST BROMWICH BUILDING SOCIETY [1998] 1 WLR 896, [1998] 1 ALL ER 98

This case concerned an agreement between ICS and investors it was representing in claims against West Bromwich Building Society. It concerned which aspects of the right to take action it had assigned to ICS.

Held: in construing the meaning of the contract between ICS and the investors, Lord Hoffmann set out the following five principles:

1. Interpretation of the meaning of the contractual term is as understood by the reasonable person taking into account the background available to the parties;
2. The background can include absolutely anything which would affect how the contractual document would have been understood by the reasonable person;
3. Evidence of negotiations and subjective intent are excluded as they should be the subject of an action for rectification;
4. The meaning of the document is not the same as the meaning of the words, and therefore ascertaining the meaning has to be contextual rather than an exercise in consulting dictionaries;
5. The rule regarding giving 'ordinary everyday meaning' to words is because it should not be easily accepted that people make linguistic mistakes in formal legal documents.

---

15 See, for example, *Photo Production v Securicor Transport Ltd* [1980] AC 827, *Andrews Bros (Bournemouth) Ltd v Singer & Co Ltd* [1934] 1 KB 17.

These principles were restated in a simplified form by Lord Neuberger in *Marley v Rawlings*,[16] who stated that, in order to identify the meaning of a contractual term, you include:

i)   the natural and ordinary meaning of the words
ii) the overall purpose of the document
iii) the other provisions in the document
iv) facts known or assumed by the parties at the time of execution of the document
v)   common sense

He also stated that you should exclude any subjective evidence of intention of the parties.

This approach to interpretation can be seen in action in the case of *Chartbrook Ltd v Persimmon Homes Ltd*,[17] where a dispute over the calculation of the 'annual residential payment' (ARP) led the court to need to interpret its meaning as written in the contract. If the ARP was interpreted using the ordinary rules of syntax, then the court encountered the problem that it made no commercial sense. They therefore ruled that it should be interpreted according to the meaning that could reasonably be given when taking into account the background knowledge available to the parties, in accordance with principle 1 of Lord Hoffmann's judgment in the *Investor Compensation Scheme* case. This approach of taking the meaning as understood by someone having all the background knowledge had been previously taken by the court in *Bank of Credit and Commerce International v Ali*.[18] In this case Lord Hoffmann made the point that there was no conceptual limit to what could be considered 'background'.

It is possible to see the point behind this approach – that the courts have attempted to take a more contextual approach to the interpretation of terms, rather than one of slavish adherence to the dictionary meaning of words. However, one of the criticisms of this approach has been that the older approach, although somewhat rigid, nevertheless has promoted legal certainty, something which the contextual approach can be criticised for.

A balance between these two approaches was needed, and in *Arnold v Britton*[19] Lord Neuberger attempted to provide it. His approach was not to allow the background and context to be used as a reason to avoid a meaning based on the ordinary meaning of words used in the contract, as in his view this would 'undervalue the importance' of those words. This was therefore a recognition that the parties should still be held to

16 [2015] AC 157.
17 [2009] 1 AC 1101.
18 [2001] 2 WLR 735.
19 [2015] AC 1619.

account for the wording used in the contract according to its ordinary meaning, and was not an opportunity to escape the consequences of bad drafting of contractual terms. This is because the parties have control over the drafting of the contract, but not so much over the background or business context within which they are entering into contractual agreements. It would only be in circumstances of bad drafting or where the meaning of the term is unclear where the court can use the background rather than just the ordinary dictionary meaning of words to ascertain what they should mean.

An example of the court applying 'commercial common sense' to a dispute over the meaning of a term was in *Pink Floyd Music Ltd v EMI*,[20] where the court agreed with Pink Floyd's interpretation of a restriction in a licensing agreement regarding the selling of their music only as a whole album to extend to digital sales (and not just 'old-fashioned 'records' and 'singles' in the traditional sense). This was because they objected to EMI's selling of individual tracks for download or songs as ringtones. This term had been included due to Pink Floyd's desire to preserve the artistic integrity of their albums as whole artistic works, and the court recognised the commercial purpose of this applying to all music sales.

5.10 CATEGORISATION OF THE CONTENTS OF THE CONTRACT

Once it has been established that a term is part of the contract, one might assume that this settles the matter; however this is not the case. A term is subcategorised in order to establish its importance, and how the contract is treated in the event of a breach. This is because the consequences of breach will vary greatly depending upon how a contractual term is categorised. It is therefore necessary to also consider whether a term is a condition or a warranty, as these are the two main categorisations for contract terms.

There is a reason for such categorisation: the amount of contractual certainty that this provides for the parties concerned. If it is clear from the outset what the consequences of breach are likely to be, this makes it clear to the parties which are the more important terms of the contract from the outset.

There are a number of terms that have been categorised as conditions based upon statute; for example, prior to the introduction of the Consumer Rights Act 2015 the Sale of Goods Act implied terms into consumer agreements and categorised them as conditions of the contract (the CRA now merely describes them as 'terms', see the discussion later in this chapter on

20 [2011] 1 WLR 770.

implied terms). Terms are also categorised at common law based upon the decisions of the judiciary, and also may be categorised as such within the contract, at the agreement of the parties involved.

However, the categorisation of terms by the parties as conditions is not necessarily conclusive, and we can see from cases below that the view of the court can often differ from the view of the parties as evidenced in the contract. There does need to be some consideration of the balance between the interests of 'justice' compared to 'certainty'. The evolution of innominate terms, discussed below, has attempted to deal with the former of these two interests.

5.11 CONDITIONS

Out of the two main categorisations, **conditions** are considered the most important, mainly because of the consequences of breach. A breach of condition will result in the repudiation of the contract at that point, and any remaining obligations from either party will cease to be due.

ESSENTIAL DEFINITION: CONDITION

'Condition' is a term commonly used to denote a term of the contract that is of such vital importance to the agreement that the contract would be so fundamentally changed and the other party would be deprived of a substantial benefit of the contract without it that the contract should be terminated at the point that it is breached.

ANALYSING THE LAW: THE MEANING OF CONDITION

One of the least helpful aspects of this word in understanding contract law is that as well as the word 'condition' having a meaning different to that used in everyday life, it is also one that is used differently in different contexts.

So, for the purposes of discussing the content of an agreement, a 'condition' is as has been described above. However, it is also used in other contexts, and therefore you will see mention of 'condition precedent' and 'condition subsequent'. These uses are much more in line with the everyday definition of condition, as they describe a requirement upon which validity of the contract is conditional.

A 'condition precedent' is some requirement that must be met before the contract is considered to be valid.

A 'condition subsequent' is some requirement that, if it ceases to be the case, will result in the contract being considered no longer valid.

There are examples of each of these meanings of condition. For example in *Head v Tattersall*,[21] a horse was sold on the understanding that it had been hunted with the Bicester Hounds; when it was discovered that this was untrue, the contract was considered null and void and the horse could be returned.

Categorisation of terms as conditions therefore results in breach being treated as repudiatory – the contract is brought to an end at that point, and all obligations are released. There are implications regarding breach of contract that are dealt with in Chapter 11 on discharge of contract. There have therefore been attempts to specifically categorise express terms in written agreements as conditions in order to give the parties certainty regarding the outcome of a breach of that particular term.

L SCHULER AG V WICKMAN MACHINE TOOL SALES LTD [1973] 2 WLR 683; [1974] AC 235

This case involved a contract for the exclusive right to sell machine presses on behalf of the manufacturer. The contract stipulated the regularity with which the sales company had to visit potential customers to elicit orders, and listed it as a condition. They failed to meet this early on in the performance of the contract, but the parties continued as normal. There were other, minor, breaches of the agreement that took place subsequent to this, but then one of the parties sought to repudiate the contract because of the breach of the visiting obligation and treat the agreement as terminated.

The House of Lords (now Supreme Court) held: the parties' own characterisation of the term as a 'condition' did not automatically mean that it was seen as such in the eyes of the law, and therefore did not automatically mean that the contract could be treated as repudiated. Lord Reid said:

We must remember that we are seeking to discover intention as disclosed by the contract as a whole. Use of the word 'condition' is an indication – even a strong indication – of such an intention but it is by no means conclusive.

The fact that a particular construction leads to a very unreasonable result must be a relevant consideration. The more unreasonable the result the more unlikely it is that the parties can have intended it.

21 (1871–72) LR 7 Ex 7.

The court felt in the circumstances that the term could not be classified in this way: that a breach, however small and however trivial, could result in the termination of the contract. To do so would treat all breaches as repudiatory. On that basis, the party seeking to rescind the contract was not entitled to do so.

RICE (T/A GARDEN GUARDIAN) V GREAT YARMOUTH BOROUGH COUNCIL [2003] TCLR 1, (2001) 3 LGLR 4

This case concerned a contract for leisure management and grounds maintenance. There was a term in this contract that provided that 'if the contractor committed a breach of any of its obligations … the council may … terminate the contractor's employment … by notice in writing'. Therefore, on an ordinary construction of the meaning of this term, it would purport to cover all terms of the agreement, particularly as there was no indication as to which terms were considered conditions and which warranties, or any indication regarding which terms were ranked as more important or central to the contract than others. A normal interpretation would therefore allow termination for *any* breach of the contract, which should be read in the light of Lord Reid's comments in the *Schuler* case.

During the period of the contract, there were minor breaches of the contract committed by Rice, for which Great Yarmouth Council served 'default notices'. Approximately three months into the contract, the council terminated the agreement on the basis of these breaches. Rice claimed that there had been a wrongful repudiation of the contract.

The court held: a common-sense interpretation would have to be applied to the term that allowed repudiation. They decided that breach of a term of the contract could only be considered to be repudiatory if the breach had deprived the other party of a substantial benefit of the contract, and only then would it be considered to be a condition in the contractual sense of the word. In this way, termination of the contract would be limited only to circumstances where repudiation had occurred.

ASSESSMENT TIP

The end result of this is important, as it means that parties' attempts to categorise a term as a condition will not be successful where it is clear that to do so would go against a common-sense approach towards the consequences of breach. It is therefore important to bear in mind the characteristics of a term, and not just what the parties call it in any contractual document.

5.11.1 TIME STIPULATIONS AS CONDITIONS

Terms regarding time stipulations are one category where the courts have been happy to classify them as conditions. This comes from the commercial contract approach that stipulations as to time are crucial, and therefore the notion that 'time is of the essence', and so if breached should result in repudiation of the contract. This gives the parties the certainty that if this type of term is breached, there is clarity that it will always result in the right to rescind the contract.

For example, *The Mihalis Angelos*[22] was a case where such a time stipulation was ruled to be a condition of the contract.

MAREDELANTO COMPANIA NAVIERA SA V BERGEBAU-HANDEL GMBH (THE MIHALIS ANGELOS) [1971] 1 QB 164, [1970] 3 WLR 601, [1970] 3 ALL ER 125

The contract was for a charterparty, which stated that the vessel was 'expected ready to load' on 1 July 1965, and there was a term which allowed the contract to be terminated if the vessel was not ready by 20 July 1965.

The charterers of the ship had no cargo available to load on 17 July, and attempted to rescind the contract as a result of this. It transpired that, had the contract not been subject to this rescission, that it would not have been ready to receive a cargo by 20 July.

Held: the 20 July deadline was a condition, and therefore the contract could be successfully rescinded as a result of the failure to meet this deadline.

5.12 WARRANTIES

The other major category of term is a **warranty**. The most obvious difference between a condition and a warranty is that a warranty is non-repudiatory: it does not result in the immediate termination of the contract.

ESSENTIAL DEFINITION: WARRANTY

A warranty is a term of the contract that, if breached, will result in the non-breaching party being entitled to a remedy. However, it does not substantially deprive the

---

22 *Maredelanto Compania Naviera SA v Bergebau-Handel GmbH (The Mihalis Angelos)* [1971] 1 QB 164, [1970] 3 WLR 601, [1970] 3 All ER 125.

other party of the core purpose of the contract, and therefore the other contractual obligations will continue to be owed by both parties, and the contract will run until discharged in some other way (e.g. by performance, breach, or frustration).

The term 'warranty' is also used in other contexts and with other meanings but, for the purposes of this discussion, the meaning concerns the consequences of its breach. A breach of a term will always be considered a breach of contract, but warranties limit the non-breaching party's actions to recovery of a remedy, e.g. damages, for that breach. The contract will not be repudiated, and the obligations of *both* parties will continue to exist.

An example of a breach of warranty can be found in the case of *Bettini v Gye*.[23]

BETTINI V GYE (1876) 1 QBD 183

This case concerned a contract for a singer to perform in theatres, halls and drawing rooms. As part of the agreement, it was stated that the singer had to present themselves six days in advance of the first performance, in order for rehearsals to take place prior to the opening performance. This was listed in the contract as a condition precedent.

Unfortunately, due to illness of the singer, he was three days late for rehearsals. When he did arrive, the other party refused to receive him into his service, and claimed that the contract had been repudiated. The singer brought an action for wrongful repudiation.

Held: the core purpose of the agreement was the performance of the singer at the arranged venues, and the failure to arrive on time, although it did affect the amount of available rehearsal time, did not prevent the contract being performed, and therefore was to be treated as a warranty, for which damages, but not termination of the contract, would be available.

This case can be contrasted with that of *Poussard v Spiers*.[24]

POUSARD V SPIERS AND POND (1876) 1 QBD 410

This case concerned the employment of an opera singer who, as in the *Bettini* case, had been engaged to perform in certain performances. She had missed some of the

---

23 (1876) 1 QBD 183.
24 (1876) 1 QBD 410.

initial rehearsals, and the other party engaged an understudy in case she was not ready for the performances.

When she missed the first few performances, the understudy undertook these performances and was paid for them, but once the singer had recovered she made herself available to perform. The other party refused to accept this, and the singer sued for wrongful dismissal.

Held: the singer's inability to perform either the opening performance or any of the other early performances went to the root of the contract, and therefore this allowed the other party to rescind the contract.

5.13 INNOMINATE TERMS

The traditional notion of categorising terms as either conditions or warranties has more recently been challenged by the notion of innominate terms. This was established in English law through *The Hongkong Fir* case.

HONG KONG FIR SHIPPING V KAWASAKI KISEN KAISHA (THE HONGKONG FIR) [1962] 2 QB 26, [1962] 2 WLR 474, [1962] 1 ALL ER 474

This case involved a ship that was chartered for 24 months, with the contract stipulating the ship 'being in every way fitted for ordinary cargo service'. It was also to be maintained 'in a thoroughly efficient state in hull and machinery during service'. The ship was delivered to begin the charter in February 1957 to begin service; however due to inadequate maintenance staff, it broke down and needed extensive repairs to make it usable again.

In June 1957, the charterers were concerned about whether the ship would be ready by September, and repudiated the agreement. The ship was repaired by the middle of September, and the ship owners sued for a wrongful repudiation of the contract.

Held: the ship owners had clearly breached their obligations regarding maintenance of the ship, but this was not a repudiatory breach of the contract and did not entitle the charterers to rescind the contract.

KEY LEARNING POINT

The key point regarding this case was that, in making their decision, the court did not classify the term regarding seaworthiness of the ship as a 'condition' or a 'warranty'. Instead it was considered to be an innominate term, and therefore in certain circumstances breach could be repudiatory, but in others would entitle the non-breaching party to damages only. It signalled a contextual approach, where the remedy applied would depend upon the situation, rather than an overall assessment of the term as a whole.

DEFINITION: INNOMINATE TERM

'Innominate' basically means 'without name', and therefore merely signifies that the term in question is not classified generally along the usual lines of condition or warranty.

The effect of this in *The Hongkong Fir* case was that the court's assessment of the term in the context of the breach was that they felt that it was not substantially depriving the other party of the benefit they should obtain under the contract, and therefore the remedy should be damages only. As it stood, because the charterers had repudiated the contract, damages were owed to the ship owners for wrongful repudiation.

This approach, when contrasted to the previous one of classifying 'conditions' and 'warranties', has a number of consequences. It does give the court the flexibility to apply an appropriate remedy to the circumstances of the breach, rather than relying upon a general classification of terms; however it also introduces an amount of uncertainty in the minds of the parties regarding how a term will be construed.

The case also brought an additional problem that had not previously been encountered, and that was the issue of establishing when a breach of an innominate term would be considered repudiatory. The stated approach of Diplock LJ in his judgment in *The Hongkong Fir* was that of 'substantially depriving the other of a benefit'. If this has occurred, the breach will be considered to be repudiatory. An example of where it was not was the case of *The Hansa Nord*.[25]

CEHAVE NV V BREMER HANDELSGESELLSCHAFT MBH (THE HANSA NORD)
[1976] QB 44, [1975] 3 WLR 447, [1975] 3 ALL ER 739

In this case, the term in question concerned the requirement that delivery of the goods be 'made in good condition'. When part of it was not, the buyer rejected the whole

---

25 *Cehave NV v Bremer Handelsgesellschaft mbH (The Hansa Nord)* [1976] QB 44, [1975] 3 WLR 447, [1975] 3 All ER 739.

cargo, but later bought the cargo from a third party who had bought the rejected cargo from the original seller at a third of its original price.

Held: the term was an 'intermediate' one, rather than a condition or warranty, and the fact that the cargo could still be used for its original purpose meant that the breach did not substantially deprive the other party of a benefit. On this basis, only damages were available, and the buyer was not entitled to rescind the contract.

This goes back to the balancing of competing interests discussed above, regarding 'certainty' versus 'justice'. It is up to the court to weigh up the balance between these interests, and to evaluate which one is most important in the circumstances of the case – for example, *Grand China Logistics Holding (Group) Co Ltd v Spar Shipping AS*,[26] where the court's decision not to classify a term as a condition was one where they considered that the importance of certainty was not enough to classify the term as a condition and therefore repudiatory.

This has led to the so-called 'modern approach' regarding the classification of contractual terms. This seems to involve a shying away from the certainty provided by a hard-and-fast classification of terms, and a move towards an approach that promotes greater flexibility. This involves treating a term as innominate unless there are clear intentions demonstrated in the contract one way or the other regarding a term's classification. This approach was acknowledged by Hamblen LJ in *Tullow Uganda Ltd v Heritage Oil and Gas Ltd*.[27] The end result of this approach would be to treat it as repudiatory predominantly only based upon the criteria for innominate terms – sacrificing certainty for the more flexible approach of repudiation only where the nature of the breach deems it necessary.

One further point is with regard to rescinding the contract in the event of an innominate term fulfilling the requirement of the 'substantial deprivation' test mentioned above. The issue of availability of rescission is discussed in Chapter 11 regarding discharge of contract, but it should be noted here that it is up to the non-breaching party to make a decision regarding whether they choose to rescind or not. It has to be their decision and, where that right is not exercised, the right itself may be lost.

5.14 IMPLIED TERMS

DEFINITION – IMPLIED TERMS

Those items that, although not expressly included by the parties, are nevertheless still held to be part of the content of the contract. They can be implied by a number of means.

---

26 [2016] EWCA Civ 982, [2017] 4 All ER 124.
27 [2014] EWCA 1048.

The content of a contractual agreement extends beyond the terms expressly agreed by the parties, and can also in certain circumstances include implied terms. These are terms that are brought into the contract because by some mechanism they should also apply and the parties should be subject to their requirements as part of the contract. Because this goes against the pure nature of the contract as an agreement arrived at by a meeting of minds, such implied terms are only used in certain limited circumstances.

The main purpose of implied terms is often to fill gaps left by the parties, either through their own carelessness or because such matters are already dealt with by a statutory provision that implies certain terms into a contract. However, where they are implied into the agreement, it is because they are intended to deal with some matter that is important to the interpretation or meaning of the contract itself.

Implied terms may fall into one of the following three categories (see Figure 5.5):

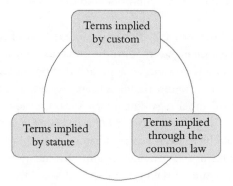

Figure 5.5 Types of implied term

5.15 IMPLIED BY CUSTOM

Custom, as we have seen from earlier in this chapter, can have an influence upon how a contract is construed or interpreted. Traditional practices can have a great influence on the way a contract is carried out, as discussed previously in *Hutton v Warren*. The custom of a particular area regarding animal husbandry had an influence on the terms of a contract between a tenant farmer and his landlord.

This influence of custom therefore also extends to, where deemed necessary, implying terms into a contract that can then be enforced. This will take place if it can be shown that there is an established custom that would be discovered by making reasonable inquiries about the existence of possible customs. Customs are generally to be found either:

- in a particular locality; or
- in a particular trade.

Often it can be a combination of both of these. Where it can be shown to exist, it binds both parties to the contract, regardless of whether they knew about it or not. This was illustrated in the *Hutton v Warren* case because the court accepted that the particular method of farming, which stipulated retention of seed and other issues at the end of a farmer's tenancy, was a binding part of the contract because of the established custom. It requires one party to demonstrate what the court referred to as 'extrinsic evidence of custom and usage' of the relevant requirement.[28]

Although ignorance of a custom cannot excuse a party from it, contracting parties may avoid a custom becoming an implied term by expressly excluding it. This is because the normal approach regarding custom is that there is an assumption that both parties would have intended to be bound by the custom, based upon it being readily discoverable by a reasonable inquiry. However, if they explicitly exclude the custom, the court is entitled to infer that, notwithstanding the custom, the parties were specifically departing from it in their agreement.

An example of this was *Les Affréteurs Réunis Société Anonyme Walford*.[29]

LES AFFRÉTEURS RÉUNIS SOCIÉTÉ ANONYME WALFORD [1919] AC 801

The custom in payment of commission for earning a charterparty was that it would happen when the hire had been earned. The contract in this instance specifically provided for commission payment on signature of the charter. This became an issue because of the requisitioning of the ship by the French Government *after* the charter was signed, but *before* the performance of the charter.

Held: the custom had been specifically excluded by the parties and could not be implied into the contract.

5.16 IMPLIED AT COMMON LAW

Terms may also be implied by the judge in common law. Such terms are 'filling the gaps' in the true sense of the word, because they will often cover circumstances in which there is ambiguity or a gap in the terms and therefore a situation in dispute which is not covered by what the parties have expressly agreed. This is referred to as covering terms 'implied in fact', as it is about some intention of the parties that has not been expressed that is the foundation of the implied term. A second type of implied term is one referred to as 'implied in law'. This covers situations where the term to be implied is not based upon the facts of the situation, but a broader idea of a term to be implied into a contract of a particular type.

---

28 *Hutton v Warren* (1836) 150 ER 517.
29 [1919] AC 801.

In order to deal with both of the above situations, the law has developed a series of tests to allow the courts to judge when an implied term was required. They all revolve around the same theme – that a term will be implied into a contract where it is deemed to be necessary to the contract. However, where the tests differ slightly from each other is in the idea of what is thought as being 'necessary'.

The traditional test that has seen common usage is referred to as the 'officious bystander test', and originates from the case of *Shirlaw v Southern Foundries*.[30]

SHIRLAW V SOUTHERN FOUNDRIES (1926) LTD [1939] 2 KB 206

This case concerned a managing director who was appointed for a period of ten years. During his tenure, there was an attempt to alter the articles of association of the company to remove him before the end of his tenure.

Held: there should be an implied term concerning the right not to have the articles of association changed in order to remove the managing director, and that in order to decide what terms it would be appropriate to imply into the contract, MacKinnon LJ made the following comment, which has been referred to as the 'officious bystander test':

> Prima facie that which in any contract is left to be implied and need not be expressed is something so obvious that it goes without saying; so that, if, while the parties were making their bargain, an officious bystander were to suggest some express provision for it in their agreement, they would testily suppress him with a common 'Oh, of course!'[31]

Similar ideas have been put forward in other cases arguing similar rules for implying terms. For example, in *The Moorcock*,[32] a rule was developed to imply terms necessary to give effect to 'business efficacy'.

THE MOORCOCK (1889) 14 PD 64

This case involved an agreement between the owner of a ship and the owner of a wharf on the river Thames. The plaintiff could unload his ship at the defendant's wharf under the agreement, although the contract contained no express guarantee of the condition of the riverbed at the wharf. This was relevant because, as the wharf was in a tidal section of the river, there would be periods of time when ships docked at the wharf would be resting on the riverbed rather than floating, because when the tide

---

30 [1939] 2 KB 206.
31 [1939] 2 KB 206 at 227.
32 (1889) 14 PD 64.

went out, the water level dropped. The riverbed next to the wharf was in a poor state and the plaintiff's ship was damaged by objects that had settled on riverbed, when the water level dropped at low tide.

Held: the court was giving effect to business efficacy by implying a term guaranteeing the state of the riverbed at low tide, and therefore entitling the ship owner to damages for the cost of repair of the ship.

This case gives us an illustration of the type of term that might be implied by the concept of 'business efficacy'. In this circumstance it might be considered obvious that the riverbed should be maintained if ships were likely to come into contact with it, but we can see that this is really just a variation on the officious bystander test, but with its emphasis on what would be appropriate in the business environment.

An example of the type of 'implied by law' term as per the earlier discussion was seen in *Lister v Romford Ice & Cold Storage*.[33] The case concerned the idea that business efficacy would be served by implying certain types of terms into contracts of employment to govern the employer–employee relationship. In this case, it was argued that an appropriate implied term in such a contract would be for the employee to promise to be faithful to the service of his employer, and to indemnify him against any wrongful acts he might commit during his employment.

Liverpool City Council v Irwin[34] is another example like the previous case, but in a different context. This case concerned the contractual relationship between landlord and tenant.

LIVERPOOL CITY COUNCIL V IRWIN [1977] AC 239

The city council let out flats and maisonettes to tenants and, in doing so, entered into tenancy agreements with them. The tenants' obligations were detailed in contract; however, that contract was of a one-sided nature, and did not express the obligations of the council.

The dispute arose because of a failure by the council to maintain lifts, stairwells and rubbish chutes. In response to this, the tenants withheld their rent and were subsequently sued by the council for non-payment of rent. The action brought by the council was for breach of contract.

Held: because of the one-sided nature of the written agreement, terms should be implied into the agreement for maintenance by the city council. Where, in a block of flats, there are common areas such as stairways, lifts, rubbish chutes, and so on, the landlord has an obligation 'to take reasonable care to keep in reasonable repair and usability' the communal areas.[35]

33 [1957] AC 555.
34 [1977] AC 239.
35 Ibid, at 256, per Lord Wilberforce.

The test that was applied was 'whether in the general run of such cases the term in question would be one which it would be reasonable to insert'.[36] In the circumstances, it was felt unreasonable to have an agreement for dwellings with communal areas, but with no provision for the care of those communal areas. If the council had intended that the tenants were supposed to bear the responsibility for their maintenance, this should have been provided for in the contract. This concept of 'reasonable in the circumstances' therefore sits within the general area of previous cases that had discussed the efficacy of implied terms.

ANALYSING THE LAW

What we are left with as a result of these cases is a general idea of necessity when it comes to implied terms – they must in one way or another satisfy the requirement of necessity in order to be applicable. This has been carried on with the recent case of *Marks & Spencer plc v BNP Paribas Securities Services Trust Co (Jersey) Ltd*,[37] where the Supreme Court confirmed that the requirement for implied terms was one of 'business necessity'. This has meant that the traditional tests we have discussed here are still applicable as the *Marks & Spencer* case acted to confirm the validity of these tests – not as individual tests, but as alternatives in a general blanket requirement within 'business necessity'. Lord Neuberger did however point out that this was about *business* necessity, and not just 'necessity', thereby narrowing the requirement down from what could have been a very wide definition.

5.17 TERMS IMPLIED BY STATUTE

Terms can also be implied into contracts through statute. These tend to be areas where it is accepted that a certain type of term needs to be inserted into all contracts of a particular type, regardless of whether the parties consider that term or not. For this reason, this is an area where the implied term is not expressing the will of the parties, but is for a particular purpose. For example, consumer protection has long been included in consumer agreements through the Sale of Goods Act, and now the Consumer Rights Act.

5.17.1 THE CONSUMER RIGHTS ACT 2015

There have been several examples of statutes that have implied terms into a contract with the intention of protecting the consumer. We have become used to several consumer rights being available to us as a matter of course, whether expressly provided for in the contract that we enter into with a business, or not. The rights under the Consumer Rights Act 2015 are therefore *only* for situations involving a business–to–consumer transaction.

36 Ibid, at 258, per Lord Cross.
37 [2015] UKSC 72, [2016] AC 742.

The Consumer Rights Act 2015 was an attempt to bring the consumer rules together in one place, to make them clearer, and also to expand them. The provisions concerning implied terms are contained within ss. 9–18 and ss. 49–52 of the Act. The first of these deal with contracts for the supply of goods, and the other deals with contracts for the supply of services.

5.17.1.1 SECTION 9: SATISFACTORY QUALITY

Like the Sale of Goods Act 1979, prior to the enactment of the Consumer Rights Act the implied terms concerning goods are focussed upon a series of requirements setting out a minimum standard that goods must meet when being sold to a consumer. The first of these in s. 9 is that of satisfactory quality. The Act says:

9 GOODS TO BE OF SATISFACTORY QUALITY

1) Every contract to supply goods is to be treated as including a term that the quality of the goods is satisfactory.
2) The quality of goods is satisfactory if they meet the standard that a reasonable person would consider satisfactory, taking account of –

   a) any description of the goods,
   b) the price or other consideration for the goods (if relevant), and
   c) all the other relevant circumstances (see subsection (5)).

The requirement of 'satisfactory quality' is therefore a relative one – it is dependent upon price, how the goods are described, any statements that the seller may have made about the goods (see s. 9(5)), unless that statement was withdrawn before the sale or the seller was unaware of the statement at the time of sale. Section 9(3) also provides a non-exhaustive list of factors that may contribute to an assessment of whether the goods are of satisfactory quality or not:

a) fitness for all the purposes for which goods of that kind are usually supplied;
b) appearance and finish;
c) freedom from minor defects;
d) safety;
e) durability.

Under s. 9(4), it is still possible for a retailer to sell items that are not satisfactory according to the general criteria above; however, this is only for situations where it was drawn to the attention of the consumer at the time of the sale, or an examination of the goods or a sample of the goods by the consumer should have revealed the defect. In these types of circumstance, the price is likely to reflect the nature of the goods as being defective and therefore be a consideration regarding the issue of reasonableness in s. 9(2).

5.17.1.2 SECTION 10: FITNESS FOR A PARTICULAR PURPOSE

Section 10 requires that goods be fit for their purpose, if one is stated by the consumer prior to the sale. This is different from previous law, which only referred to the general provision of 'fitness for all the purposes for which goods of the kind in question are commonly supplied', as in s. 9 Consumer Rights Act 2015. This means that where a consumer states a purpose for the goods, the retailer supplies them on that basis, because the consumer is relying on their skill and knowledge to be able to ascertain whether the goods would meet that purpose or not.

5.17.1.3 ACCURACY OF DESCRIPTIONS, MODELS AND SAMPLES

There are three sections of the Consumer Rights Act 2015 that deal with information supplied to the consumer at the time that they make the decision to buy. Section 11 covers contracts entered into after the seller provides a description of the goods, rather than the consumer viewing the goods themselves – for example, if a consumer goes to a shop and orders goods after viewing them in a catalogue or on computer screens in the shop, rather than viewing the goods, and after they have made their purchasing decision, they are brought to the consumer from the stock room. Section 11 requires that a term is implied into the contract with the consumer that the goods must conform to the description. If there is also a sample provided, this does not release the seller from their obligation – even if the goods comply with the sample, they must also comply with the description (see s. 11(2)).

Similarly, under s. 13, where goods are sold by sample, a term is implied into the contract that the goods will comply with the sample. This may be particularly relevant where a large quantity of goods is being sold, and therefore, at the time of sale, only a sample of the goods is available. The only exception to this requirement is if the consumer is specifically informed of differences between the sample and the goods themselves. The CRA refers to 'being brought to the consumer's attention' in s. 13(2)(a), which indicates a need to deliberately inform the consumer of the differences.

Finally, s. 14 refers to goods sold by reference to a model. Where the consumer has entered into a contract for goods as a result of inspecting a model, as with the previously mentioned sections, this also implies a term into the contract. The goods are required to comply with the model. As with the sample in s. 13, differences between the model and the goods must be brought to the attention of the consumer at the time of sale.

5.17.1.4 IMPLIED TERMS IN SERVICE CONTRACTS

The Consumer Rights Act 2015 also contains several provisions regarding implied terms in service contracts. Section 49 requires a term to be implied into consumer contracts for the performance of services regarding the exercise of 'reasonable care and skill'.[38]

Section 50 makes any statement about the trader or the service made orally or in writing, by or on behalf of the trader, an implied term of the contract if it is taken into account by the consumer when entering into the contract. This is an interesting implied term, because it means that traders have to take care when making statements to consumers that might

---

38 Consumer Rights Act 2015, s. 49(1).

subsequently be relied upon by them when making their decisions to enter the contract. As the trader has no control over whether the information will be 'taken into account by the consumer when deciding to enter into the contract' (s. 50(1)(a)) or 'taken into account by the consumer when making any decision about the service after entering into the contract', it means there is a very wide scope for statements made carelessly to be implied into agreements. It certainly removes the opportunity for traders to claim that statements made before the contract was agreed are 'mere puffs' and therefore throwaway comments. The consumer may not be able to easily ascertain the difference between throwaway comments not to be taken seriously and statements to be relied upon, so the emphasis is therefore placed upon the trader to ensure that they are careful about their communications with the consumer, and clear that information that they give will form part of their agreement.

5.17.1.5 REMEDIES

Remedies for breach of implied terms are discussed in s. 19 (goods) and s. 54 (services). In the case of goods, this sets out a complex set of remedies available to the consumer in the event of a breach of an implied term, including:

a) a short-term right to reject
b) the right to repair or replacement
c) the right to a price reduction or the final right to reject.[39]

Interestingly, the right to treat the contract as at an end in s. 19(11) is restricted to only express terms of the contract, and therefore this suggests that implied terms under the Consumer Rights Act 2015 will not be considered to be repudiatory. There is no language in the Act to classify terms as conditions, so remedies for goods contracts will be restricted to those contained in s. 19.

The remedies for a breach of an implied term in a service contract are contained in s. 54. The consumer has a right to:

a) price reduction; or
b) repeat performance of the service.[40]

The extent to which a consumer can treat a service contract as being at an end (the right to repudiate) is contained in s. 54(7)(f). It is listed as one of the 'other remedies' in that subsection. There is no stipulation in s. 54 regarding the availability of repudiation for breach of terms implied under the Consumer Rights Act 2015 in services contracts, and therefore such remedies will be available for implied as well as express terms.

---

39 Consumer Rights Act 2015, s. 19(3).
40 Consumer Rights Act 2015, s. 54(3).

5.18 BRINGING IT TOGETHER

You should now have a good understanding of the varied forms of content of the contractual agreement. We have examined the range of different sources, and different ways in which terms can form part of an agreement.

As these issues will often arise because of disputes over the contract, it is firstly important to establish what is and is not part of the contractual agreement, and for that you need to ensure that you are able to classify statements made by the parties as part of negotiations. Those items that do not form part of the contract are not dealt with in the same way as terms of the contract.

Secondly, it is important to ensure that both express and implied terms are considered when establishing the content of the agreement. Implied terms will not have been agreed by the parties, but they will nevertheless form part of the agreement in situations where they are applicable – whether by custom, statute, or by the common law.

Finally, once you have established what is a term of the contract, the consequences of its breach should also be considered. Some terms once breached will end the contract at that stage, and others will not, but will result in damages being owed. Understanding the distinction is an important part of resolving any problems that arise with the contract itself.

KEY LEARNING POINTS

Remember that you need to understand the following key areas when ascertaining the content of a contractual agreement:

- The distinction between terms, representations and 'mere puffs'
- Whether an express term has been successfully incorporated into the contract, and therefore whether the parties are bound by it
- The current approach towards interpretation of the meaning of terms, once they are recognised as part of the contract
- The distinction between conditions, warranties, and innominate terms, and the appropriate remedies to be applied
- The incorporation of implied terms by custom, common law or statute

TAKING IT FURTHER

Beatson & Burrows, *Anson's Law of Contract*, 29th edn, Oxford University Press, 2010

Bojeczuk, 'When is a condition not a condition?' (1987) JBL 353

Goh, 'Lost but found again: the traditional tests for implied terms in fact: *Marks & Spencer plc v BNP Paribas Securities Services Trust Company (Jersey) Ltd*' (2016) JBL 231

Macdonald, 'Incorporation of contract terms by a "consistent course of dealing" ' (1988) 8 Legal Studies 48

Macdonald, 'The duty to give notice of unusual contract terms' (1988) JBL 375

McCaughran, 'Implied terms: The journey of the man on the Clapham Omnibus' [2011] CLJ 607

Peden & Carter, 'Incorporation of terms by signature: *L'Estrange* rules!' (2005) 21 JCL 96

Peel, 'Terms implied in fact' (2016) 132 LQR 531

Peel, *Treitel on the Law of Contract*, 14th edn, Sweet & Maxwell, 2015

Phang, 'Implied terms, business efficacy and the officious bystander – a modern history' (1998) JBL 1

6

CHAPTER 6
EXCLUSION CLAUSES AND UNFAIR TERMS

6.1 INTRODUCTION

This chapter deals with exclusion clauses and unfair terms within a contract. Exclusion or limitation, often referred to collectively as 'exemption' clauses, can be extremely contentious, as consequential losses incurred by a party that the other party is seeking to avoid due to a failure in performance can be substantial. It is neither immoral, nor abnormal, for parties to seek to control any risks that may arise in relation to the contract. Indeed, under the freedom of contract doctrine, parties should be free to agree whatever terms they wish with minimal interference. However, owing to the impact that the clause(s) can have on the respective liability of the parties, the clause(s) must meet certain requirements to be enforceable before the courts. In particular, the consumer is often the party who stands to lose out as a result of a more powerful party who has included broad clauses to exclude liability from the contractual terms. Against this backdrop, the law must achieve a balance in retaining a legitimate function for such clauses, whilst also ensuring that the use of such clauses is regulated to prevent abuse by the dominant party. The law attempts to achieve this balance through common law rules on incorporation, appropriate interpretation of exclusion clauses and in conformity with various statutes that govern this area. Legislation in this area can have the effect of invalidating a clause outright in some cases or, in others, nullifying a clause on the grounds that it is unreasonable or unfair. As well as examining exclusion clauses and limitation clauses, this chapter will also consider the judicial and statutory approach towards unfair clauses in general, incorporating the recently enacted Consumer Rights Act 2015.

AS YOU READ

At the end of this chapter you should be able to:

- Identify the existence of an exclusion/limitation clause or unfair term

- Understand how to assess whether or not a clause is valid

- Identify the methods through which a clause can be incorporated into a contract

- Understand the difference between a business to business (B2B) contract and a business to consumer (B2C) contract and understand which statute will apply in each particular instance (UCTA 1977 or CRA 2015)

- Be able to apply the reasonableness test (UCTA 1977) or the test of fairness (CRA 2015) to a given set of circumstances to assess whether a clause is enforceable

6.2 DEFINITION AND COMPONENTS

An exclusion or limitation clause is a statement that dictates that one party will

1) not be liable, or
2) will limit liability

to another in a specific set of circumstances. Exclusion clauses are often found in standard form contracts (see previous chapter on terms), for example those used by mobile phone companies or utility providers, sports and recreation memberships and public transport providers.
A standard form contract is a uniform contract that is used by a large organisation in all its dealings with customers. Exclusion clauses are also present in individually negotiated contracts.

An exemption clause can play a useful part in helping to regulate risk within a contractual agreement, as was evidenced in the case of *British Fermentation Products Ltd v Compare Reavell Ltd*,[1] when the court held that a contractual term that the sellers' liability to make good or replace defective equipment was acceptable instead of warranties implied by law as to quality or fitness for purpose. The term made business common sense and had been accepted by the parties. On these facts and on the taking into account that the clause did not infringe the Unfair Contract Terms Act 1977 (UCTA 1977), this was probably a reasonable outcome for two parties who had engaged in a commercial contract. However, cases such as *Parker v South Eastern Railway*[2] enable us to look at the outcome of exclusion clauses from a different perspective; that of the consumer.

PARKER V SOUTH EASTERN RAILWAY (1877) 2 CPD 416

Mr Parker left a bag in the cloakroom at a railway station operated by SE Railway Company. On depositing his bag and making payment he received a ticket. On the front it said 'see back'. On its back, it stated that the railway was excluded from liability for items worth £10 or more. Mr Parker did not read the clause as he thought the ticket was a receipt of payment. Mr Parkers bag, which was worth in excess of £10, was lost.

Held: The COA said that if Mr Parker knew of the conditions he would be bound. If he did not know, he would still be bound if he was given the ticket in such a way as amounted to 'reasonable notice'. It was held that the writing on the ticket amounted to reasonable notice.

The harsh result in *Parker* provides a good illustration of how broad and generalist clauses can produce tough outcomes for the ordinary unassuming consumer, who may have had little or

---

1   [1999] BLR 352.
2   (1877) 2 CPD 416.

no input into the terms of the agreement and quite probably would have been oblivious to the consequences of the operative exclusion clause when engaging in a simple or somewhat uneventful transaction like buying a ticket for a train journey.

Thus, a balance must be reached between the legitimate aims, in one sense of achieving fairness in assessment of reasonable clauses where mechanisms to deal with liability have been agreed between the contracting parties and the less legitimate practice of a more experienced or powerful party taking advantage of the inexpert consumer. The courts play an important role in facilitating this balance and there are certain barriers that an exclusion clause must overcome before it will be enforced. From the outset, an exclusion clause or contractual term must have been validly incorporated into the agreement to be relied upon. If successfully incorporated, the wording of an exclusion clause must be shown to cover the loss that is the subject of any attempt to exclude liability, and the wording must be clear. Finally, the clause must not violate any statutory provision contained in the UCTA 1977, which applies to exclusion and limitation clauses in commercial contracts (but not all unfair terms in contracts). An exclusion clause in a consumer contract must not infringe the rules on fairness set out in the Consumer Rights Act 2015 (CRA 2015).

Figure 6.1 summarises the components of a valid exclusion or limitation clause.

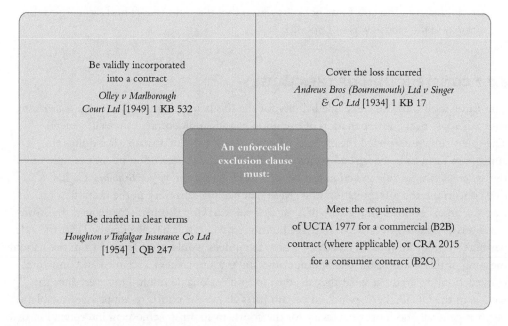

Figure 6.1 Requirements of an exclusion clause

6.2.1 INCORPORATION

A party who is seeking to rely on an exclusion clause to exclude or limit liability must prove that the clause has been validly incorporated into the contract. The subject of incorporation was discussed in the previous chapter on terms of a contract. In many instances, the cases already discussed relate to the incorporation of an exclusion clause,[3] so whilst it is important to note their relevance here, it is unnecessary to review these cases again. When considering the level of notice that must be given of the presence and impact of an exclusion clause, it is important to note that a higher degree of notice for onerous or unusual terms is required.[4]

INTERFOTO PICTURE LIBRARY LTD V STILETTO VISUAL PROGRAMMES LTD [1987] EWCA CIV 6

The proprietors of a photo library allowed the defendant to take away a large selection of pictures to look at to enable him to choose which photos he wished to use in his advertising business. The package containing the photos included a document that stated that any retention of the materials for longer than 14 days would incur a fee of £5 + VAT per photo for each day overdue. The defendant did not read the document and forgot to return the photos, which were eventually returned six weeks late. The claimants demanded a fee of £3,783.50 in line with the contractual terms.

Held: the term had not been properly incorporated into the contract. Where a contractual term is particularly onerous, the court adjudged that the party seeking to enforce the term must take greater measures to bring it to the attention of the other party. In this case the court was not persuaded that the defendants had discharged this burden and the clause was not upheld.

6.2.2 CONSTRUCTION OF THE CLAUSE

The clause itself must fully exclude liability for the loss being claimed. The *contra proferentem* rule will apply in the interpretation of exclusion clauses and contract clauses in general.[5] The rule strictly interpreted means 'interpretation against the draftsman'. It requires an ambiguous term to be construed against the party seeking to rely upon it. An example of the *contra proferentem* rule in action can be seen in *Houghton v Trafalgar Insurance Co Ltd*[6] a case concerning the interpretation of a clause that excluded liability in the event of a car carrying an excess load. In the case of a car that was carrying too many passengers, the word 'load' was considered to relate to baggage but not passengers. It has been argued that the rule permitted significant judicial creativity where the judges would often 'depart from the natural meaning of the words of the exemption clause and put upon them a strained and unnatural construction'[7] to arrive at what they deemed to be a reasonable result. However, since the passage of the UCTA 1977, which in certain parts allows the courts to adopt a 'reasonableness' test, it is generally no longer necessary for the courts to strain to achieve an interpretation that

---

3   *Olley v Marlborough Court Ltd* [1949] 1 KB 532; *Thornton Shoe Lane Parking* [1971] 2 QB 163; *Parker v South Eastern Railway* (1877) 2 CPD 416.

4   *Spurling v Bradshaw* [1956] 1 WLR 461, *Interfoto Picture Library Ltd v Stiletto Visual Programmes Ltd* [1987] EWCA Civ 6.

5   *Tan Wing Chuen v Bank of Credit and Commerce Hong Kong Ltd* [1996] 2 BCLC 69.

6   [1954] 1 QB 247.

7   Per Lord Denning MR in *George Mitchell (Chesterhall) Ltd v Finney Lock Seeds Ltd* [1983] QB 284.

is fair to the weaker party. You will recall from the previous chapter on terms that the case of *ICS v West Bromwich Building Society*[8] laid down principles that should be followed by the courts when interpreting contractual terms; this will also include exclusion clauses.

6.2.3 EXCLUSION OF LIABILITY FOR NEGLIGENCE

A strict approach is taken where a party is seeking to exclude liability for negligence. A clause would need to be worded very clearly to persuade the courts to enforce clauses within this category. Generally, it is not in the public interest to enforce agreements that are illegitimate in nature, and it goes without saying that most parties would want the other party to take reasonable care in executing their obligations under an agreement; whether that be the supply of goods or the provision of a service. Guidance on the exclusion of negligence was laid down by Lord Morton in *Canada Steamship Lines v The King*[9] and is summarised in Figure 6.2.

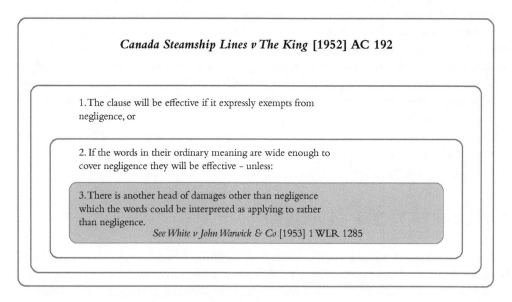

Figure 6.2 Common law exclusion of negligence

It should be remembered that the *Canada Steamship* guidelines are not rules of law and can be departed from where the court deems it appropriate to do so.[10] This point was emphasised by the Court of Appeal in *Mir Steel UK Ltd v Morris*[11] where it was stated that the guidelines 'should not be applied mechanistically and ought to be regarded as no more than guidelines'. Additionally, the guidelines 'should not be applied in a manner that would frustrate the intention of the parties'.[12]

----

8 [1998] 1 WLR 896.

9 [1952] AC 192.

10 *Hollier v Rambler Motors (AMC) Ltd* [1972] 2 QB 71.

11 [2012] EWCA Civ 1397, [2013] 2 All ER (Comm) 54.

12 *Greenwich Millennium Village Ltd v Essex Services Group plc* [2014] EWCA Civ 960, [2014] 1 WLR 3517.

To sum up the position, where a clause clearly excludes liability for negligence, it will be effective[13] and an exemption clause that does not spell out the actual word 'negligence' may also be regarded as sufficiently broad to cover negligence provided it cannot be interpreted to cover another potential (non-negligence) liability.[14] If it could be interpreted to cover another liability within the contract, the clause will not be effective to protect against negligence.[15]

6.3 FUNDAMENTAL BREACH

A fundamental term of the contract is one that goes to the root of the contract or is part of its essential character. A fundamental breach will occur where a party is seeking to exclude liability for a fundamental term, and also in cases involving a deliberate refusal to perform obligations under a contract that has serious consequences for the other party. Prior to the enactment of the UCTA 1977, the doctrine was used as a mechanism by the courts to control unreasonable exclusion clauses. As a matter of law, exclusion clauses were deemed non-available to a party responsible for a fundamental breach of contract. Nowadays, as recognised by the House of Lords in *Photo Production Ltd v Securicor Transport Ltd*,[16] since the enactment of UCTA 1977, which provides a statutory basis for regulating unreasonable exclusion clauses, the doctrine of fundamental breach is no longer required to provide a remedy. It is acknowledged that the doctrine did provide a useful function in that it prevented a guilty party from relying on an exemption clause where s/he had committed a fundamental breach of contract that was sufficient to bring a contract to an end.[17]

6.4 LIMITATION CLAUSES

So far we have looked at exclusion clauses as a mechanism for excluding liability in totality. However, rather than seeking to exclude liability *per se*, a party may simply be wanting to limit liability in certain specific areas of a contract. Evidence suggests that the judiciary tenders a more relaxed approach towards a limitation clause, mainly because a limitation clause is perceived as a more genuine attempt to apportion losses rather than a complete refusal to acknowledge any responsibility where morally some accountability should be borne by the reliant party. *Ailsa Craig Fishing Co Ltd v Malvern Fishing Co Ltd*[18] provides authority that where a clause is 'clear and unambiguous' this will be sufficient to ensure its enforceability and the application of the more rigorous rules that exist for exclusion clauses are unnecessary.

13 *Monarch Airlines v Luton Airport* (1998) 1 Lloyds Rep 403.
14 *Alderslade v Hendon Laundry* [1945] 1 KB 189.
15 *White v John Warwick* [1953] 1 WLR 1285, [1953] 2 All ER 1021, (1953) 97 SJ 740; *EE Caledonia v Orbit Valve* [1994] 1 WLR 1515.
16 [1980] AC 827.
17 *Harbutt's Plasticine Ltd v Wayne Tank and Pump Co Ltd* [1970] 1 QB 447.
18 [1983] 1 WLR 964.

APPLYING THE LAW

Mia joined the Infinity Spa and Gym. When signing up, she signed a contract without reading it. The contract had a clause in it which stated that the club would not be liable for loss or damage to any property left by the members on the club's premises.

On her first visit, Mia's gym bag was stolen from her locker. When Mia complained to the club's management they denied liability, relying on the contract Mia had signed. Mia argued that she should not be stopped from claiming as she had not read the contract.

Has the exclusion clause been incorporated into the contract?

ADVICE TO MIA

In advising Mia you should identify the area of law and explain the rules on validity of exclusion clauses. At this stage you have covered incorporation and construction of the clause. Define the law and discuss any case law or statute that prevails in this area. Then apply the rules to the issues raised.

The area of law is exclusion clauses. First set out the facts that need to be considered to answer the question. Next, a brief definition of an exclusion clause is required. Follow this by looking at the legal requirements that must be fulfilled for the clause to be enforceable:

- Incorporation
- Construction
- Statutory control (not yet covered, so we will not discuss at this stage)

Incorporation: Using case law to support your discussions, consider factors such as:

- Was reasonable notice given? (*Olley v Marlborough Court Ltd* [1949] 1 KB 532)
- Was the term referred to in the document that is intended to be contractually enforceable (*Chapleton v Barry UDC* [1940] 1 KB 532)?
- Have reasonable steps been taken to bring the clause to the attention of the other party? (*Parker v South Eastern Railway* (1877) 2 CPD 416; *Thompson v London, Midland and Scottish Railway* [1930] 1 KB 41)
- Nature of the clause: How onerous was the clause? If the clause is particularly onerous, it must be very clear (*Interfoto Picture Library Ltd v Stilleto Visual Programmes Ltd* [1989] 1 QB 433)

Construction: Explore whether the clause in question was appropriately worded to cover the occurrence that is being avoided

Apply the law: You would probably conclude that the clause has been incorporated into the contract. It is included in the membership contract that was signed at the time that Mia joined the gym, and the wording appears to be clear and the clause would probably not be considered onerous.

6.5 UNFAIR CONTRACT TERMS ACT 1977

Prior to the enactment of the UCTA 1977, a court had no power to strike down an unreasonable exclusion clause unless:

1) the clause had not been incorporated, or
2) the clause failed to include the liability that it sought to exclude.

The enactment of UCTA 1977 provided the judiciary with far greater powers to declare certain terms invalid. It is still necessary to verify that an exclusion clause has been incorporated and includes the liability it seeks to exclude, but the clause itself can now be scrutinised under statutory rules that enable a more transparent interpretation.

Under UCTA 1977 some exclusion clauses will be completely ineffective, whereas other clauses will be effective only if they pass the test of 'reasonableness'. It is important to note that the Act has been subject to significant change since the passage of the CRA 2015, which has taken over the regulation of consumer contracts. Prior to the enactment of the CRA 2015, exclusion clauses in both business to business (B2B) and in business to consumer (B2C) contracts were controlled by UCTA 1977. In addition, the Unfair Terms in Consumer Contract Regulations (UTCCR) 1999[19] also governed terms in consumer contracts, but this instrument has now been revoked and replaced by the CRA 2015.

The CRA 2015 has taken over the regulation of B2C clauses, leaving UCTA 1977 to regulate B2B clauses. We considered many CRA 2015 provisions in the previous chapter on contractual terms, and CRA 2015 will be analysed later in this chapter in relation to its regulation of B2C clauses. But, for now, we will look at the provisions of UCTA 1977 and how it controls exclusion clauses in B2B transactions.

6.5.1 APPLICATION OF THE UCTA 1977

As a result of the amendments in Sch. 4 of the CRA 2015, UCTA 1977 now only applies to B2B contracts. Part 1 of UCTA 1977 applies to England, Wales and Northern Ireland and Part III applies to the whole of the UK. Scotland has its own provision in Part II of the Act. Let us turn first to s. 1(3) of the Act, which clarifies the scope of the Act in relation to exclusions or restrictions in business liability.

---

19 S.I. 1999/2083.

EXPLAINING THE LAW

Business liability is defined in s. 1(3) of UCTA 1977 as 'liability for breach of obligations or duties arising from things done or to be done by a person in the course of a business (whether his own business or another's); or from the occupation of premises used for business purposes of the occupier'. For an expansion of what is included under the term 'business', s. 14 specifies that a business includes 'professions and the activities of any government department, or local or public authority'.

UCTA 1977 deals with situations where a business is contracting with another business but does not govern instances where two non-business parties are making an agreement. So, any attempt to exclude liability in a private sale, for example an agreement made to sell your iPhone to a friend, will fall outside the remit of the Act.

ASSESSMENT TIP

The CRA 2015 has replaced the UTCCR 1999 and the UCTA 1977 in relation to business to consumer contracts (B2C). When embarking upon a problem question concerning an exclusion clause it is extremely important to determine the relationship between the parties to an agreement. For example, if it is a B2C transaction, the CRA 2015 will apply, whereas if it is a B2B transaction, UCTA 1977 will apply. *It is crucial that this determination is made before you move on to advise the parties:*

Table 6.1

Type of Contract	UCTA 1977	CRA 2015
B2B	✓	✗
B2C	✗	✓

6.5.2 CLAUSES NOT COVERED BY UCTA 1977

Under Sch. 1 certain types of contract are excluded from the governance of UCTA 1977. These include insurance contracts, international supply contracts, contracts relating to interests in land, contracts relating to intellectual property law, formation, dissolution or constitution of a company or to the rights or obligations of its members, contracts relating to the creation or transfer of securities or rights in securities, and certain maritime contracts.

6.5.3 INEFFECTIVE CLAUSES

Certain contractual clauses are classified as ineffective under UCTA 1977 and are never enforceable. These clauses typically involve a more serious nature of exclusion that can have a harsh impact on the other party to the contract. The main section to consider is s. 2(1), which states that liability for death or personal injury caused by negligence cannot be excluded. This rule applies to contract terms as well as exclusion clauses. The definition of negligence is provided in s.1(1) of UCTA 1977 (below). Section 2(3) of UCTA 1977 provides that where a contract term or notice purports to exclude or restrict liability for negligence, a person's agreement to or awareness of it should not, of itself, be taken as indicating voluntary acceptance of any risk. So, to be clear, it cannot be argued that simply because someone has read a particular clause, the clause will be effective and binding upon them.

6.5.4 NEGLIGENCE

Whilst exclusion for negligence in the case of death or personal injury is excluded under UCTA 1977, s. 2(2) will allow exclusion of liability for negligence in regard to other loss or damage provided that the term or notice satisfies the requirement of reasonableness. The question of what is reasonable is determined by applying the reasonableness test, which is covered in s. 11 of the Act and will be discussed later on.

Negligence is defined below:

SECTION 1(1) UCTA 1977

1(1) For the purposes of the Part of this Act, 'negligence' means the breach-
   (a) Of any obligation, arising from the express or implied terms of a contract, to take reasonable care or exercise reasonable skill in the performance of the contract;
   (b) Of any common law duty to take reasonable care or exercise reasonable skill (but not any stricter duty);
   (c) Of the common duty of care imposed by the Occupiers' Liability Act 1957 or the Occupiers' Liability Act (Northern Ireland) 1957.

We should also note s. 6(1)(a) UCTA 1977, which prohibits exclusion of liability for obligations arising under s. 12 of the Sale of Goods Act 1979, relating to the seller's implied undertakings as to title and s. 7(3A), which prohibits exclusion of liability for breach of s. 2 of the Supply of Goods and Services Act 1982, which relates to the transfer of goods in a work and materials contract.

6.5.5 EFFECTIVE CLAUSES

Section 3 of UCTA 1977 governs instances where liability can be excluded if the test of reasonableness is satisfied. This section covers the exclusion of liability for breach of contract (except for implied obligations covered under ss. 6 and 7) where the parties have dealt with each other under their 'standard terms of business'. Section 3(2) states:

> As against that party, the other cannot by reference to any contract term –
>
> (a) when himself in breach of contract, exclude or restrict any liability of his in respect of the breach; or
> (b) claim to be entitled –
>   (i) to render a contractual performance substantially different from that which was reasonably expected of him, or
>   (ii) in respect of the whole or any part of his contractual obligation, to render no performance at all, except in so far as (in any of the cases mentioned above in this subsection) the contract term satisfies the requirement of reasonableness.

Let us consider s. 3 of the Act. Section 3(2) seeks to prevent the parties from excluding liability for breach of strict contractual obligations where one of the parties deals on the other's written standard terms of business except in so far as the term satisfies the requirement of reasonableness. There are no definitions provided to aid interpretation of what is meant by 'on the other's standard written terms of business'. Case law suggests that, for terms to be standard, 'they should be regarded by the party that advances them as its standard terms and that it should habitually contract in those terms'.[20] In addition, although the fact that negotiations have taken place will not mean that the contract is non-standard,[21] the extent of negotiations is a relevant factor. Overall, it appears that the courts will only find for a non-standard contract over a standard contract in instances where there has been significant discussion and negotiation over the standard terms and material alterations have been made.

Two further important sections of UCTA 1977 are ss. 6(1A) and 7(1A). Both these sections permit the exclusion of liability where the test of reasonableness is discharged:

---

20 *Chester Grosvenor Hotel Co Ltd v Alfred McAlpine Management Ltd* (1991) 56 Build LR 115.

21 *Yuanda v WW Gear Construction Ltd* [2010] EWHC 720 (TCC), [2011] Bus LR 360, [2011] 1 All ER (Comm) 550.

Section 6(1A) presides over attempts to exclude liability for breaches of ss. 13–15 of the Sale of Goods Act 1979 in commercial contracts. These sections cover sale by description, satisfactory quality, fitness for purpose and sale by sample for which liability can be excluded or restricted if the clause satisfies the requirement of reasonableness. Section 7(1A) is similar to s. 6(1A) in that it covers attempts to exclude the obligations relating to description, satisfactory quality, fitness for purpose and sale by sample in contracts for work and materials and hire contracts. Again, liability can only be excluded if the requirement of reasonableness is satisfied.

6.6 THE REASONABLENESS TEST

The reasonableness test is set out in s. 11 of UCTA 1977. It has a wide application and is applicable to ss. 2(2), 3, 6(1A), 7(1A), 7(4) and 8 of the Act. The reasonableness test will apply to the circumstances that prevailed when the contract was created (s. 11(1)); not at the time that a breach has occurred. The aim of the reasonableness test is to assess the equability of the allocation of risk and responsibility between the parties when they entered into the agreement and it is for the party seeking to show that a clause is reasonable to demonstrate that it satisfies the test (s. 11(5)).

In considering whether a contractual term satisfies the reasonableness test for the purposes of s. 6 or s. 7 of UCTA 1977, regard should be had to the matters specified in Sch. 2 to the Act (s. 11 (2)); however the court tends to also defer to Sch. 2 when assessing clauses for reasonableness under other relevant areas of the Act. The specifics of the test are set out in Figure 6.3.

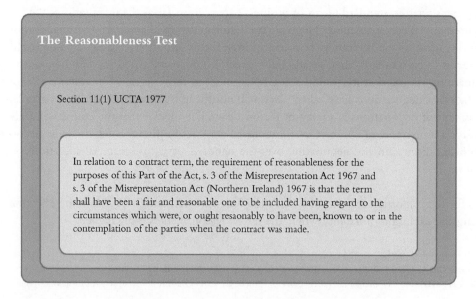

The Reasonableness Test

Section 11(1) UCTA 1977

In relation to a contract term, the requirement of reasonableness for the purposes of this Part of the Act, s. 3 of the Misrepresentation Act 1967 and s. 3 of the Misrepresentation Act (Northern Ireland) 1967 is that the term shall have been a fair and reasonable one to be included having regard to the circumstances which were, or ought resaonably to have been, known to or in the contemplation of the parties when the contract was made.

Figure 6.3 The reasonableness test

In relation to a notice (s. 11(3)), the requirement of reasonableness is that it should be fair and reasonable to allow reliance on it, having regard to all the circumstances pertaining when the liability arose or would have arisen. In addition, where a party seeks to limit liability to a specified sum of money, in deciding whether or not the clause satisfies the requirement of reasonableness, regard will be had (without prejudice to Sch. 2 criteria) to:

1) the resources which the party seeking to rely on the clause could expect to be available to him for the purpose of meeting any liability that may arise, and
2) how far it was open to the party to cover himself by insurance (s. 11(4)).

The burden of proving reasonableness lies with the party seeking to rely on the exclusion clause (s. 11(5)).

The case of *George Mitchell (Chesterhall) Ltd v Finney Lock Seeds Ltd*[22] is a good starting point to analyse the approach taken by the courts in assessing reasonableness.

GEORGE MITCHELL (CHESTERHALL) LTD V FINNEY LOCK SEEDS LTD
[1983] 2 AC 803

The contract involved the sale and supply of cabbage seed. It transpired that the seed was defective and the crop did not grow properly. The monetary loss of production equated to many thousands of pounds; a figure substantially in excess of the cost of the seed. The contract had a limitation clause restricting the liability of the supplier to the amount of the contract price.

Held: the court found the clause to be unreasonable. The fact that the industry's practice had always been to negotiate damages claims if they seemed genuine and justified was sufficient to demonstrate to the court that the suppliers themselves did not consider the clause to be fair or reasonable. Also, the fact that the suppliers could have insured themselves for claims of this nature was a decisive factor in this case.

In summary, the key factors to be taken into account in assessing the reasonableness of a clause in a commercial contract are:

- Equality of bargaining powers
- Whether the clause is usually operative in the industry in question
- Whether the party seeking to limit liability could have resources available to meet the type of liability, i.e. insurance cover
- Whether the party agreeing to the clause received an inducement (did they pay a lower price for example?)

---

22 [1983] 2 AC 803.

ESSENTIAL DEFINITION: EQUALITY OF BARGAINING POWERS

Where both parties to an agreement are of equal status. If one party to an agreement has more and better alternatives than the other party or greater power it is more likely that this party will gain more favourable terms leading to inequality of bargaining powers. Where an inequality of bargaining power exists, freedom of contract will no longer prevail and judicial or legislation interventions will often be observed.

In deciding whether the requirement of reasonableness has been satisfied, an important prior factor for the courts to ascertain is that the meaning of the clause is understood. In *Watford Electronics Ltd v Sanderson CFL Ltd*,[23] Chadwick LJ stated:

it is necessary, as it seems to me, to determine, first, the scope and effect of that term as a matter of construction. In particular, it is necessary to identify the nature of the liability which the term is seeking to exclude or restrict. Whether or not a contract term satisfies the requirement of reasonableness within the meaning of section 11 of the Unfair Contract Terms Act 1977 does not fall to be determined in isolation. It falls to be determined where a person is seeking to rely upon the term in order to exclude or restrict his liability in some context to which the earlier provisions of the 1977 Act (or the provisions of section 3 of the Misrepresentation Act 1967) apply.

Thus, the scope of the clause will have a strong influence on the prospect of it passing the reasonableness test. A very narrow clause is less likely to pass the test.[24]

In contrast to the decision in *George Mitchell*, it is useful to consider the outcome and the reasoning in *Watford Electronics*,[25] where the courts were reluctant to interfere with an agreement made. The difference was that his agreement was made at arm's length by two commercial parties:

WATFORD ELECTRONICS LTD V SANDERSON CFL LTD [2001] EWCA CIV 317, [2001] 1 ALL ER (COMM) 696

The case involved a claim for a breach of contract in an agreement to supply a custom-made software system. The contract contained a clause which stated 'Neither the Company nor the Customer shall be liable to the other for any claims for indirect or consequential losses whether arising from negligence or otherwise. In no event shall the company's liability under the contract exceed the price paid by the customer to

23 [2001] All ER (Comm) 696.
24 *Regus (UK) Ltd v Epcot Solutions Ltd* [2008] EWCA Civ 361, [2009] 1 All ER (Comm) 586.
25 [2001] All ER (Comm) 696.

the company for the equipment connected with any claim.' The system was defective and the claimant sued for damages of £5.5 million, which covered the cost of a replacement, working costs and loss of profit.

Held: the Court of Appeal reversed the first instance decision and held the clause to be reasonable. The contract had been negotiated between experienced parties of equal bargaining power and skill, who had chosen to allocate the risks in a specified way. The court took the view that it should not interfere in the allocation of risks agreed between commercial parties. This decision supports the general notion that freedom of contract is far more likely to prevail when the parties are in a position to protect themselves.

ANALYSING THE LAW – *GEORGE MITCHELL* CASE AND *WATFORD ELECTRONICS*

In analysing the House of Lords decision in *George Mitchell (Chesterhall) Ltd v Finney Lock Seeds Ltd*, the court appears to have taken an interventionist approach. The scope and effect of the clause was effective to limit the liability to the replacement of the seed or the refund of the price paid, so this was not problematic in itself. However, one of the crucial deciding points came from an admission by the seed company that it had always been its practice to negotiate settlements where farmers had made claims in excess of the seed price, if the claims were believed to be genuine and justified. This evidence was interpreted by the court to indicate a clear acknowledgement by the seed sellers that reliance on the limitation clause was not fair and reasonable. The clause had not been negotiated with the relevant trade bodies. The final factors in deciding that the clause was not reasonable included the fact that the seed company had been negligent in its supply of the incorrect and inferior seed and the fact that it was open to seed sellers to insure against the risks of crop failure caused by an inaccurate supply of seeds, without incurring any substantial cost. Lord Bridge emphasised that it was not a matter of 'discretion', but more a matter of the court entertaining 'a whole range of considerations' which should then be put 'in the scales on one side or the other, and decide at the end of the day on which side the balance comes down'. The courts are also generally keen to avoid setting a precedent, emphasising that each case should be treated on its own merits.

Watford Electronics, on the other hand, symbolises that equality of bargaining power is a relevant factor for the courts in looking at the reasonableness of a clause and, where the bargaining power between the parties is equal or fairly strong, a clause will generally be declared reasonable. In contemplation of businessmen representing substantial companies of equal bargaining power, Chadwick LJ put out a very strong message that those parties should in his view 'be taken to be the best judge on the question whether the terms of the agreement are reasonable. The court should not assume that either is likely to commit his company to an agreement which he thinks is unfair, or which he thinks includes unreasonable terms. Unless satisfied that one party has, in effect, taken unfair advantage of the other or that a term is so unreasonable that it cannot properly have been understood or considered the court should not interfere.'

Thus, the position appears quite clear: where it is apparent that parties are on an equal commercial footing, the court will adopt an arm's length approach and invoke minimal interference.

The minimal interference approach is in step with the principle of freedom of contract and shows that the *laissez faire* approach still permeates the courts' attitude towards commercial contracts. There have been a wealth of cases since *Watford Electronics* that support a minimal intervention approach where an agreement has been made between two commercial parties. Another example can be seen in *Granville Oil & Chemical v Davis Turner.*[26]

GRANVILLE OIL & CHEMICAL V DAVIS TURNER [2003] EWCA CIV 570, [2003] 2 LLOYD'S REP 356

The contract involved a shipping contract to transport a consignment of paint. The defendant arranged insurance for the voyage. The contract was said to be subject to a standard term in the British International Freight Association standard trading conditions. The dispute centred on a limitation clause, which stipulated that the insurer could only claim if a claim was submitted within nine months of the event. The paint was damaged in transit and the claimant submitted a claim which was rejected as it was made one day after the expiry of the nine-month period. The claimant then sued for breach and the defendant sought to rely on the limitation clause. Although going one day over may seem unreasonable, the court was not required to assess this, as the judgment had to be based upon the reasonableness of the clause at the time that the contract was made.

Held: the court held that the defendant could rely on the clause. They imported all of Sch. 2 into the judgment. The court could not look directly at Sch. 2, because this was a s. 3 claim (Sch. 2 is relevant to ss. 6 and 7); however, the court did incorporate Sch. 2 as a set of 'relevant criteria'. The court did not label this as Sch. 2, but the factors were very similar. The main deciding factor for the court was that the contract was between two business parties in the same industry and they could have insured themselves separately if necessary – they were saving money by not doing so. The court also considered nine months to be a reasonable period of time for this industry.

In *Röhlig (UK) Ltd v Rock Unique Ltd*[27] the Court of Appeal had to determine whether two clauses within a contract were unreasonable and thus unenforceable under s. 3 of UCTA 1977. The first clause incorporated the British International Freight Association ('BIFA') standard terms and conditions, which excluded the remedy of set-off for all claims; and the second clause barred any claims that had not been notified to the offending party within nine months after they arose. In finding that such terms were indeed reasonable and enforceable, the Court of Appeal made reference to two earlier Court of Appeal decisions (namely *Overland Shoes Ltd v Schenkers International Deutschland GmbH*[28] and *Granville Oil & Chemicals Ltd v Davies Turner & Co Ltd*[29] (discussed above)), which had determined very similar clauses to those in the instant case to be reasonable. Although the Court of Appeal stated that the question of reasonableness must be considered on a case-by-case basis, it did stress that where a standard condition was involved, the courts should not draw unnecessarily fine distinctions between cases that are, for all intents and purposes, very similar. A further significant factor was that the parties to the contract in question had done business with each other over a considerable period of time and therefore ought to have been aware of the terms of the contract that they had negotiated. Although the contracts incorporated the BIFA standard terms and conditions,[30] the fact that these terms had been negotiated by the parties themselves was taken as a clear indication that they represented a fair balance of each party's respective interests. The Court of Appeal also concluded that the relative sizes in corporate terms of the parties to a contract is not a significant factor in cases of this kind where a 'small but commercially experienced organisation' contracts to obtain services of a kind that are available from a large number of competing suppliers.

Notwithstanding this point, where a clear imbalance in equality of bargaining power is evident, there is evidence to show that the courts will still adopt an interventionist approach, as observed in *Kingsway Hall Hotel Ltd v Red Sky IT (Hounslow) Ltd*[31] and *Barclays Bank plc v Grant Thornton*.[32]

As a final comment on this point, it should not be taken for granted that all clauses between businesses will be held reasonable. *Britvic Soft Drinks v Messer UK Ltd*[33] and *Bacardi-Martini Beverages Ltd v Thomas Hardy Packaging*[34] both involved exclusion clauses exempting the suppliers from liability for contamination of a component of their soft drinks. The clauses were declared unreasonable. The clauses had not been negotiated and the contamination, which had been caused by the supplier's own negligence, was not something that would have

---

27 [2011] EWCA Civ 18.
28 [1998] 1 Lloyd's Rep 498.
29 [2003] EWCA Civ 570, [2003] 2 Lloyd's Rep 356.
30 British International Freight Association standard terms which can be used by members.
31 [2010] EWHC 965 (TCC).
32 [2015] EWHC 320 (Comm), [2015] 2 BCLC 537.
33 [2002] EWCA Civ 548, [2002] 2 Lloyd's Rep 368.
34 [2002] EWCA Civ 549, [2002] Lloyd's Rep 379.

been anticipated as a commercial risk. Further examples of clauses held to be unreasonable due to unequal bargaining powers between commercial parties can be found in *Motours Ltd v Euroball (West Kent) Ltd* and *Kingsway Hall Hotel Ltd v Red Sky IT (Hounslow) Ltd*.[35]

ANALYSING THE LAW – REASONABLENESS TEST

Having looked at a variety of cases where the courts were required to assess the reasonableness of a clause, the flow of decisions appears to indicate a willingness on the part of the courts to deal robustly and practically with disputes arising out of standard exclusion clauses. It is also evident from Court of Appeal decisions that where exclusion clauses have been negotiated by the parties to the contract, the difference in size of the contracting parties is unlikely to affect the courts' decision, but inequality in bargaining power will usually be relevant. The wider a clause, the less likely it is to be reasonable, but this will not necessarily prevent wide clauses from being implemented particularly where the parties are of equal bargaining power. Businesses seeking to rely on exclusion clauses are best advised to take extra care to ensure that they fully understand and appreciate the effect of the terms they agree and give consideration to whether such terms will generally be regarded as reasonable.

Figure 6.4 summarises the factors that will be observed by the courts in ascertaining whether or not a clause is reasonable in the context of an exclusion or limitation clause.

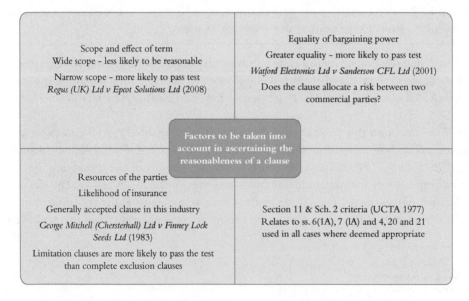

Figure 6.4 Factors to be considered in ascertaining reasonableness

---

35 *Motours Ltd v Euroball (West Kent) Ltd* [2003] EWHC 614 (QB), [2003] All ER (D) 165; *Kingsway Hall Hotel Ltd v Red Sky IT (Hounslow) Ltd* (2010) 26 Const. L.J. 542.

In addition to the factors established by precedent, s. 11(2) UCTA 1977 incorporates specific guidelines on reasonableness into the equation under Sch. 2 to the Act. The factors that must be taken into account are shown in Figure 6.5.

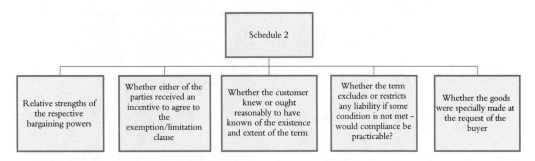

Figure 6.5 Schedule 2 guidelines

When prescribing the particular clauses Sch. 2 applies to, the Act only specifically mentions exclusions relating to implied terms in sale and supply contracts. In practice, however, the guidelines have been applied more generally in assessing the reasonableness of clauses falling under a variety of sections in the Sale of Goods Act 1979.[36] Where the test of reasonableness is not met, the clause cannot be relied upon to exclude liability that would otherwise be enforceable under a contract.

ASSESSMENT TIP

- It is important to remember the scope of application of UCTA 1977 (which has changed considerably since the introduction of the CRA 2015), otherwise you may apply the wrong piece of legislation to a scenario involving an exclusion/limitation clause.
- Prior to the enactment of the CRA 2015 on 1 October 2015, the provisions of UCTA 1977 also applied to consumer contracts, i.e. in situations where the clause in question was used against a party who was 'dealing as consumer'.
- In analysing an exclusion or limitation clause, remember that a clause is sometimes branded ineffective right from the outset and the reasonableness test cannot be applied, whereas other clauses will be subject to the reasonableness test.

---

36 *St Albans City and District Council v International Computers Ltd* [1996] EWCA Civ 1296.

The categories are summarised below:

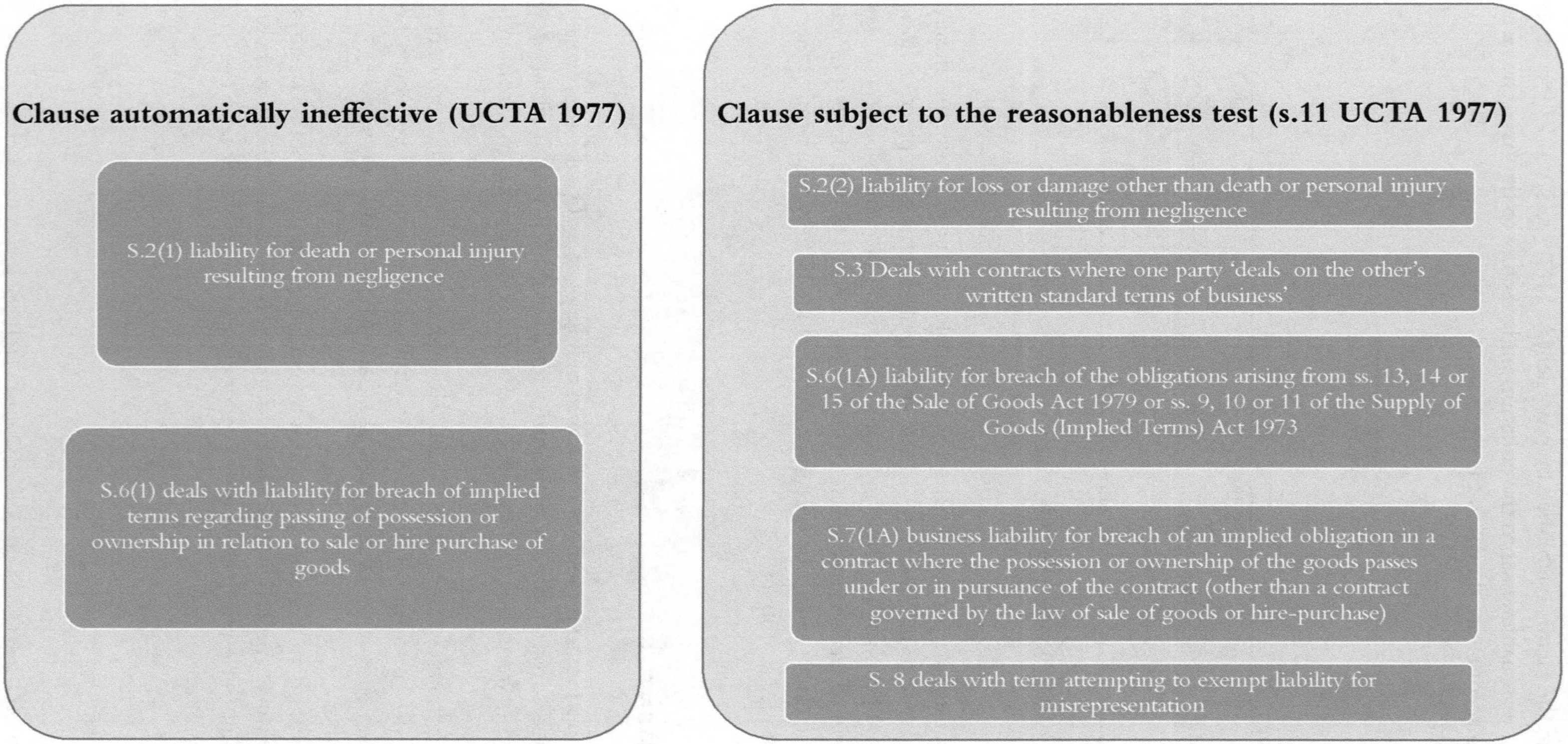

Clause automatically ineffective (UCTA 1977)

S.2(1) liability for death or personal injury resulting from negligence

S.6(1) deals with liability for breach of implied terms regarding passing of possession or ownership in relation to sale or hire purchase of goods

Clause subject to the reasonableness test (s.11 UCTA 1977)

S.2(2) liability for loss or damage other than death or personal injury resulting from negligence

S.3 Deals with contracts where one party 'deals, on the other's written standard terms of business'

S.6((1A) liability for breach of the obligations arising from ss. 13, 14 or 15 of the Sale of Goods Act 1979 or ss. 9, 10 or 11 of the Supply of Goods (Implied Terms) Act 1973

S.7(1A) business liability for breach of an implied obligation in a contract where the possession or ownership of the goods passes under or in pursuance of the contract (other than a contract governed by the law of sale of goods or hire-purchase)

S. 8 deals with term attempting to exempt liability for misrepresentation

Figure 6.6 Categorisation of UCTA clauses

6.7 CONSUMER RIGHTS ACT 2015 AND UNFAIR TERMS IN BUSINESS TO CONSUMER CONTRACTS

In order to fully appreciate the changes made by the CRA 2015, it is important to be aware of previous legislation on unfair terms in consumer contracts (see Figure 6.7).

6.7.1 TIMELINE

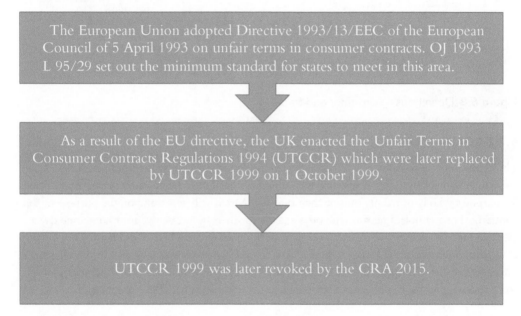

The European Union adopted Directive 1993/13/EEC of the European Council of 5 April 1993 on unfair terms in consumer contracts. OJ 1993 L 95/29 set out the minimum standard for states to meet in this area.

As a result of the EU directive, the UK enacted the Unfair Terms in Consumer Contracts Regulations 1994 (UTCCR) which were later replaced by UTCCR 1999 on 1 October 1999.

UTCCR 1999 was later revoked by the CRA 2015.

Figure 6.7 Unfair terms statutes – consumer contracts

Prior to the enactment of the CRA 2015, when considering whether an exclusion clause in a consumer contract was valid, it was necessary to consider both the UCTA 1977 and the UTCCR 1999. The law is now consolidated into Part 2 of the CRA 2015, which replaces the UTCCR and applies to contracts entered into, and relevant notices issued, on or after 1 October 2015.

The CRA 2015 is significant in that it consolidates the legislation governing unfair contract terms in relation to business to consumer (B2C) contracts. In addition to revoking and replacing the UTCCR 1999, it also replaces UCTA 1977 in respect of B2C contracts.

As mentioned in the previous chapter, the CRA 2015 is split into three parts. Parts 1 and 2 of the Act consolidate and replace the UTCCR 1999 and relevant provisions of UCTA 1977. In this chapter we are concerned in particular with contract terms and notices that are classified as unfair to consumers and are unenforceable.

The CRA 2015 regulates contracts between a trader and a consumer (s. 61(1)), referred to as consumer contracts, but specifically exclude a contract of employment or apprenticeship (s. 61(2)): Some vital definitions are provided in Figure 6.8.

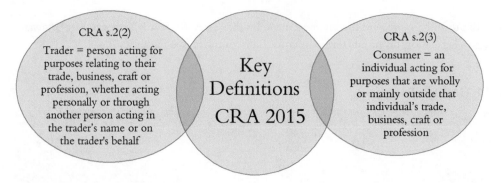

Figure 6.8 Definitions – consumer and trader

6.7.2 CONSUMER

The definition of a consumer clearly specifies 'an individual', which by definition excludes companies and partnerships. A sole trader could possibly fall into the consumer category if acting for purposes wholly or mainly outside their business. Much will depend upon the purpose of the contract.[37] For example, a person who buys a kettle for their home, works from home one day a week and uses it on the days when working from home would still be a consumer for the purpose of a claim in respect of the kettle (example taken from CRA explanatory notes). In this chapter on unfair terms, we will concentrate on Part 2 of the CRA 2015, which relates to contractual terms and notices applicable to obligations between a trader and consumer (B2C contracts).

In considering unfair terms, s. 62 of the CRA 2015 is the main instructor. Section 62(1) dictates that an unfair term of a consumer contract is not binding on the consumer and s. 62(2) provides the same consequence for an unfair **consumer notice**.

ESSENTIAL DEFINITION: CONSUMER NOTICE

A consumer notice is broadly defined as a notice that relates to rights or obligations between a trader and a consumer, or a notice that appears to exclude or restrict a trader's liability to a consumer. It includes an announcement or other communication, whether or not in writing, as long as it is reasonable to assume that it is intended to be seen or heard by a consumer. Consumer notices are often used, in public places such as shops or car parks as well as online and in documentation that is otherwise contractual in nature.

---

37 *Overy v Paypal (Europe) Ltd* [2012] EWHC 2659 (QB), [2013] Bus LR D1.

The Act may be particularly significant for consumer notices involving digital content. Software and other digital products are sold to consumers subject to end user licence agreements (EULAs).[38] The terms of EULAs may not in all cases be clearly part of the contract with the consumer and, where this is the case, they are still assessable for fairness and transparency, as consumer notices under CRA 2015.

Digital content means data that is produced and supplied in digital form. The digital content can be contained both within a physical product, such as music, films, games or software contained in CDs and DVDs; alternatively it may be in a less tangible format such as an app or a music download. The requirements of fairness and transparency under Part 2 of the Act will apply to contracts and notices for these product types (see Figure 6.9).

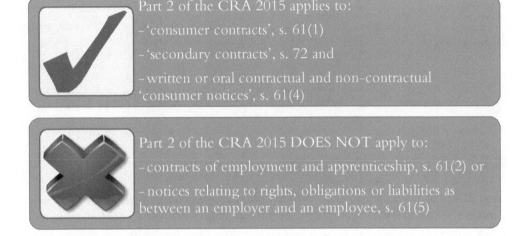

Figure 6.9 Scope of the Act

6.7.3 APPLYING THE TEST OF FAIRNESS

Where a term is found to be unfair, it does not necessarily mean that the whole of the contract is non-binding; in most cases the contract can continue with the exclusion of the unfair term (s. 67). However, a consumer can rely on the term or notice if s/he chooses to do so (s. 63(3)). The assessment of fairness should be determined at the time that the term was agreed and not at the time of breach. No assessment of fairness will be undertaken in relation to a term relating to the subject matter of the contract or the price (s. 64(1)). The CRA enables the fairness test to be applied to both standard form contracts and individually negotiated contracts, which is a change from the previous position under the UTCCR where the fairness test could only be applied to standard form contracts.

---

38 A legal contract between the manufacturer and the end user of a software application. The end user licence agreement details how the software can and cannot be used and any restrictions that the manufacturer imposes. A common restriction in many agreements is the prohibition of the user from sharing the software with other parties.

Figure 6.10 provides a summary of s. 62, which governs unfairness in contract terms and notices.

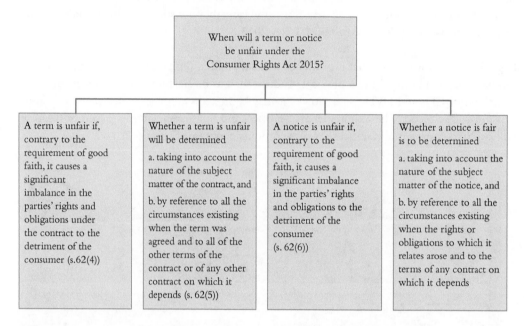

Figure 6.10 S.62 Summary test of fairness

Section 71(2) CRA 2015 permits the court to consider whether a term is fair even if none of the parties to the proceedings has raised the issue. Although the court is not required to do this as a matter of course, it can do so to ensure that justice is achieved for the undiscerning customer who may be unaware of the opportunity to make a challenge.

6.7.4 THE CORE EXEMPTION

Provided that the term(s) are transparent and prominent Part 2 of the CRA 2015 permits an exemption from the test of fairness where a term relates to:

1) the main subject matter of the contract, or
2) the adequacy of the price.

Whilst this exemption does not extend to consumer notices, it is anticipated that businesses are unlikely to wish to use wording in their notices that has no legal force to determine core contractual issues. The core exemption prevents unnecessary regulation of key obligations in a contract and the price. Within a free market economy, such areas should endure minimal judicial interference and be left to the parties to agree as they consider appropriate. That said, if such terms are not prominent and transparent, the exemption will not apply and the terms can be assessed for fairness. Remember: only terms that are regarded as the 'very essence of the contractual relationship' will fall under the core exemption; in other words, the main subject matter of the contract. Such terms will lay down the essential obligations of the contract rather than terms that are ancillary to essential obligations.

Terms that have the same object or effect of those on the grey list (see later) cannot fall within the core exemption, and can be assessed for fairness. Thus, a term may not benefit from 'the core exemption' merely on the basis that it can be said to have an impact on the main subject matter of the contract or the price. Terms granting the trader unfettered discretion to vary the price or the definition of the main subject matter are examples of terms included in the grey list, which can be assessed for fairness.

6.7.5 THE MAIN SUBJECT MATTER OF A CONTRACT

Only terms that specify what the CJEU has called the 'very essence of the contractual relationship' fall within the ambit of the core exemption, i.e. 'the main subject matter of the contract'. Such terms 'must be understood as being those that lay down the essential obligations of the contract' as against terms that are 'ancillary to those that define the very essence of the contractual relationship'. The CMA considers that in a contract for the sale of goods, for instance, terms that describe the nature of the goods to be sold are likely to be seen as setting out 'essential obligations'. Provided such terms are transparent and prominent, they can benefit from 'the core exemption'. In contrast, a term describing the arrangements for delivery of the same goods would (depending on the circumstances) likely be considered ancillary and, as such, would not benefit from the exemption.[39]

A price-setting term can be assessed for fairness except to the extent that the assessment relates to the appropriateness of the price as against the services, goods or digital content supplied in exchange. This means that the level of the price cannot be assessed against the value of the product. Such a term may still be assessed, however, on grounds other than the appropriateness/adequacy of the price. This could include areas such as the timing, method or variation of the payment.

6.7.6 DUTY TO CONSIDER FAIRNESS

The CRA 2015, like the UCTA 1977, also provides a mechanism to enable certain terms to be automatically invalidated. These are widely referred to as 'blacklisted' terms. Terms falling into blacklisted categories will be automatically ineffective and the fairness test will not be applied. Section 31 of the Act contains certain mandatory statutory or regulatory provisions or requirements that derive from international conventions (such as the requirements that goods are of satisfactory quality and fit for purpose), and specifically states that these obligations or liability for them cannot be excluded or restricted.

The other main areas of invalid terms are set out in Figure 6.11.

---

39 www.gov.uk/government/uploads/system/uploads/attachment_data/file/450440/Unfair_Terms_Main_Guidance.pdf.

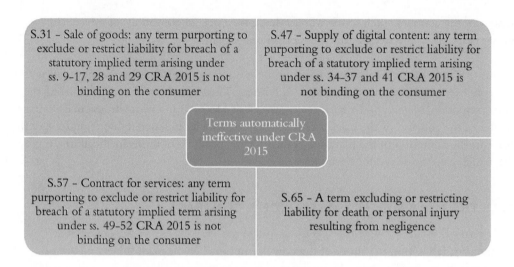

Figure 6.11 Ineffective terms under CRA 2015

6.7.7 NEGLIGENCE LIABILITY AND THE CRA 2015

So what does the CRA 2015 say about exclusion of liability for negligence?

The CRA provisions are largely equivalent to s. 2(1) of UCTA 1977. Section 65(1) specifies that a trader cannot by a term of a consumer contract or notice exclude or restrict liability for death or personal injury resulting from negligence. The fairness test should not be applied in such instances. Nor can a consumer be assumed to have accepted any risk simply by agreeing to or having knowledge of a particular term. If the term purports to exclude or restrict other loss or damage that has occurred not as a result of negligence, it will be subject to the fairness test. As far as is practicable, where a term is deemed unfair, the remainder of the contract will continue and can be enforced unless it is incapable of continuing in the absence of the term.

The Act is wider in scope than UCTA 1977, which covers exemption clauses in B2B contracts. The CRA regulates 'unfair terms' in consumer contracts or unfair consumer notices. This wider scope of the Act also enables it to cover unreasonable deposits and penalty clauses. Not all terms may be subjected to the fairness test. As mentioned earlier, the courts will not assess the fairness of terms regarding the price and subject matter of the contract, unless those terms are either non-transparent or non-prominent. A transparent term is one that is 'expressed in plain and intelligible language' (mirroring the previous requirement under reg. 7(1) UTCCR 1999), and a prominent term is one that will have been 'brought to the customers attention in such a way that an average consumer would be aware of the term' (s. 64(4) CRA). The average consumer is one who is reasonably well informed, observant and circumspect (s. 64(5) CRA). Previous case law under the UTCCR relating to the requirements of fairness and transparency is relevant to understanding the corresponding provisions in the CRA. The issue on whether a 'core term' could be assessed for fairness was considered in the following case:

DIRECTOR GENERAL OF FAIR TRADING (DGFT) V FIRST NATIONAL BANK PLC [2001] UKHL 52, [2002] 1 AC 481

In its standard loan agreement, one of the conditions entitled the bank to interest at the contractual rate both after and before any judgment had been made until repayment of the loan and any interest. Under general law the interest is merged into the judgement and the interest is not payable. Thus the Director General sought an injunction to prevent the bank from relying upon the condition on the grounds that it was an unfair term.

Held: the House of Lords held that the condition was not a core term, as it dealt with the consequences of a default by the borrower, rather than the bank's remuneration for the agreement; thus it could be assessed for fairness. The court then went on to consider whether the condition satisfied the test of fairness and concluded that it did, resulting in the interest being payable.

Shortly after the *First National Bank* case, in *Bairstow Eves London Central Ltd v Smith*[40] the commission price for a property sale was stated as 1.5% for early payment. This was a core term, i.e. the price for the service, and was not disputed. A further term specifying that commission payment would be 3% if payment was not made within ten days of completion was disputed and found not to be a core term. An assessment of the fairness of the clause then followed and it was found to be unfair.

Another prominent case in which the issue of whether clauses in respect of bank charges could be considered unfair was *Office of Fair Trading v Abbey National plc.*[41] The issue at stake was whether the bank charge clauses being sought from the customer should be interpreted as ancillary to the main price agreement and therefore not part of the core terms. Of course, if they were found to be ancillary, the court would be able to assess the charges for fairness. A Court of Appeal decision found the charges to be ancillary and the decision was appealed to the Supreme Court. Instead of distinguishing between core or ancillary terms, the Supreme Court determined the issue by looking at whether the charges represented the monetary price for the service provided. The fact that the charges amounted to over 30% of the bank's revenue stream from personal account holders was a strong indication that they must be part of the core or essential bargain. Having concluded that the bank charges were core, the court could not then assess them for fairness.

Section 62(4) requires further analysis to determine what is meant by the terms 'significant imbalance' and the 'requirement of good faith'.

---

40 [2004] EWHC 263 (QB), [2004] 2 EGLR 25.
41 [2009] UKSC 6, [2010] 1 AC 696.

EXPLAINING THE LAW – WHAT IS MEANT BY 'CONTRARY TO GOOD FAITH'

Assessing what exactly is meant by 'contrary to good faith' presents us with a challenge, as there is no recognised doctrine of good faith in English contract law. Guidance can be drawn from the House of Lords judgment in *Director General of Fair Trading v First National Bank plc*, where Lord Bingham defines the requirement of good faith as 'one of fair and open dealing'. He talks of openness as requiring that the terms are 'expressed fully, clearly and legibly, containing no concealed pitfalls or traps'. Fair dealing, he stated, meant that a supplier should 'not take advantage of the consumer's necessity, indigence, lack of experience, unfamiliarity with the subject matter of the contract, weak bargaining position or any other factor listed in or analogous to those listed in Schedule 2'. Good faith looks to 'good standards of commercial morality and practice'. Lord Steyn in the same judgment defined good faith as an 'objective criterion'. He stated that an argument that 'good faith is predominantly concerned with procedural defects in negotiating procedures' cannot be sustained.

The case of *Aziz v Caixa d'Estalvis de Catalunya, Tarragona I Manresa*,[42] concerning the fairness of three provisions in a loan agreement, also offers some assistance when determining what is meant by good faith: the Court of Justice of the EU (CJEU) stated that 'in considering whether the imbalance is contrary to the requirements of good faith, the court will also have regard to whether the trader, dealing fairly and equitably with the consumer, could reasonably have assumed that the consumer would have agreed to the disputed term in individual contract negotiations'. Thus, it is clear that good faith embodies a general principle of 'fair and open dealing'.

Section 62(5) makes it clear that the assessment of fairness will be undertaken in respect of all of the terms of the contract, not simply the term that is the subject of challenge. A consumer contract may be considered balanced if both parties enjoy rights of equal extent and value in reality, particularly taking into account the nature of the goods, services or digital content provided under the contract. Thus, in *West v Ian Finlay & Associates*,[43] where the consumer had extensive knowledge of the issue covered by the clause and associated risks, the clause was determined to be a fair one.

The Supreme Court also provided guidance on 'fairness' in *ParkingEye Ltd v Beavis*,[44] a recent appeal case conjoined with *Cavendish Square Holding BV v Talal El Makdessi*. The cases concerned penalty clauses (which are covered the later chapter on remedies; but it is helpful to look at the *ParkingEye* case at this point as one of the important matters considered by the court was whether a rather contentious contractual term was unfair).

---

42 (2013) Case C–415/11.
43 [2014] EWCA Civ 316.
44 [2015] UKSC 67, [2015] 3 WLR 1373.

PARKINGEYE LTD V BEAVIS [2015] UKSC 67, [2015] 3 WLR 1373

The case involved the imposition of a parking charge of £85 levied upon Mr Beavis by ParkingEye for overstaying in a retail shopping centre car park. He argued that the charge was a penalty clause and was far too high to constitute a genuine pre-estimate of the loss that ParkingEye had suffered as a result of his breach of contract.

The two issues that the Supreme Court had to determine were:

1) Whether a charge of £85 for exceeding a maximum car parking period was an unenforceable penalty
2) Whether a charge of £85 for exceeding a maximum car parking period was unfair under the UTCCR (the regulations preceding CRA 2015).

The law on penalty clauses as it stood allowed contracting parties to agree in advance the amount of damages that should be paid if a particular contractual obligation is subsequently breached. The provision that sets such an amount of damages is called 'a liquidated damages clause'. Nevertheless, there is a limit to the extent to which enforcement of such clauses is permitted. A penalty clause cannot be enforced, in the sense that the detriment imposed is disproportionately excessive in comparison with the legitimate interest of the innocent party in enforcing those provisions. The penalty clause side will be dealt with in greater detail in a later chapter, so we will just look at the issue of 'fairness' of the term here.

You will see later on that the parking charge of £85 was held to be enforceable. The charge was not regarded as an unfair term since the court recognised that ParkingEye had a legitimate interest in charging overstaying motorists, which extended beyond the recovery of any loss. The company was managing car parks in the interests of the retail outlets, their customers and the public at large and as such had a legitimate interest in influencing the conduct of the contracting party, which is not satisfied by the mere right to recover damages for breach of contract. ParkingEye could not charge a sum out of all proportion to its interests, but the sum of £85 was not deemed to be out of all proportion.

ANALYSING THE LAW

As a result of *ParkingEye*, the general test now appears to be based upon whether the sum or remedy stipulated as a consequence of a breach of contract is exorbitant or unconscionable when regard is had to the innocent party's interest in the performance of the contract. The major shift in interpretation of the penalty rule is acknowledgment that the traditional test based simply on the comparison between the stipulated sum and the greatest amount of loss that could be caused by the breach will usually be inapt, and regard may need to be had to the wider interest of the innocent party in enforcing the claim for the specified sum. This change in approach will most likely make it more difficult to challenge the enforceability of the liquidated damages clause. For example, consider the enforceability of a liquidated damages clause in a building construction project. In such a situation, if there is evidence that the figure set for liquidated damages was set entirely with regard to losses that the innocent party might be able to recover under the relevant contract, it is likely that the court will not apply the test of wider interest. If looking at the wider interest, however, one of the matters the court might take into account is whether the relevant construction project was an individual project or an important component in a bigger project. If the latter is the case, it may be easier for the court to identify a wider legitimate interest of the innocent party in enforcing the disputed clause than merely the need for financial compensation for loss. Where such an interest is acknowledged, the court might uphold the enforceability of the disputed clause, even if the amount of the stipulated sum is such that the court would previously have treated the clause as a penalty clause and therefore unenforceable.

On the second question of whether the charge was unfair under the UTCCR, the clause was not found to be 'contrary to the requirements of good faith' and did not 'create a significant imbalance in the parties' rights and obligations under the contract, to the detriment of the consumer' as any imbalance in the parties' rights was not considered to have arisen contrary to the requirement of good faith. The reason for this was because the operator and the landlord had a legitimate interest in imposing a liability on Mr Beavis in excess of the damages that would have been recoverable at common law.

ASSESSMENT TIP

The test now is whether a contractual clause is extravagant or extortionate compared to the legitimate purpose to be achieved.

6.7.8 SIGNIFICANT IMBALANCE

The meaning of the term 'significant imbalance' is not defined in the CRA 2015 and is somewhat elusive. A definition was attempted by Lord Bingham: *Director General of Fair Trading v First National Bank* (see Figure 6.12).[45]

45 [2002] UKHL 52, [2002] 1 AC 481.

Figure 6.12 Definition: significant imbalance

Significant imbalance will not necessarily be restricted to cases where a purely financial burden or cost is imposed on the consumer. The focus of the fairness test, particularly in relation to imbalance, is upon the consumer's legal rights and obligations generally. An example of a term that could impose non-financial disadvantage is one that purports to allow the trader to pass on information it holds on the consumer more widely than is permitted under the Data Protection Act 1998. This term may not result in a financial cost to the consumer, but it would nevertheless take away his/her rights. To be unfair an imbalance must be of tangible significance, but a finding of unfairness does not require proof that a term has already caused loss or damage. The fairness assessment is concerned with consumer rights and sellers' duties and, as such, the onus is on possible not actual outcomes. A term may be contested if it could be used to cause consumer detriment even if it is not currently being used to produce that outcome. Where it appears that a potentially unfair term is not currently being used to the disadvantage of a consumer, it could be narrowed to reflect the specific nature of a business. The narrower a clause, the more likely it is to be reasonable. The question of significant imbalance was raised in the case of *Office of Fair Trading v Ashbourne Management Services Ltd*[46] where minimum gym membership periods imposed upon customers were found to constitute unfair terms as they were heavily weighted against the consumer and contravened the requirement of good faith.

6.7.9 TRANSPARENCY

A written term of a consumer contract or notice must be transparent (s. 68(1) CRA). A consumer notice is transparent if it is expressed 'in plain and intelligible language and it is legible' (s. 68(2)). Where a term in a consumer contract or notice is argued to have more than one meaning, the most favourable meaning to the benefit of the consumer must prevail (s. 69(1) CRA). The effect of s. 69(1) is to give statutory effect to the *contra proferentem* construction rule. You will recall that the *contra proferentem* rule requires any ambiguity in a term to be resolved against the party who is seeking to rely upon it. To meet the statutory requirement of transparency, obligations and rights should be set out fully, and in a way that is not only comprehensible but also in a way that places the consumer in a position where s/he can understand their practical significance. On entering the contract, the consumer should

---

46 [2011] EWHC 1237 (Ch), [2011] EEC 31.

be able to see how the obligations and rights relate to each other, and be able to foresee and evaluate the consequences the terms may have in the future and make an informed choice whether or not to enter into the contract.

6.7.10 THE 'GREY' LIST – TERMS ASSESSABLE FOR FAIRNESS

Section 63 CRA 2015 refers to Part 1 of Sch. 2, which is widely known as 'the grey list'. Schedule 2 provides an indicative non-exhaustive list of terms in consumer contracts that are not regarded as 'automatically' unfair but that *may* be regarded as being unfair. Schedule 2 derives from the 'grey list' that was contained previously in the UTCCR 1999. Whilst the list can be used by the court as a guide to terms that 'may' be unfair, it should be stressed that the list is not conclusive on the matter, and any such term must be assessed under the fairness test. Section 63(5) of the Act also gives the Secretary of State the power to amend the grey list if appropriate to do so.

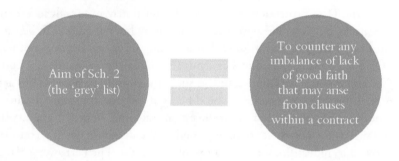

Figure 6.13 The grey list

ASSESSMENT TIP

Take care not to assume that a term will be unfair just because it is on the grey list. Remember, the list gives an indication of the types of terms that are likely to be considered unfair without any justification being provided. However, it is possible that a term can be found to be fair even if it is included on the grey list; likewise, a term can be found unfair even if it is not included on the list.

The CRA 2015 adds an additional three terms to the previous grey list. These are terms that have the effect of:

- allowing the trader to decide the characteristics of the subject matter after the consumer is bound;
- allowing disproportionate charges or requiring the consumer to pay for services that have not been supplied when the consumer ends the contract;
- allowing the trader discretion over the price after the consumer is bound.

Schedule 2 is reproduced below:

SCHEDULE 2

CONSUMER CONTRACT TERMS WHICH MAY BE REGARDED AS UNFAIR

PART 1

List of terms

1 A term which has the object or effect of excluding or limiting the trader's liability in the event of the death of or personal injury to the consumer resulting from an act or omission of the trader.
2 A term which has the object or effect of inappropriately excluding or limiting the legal rights of the consumer in relation to the trader or another party in the event of total or partial non-performance or inadequate performance by the trader of any of the contractual obligations, including the option of offsetting a debt owed to the trader against any claim which the consumer may have against the trader.
3 A term which has the object or effect of making an agreement binding on the consumer in a case where the provision of services by the trader is subject to a condition whose realisation depends on the trader's will alone.
4 A term which has the object or effect of permitting the trader to retain sums paid by the consumer where the consumer decides not to conclude or perform the contract, without providing for the consumer to receive compensation of an equivalent amount from the trader where the trader is the party cancelling the contract.
5 A term which has the object or effect of requiring that, where the consumer decides not to conclude or perform the contract, the consumer must pay the trader a disproportionately high sum in compensation or for services which have not been supplied.
6 A term which has the object or effect of requiring a consumer who fails to fulfil his obligations under the contract to pay a disproportionately high sum in compensation.
7 A term which has the object or effect of authorising the trader to dissolve the contract on a discretionary basis where the same facility is not granted to the consumer, or permitting the trader to retain the sums paid for services not yet supplied by the trader where it is the trader who dissolves the contract.
8 A term which has the object or effect of enabling the trader to terminate a contract of indeterminate duration without reasonable notice except where there are serious grounds for doing so.
9 A term which has the object or effect of automatically extending a contract of fixed duration where the consumer does not indicate otherwise, when the deadline fixed

for the consumer to express a desire not to extend the contract is unreasonably early.

10 A term which has the object or effect of irrevocably binding the consumer to terms with which the consumer has had no real opportunity of becoming acquainted before the conclusion of the contract.

11 A term which has the object or effect of enabling the trader to alter the terms of the contract unilaterally without a valid reason which is specified in the contract.

12 A term which has the object or effect of permitting the trader to determine the characteristics of the subject matter of the contract after the consumer has become bound by it.

13 A term which has the object or effect of enabling the trader to alter unilaterally without a valid reason any characteristics of the goods, digital content or services to be provided.

14 A term which has the object or effect of giving the trader the discretion to decide the price payable under the contract after the consumer has become bound by it, where no price or method of determining the price is agreed when the consumer becomes bound.

15 A term which has the object or effect of permitting a trader to increase the price of goods, digital content or services without giving the consumer the right to cancel the contract if the final price is too high in relation to the price agreed when the contract was concluded.

16 A term which has the object or effect of giving the trader the right to determine whether the goods, digital content or services supplied are in conformity with the contract, or giving the trader the exclusive right to interpret any term of the contract.

17 A term which has the object or effect of limiting the trader's obligation to respect commitments undertaken by the trader's agents or making the trader's commitments subject to compliance with a particular formality.

18 A term which has the object or effect of obliging the consumer to fulfil all of the consumer's obligations where the trader does not perform the trader's obligations.

19 A term which has the object or effect of allowing the trader to transfer the trader's rights and obligations under the contract, where this may reduce the guarantees for the consumer, without the consumer's agreement.

20 A term which has the object or effect of excluding or hindering the consumer's right to take legal action or exercise any other legal remedy, in particular by –
   (a) requiring the consumer to take disputes exclusively to arbitration not covered by legal provisions,
   (b) unduly restricting the evidence available to the consumer, or
   (c) imposing on the consumer a burden of proof which, according to the applicable law, should lie with another party to the contract.

6.8 THE CONSUMER CONTRACTS (INFORMATION, CANCELLATION AND ADDITIONAL CHARGES) REGULATIONS 2013

In discussing consumer rights, it is also important to understand the function of the Consumer Contracts (Information, Cancellation and Additional Charges) Regulations 2013[47] (CCR 2013). For contracts entered into on or after 13 June 2014, the regulations supersede two previous sets of regulations:

- Consumer Protection (Distance Selling) Regulations 2000
- Cancellation of Contracts made in a Consumer's Home or Place of Work etc Regulations 2008.

Amongst other things, the CCR 2013 require traders to provide certain pre-contract information to consumers, and to do so 'in a clear and comprehensible manner'. This statutory pre-contract information is to be treated as legally binding on the business in the same way as what is said in the contract itself. The goods, services or digital content must be provided as stated in the pre-contract information, and any change will not be effective unless expressly agreed between the consumer and the trader.

The CCR 2013 set out certain requirements:

- the information that a trader must give to a consumer before and after making a sale
- how that information should be given
- the right for consumers to change their minds when buying at a distance or off-premises
- delivery times and passing of risk
- a prohibition on any additional payments that appear as a default option
- a prohibition on consumers having to pay more than the basic rate for post-contract customer helplines.

The provisions of the CCR should particularly be borne in mind in connection with the use of variation clauses – that is, wording that could be used to allow changes to be made to any aspect of the contract. Where a variation clause allows changes to be made to any details as to (for instance) the product or its price as set out in the pre-contract information, businesses need to carefully consider whether their use of such clauses with consumers will meet the requirements of the CCR and the Act.

6.9 ENFORCEMENT

Section 70 of CRA 2015 states that the general enforcement of the law in relation to unfair contract terms is the function of the Competition and Markets Authority (CMA). The CMA

---

47 S.I. 2013/3134.

took over the function from the Office of Fair Trading and other regulators (see Part 1 of Sch. 5 to the CRA 2015).

In addition to the CMA, there are a number of additional bodies that are involved in enforcement of consumer law, including local authority trading standards services ('trading standards'), and the Department of Enterprise, Trade and Investment in Northern Ireland ('DETI').

Schedule 3 to CRA 2015 provides a regulator with statutory power to consider a complaint under Part 2 of the Act. The regulator may apply for an injunction to prevent the use of a specific term or notice, or to prevent the future use of a term or notice. Schedule 5 to the CRA sets out the enforcement and investigative powers available to the various enforcement bodies.

6.10 BRINGING IT ALL TOGETHER

Figure 6.14 shows the tests that need to be applied to ascertain whether an exclusion clause is valid and enforceable.

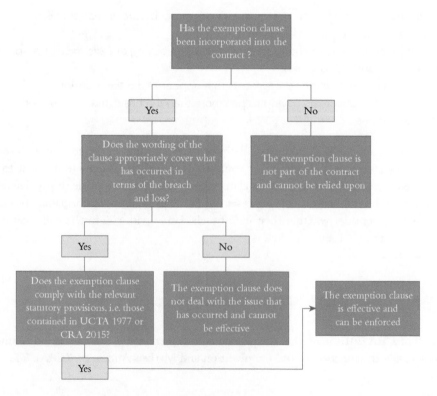

Figure 6.14 Exclusion clause – is it enforceable?

6.11 SUMMARY

- UCTA 1977 regulates B2B contracts
- UCTA 1977 incorporates a reasonableness test to assess the validity of some exemption clauses
- The CRA 2015 regulates B2C contracts only
- Under CRA 2015, the UCTA 1977 'reasonableness' test is replaced by the 'fairness' assessment previously contained in the UTCCR. Previous case law used to assess fairness is still valid
- The fairness test applies to both negotiated and non-negotiated (standard term) contracts, providing further scope than the UTCCR, which only applied to standard terms
- The fairness test applies to consumer contracts and consumer notices
- Unfair terms and notices are not binding on a consumer but they can choose to rely on them
- Terms which specify the main subject matter of the contract or the price are not subject to an assessment for fairness provided that:
  1) the term is transparent (in plain and intelligible language and, if in writing, legible)
  2) prominent (presented in a way that an average consumer would be aware of them)
- A contract term cannot exclude or restrict liability for death or personal injury resulting from negligence (s. 65 CRA 2015)
- The CRA 2015 contains additional 'grey list' terms – terms that may be regarded as unfair and the fairness test must be applied
- A trader must ensure that a written term of a consumer contract or a written consumer notice is transparent. To be transparent the term must be expressed in plain and intelligible language and be legible. This reflects the previous UTCCR
- Where a term in a consumer contract or consumer notice has different meanings, the most favourable term to the consumer will prevail. This reflects the UTCCR and is in line with the *contra proferentem* rule
- The courts are duty bound to consider the fairness of a term in a consumer contract whether or not a party has raised the issue

APPLYING THE LAW

Simon received a publicity brochure from the newly opened Starlight Snow Centre inviting him to take a reduced-price skiing lesson at an introductory fee of £25 for two hours. The brochure contained the following statements:

(1) Starlight Snow Centre cannot guarantee the provision of an instructor throughout the period of a trial lesson;
(2) Starlight Snow Centre cannot accept responsibility for loss or damage caused to customers' personal property during the course of a trial lesson.

Simon went to the Snow Centre, paid £25 and, without any reference being made to the above statement, was put on the ski lift and told to wait for his instructor by the red post at the top of the slope. Simon waited by the red post for half an hour, awaiting instruction, and then decided to go back to the base of the slope and complain. He bravely commenced his descent down the slope. However, as a beginner, he really needed instructor assistance and, being unfamiliar with skiing, his technique was poor and he fell over, rolled to the bottom of the slope and broke both of his ski poles worth £120. Simon is most upset as he had purchased the poles especially for his first ski lesson.

Simon is now claiming a refund of £25 and £120 for a replacement set of ski poles.

ADVICE TO STARLIGHT SNOW CENTRE

In advising Starlight Snow Centre you should identify the area of law and explain the rules on validity of exclusion clauses.

You should define the law that covers this area and discuss any applicable case law or statute relevant to the problem.

Finally apply the rules to the problem.

AREA OF LAW – EXCLUSION CLAUSES

Set out the issues that need to be addressed to compile the advice for Starlight Snow Centre.

Next, a brief definition of an exclusion clause is required.

Follow this by looking at the legal requirements that must be fulfilled for an exclusion clause to be enforceable:

- Incorporation
- Construction
- Statutory control

Incorporation and construction: Was the clause incorporated into the contract and is it appropriately worded to cover the occurrence that is being avoided?

Remember the rule: the clause must be visible or brought to the attention of the contracting party either before, or at the time that, the contract was entered into (*Olley v Marlborough Court Hotel* [1949] 1 KB 532).

Was the document within the nature of a document that one would expect to contain contractual terms? (Discuss cases such as *Chapleton v Barry UDC* [1940] 1 KB 532; *Parker v South Eastern Railway* (1877) 2 CPD 416; *Thompson v LM & S Railway* [1930] 1 KB 41.)

Nature of the clause: How onerous was the clause? If the clause is particularly onerous, it must be very clear (*Interfoto Picture Library Ltd v Stiletto Visual Programmes Ltd* [1989] 1 QB 433).

Also, remember the words of Lord Denning in *Spurling v Bradshaw* [1956] 1 WLR 461: 'Some clauses I have seen would need to be printed in **red ink** on the face of a document with a red hand pointing to it.'

Apply: The brochure would probably suffice as a document in which a claimant would expect to contain contractual terms. But were the onerous terms clear? They are more likely to be incorporated if specifically brought to claimant's attention. In this case they were not referred to when the contract was agreed; thus they may not be incorporated.

STATUTORY CONTROL

(i) Starlight Snow Dome cannot guarantee the provision of an instructor throughout the period of a trial lesson.

Due to the type of contract, it could surely be argued that provision of an instructor is fundamental to the performance of the contract. You would raise the point that the Snow Dome have a duty to carry out their instruction duties with 'reasonable skill and care' (s. 49 CRA 2015). Section 57 of the CRA 2015 prohibits exclusion of rights or remedies in such instances.

Apply: it is highly unlikely that the instruction duties can be carried out with reasonable skill and care if there was no instructor present.

(ii) Starlight Snow Dome cannot accept responsibility for loss or damage caused to customers' personal property during the course of a trial lesson.

Look at the CRA 2015 provisions governing liability for negligence, can this be excluded?

SECTION 65 CRA 2015 – LIABILITY FOR NEGLIGENCE

A contract term cannot exclude or restrict liability for death or personal injury resulting from negligence.

A contract term can only exclude or restrict other liability resulting from negligence if it satisfies the requirement of fairness. CRA s. 65(2) extends liability for the trader's negligence, so that they cannot restrict liability using a contractual term or notice to cover the loss or damage they caused unless it is fair.

Section 65(2) also provides that a 'person is not to be taken to have voluntarily accepted any risk merely because the person agreed to or knew about the term or notice'.

Does the term satisfy the requirement of 'fairness'? A term is unfair if 'contrary to the requirement of good faith, it causes a significant imbalance in the parties' rights and obligations under the contract to the detriment of the consumer' (s. 62(4)).

In order to determine the fairness of a term, the court has to take into account 'the nature of the subject matter of the contract' under CRA s. 62(5)(a) and look at all the existing circumstances 'when the term was agreed and to all of the other terms of the contract or of any other contract on which it depends' under s. 62(5)(b).

Notices under s. 62 are treated the same as contractual terms, i.e. the notice must be fair. It will be unfair if it is contrary to the requirement of good faith causing a 'significant imbalance in the parties' right and obligations to the detriment of the consumer' as per s. 62(6). To establish if a notice is fair, as in contract terms, it takes 'into account the nature of the subject matter' of the notice under s. 62(7)(a) and looks at all the circumstances 'existing when the rights or obligations to which it relates arose and to the terms of any contract on which it depends' as per s. 62(7)(b).

Apply: it is a consumer transaction that has not been individually negotiated. Simon had no influence over the main substance of the terms. The clause does create an imbalance to the detriment of the consumer, Simon. If it is deemed to be unfair, Simon will be able to claim for his wasted lesson fee and his broken poles.

ANALYSING THE LAW

> It is important that unfair terms legislation continues to fulfil its primary role, which is to protect consumers against unfair surprise. Unfair terms legislation cannot, however, solve all the problems of the market place and it should not protect consumers against the consequences of their own poor decisions.
>
> (Law Commission, 2012, para. 3.4)

This quotation demonstrates the difficult balance that the courts and Parliament have to strike between protecting the rights of consumers and upholding the traditional notion of freedom of contract. This notion views the role of the law as being to uphold the obligations the parties have agreed without trying to protect either party or rewrite the contract in any way

Do you think the current law achieves this and appropriately addresses the tensions that exist between freedom to contract and consumer protection?

KEY LEARNING POINTS

Remember that you need to understand the following key areas when testing to see whether an exemption clause is valid:

- Incorporation – Has the exemption clause been incorporated into the contract, i.e. has it become a term of the contract?
- Construction/Interpretation – Does the exemption clause cover the breach, i.e. is it appropriately worded to cover what has occurred?
- Statutory provisions – Is the exemption clause affected by statutory provisions (UCTA 1977 or CRA 2015), i.e. is the clause in question subject to legislation?

It is then crucial to understand the importance of consulting the correct statute; this will hinge on whether the clause is contained in a B2B contract or a B2C contract:

- For a B2B contract you must understand the provisions of UCTA1977
- For a B2C contract you must understand the provisions of the CRA 2015
- Remember, whether it is a B2B contract or a B2C contract, some clauses will be automatically invalid, whereas others will be subject to a further test
- You must understand the reasonableness test for B2B contracts
- You must understand the fairness test for B2C contracts

TAKING IT FURTHER

Brannigan and Packman, 'It's not fair' (2016) 27(6) Cons Law 26

Hare, 'Further twists and turns in the labyrinth of statutory liability for misrepresentation' (2017) 9 JIBFL 535

Waters, 'Implementing the Unfair Terms Directive in accessible language: an impossible challenge?' (2012) 10 JIBFL 605.

Ovey, 'Consumer Rights Act 2015: clarity and confidence for consumers and traders?' (2015) 8 JIBFL 504

Samuels, 'Consumer confusion' (2015) 65 NLJ 7679

7

CHAPTER 7
ILLEGAL AND UNENFORCEABLE CONTRACTS

AS YOU READ

At the end of this chapter you should be able to:

- Identify the categories of contract that are **illegal** and unenforceable

- Appreciate how the law has evolved in this area

- Understand the impact on the agreement where it is found to be void

- Understand how the rules operate where a restraint of trade clause is used

- Analyse a problem involving a restraint of trade clause and apply the relevant law

---

ESSENTIAL DEFINITION: ILLEGAL CONTRACT

An illegal contract is an agreement that has been made for an illegal purpose and, consequently, breaks the law. Contracts are illegal if the performance or creation of the agreement will cause the parties to engage in activity that is illegal.

An illegal contract is void ab initio; and the contract will be treated as though it has never existed. In a legal context void means 'of no legal effect'. An action, document or transaction which is void is of no legal effect whatsoever. The law treats it as if it had never existed or happened. The term void ab initio, means that something is invalid from the outset. *Ab initio* is Latin for 'from the beginning'.

The principle is underpinned by the principle *ex turpi causa non oritur actio* (an action cannot arise from a bad cause). Thus, it follows that because the contract never existed, no action can be taken for breach of contract and, as a general rule, the law will not allow recovery of benefits conferred by such a contract.

Contractual illegality is aptly summarised in Lord Mansfield's classic statement of law in *Holman v Johnson*[1] that no court will lend its aid to a person:

> who founds his cause of action upon an immoral or an illegal act. If, from the plaintiff's own stating or otherwise, the cause of action appears to arise *ex turpi causa*, or the transgression of a positive law of this country, there the court says he has no right to be assisted. It is upon that ground the court goes; not for the sake of the defendant, but because they will not lend their aid to such a plaintiff.

This area of contract law represents an area where the courts will interfere with the contracting parties' freedom to agree the main body and constituent elements of their contract. Such contracts concern areas where an agreement has been made but where the law does not approve of the subject matter.

This is illustrated in the case of *Pearce v Brooks*,[2] where the owner of a coach of unusual design was unable to recover the cost of hire from a prostitute who had hired it to attract clients. There are a few exceptions where the courts will allow recovery, for example where one of the parties was unaware of the illegality, or where a party can prove without reliance on the illegal act that they are entitled to money or property transferred.[3]

As a more modern-day example, if Josh agreed to supply Brad with 12 kilos of cocaine and later did not deliver the product, the approach of the courts would be to treat the contract as if it did not exist and the law will not assist with the recovery of any monies that have changed hands. Clearly the police would also be involved due to the crime of possession with intent to supply a class A drug having been committed under s. 5(3) of the Misuse of Drugs Act 1971.

Illegal agreements can be broken down into two broad areas:

1) Contracts illegal by statute
2) Contracts illegal at common law (including contracts contrary to public policy).

7.1 CONTRACTS ILLEGAL BY STATUTE

Figure 7.1 gives a broad overview of contracts that will be regarded as illegal by statute:

---

1   [1775] 1 Cowp 341.
2   (1866) LR 1 Ex 213.
3   *Tinsley v Milligan* [1993] 3 WLR 126, [1993] 2 All ER 65.

> ## Contracts illegal by statute
>
> - Statute may declare a contract illegal, for example the Competition Act 1998
>
> - Statute may prohibit an act, but declare that it shall not affect validity of contract, for example the Consumer Protection Act 1987
>
> - Statute may prohibit an act but not stipulate its effect on the contract. The status of the contract will be a matter of interpretation for the court: *Re Mahmoud and Ispahani* [1921] 2 KB 716
>
> - The courts are reluctant to imply a prohibition when this is not clearly indicated in the statute: *Hughes v Asset Managers* [1994] EWCA Civ 14, [1995] 3 All ER 669

Figure 7.1 Illegal contracts under statute

Where the legislature has specifically enacted a statute prohibiting a certain act, or requiring compliance in a specific manner, such actions provide clear evidence of an intention to prevent the specified act. Thus, contracts in breach of the statutory provision are illegal and will be void, as illustrated in *Re Mahmoud and Ispahani*:[4]

RE MAHMOUD AND ISPAHANI [1921] 2 KB 716

Under the Defence of the Realm Regulations, parties were prohibited from dealing in linseed oil without a licence. The defendant had initially contracted with the plaintiff on the basis that he had a licence, but subsequently refused delivery of the oil on the grounds that the contract was illegal as he did not possess the requisite licence.

Held: even though the plaintiff was not to blame, the contract was unenforceable as to enforce the contract would be in direct conflict with the statute that set out the licence requirement. Scrutton LJ said:

> In my view the court is bound, once it knows that the contract is illegal, to take the objection and to refuse to enforce the contract, whether its knowledge comes from the statement of the party who was guilty of the illegality, or whether its knowledge comes from outside sources. The court does not sit to enforce illegal contracts. There is no question of estoppel; it is for the protection of the public that the court refuses to enforce such a contract.

---

4   [1921] 2 KB 716.

A contract will be regarded as illegal, and thus void ab initio, if creation in itself is prohibited. In *Cope v Rowlands*[5] statute required anyone acting as a broker in the City of London to hold a licence or pay £25 to the City for transactions entered into without a licence. An action by an unlicensed broker, who sued for his commission in buying and selling the defendant's stock, was dismissed on the basis that he neither had a licence nor had he paid the specified sum to enable him to carry out the work.

In *Mohamed v Alaga & Co (a firm)*[6] a contract whereby the plaintiff introduced Somali refugees to a solicitor for a fee, in order for the solicitor to take them on and represent them as clients, was held to be void as the Solicitors' Practice Rules prohibited solicitors from entering into contracts of this nature.

The case of *Anderson Ltd v Daniel*[7] further illustrates that a contract that was lawful upon creation can later become illegal due to its mode of performance. In this case, statute required vendors of artificial fertilisers to state the chemical breakdown of the product on their invoice. The plaintiff sold fertiliser to the defendants but failed to comply with the statutory requirement. When the defendants failed to make payment, the plaintiff sued. The court held that the contract had been lawful in its inception but had subsequently became illegal in its execution, and thus unenforceable. This resulted in a loss for the plaintiff who was unable to recover his payment. The case provides a good example of the court enforcing the will of parliament, as to enable an illegal performer to enforce a contract would undermine the purpose of the statute.

In some instances, the party at fault may enforce the contract, if the illegality is incidental. For example, in *Shaw v Groom*,[8] a landlord who failed to provide his tenant with a rent book, as required by s. 4 Landlord and Tenant Act 1962, was allowed to sue for unpaid rent. The purpose of the statute was to punish the landlord's failure to supply a rent book, not to render the contract void. A useful case to look at where the courts had to decide which approach to adopt is considered below.

ST JOHN SHIPPING CORPN V JOSEPH RANK LTD [1956] 3 ALL ER 683

This case involved a dispute between the defendant company that withheld part of the freight due to the plaintiffs on the basis that whilst carrying the cargo the master of the ship had overloaded the ship, in breach of the Merchant Shipping Act 1932. The defendants argued that the plaintiffs could not enforce the contract because it had been performed in an illegal manner.

---

5   (1836) 2 M & W 149.
6   [2000] 1 WLR 1815 (CA).
7   [1924] 1 KB 138.
8   [1970] 2 QB 504.

Held: the court declared that the deciding factor in such cases was whether the statute that had been breached had been enacted to

1) penalise a party for its conduct or
2) whether its intention was to invalidate the contract.

In concluding that the intention behind the statute was to penalise a party in breach, the court allowed the plaintiff to enforce the contract.

ANALYSING THE LAW

In analysing the above judgments, it can be deduced that the courts will place significant weight on the intention of the legislature in passing the specific statute when deciding whether a contract shall be rendered void and the decision on whether a contract is void will largely depend upon the court's interpretation of the intention behind the statute.

But what factors will be considered in assessing the intention behind the statute?

If it appears that Parliament's aim was to further an aspect of public policy or to protect the public, it is likely that a contract resulting in a breach of statute will be void.

But what if the plaintiff is unaware of the illegality? In *Archbolds (Freightage) Ltd v S Spanglett,*[9] Spanglett contracted to carry Archbold's whisky in a van that was not licensed to carry any goods other than his own. Archbold was unaware of this and could therefore recover damages for breach of contract. And what if the other party is aware of the illegality? Contrast the outcome in *Archbolds* with *Ashmore, Benson, Pease & Co v Dawson Ltd,*[10] where a lorry had been overloaded but the other party was aware of this breach. Here, the claimant could not recover damages as he had participated in the illegality. It is fairly apparent that the courts seek to distinguish between innocent and non-innocent participants when reaching decisions in this area.

7.2 CONTRACTS ILLEGAL AT COMMON LAW

Historically, an analysis of common law provides a fairly clear indication that the judges have strived to conserve a concept of public policy. Whilst freedom of contract must be sustained, it must be balanced against any prejudicial impact on social and economic interests of the wider populace.

9 [1961] 1 All ER 417.
10 [1973] 1 WLR 828.

In *Saunders v Edwards*,[11] Bingham LJ stated that the position of the courts is to

steer a middle course between two unacceptable positions. On the one hand it is unacceptable that any court of law should aid or lend its authority to a party seeking to pursue or enforce an object or agreement which the law prohibits. On the other hand, it is unacceptable that the courts should, on the first indication of unlawfulness affecting any aspect of a transaction, draw up its skirts and refuse all assistance to the plaintiff.

Over the centuries, views on whether certain agreements are immoral or insubordinate to society have changed. Whereas one generation may have displayed abhorrence to certain agreements, a later generation may have considered the same agreements to be harmless. Sexually 'immoral' contracts are an example of where attitudes have changed over a wider period of time. And, of course, there are different levels of gravity when considering illegality. For example, a contract to hire a hitman to kill your husband or wife is clearly more reprehensible than a contract to hire out a room for illegal gambling, or maybe an agreement preventing another person from engaging in business for a certain period of time in a particular geographical area.

It is not a straightforward exercise to categorise the different types of illegality and to predict the outcome on a challenge of illegality. In some cases where a contract potentially would be declared illegal, a court may allow a contract to stand if it is still viable once the illegal clause has been removed. The court will reach a balanced judgment, taking on board policy implications, including maintenance of integrity of the legal system, deterring future illegal behaviour and ensuring that the claimant does not profit from their own wrong alongside an examination of the parties' positions and circumstances[12]

Figure 7.2 gives an overview of contracts regarded as illegal at common law.

Contracts illegal at common law

- An agreement to commit a crime, a tort or a fraud
- An agreement to defraud Revenue and Customs (HMRC) (*Napier v Business Associates* [1951] 2 All ER 264)
- Contracts damaging to the public safety or foreign relations (*Furtado v Rogers* [1802] 3 B & P 191)
- Contracts prejudicial to the administration of justice, for example contracts to give false evidence
- Contracts that are sexually immoral (*Pearce v Brooks* [1866] LR 1 Ex 213)
- Contracts leading to corruption in public life (*Parkinson v Royal College of Ambulance* [1925] 2 KB 1)

Figure 7.2 Contracts illegal at common law

11 [1987] 2 All ER 651.
12 *ParkingEye Ltd v Somerfield Stores Ltd* [2012] EWCA Civ 1338, [2013] QB 840.

You will not be surprised to learn that an agreement to commit a crime, tort or a fraud is illegal and void. In *Bigos v Bousted*[13] a contract that was contrary to exchange control regulations (which placed restrictions on English money) was held to be unenforceable. Unsurprisingly, it follows that a contract to defraud or deceive[14] or assault[15] a third party will also be illegal. The principle that a person cannot benefit from their own crime was also upheld in *Beresford v Royal Insurance Co Ltd*[16] where the relatives of a person who had committed suicide were not permitted to benefit from a life insurance policy (suicide at this time was classified as a crime). The same principle can also be observed in *Gray v Thames Trains Ltd*,[17] when the House of Lords refused to grant damages against a negligent rail operator to a train crash victim. The crash had been caused by the railway operator's negligence but the victim later went on to commit manslaughter as a result of the psychological injuries sustained as a result of the crash. Damages claimed by Gray for loss of earnings and loss of liberty and reputation were not, however, awarded against the rail operator as they flowed from a criminal act.

Contracts to defraud Revenue and Customs (HMRC) are also illegal. In *Napier v Business Associates*[18] an employment contract that had been deliberately set up to defraud the Revenue in respect of expenses payments was void, and again in *Alexander v Rayson*[19] a contract to make the value of a property appear lower than its actual value to defraud the local authority was illegal and void.

Contracts that are damaging to public safety or foreign relations will be illegal. Lord Alvanley in *Furtado v Rogers*[20] stated that

> it is not competent to any subject to enter into a contract to do anything which may be detrimental to the interests of his own country; and that such a contract is as much prohibited as if it had been expressly forbidden by Act of parliament.

Such acts would include agreements that could disrupt relations between our country and other nations.

A further category of illegality concerns contracts that are prejudicial to the **administration of justice**. An agreement to suppress a prosecution would be illegal: 'it is to the interest of the public that the suppression of a prosecution should not be a matter of private bargain'.[21] An agreement not to proceed with divorce proceedings will be unenforceable.[22] Furthermore, in *Hyman v Hyman*[23] an agreement between a husband and wife not to apply to the courts

---

13 [1951] 1 All ER 92.
14 *Brown Jenkinson & Co Ltd v Percy Dalton (London) Ltd* [1957] 2 QB 621, [1957] 2 All ER 844.
15 *Allen v Rescous* (1676) 2 Lev 174.
16 [1937] 2 KB 197.
17 [2009] UKHL 33, [2009] 1 AC 1339.
18 [1951] 2 All ER 264.
19 [1936] 1 KB 169.
20 (1802) 3 Bos & P 191.
21 *Clubb v Hutson* (1865) 18 CBNS 414 at P 417.
22 *Cooper v Willis* (1906) 22 TLR 582.
23 [1929] AC 601.

for maintenance was unenforceable although, on this point, it should be noted that since the Supreme Court judgment in *Granatino v Radmacher*[24] pre- or post-nuptial agreements may be given effect where they have been entered into freely with a full appreciation of the implications of the agreement.

ESSENTIAL DEFINITION: ADMINISTRATION OF JUSTICE

The process and structure that allows conflicts between parties to be settled by a body dedicated to that purpose, generally acknowledged as Her Majesty's Court Service.

Contracts that are sexually immoral may be unenforceable, but this area has been subject to change over the years due to a shift in societal attitudes and it is difficult to isolate specific rules in this area. The age-old case of *Pearce v Brooks*,[25] which involved the hire of a carriage for prostitution, is perhaps the best-known example where the court held a sexually immoral contract void. And indeed, the promise of a payment to a woman to become a man's mistress was held to be unenforceable in *Benyon v Nettlefold*.[26] Generally these contracts were illegal as they went against public policy and morality. But if we consider more recent cases, a more lenient approach can be observed. Take for example, the case of *Armhouse Lee Ltd v Chappell*.

ARMHOUSE LEE LTD V CHAPPELL (1996) TIMES, 7 AUGUST

The publishers of a magazine sought to recover payment for advertisements that had been placed by the defendants. The advertisements related to telephone 'sex lines'. The defendants contested the claim on the basis that the content of the advertisements was illegal or immoral.

Held: the Court of Appeal considered several areas under which the advertisements could fall to be illegal, including prostitution, obscenity, and conspiracy to corrupt public morals, but all of these grounds were rejected. In considering 'public policy' the court found no evidence that any generally accepted moral code condemned these sex lines. Nor was the court prepared to impose its own moral attitudes, when exercising a civil jurisdiction in an area regarded as the province of the criminal law.

---

24 [2010] UKSC 42, [2011] 1 AC 534.
25 (1866) LR 1 Ex 213.
26 (1850) 3 Mac & G 94.

Contracts leading to corruption in public life will be illegal. There is a clear interest in protecting the public from activities that will corrupt the administration of central or local state services, or will interfere with the performance of public officials in conducting their duties. For example, in *Parkinson v College of Ambulance Ltd*[27] the plaintiff, Colonel Parkinson, was unable to recover money he had donated to the defendants on the understanding that they would secure him a knighthood, because such an agreement was corrupt.

7.3 CONTRACTS IN RESTRAINT OF TRADE

Any intervention by the courts where a contract has been agreed between parties involving a **restraint of trade** will conflict with the doctrine of freedom of contract; the foundation upon which contract law is based. The restraint of trade doctrine exists only in limited form and has developed since the nineteenth century, which was a period where interference in consensual agreements was deemed undesirable when weighted against the more important objective of maintaining certainty in agreements and upholding the freedom of individuals to agree contracts with minimal interference from external sources.

ESSENTIAL DEFINITION: RESTRAINT OF TRADE DOCTRINE

A legal contract between a buyer and a seller of a business, or between an employer and employee, that prevents the seller or employee from engaging in a similar business within a specified geographical area and within a specified period. Its purpose is to protect trade secrets or proprietary information but is enforceable only if it is reasonable with reference to the party against whom it is made and if it is not contrary to public policy.

The initial presumption with regard to a contract which places a restraint on trade is that the contract is void. It is then up to the party seeking to enforce the contract to rebut the presumption by proving that the restraint clause is reasonable.

27 [1925] 2 KB 1.

But what types of clauses will be classed as reasonable in the eyes of the court?

EXPLAINING THE LAW: DEVELOPMENT OF THE DOCTRINE OF RESTRAINT OF TRADE

Under the common law, a general principle exists that an individual or body is entitled to exercise any lawful trade or calling as and where they see fit.

In the nineteenth century all contracts in restraint of trade would probably have been void, in alignment with the doctrine of freedom of contract; but, as time has progressed, the harshness of this principle has gradually relaxed.

Nowadays, the position is that contracts in restraint of trade are prima facie void because they are contrary to public policy, but a partial restraint may be acceptable if reasonable.

The main reason for the doctrine of restraint of trade is to prevent an individual from negotiating away his means of support and revenue, possibly to a stronger negotiating person or body. If the restraint is a very general one, it can destroy an individual's future business opportunities or prevent him/her from being employed as a result of an agreement he may have naively agreed to. It is also acknowledged that it is not in the public interest to deprive a group of persons of a valuable benefit by preventing someone carrying out a lawful trade or business.

The main precedent derives from the *Nordenfelt*[28] case that was determined at a time when industrialisation was profound. This case is usually referred to as the leading case on the doctrine of restraint of trade.

NORDENFELT V MAXIM NORDENFELT GUNS AND AMMUNITION CO [1894] AC 535

The case arose following the sale of a guns and ammunition business. As part of the sale agreement the vendor contracted not to engage in this type of business anywhere in the world for 25 years.

Held: the worldwide ban was upheld by the House of Lords for its full duration. Lord MacNaghten stated that in normal circumstances restraints of trade are void, but acknowledged an exception to the rule where the restraint can be proven to be reasonable. In defining the term 'reasonable' he declared that a restriction needs to be

---

28 *Nordenfelt v Maxim Nordenfelt Guns and Ammunition Co* [1894] AC 535.

reasonable with reference to the interests of the parties concerned, and reasonable in the interests of the public. His emphasis in particular was the fact that the public has an interest in all persons being able to carry out their trade freely and in a fashion that is not injurious to the public.

ASSESSMENT TIP

When answering question relating to a contract in restraint of trade, follow the steps below:

1) Initial statement that prima facie contracts in restraint of trade are void
2) Consider whether there are there any special circumstances that should be taken into account which justify the restraint and make it reasonable

Look at whether the restraint meets the test of reasonableness:

a) Is there a **legitimate interest** that is worthy of protection?
b) Is it reasonable with reference to the interests of the parties involved?
c) Is it reasonable in the **public interest**?

If the above criteria (a)–(c) are not met then the restriction will be unenforceable and the contract void.

Clearly since the judgment in *Nordenfelt* in 1894, industrialisation has increased profoundly and the commercial world has undergone significant transformation. So how have the courts interpreted and applied the precedent extending from this judgment? Let us look at each *Nordenfelt* criteria in turn.

7.4 LEGITIMATE INTEREST

In examining the types of interest that merit protection, Lord Parker in *Herbert Morris Ltd v Saxelby*[29] summarised the position as follows:

Wherever such covenants have been upheld it has been on the ground, not that the servant or apprentice would, by reason of his employment or trade, obtain the skill and knowledge necessary to equip him as a possible competitor in the trade but that

29 [1916] 1 AC 688.

he might obtain such personal knowledge of and influence over the customers of his employer, or such an acquaintance with his employer's trade and secrets as would enable him, if competition were allowed, to take advantage of his employer's trade connection or utilize information confidentially obtained.

In the same case, Lord Shaw set out the two types of interest that can legitimately be protected:

1) Sale of business – clause to prevent seller from acting in direct competition. This type of clause is intended to prevent the vendor of a business from acting in direct competition with the business he has just sold. The purchaser will have paid an element for the 'goodwill' of the business; thus he would argue that it is a legitimate venture to protect this goodwill interest.

ESSENTIAL DEFINITION: GOODWILL

Goodwill is an asset of a business that may be bought and sold in conjunction with the business. Goodwill is a marketplace advantage of customer loyalty developed with continuous business that has extended over a period of time. It may be bought and sold in connection with a business, and the valuation is a subjective one. Any person engaging in competitive business that offers goods or services may acquire goodwill and insist on its protection. Goodwill can be sold in a sales contract and will be governed by the ordinary rules of contract law.

ESSENTIAL DEFINITION: LEGITIMATE INTEREST

The value of any relationships the employee develops with clients during the course of employment. These relationships are of value to the employer and the value is treated as an interest that justifies some protection when the employment ceases. Accepted legitimate interests include: trade secrets, confidential information, trade connections and goodwill.

2) Contract of employment – clause to protect trade secrets and to prevent **solicitation** of clients. A clause preventing the employee from working for a competitor would not be enforceable, but a clause preventing a former employee from benefitting from 'insider' knowledge accrued during his past employment with a new employer could be upheld.

Overall, the business interests recognised as legitimate by the law as being worthy of protection include trade secrets, customer connections, relationships with suppliers, and senior employees.

> **ESSENTIAL** DEFINITION: SOLICITATION
>
> Involves approaching customers in a direct or targeted manner with a view to appropriating the customer's business or custom. There must be an active approach alongside a positive intention to poach the customer.

In considering the legitimacy of the interest that is the source of the restriction, the court must be satisfied that there is a genuine reason for protection and that the covenant is not simply an attempt to prevent competition *per se*. The reasonableness of a particular restraint depends on all the facts of the case,[30] but factors that are likely to be relevant in every case include the nature of the business or interest for which the employer seeks protection and the status or position of the employee.

An instance in which the courts had to consider this issue occurred in *Forster & Sons Ltd v Suggett*.[31] The agreement involved a covenant that had been entered into by a works manager on leaving his former company, restricting him from engaging in glass-making anywhere within the UK. Throughout his term with the company the manager had acquired knowledge of a secret glass-making process and the covenant was in place to protect the trade secret; therefore the covenant was held to be reasonable and enforceable. An employer is entitled to prevent the employee taking unfair advantage of confidential information and business connections to which he had access in the course of his employment. That said, the courts do not take decisions of this nature lightly due to the impact upon the covenanter's livelihood. Contrast the decision in *Forster* with the following case.

BRITISH REINFORCED CONCRETE ENGINEERING CO LTD V SCHELFF [1921] 2 CH 563

A national company making road reinforcement products took over the business of a small company specialising in the selling of loop road reinforcements. The contract contained a covenant restricting the smaller company from establishing a new business within a ten-mile radius.

Held: the restriction was void as it did not protect a proprietary interest. The small company specialising in loop road reinforcements was no threat to the much larger business that sold road reinforcements in general.

---

30 *Dairy Crest v Pigott* [1989] ICR 92.
31 (1918) 35 TLR 87.

7.5 REASONABLENESS TEST

In looking at whether the agreement is reasonable with reference to the interests of the parties involved, the main areas of contention tend to concern nature, geographical span and duration. The courts will only enforce restrictions so far as they protect an interest. If the duration of the restriction is excessive the courts will not enforce it:

FITCH V DEWES [1921] 2 AC 158

The defendant was employed as a manager at a solicitors' practice in Tamworth. The contract contained a clause that restricted him from working in a solicitors' office within seven miles of Tamworth for a period that could be extended to cover the rest of his life. After he left the company, the defendant intentionally committed a breach of the covenant to test its validity.

Held: the House of Lords held that the clause was reasonable and accepted that it was necessary to protect the plaintiff's business, as the business was one to which clients were likely to return over a long period of time.

7.6 GEOGRAPHICAL EXTENT

In *E Underwood & Con Ltd v Barker*,[32] a restriction extending throughout the whole of the UK was permitted and, again, in *Forster & Sons Ltd v Suggett*, mentioned earlier, the fact that the restriction operated throughout the UK was deemed reasonable to prevent the outing of secret and sensitive information.

In contrast, *Attwood v Lamont*[33] tested the radius of a covenant in a contract of employment restricting a person who had previously worked as a tailor within the tailoring department of a store from being able to work as a tailor, dressmaker or draper within ten miles of Kidderminster. In looking at the nature of the activity covered by the restraint, the court held that the restriction was unenforceable as it was too wide in geographical scope. Similarly, in *Mason v Provident Clothing Co*[34] a clause restricting a canvasser in the clothing business from working within a 25-mile radius in a densely populated area of London was found excessive, particularly when taking into account that he had previously worked in a very small shop in a London suburb and the relatively minor potential of influence in this domain. To sum up, there appears to be no precise rule of thumb to govern disputes on geographical span.

---

32 [1899] 1 Ch 300.
33 [1920] 3 KB 571.
34 [1913] AC 724.

The validity of this type of clause will very much depend upon the circumstances in each individual case. Some cases will merit a far wider restraint in geographical terms than others.

7.7 DURATION

As well as not extending over an excessive geographical span, the covenant must not be excessive in duration. In *J A Mont (UK) Ltd v Mills*[35] a restriction on the former manager of a paper tissue company, made redundant after 20 years of service, was found to be too wide, as there were no specifics of any trade secret mentioned in the clause. His severance package had included a clause that he would not work for another paper tissue company for 12 months. The Court of Appeal took a very narrow view of the restrictive clause as they were aware that the effect of the clause would mean that the individual could not be gainfully employed in his area of knowledge at all, and as such was not reasonable. Similarly, in *M & S Drapers (A Firm) v Reynolds*[36] a covenant that prevented a sales representative from soliciting former customers for five years was declared unenforceable due to excessive duration. In *Home Counties Dairies v Skilton*[37] a restraint on a milkman not to serve or sell milk or dairy produce to, or solicit orders for milk or dairy produce for a period of one year from, any person or company he had dealt with in the last six months as an employee in the course of his employment was determined unreasonable by the court. Here the deciding factor for the court was based on an analysis of the objectives that the parties were trying to pursue rather than the literal wording of the contract. The clause, if literally interpreted, would extend far wider than necessary to safeguard the interest that it intended to protect. For example, the covenanter would not be able to work for any retailer selling this type of produce. The court took the view that the parties had not intended the clause to operate in such an oppressive manner and interpreted it to include milk only. Under the narrower interpretation, the court found the clause to be valid.

Whilst extensive time restrictions need to be probed with caution, the fact that a restriction extends over a long period of time will not always render the agreement void. Take the case of *Nordenfelt* above, where a ban on the sale of ammunition for 25 years was held to be reasonable. There is no rule of thumb; the crucial test is whether the circumstances in an individual case and the nature of the interest that is being protected can warrant the specific restriction.

7.8 PUBLIC INTEREST

As well as looking at the interest of the parties themselves, consideration must also be given to the interests of the wider public. Whether the clause is reasonable in the public interest

35 *J A Mont (UK) Ltd v Mills* [1993] IRLR 173.
36 [1957] 1 WLR 9.
37 [1970] 1 All ER 1227.

must be affirmed if a challenged clause is to be upheld. The conclusion as to whether a clause is reasonable in the interest of the public is not always a straightforward matter, as the concept of public interest has no precise definition. Where a clause has been agreed to restrict competition in the marketplace, it is highly unlikely to be upheld. In *Herbert Morris Ltd v Saxelby*[38] the House of Lords stated that a covenant which restrains a person from competition is always void and unreasonable, unless the proprietary interest to be protected is exceptional. In *Mallan v May*[39] it was stated that 'The test appears to be whether the contract be prejudicial or not to the public interest, for it is on grounds of public policy alone that these contracts are supported or avoided.' But what is meant by term 'public interest'? There is no precise definition. Deliberation on a clause and its impact upon the public interest was undertaken in the following case.

WYATT V KREGLINGER AND FERNAU [1933] 1 KB 793

The defendants wrote to a long-serving employee, intimating that when he retired they proposed to provide him with an annual pension on the condition that he did not compete against them in the wool trade. Following his retirement, the pension was paid to the ex-employee for a number of years. The case involved various contractual issues, one of which was the restraint of trade clause.

Held: the Court of Appeal found that the clause was too wide, but also addressed the issue of public interest. The contract itself was found to be injurious to the interests of the public, as a ban on the plaintiff from trading in the wool trade served to deprive the community of a service from which it could derive an advantage.

In *Hanover Insurance Brokers Ltd and Christchurch Insurance Brokers Ltd v Schapiro*[40] the court had to interpret a restraint of trade clause that was to become operative following the sale of a business in order to prevent solicitation of clients by the former directors. Matters were not helped by the fact that not all the agreements were the same and some contained wider restrictions than others, restricting activity in other areas in addition to the insurance business. The courts adopted a purposive approach in interpreting the restraint of trade clause and read it narrowly to ensure that it was enforced in the spirit of its intended scale, which was to prevent the solicitation of insurance clients, and not wider business.

What is clear is that where the agreement concerns a restrictive clause in a contract of employment or the sale of a business, the covenant will always be subject to a test of reasonableness. It is important to note, however, that in some areas of trading restrictive

---

38 [1916] 1 AC 688.
39 (1843) 11 M & W 653.
40 [1994] IRLR 82.

agreements are now regarded as the norm in certain commercial areas and agreements. One example is in the licensed trade sector, where a lessee of a public house agrees to only sell beer that has been brewed by the lessor. There is no set rule that exists to inform when the court will or will not approve a covenant with each case being judged upon its own facts. It is not possible to set up 'categories' of where the courts will intervene. Indeed, in the *Esso* case,[41] outlined below, Lord Wilberforce clearly stated that 'the classification must remain fluid and the categories can never be closed'.

ESSO PETROLEUM CO LTD V HARPER'S GARAGE (STOURPORT) LTD [1968] AC 269, [1967] 1 ALL ER 699

The respondent company (Harper's Garage) entered into a solus agreement, which, inter alia, included a clause covenanting to buy all fuel from Esso for its two garages. In return the appellant agreed a rebate of 1d per gallon on all fuel purchased. The duration of the agreements were four years five months, and 21 years respectively. The second garage was mortgaged to Esso for 21 years and was not redeemable before the end of the 21-year period. The respondents argued that the contract was in restraint of trade when they were sued under the contract for selling another brand of petrol.

Held: both of the contracts fell into the category of contracts that were prima facie in restraint of trade and needed to be assessed for reasonableness in the interests of both the parties themselves and in the interest of the public. As between the parties themselves, the House of Lords were content that the agreements protected a legitimate interest between the parties and the first agreement was approved as being reasonable. In contrast, the House of Lords found the second agreement to be unreasonable as it operated for an excessive period.

7.9 EFFECT OF A VOID CONTRACT

An illegal contract is void ab initio and is treated as though it was never formed at all. Neither of the parties will be allowed to seek a remedy and no action will lie in damages.

In many contracts that fall within the 'illegality' category, it is often the case that only part of the agreement is objectionable. In such instances, it can be possible to split the contract into its constituent parts, with one part being valid and enforceable, and the objectionable part being void and unenforceable. But how can this be achieved?

---

41 *Esso Petroleum Co Ltd v Harper's Garage (Stourport) Ltd* [1968] AC 269, [1967] 1 All ER 699.

7.10 SEVERANCE

Before an entire covenant can be struck out of an agreement it must be ascertained that the lawful part of the agreement is of greater importance than the unlawful part. This may occur if it is possible to assign a precise value to different parts of the contract, as was the case in *Ailion v Spiekermann*,[42] where the contract to pay the illegal premium could be severed, because a precise amount could be assigned to the illegal part of the agreement. **Severance** cannot take place if the objectionable part forms the main consideration of the agreement.

Severance cannot occur where contracts are illegal because the act that is the subject of the contract is a criminal offence, or is contrary to public policy. The attempt to sever promises occurs most frequently in relation to restraint of trade cases, where the wish is to delete from a list of restrictions those that make the restraint too wide and leave the remainder of the agreement in force. There have traditionally been two elements to the courts' approach:

1) The 'blue pencil test', and
2) The requirement that the nature of the contract must be retained.

The blue pencil test means the severance must be possible simply by taking out the offending words. The court will not become involved in redrafting the contract. So, for example, in *Mason v Provident Clothing Co*,[43] the court refused to replace the phrase 'in Islington' with the words 'within 25 miles of London'. On the other hand, where a simple deletion is possible and the contract is still workable, this can provide a resolution.

> **ESSENTIAL** DEFINITION: SEVERANCE
>
> Severance refers to striking out of an offending part of a contract, leaving the legal segments intact. The severed parts should not affect the meaning of the remaining parts.

> **ESSENTIAL** DEFINITION: BLUE PENCIL TEST
>
> The blue pencil test is a method that the courts use to decide whether to invalidate the whole contract or only the offending words. The offending words are only invalidated if it would be possible to delete them simply by running a blue pencil through them, as opposed to changing, adding or rearranging words.

---

42 [1976] Ch 158, [1976] 1 All ER 497.
43 [1913] AC 724.

GOLDSOLL V GOLDMAN [1915] 1 CH 292

The issue involved a covenant in the sale of an imitation jewellery business that contained a restriction on the vendor in dealing in real or imitation jewellery in any of a long list of countries.

Held: the restriction was too wide with regard to its extent and geographical span. The business itself only traded in imitation jewellery; thus a restriction on 'real' jewellery could not be substantiated. Again, on geographical area, the long list of countries could not be substantiated as the business itself was limited to the UK. The contract survived, as both restrictions could be narrowed by simple deletions of the words 'real or', and the list of countries other than the UK.

The requirement that the nature of the contract must be retained stems from *Attwood v Lamont*,[44] considered earlier. The restraint on a tailor upon leaving his employment required him not to engage in the trade or business of a tailor, dressmaker, general draper, milliner, hatter, haberdasher, gentlemen's, ladies' or children's outfitter. It was suggested that the clause could be reasonable if the list of all the additional trades except 'tailor' were severed. The Court of Appeal refused to do this, on the basis that severing these particular words would affect the nature of the agreement as a whole. The covenant had to be looked at in its entirety and was not capable of severance. In the view of the court the parties had made a single indivisible agreement to protect the entire business interest of the employer and the covenant had to 'stand or fall in its unaltered form'. It should also be noted that the court will not add or alter existing words, as to do so would be changing an undertaking to one that the parties may have intended to make but one that they did not make.[45]

ASSESSMENT TIP

Faced with the task of deciding whether or not severance of an objectionable clause can take place, ask yourself: Can the substantial nature of the covenant remain operational if one of its components is taken away? If the answer is 'yes' then severance is likely to be an acceptable remedy; but if the answer is 'no' then it is likely that the covenant will be void.

44 *Attwood v Lamont* [1920] 3 KB 571.
45 *Putsman v Taylor* [1927] 1 KB 637.

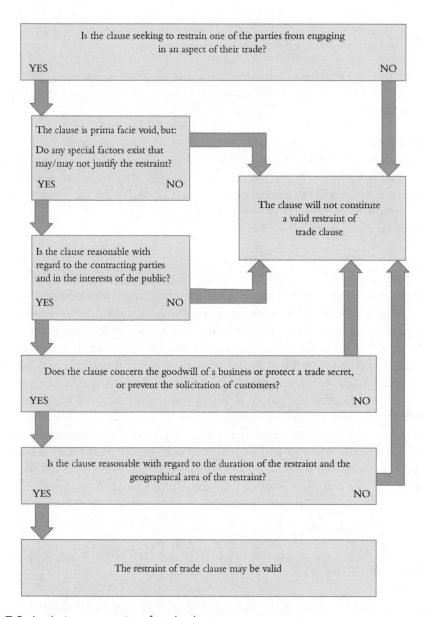

Figure 7.3 Analysing a restraint of trade clause

APPLYING THE LAW

Use Figure 7.3 and attempt the following problem.

You are acting on behalf of a client who owns a shop in the centre of Nezzlebrooke, a large town in the north east of England. His business mainly consists of selling and repairing Eco-care energy saving refrigerators. The shop is the only retail outlet in

Nezzlebrooke that deals in Eco-care products. Your client is now considering opening another shop in a small village called Bloom, located approximately six miles away from Nezzlebrooke. Your client plans to sell his shop in Nezzlebrooke. The prospective purchaser is Cooljoe's plc, a national firm that owns a chain of electrical shops, and specialises in Eco-care refrigerators. This firm wants your client to agree not to open another shop selling 'Eco-care' refrigerators, or any other make of refrigerator, or any other kitchen equipment, anywhere in the UK for the next ten years. Advise your client.

ADVICE TO CLIENT – PLAN

The issue here is whether Cooljoe's clause would be valid and enforceable,

What does the law say?

In providing advice to the client you should immediately identify that such a restriction will be regarded as being in restraint of trade and therefore prima facie void. Define what is meant by an agreement 'in restraint of trade' and state the legal source of this rule, setting out the full criteria.

Refer to other relevant cases that drill down on the constituent parts of the rule.

The starting point for this kind of restraint is *Nordenfelt v Maxim Nordenfelt*.

Precedent flowing from this case is that all covenants in restraint of trade are prima facie contrary to public policy and void. Here the presumption could be rebutted if the restraint could be shown to be reasonable with reference to both the interests of the parties and the public interest. For the restraint to be reasonable, Cooljoe's must show that they have a legitimate interest to protect; that the scope of the restraint does not extend further than is reasonable to protect that interest, and that there is no general public interest at stake in permitting the restriction.

APPLY THE LAW

Your client will only be bound by the clause if Cooljoe's can rebut the presumption of illegality by showing that the restraint is **reasonable** to protect a **legitimate interest**. Apply these two requirements to the facts in the scenario.

Legitimate interest: The legitimate interest test is satisfied. Where a person sells a shop as an ongoing business, goodwill is an important aspect of the sale. Good reputation and established customers are both valuable business assets. It is highly likely that your client will increase the price of the business to include these elements in its value.

It is accepted that the protection of the goodwill in a business being bought is a legitimate interest that can be protected by a reasonable restriction. This type of clause will benefit the vendor as well as the purchaser, because if the vendor were not prepared to accept an obligation not to compete, it is likely that he would have difficulty selling his business, or he would almost certainly have to accept a lower sale price.

On whether the restraint is reasonable to protect that interest, let us look more closely at the restraint. Cooljoe's clearly have an interest to protect. The restraint covers the sale of any make of refrigerator and other kitchen equipment, anywhere in the UK for ten years. In order for the restraint to stand, it will have to be considered reasonable in respect of scope, area and time. Does the clause pass these tests?

Your client's business mainly concerns Eco-care refrigerators, whereas the restraint extends to refrigerators and other kitchen equipment. It seems that the bulk of your client's business is in Eco-care refrigerators. Such a restraint that extends significantly beyond this area is likely to be regarded as unreasonable.

Cooljoe's must tailor the restraint to the scope of the business that they are purchasing, not the scope of their own business (*British Reinforced Concrete Engineering Co Ltd v Schelff*). In *Nordenfelt*, a worldwide restriction was found to be reasonable. In this case the restriction is to the UK market only.

From this case, it seems that the area must relate to the interest being protected. It is unlikely that your client would have a serious impact on Cooljoe's business by opening up a shop in an area in which he was unknown. There are likely to be areas in the UK where Cooljoe's have no existing shops that would be affected by your client's competition.

REMEDIES

Explain the concept of **severance.** Even if the clause is unreasonable as worded, the court may be prepared to enforce it if the scope can be narrowed by taking out some part of the restriction.

Explain the blue pencil test.

Apply the law on the length of restriction – On the length of the restriction. One needs to ask the question as to whether, if your client opened a shop within the next ten years, would he be likely to retain any of his existing customers? This must be explored as there could be an impact on the goodwill of the business sold to Cooljoe's.

This aspect of the restraint may be reasonable. The courts could sever the unreasonable parts of the restraint and give effect to what is reasonable (*Goldsoll v Goldman*). The court can strike out offending words and, if what is left makes sense, the agreement can continue.

It is fairly simple to narrow the scope of this clause by cutting out the phrases 'any other make of refrigerator, or any other type of kitchen equipment'. The courts may also narrow the geographical span, and substitute the words 'anywhere in the UK', to cover a more localised area. There is no real argument to suggest that the restraint is contrary to the general public interest.

7.11 BRINGING IT ALL TOGETHER

As we have seen, it is important to note the effect of finding a contract illegal. The contract will be void ab initio and will be treated as though it has never been made, with benefits that have been conferred being non-recoverable.

In this chapter we have looked at examples of this type of contract under very broad headings: contracts illegal at common law, contracts illegal by statute and contracts in restraint of trade. These can be further broken down into smaller areas within each main group. It is important to have an appreciation of the heads under which a court will find a contract void and unenforceable and be able to distinguish between these and situations where a court may be prepared to uphold a contract, particularly in circumstances where it is possible to sever the illegal parts and retain the main substance of an agreement. This area has evolved over the years and rules are unlikely to remain static, being very much influenced by shifts in tradition and values as patterns of behaviour change from generation to generation, particularly when dealing with areas involving cultural and moral issues. What may have been morally reprehensible at one time may, at a later time, be acceptable conduct. The law must try to retain a balance between freedom of contract on the one hand and upholding lawfulness on the other and try to 'steer a middle course between two unacceptable positions'.[46]

Contracts in restraint of trade have been the main focus of this chapter as this is an area where there has been much litigation over the years. The precedent in this area is now fairly clear, having derived from a significant body of case law. The starting point will always render a contract in restraint of trade as void, but where circumstances justify such a restraint, an exception to the rule can be permitted if it is reasonable between the parties and in the

46 *Saunders v Edwards* [1987] 2 All ER 651.

interests of the general public. It is ascertaining these two factors in any particular case that can sometimes be tricky.

> ## KEY LEARNING POINTS
>
> Remember that you should consider the following in deciding whether a contract will be void due to illegality:
>
> - What is it that makes the contract illegal?
> - What is the effect of the illegality on the contract?
> - The above will depend upon the type of illegality, as this will influence the courts on whether relief is possible
>
> Contracts in restraint of trade:
>
> - A presumption exists that these types of contract are prima facie void
> - The presumption can be rebutted if it is reasonable both in the interests of the parties themselves and in the public interest
> - The burden of proof lies with the person who is seeking to enforce the contract
> - There are two main types of contract where restraint of trade clauses will exist: contracts of employment and contracts for the sale of a business
> - Interests capable of protection include the goodwill of a business, trade secrets, prevention of solicitation of customers
> - The duration and geographical span must not be excessive for the protection of the legitimate interest

TAKING IT FURTHER

Buckley, 'Illegal Transactions: Chaos or Discretion?' (2000) 20 Legal Studies 155

Buckley, *Illegality and Public Policy*, 3rd edn, Sweet & Maxwell, 2013

Furmston, 'Illegality: The limits of a statute' (1961) 24 Modern Law Review 394

Furmston, *Cheshire, Fifoot and Furmston's Law of Contract*, 16th ed, Oxford University Press, 2012

Jefferson, 'Evading the Doctrine of Restraint of Trade' (1990) 134 Solicitors Journal 532

Smith and Atiyah, *Atiyah's Introduction to the Law of Contract*, 6th edn, Oxford University Press, 2006

Sumpton, 'Reflections on the Law of Illegality' (2012) RLR 1

Zhong Xing Tan, 'The Anatomy of contractual illegality' (2015) 44(2) CLWR 99

CHAPTER 8
MISREPRESENTATION

8.1 INTRODUCTION

This section of the book deals with what are referred to as 'vitiating factors', which affect the validity of a contract. Vitiating factors arise as a result of actions in the contractual relationship that may affect the subsequent validity of the contract. Where vitiating factors are found to exist in a contractual situation, the result may be that the contract is voidable at the discretion of the innocent party.

The first vitiating factor to be considered is misrepresentation.

Where one of the parties entering a contract makes a statement as part of the negotiating process, it could be a 'mere puff', a term of the contract, or a representation. A representation is a statement of fact that is not a term of the contract but has induced the other party to enter into the contract.

This chapter deals with situations involving false representations, otherwise known as 'misrepresentations'. A misrepresentation is a false statement of fact that induces another to enter into the contract.

The law of misrepresentation deals with situations in which one party should be able to bring the contract to an end because of a misrepresentation from the other party. This is one area where statements made by one party before the contract is agreed have an effect upon the contract after it has been entered into.

This chapter will explain the elements required to demonstrate the existence of misrepresentation, as well as the different types of misrepresentation. It will then conclude by demonstrating the remedies available to a party who has been affected by the misrepresentation of the other party.

8.2 DISTINGUISH FROM BREACH OF TERMS

It is important to note that a pre-contractual statement can be construed as a term of the contract. Any problems involving terms are dealt with by way of breach of contract. The Consumer Rights Act 2015 (s.50) specifically states that in a service contract any statements that relate to the trader or service that induce the contract will be treated as terms. If, however, the statement is a representation, we turn to the rules that govern misrepresentation which has its own rules and its own set of remedies. So, if a misrepresentation is proven, there are a completely separate set of rules that cover the remedies available, all of which will be covered towards the end of the chapter.

AS YOU READ

At the end of this chapter you should be able to:

- Identify the existence of misrepresentation by the components of its definition
- Identify the type of misrepresentation applicable to particular circumstances
- Apply the appropriate remedy based upon the type of misrepresentation

8.3 DEFINITION AND COMPONENTS

Misrepresentation can be explained by the following definition (see Figure 8.1). It is essentially a false statement of fact which induces the other party to enter into the contract. In order to consider its impact, it is therefore necessary to break it down into its constituent parts.

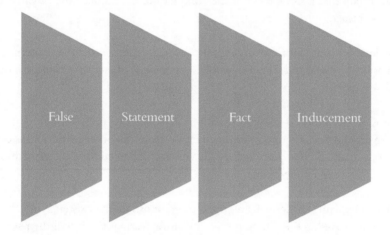

Figure 8.1 Elements of misrepresentation

In this section, we will be looking at each of these parts in turn. The key thing to remember about this definition is that, as a test, it is cumulative. Each part must be satisfied in order for the definition to be applicable. If any one of the parts is missing, it will defeat an individual's attempt to argue that a misrepresentation has occurred, and an action will not be successful if taken to court.

ASSESSMENT TIP

Remembering this simple definition for misrepresentation can be a big help in examination assessments. Working through each of the four steps listed above allows you to deal with a problem question and its set of facts in a clear methodical way, which will allow you to show a logical approach to answering the assessment question.

8.3.1 FALSE

In order for a representation to be considered a misrepresentation, it must be false. This might appear an obvious statement; however unless something can be shown to be objectively false, it cannot be a misrepresentation. This in itself may appear fairly obvious; however, where the accuracy of the statement made is a matter of degree, the court will look at whether the statement in itself was 'substantially correct'. Although not very helpful in itself, the case of *Avon Insurance v Swire Fraser*[1] clarifies this by providing that if the difference between the truth and the statement made was not enough to induce them to enter into the contract, the statement is 'substantially correct' – in the substance of the representation that mattered to the other party, it was essentially correct.

8.3.2 STATEMENT

The law requires a false statement of fact to have been made in order for there to be a misrepresentation. This therefore means that there is a distinction that has been drawn between statements of fact and other types of statement. We will deal with those later in the chapter.

One interesting point regarding the way in which the concept of 'statement' has been dealt with in the cases has meant that this has been given a rather broad meaning in the law. Ordinarily, you would expect the word 'statement' to include things that are spoken, or alternatively communicated to the other party in writing (for example in a letter or an email), but the definition of 'statement' was greatly broadened by Lord Denning in the case of *Curtis v Chemical Cleaning and Dyeing Co Ltd*.[2] Denning said: 'Any behaviour, by words or conduct, is sufficient to be a misrepresentation if it is such as to mislead the other … If it conveys a false impression that is enough.'[3] This has meant that it is the end result that is important, not whether the person has said something, or carried out a particular action. The important part appears to be giving the other party a certain impression. This is what can sometimes be referred as misrepresentation by conduct.

8.3.3 CONDUCT

Denning's comments in the *Curtis* case therefore suggest that it is possible to make a misrepresentation in this way, rather than just the traditional way of considering a statement. There are several examples of where this has happened. For example, in *Gordon and Teixeira*

---

1   [2000] Lloyd's LR IR 535, [2000] 1 All ER Comm 573.
2   [1951] 1 KB 805, [1951] 1 All ER 631.
3   [1951] 1 KB 805 at 808.

v Selico Ltd and Select Managements Ltd,[4] the misrepresentation concerned something that the seller of a house did, rather than what they said:

GORDON V SELICO (1986) 18 HLR 219

The seller of a flat, in preparing it for sale, deliberately covered up patches on the wall of the house that showed that there was dry rot in the building. In hiding these patches, the seller was deliberately concealing the dry rot from anyone who inspected the flat with a view to buying it. It was inspected by a prospective purchaser who, after having inspected it, went ahead with the purchase on the basis of what they saw. When the dry rot was later discovered, the purchaser claimed that a misrepresentation had taken place.

Held: conduct alone could constitute a misrepresentation, and therefore the act of concealing the dry rot was enough for it to constitute a false statement of the current condition of the property. They therefore found in favour of the purchaser.

The important point here is that nothing was said in the course of the sale regarding the existence of dry rot or otherwise, and therefore there was no statement in the ordinary sense of the word. It was the conduct alone that conveyed the impression that Denning referred to in *Curtis*. Other examples of this impression being conveyed have come in other cases. In *Horsfall v Thomas*[5] a defect in a gun for sale was concealed by a skilful repair that made the gun appear normal, but because the repair was superficial in nature, the gun would have malfunctioned if it were to be fired. Again, the act of concealment was in itself capable of being equivalent to a false statement in the impression that it conveyed.

A more recent case that dealt with similar issues was that of *Spice Girls Ltd v Aprilla World Service*.[6] This case concerned a misrepresentation by conduct:

SPICE GIRLS LTD V APRILIA WORLD SERVICE [2002] EWCA CIV 15, [2002] EMLR 27

A contract was entered into by the Spice Girls for sponsorship of their world tour by Aprilia in exchange for their involvement in promotional work for them. The promotional work included engaging in advertising work for Aprilia, which would then be used as part of Aprilia's advertising campaigns and would also form part of the

---

4   (1986) 18 HLR 219.
5   [1862] 158 ER 813.
6   [2002] EWCA Civ 15, [2002] EMLR 27.

advertising on the tour. Nothing was mentioned at the time of entering the agreement of any wish of any of the Spice Girls to leave the group, and therefore the expectation was that they would remain as a group for the minimum period of the contract. This was important for Aprilia because of the completed promotional work prior to going on tour, and if any member of the Spice Girls had left, at least some of the advertising materials for Aprilia would become out of date and worthless. Although Geri Halliwell ('Ginger Spice') did not confirm to the rest of the group her intention to leave until after the contract was signed, it had been discussed internally within the group prior to the tour.

When Geri Halliwell announced her departure from the group part way through the international tour, Aprilia claimed that there was a misrepresentation because it was misleading of the group to represent by their conduct in carrying out the sponsorship deal that there was no intention of any of the group members to leave.

Held: by their conduct, the Spice Girls had made a misrepresentation that affected their contract with Aprilia and, as a result, the contract they had was voidable at Aprilia's discretion.

This may appear to be an issue of misrepresentation by omission rather than by their actions; however the way in which this has been argued is on the basis that the contract was entered into and performed under the impression created by the conduct of the Spice Girls that they would remain as a whole group for the duration of the agreement, and that they should accept liability for any departure from this.

An important point here concerns the fact that it was the behaviour of the group that was held to be the misrepresentation, rather than any statements, verbal or written, about their current status. An omission would not normally be considered to be a misrepresentation. However, there are issues regarding informing the other party when things change, which can be misrepresentations, and we will deal with those later.

EXPLAINING THE LAW: CONVEYING A MISLEADING IMPRESSION

Earlier we mentioned that in *Curtis v Chemical Cleaning & Dyeing Co Ltd*, Denning said that 'conveying a false impression' was all that is required in order to show that a statement had been made that could be a misrepresentation. The way in which this has affected the idea of a false 'statement' in the law of misrepresentation means that it is more focussed upon the outcome of what has happened, rather than looking for one of the parties to have performed a particular act or said particular words. It makes this part of misrepresentation very flexible.

This means that the following will result in the 'false impression' being conveyed:

- Telling the other party something which is untrue
- Carrying out behaviour that would lead a reasonable person to a particular (untrue) conclusion
- Carrying out an act with the intent to deceive (or at least that the reasonable person would be deceived by it)

Whereas the following would not result in a false impression being conveyed:

- Failing to volunteer information without being directly asked (subject to the exceptions in the next section of this chapter)
- Carrying out conduct that would not lead the reasonable person to believe something that was untrue, because they have not been affected by it or do not know about it
- Telling the other party something that they already know is untrue

Because misrepresentations are about the other party changing their decision to enter into the contract as a result of them, having something that 'conveys a false impression' that could then influence that decision is crucial here. Whether that happens because of what a person says or does is immaterial.

The other aspect of this is about how you evaluate whether a false impression is being conveyed. This is not judged from the perspective of either party, and therefore has to be an objective one. So, in considering the above, how would a reasonable person judge whether a false impression is being conveyed? This is what should be considered as this is how a court will approach it.

8.3.4 WITHHOLDING INFORMATION

What we have seen so far is that there needs to be some form of positive statement or act to be a misrepresentation. What this does not cover is situations where there is not a positive statement or act, but rather the other party has merely failed to tell the other party something. Can a misrepresentation take place merely by someone remaining silent?

There is no general duty to tell the other party everything that may be pertinent to the sale, and in fact the law in the UK places the burden on the other party to make reasonable enquiries to find out information themselves. This relates to the general principle of *caveat emptor*, or 'buyer beware'. This indicates that you should make reasonable enquiries to find things out before going ahead with a contract, rather than the other party being obliged to volunteer information themselves.

Caveat emptor – a Latin phrase that translates as 'buyer beware'. It is the legal principle that generally accepts that the law is not there to rectify 'bad bargains' entered into by parties to a contract. If a person of sound mind and appropriate age has entered into an agreement, it is not up to the law to consider it as 'fair' or not. There are of course exceptions to this; see, in particular, the chapter on capacity to contract.

There are however, exceptions to this rule, and they are as follows.

8.3.5 FIDUCIARY OR CONFIDENTIAL RELATIONSHIP

In certain situations, there is a fiduciary relationship (one where there is implied into the nature of the relationship a special duty to the other party) or a relationship where the parties have agreed to confidentiality. Certain relationships (such as between a solicitor and client or between doctor and patient) have implied into them this duty and, where this is the case, there is a duty to disclose material information. Therefore, to withhold such information would be considered to be a misrepresentation.

These are contracts 'of the utmost good faith' and therefore there is a duty to disclose information as part of the nature of the agreement. The best everyday examples of this are contracts of insurance. When taking out insurance of whatever type (e.g. car insurance, home insurance) there is a general duty to inform the insurer of any material facts affecting the insurance.[7] Anyone who fails to disclose such information is making a misrepresentation.

8.3.6 HALF TRUTHS

Where the statement made is true, but due to an omission is in itself misleading, this can form a misrepresentation. For example, the case of *Dimmock v Hallett*[8] involved a statement that was true. This involved a sale of property. The property was described as 'fully let' as it was at that time fully occupied by tenants. This particular fact was true, but the sellers had neglected to mention that the tenants had served a notice to quit, and it was the absence of this fact that made the statement misleading. So, although the statements made were always true, and at no point was anything untruthful said, it was the act of leaving out the other half of the information that made the statement misleading – in the absence of the extra information, people will make assumptions about the information they are given.

---

7   There are a number of material facts that will affect the actuarial calculation of insurance premiums; for example with car insurance this will include information about recent claims, motoring convictions, number of estimated miles travelled per year, etc.

8   (1866–67) LR 2 Ch App 21.

8.3.7 CHANGING CIRCUMSTANCES

Another area where even though only the truth has been given, this may result in misleading the other party, is with regard to where circumstances change. A truthful statement may subsequently become misleading because of a change of circumstances. Where this occurs, there is a duty on the person who made the statement to correct this statement. This stems from the fact that where a person makes a representation, they have a continuing responsibility as to the statement's accuracy within the scope of the contract.

With v O'Flanagan[9] involved the sale of a medical practice. At the time that the sale was negotiated, a statement was made concerning the amount of money made by the practice. At the time it was made, it was accurate; however, five months lapsed between the negotiation and the eventual sale of the practice and, during this time, the seller had fallen ill, and the income had fallen away to virtually nothing. The buyer was not informed of this, and he only discovered this was the case once he had bought it. He attempted to get rescission of the contract and succeeded. The court held that he was entitled to believe the truth of the statement until either the time of sale, or until it was corrected by the other party.

This case does not introduce the idea of silence being a misrepresentation as such. Silence on its own cannot be a misrepresentation in situations where there is no obligation to inform the other party of every pertinent fact. However, it is silence in combination with a previous statement, such that failing to update the information creates the false impression. It is therefore silence in conjunction with something else that creates the situation of misrepresentation.

ANALYSING THE LAW: SILENCE AS MISREPRESENTATION – THE ISSUE OF *CAVEAT EMPTOR*

The issue here goes to the heart of the notion of freedom of contract that we discussed in the opening chapter. The freedom that individuals have to enter into a bargain of their own free will also include the responsibility to discover through reasonable enquiry anything relevant to the contract, and also the ability of the other side of the bargain to get the best possible deal for themselves.

What this also means is that, aside from a number of defined examples that have been mentioned over the past few pages, there are no obligations upon one party to reveal information unless they are asked a direct question.

This does not however apply to situations where goods are being bought from a business – in such a scenario there are consumer rules that protect a buyer and therefore mean that *caveat emptor* does not apply.

---

9   [1936] Ch 575, [1936] 1 All ER 727.

Consider the following examples and decide whether you would consider that there is any legal reason why one party should disclose certain information to the other party:

- the sale of a car between two private individuals, but the buyer failed to test drive the car. It is subsequently discovered that there is a gearbox fault
- a contract of life insurance where the insured person forgets to reveal an important fact about his health
- a private sale of a fragile ornament on eBay which is broken after the sale has taken place
- the sale of a painting where the seller fails to mention that they know that it is in fact a fake
- the sale of a piece of broken furniture as 'original and undamaged', where there has been a deliberate attempt to conceal the repair

KEY LEARNING POINTS

Is a statement really a 'statement'?

What all this means with regard to misrepresentation is that the ordinary meaning of 'statement' has been exceeded, but it still retains the essence of what we mean by 'statement'. It goes back to what Denning was discussing in the *Curtis* case. The essence of this was that an impression had to be conveyed by the person's actions or inactions, and this must be one that could be judged objectively. So a 'statement' for the purposes of misrepresentation could be:

- a statement, either spoken or written
- conduct that conveys an impression
- silence in a situation where there is a duty to make a positive statement, or where failure to correct a previous statement conveys an impression in itself

What becomes the common theme between these is therefore what is being conveyed, and therefore the concept of 'statement' has taken on this wider meaning.

8.4 FACT

Any information provided as part of a misrepresentation must be about existing fact. It is important to ensure that you do not get confused regarding what information can form a misrepresentation, and therefore there are two important categories that must be distinguished from fact. The reason why a misrepresentation must be as to existing fact is because a fact is most easily assessed as being true or untrue. There are problems with other types of statements being part of a misrepresentation.

8.4.1 STATEMENTS OF OPINION

For example, the most straightforward exception to this is opinion. A statement of opinion cannot form part of a misrepresentation because of the subjective nature of an opinion. Everyone has their own opinion, and it is not for the law to judge individuals' opinions as being right or wrong. There are some key issues here to be considered.

Opinions are subjective. Where an individual has an opinion, normally this will not be treated as fact because there may be a range of opinions that an individual might genuinely hold on a particular matter. It is only in certain circumstances that an individual might be held to account for having a particular opinion, but we will come onto that later. Ordinarily the statement maker will be in no different position to the statement receiver, and therefore there are no grounds upon which one person might be justified in relying upon the statement of the other.

A good illustration of an individual holding an opinion is the Privy Council decision in *Bisset v Wilkinson*,[10] which shows the reasons behind why opinions cannot be the basis of a misrepresentation.

BISSET V WILKINSON [1927] AC 177

This involved the sale of two pieces of land. These were being sold together, and there was an enquiry from the purchaser regarding the capacity of that land to support sheep before entering into the contract. Such considerations would depend upon the quality and area of the land in question. In response to the question, the seller stated that, in his opinion, the land could support 2,000 sheep. However, the seller was not a sheep farmer, and had no special expertise upon which to support this opinion. The statement was at best his own estimate on the capability of the land.

When it transpired that the land was not of sufficient quality to support 2,000 sheep, the buyer of the land attempted to claim that a misrepresentation had taken place.

Held: the statement made was merely an opinion, and therefore could not form the basis of a misrepresentation. An opinion is exactly that, and therefore an individual could reasonably hold an honest opinion on a subject and yet be incorrect. The law will not hold him liable for such mistaken beliefs. As long as the opinion is honestly held, and from no position of expertise, there is no misrepresentation.

---

10 [1927] AC 177.

The key thing here is that a mistaken belief will not lead to liability, as long as it is not unreasonable for that person to hold that belief, either through issues of honesty or expertise. We therefore also need to look at these two issues in more detail.

In *Bisset* above, the person making the statement was not an expert, and it was objectively clear that this was the case. Therefore, in these circumstances it would not have been reasonable for the buyer to have relied upon the statement because the seller was in no better position to make the statement and the buyer would therefore have no grounds to rely upon it. However, this is not always the case, and where an individual does have expertise, this changes the nature of his statement and how it might be regarded by others.

Expertise in this context is merely having better knowledge on a subject. Whether this is holding a qualification or experience in a particular field, or merely being in a better position than the other party to know the truth, it still puts a person in a more advantageous position, and the other person would normally be expected to react accordingly.

In *Smith v Land & House Property Corpn*[11] the seller was in a better position to know the truth about the attributes of his tenant due to being the existing landlord of a property. He was selling the property with the tenant *in situ*, and described the tenant as 'a most desirable tenant'.[12] In reality, this was far from being the case, and was something that the landlord would have known about from his dealings with the tenant. When the property was sold, and the truth was discovered, the seller was accused of misrepresentation. He claimed that his statement was merely an opinion, and therefore not capable of being a misrepresentation. However, there were two issues here. Firstly, upon the evidence of the conduct of the tenant, it was clear that this opinion of him as 'desirable' was not one that could be reasonably held and, more importantly, the opinion was one held by a person in a much better position than the buyer. Had the seller remained silent and allowed the buyer to discover the nature of his tenant for himself, this would not have been a misrepresentation; however, speaking from his position as landlord would have led a reasonable person to rely upon his statement, making it a misrepresentation.

Similar reasoning can be applied to statements made by those with expertise in the traditional sense. Cases such as *Dick Bentley Productions v Harold Smith Motors*[13] and *Esso Petroleum v Mardon*[14] (discussed elsewhere in this book) are good illustrations of this applied to 'experts'. The principle however, remains the same.

8.4.2 STATEMENTS OF LAW

The position regarding statements of law has always been that they cannot be misrepresentations and therefore must be distinguished from statements of fact. This is based upon the principle **ignorantia juris non excusat**, which means 'ignorance of the law is no excuse'. People generally are expected to know the law that applies to them, and therefore not

11 (1884) 28 Ch D 7.
12 Ibid, at 13.
13 [1965] 1 WLR 623, [1965] 2 All ER 65, (1965) 109 SJ 329.
14 [1976] QB 801, [1976] 2 WLR 583, [1976] 2 All ER 5, [1976] 2 Lloyd's Rep 305, 2 BLR 82, (1976) 120 SJ 131.

doing so and relying upon the statements of others instead was not considered acceptable. For anyone who did not know the law, they would always be in a position to get advice from a lawyer to be able to rectify this.

ESSENTIAL DEFINITION: *IGNORANTIA JURIS NON EXCUSAT*

A Latin phrase that describes the principle that a party to a contract cannot use their ignorance of the law as the basis for, in this situation, a claim of misrepresentation. It is related to the other Latin phrase mentioned earlier in this chapter in that these are both examples of where the law is not there to resolve problems that are the responsibility of the parties.

This situation (and the blanket rule that false statements of law could not be misrepresentations) seems to have been challenged by the courts in two cases regarding misstatements of law. Firstly, the case of *Kleinwort Benson Ltd v Lincoln City Council*,[15] a House of Lords judgment, casts doubt on the previously solid assertion that statements of law were not misrepresentations through the ruling that money paid out under a mistake of law was recoverable in the same way that money paid out under a mistake of fact. The logical argument from this is that if there is a remedy available in such situations, it would also follow that a false statement of law should more generally be actionable in a way that previously was considered to be exempt.

This was followed up in 2002 with the case *Pankhania v Hackney London Borough Council*,[16] where this was applied to a situation where there had been a false statement as to the legal position of the tenancy of a property, which had induced the other party to enter into the contract. *Pankhania* involved the sale of land that was partially occupied by NCP, who operated a car park on that part of the land. The sale was by auction, and the misrepresentation occurred in the auction brochure, which stated that NCP were a **contractual licensee**. In reality they were a business tenant and, as such, were protected under the relevant tenancy legislation.[17] The reality of this difference was about the legal status of the tenant – as a contractual licensee, they could be given three months' notice, but as a **business tenant** they had much more protection and would need to be bought out of their tenancy in order to require them to leave the premises.

ESSENTIAL DEFINITION: CONTRACTUAL LICENSEE

Contractual licensee – a party who has permission to perform a certain act, or a right over certain content within a contract.

---

15 [1999] 2 AC 349, [1998] 3 WLR 1095, [1999] CLC 332.
16 [2002] EWHC 2441 (Ch), [2002] NPC 123.
17 In this case, the Landlord and Tenant Act 1954.

ESSENTIAL DEFINITION: BUSINESS TENANT

Someone who has a tenancy over a piece of property or land, which gives them rights under the relevant tenancy legislation.

It might seem from these cases that the law has changed significantly from its previous position, but in reality there is very little difference between this and the previous position that, although statements of law are not actionable, statements of how the law applies to a particular situation are statements of fact and therefore are actionable. This can be seen from the case of *Solle v Butcher*.[18] Nevertheless, the judge in the *Pankhania* case ruled that the rule about 'mistakes of law' had not survived the *Kleinwort Benson* judgment, and therefore this broke down the distinction between statements of fact and law.

8.5 INDUCEMENT TO ENTER INTO THE CONTRACT

So far we have looked at the elements that must be present for something to be *capable* of being a misrepresentation. However, even if all those elements are present, an actionable misrepresentation will not be present unless it produces a particular effect. This is where it is necessary to show that the misrepresentation actually induced the other party to enter into the contract. There are four parts to this. In order to show that the contract was induced by the representation, you must show the following:

- The representation must be material
- It must be known to the other party
- It must be intended to be acted upon
- It must be acted upon.

8.5.1 REPRESENTATION MUST BE MATERIAL

There must be a fact here that would induce a reasonable person into entering into an agreement. There are two uses for this reasoning, firstly that it enables the court to dismiss any trivial claims to misrepresentation and, secondly, it introduces an objective element into the equation, which may allow the court to infer inducement through the objectivity of this requirement. If the reasonable person would be induced, there is no need to show that the person in this particular circumstance has *actually* been induced. This objective standard was shown in the case of *Pan Atlantic Insurance Co Ltd v Pine Top Insurance Co Ltd*,[19] where

18 [1950] 1 KB 671, [1949] 2 All ER 1107.
19 [1995] 1 AC 501 [1994] 3 WLR 677 [1994] CLC 868.

it was held that it was an objective assessment of whether the representation was material, and not what either party thought. This therefore shows again the objective nature of the situation required for misrepresentation. However, one thing which is important to point out about this is that some form of subjective intention to act upon the misrepresentation is still necessary. *Museprime Properties Ltd v Adhill Properties Ltd*[20] showed that the objective test regarding whether the reasonable person would have been induced to enter into the contract was merely to show that it would not have been unreasonable for that person to enter into the agreement.

8.5.2 KNOWN TO THE OTHER PARTY

This requirement really is obvious enough for it to be straightforward. It is best illustrated by a case mentioned earlier, that of *Horsfall v Thomas*, where there was a misrepresentation by conduct because the gun had been altered to conceal a defect. However, the buyer did not inspect the gun before the sale, and it was this fact that meant that he was not exposed to the misrepresentation made by the conduct of the seller. Had he inspected the gun, he could have argued misrepresentation. The concealment was set up in such a way as to fool anyone who inspected it, and when someone does not inspect it, they cannot be misled by the concealment. It is therefore this that removes the link between the misrepresentation and the inducement – you cannot be induced by something you do not know anything about, because it will not have had an effect upon your decision whether to buy or not.

8.5.3 INTENDED TO BE ACTED UPON

The intention here lies with the person making the statement. This is because when statements are made, all the above discussion regarding being in a better position to know the truth of a situation will also be clear to the person making the statement, as well as the person receiving it. This means an individual making a representation has the perfect opportunity to ensure that the other party does not rely upon their statements by encouraging them to verify the truth of what they are saying, usually by inviting them to arrange expert inspection of the subject-matter of the contract, or by making it clear that they are making no guarantees about what they are saying. However, although some might consider this an efficient get-out clause, there are some situations in which it would be better to say nothing at all. Situations in which this would be relevant are those where a positive statement has been issued by one party. Making statements that the reasonable person could subsequently rely upon leaves the statement maker in the situation of possibly laying themselves open to liability for misrepresentation, as in the *Attwood v Small*[21] case mentioned below.

8.5.4 ACTED UPON

This element requires the **misrepresentee** to have acted upon the statement being made to him or her. However, it will often be self-evident through the above circumstances, because usually in a situation where there is a clear misrepresentation that was intended to be acted

20 (1991) 61 P & CR 111, [1990] 36 EG 114, [1990] EG 29 (CS).

21 (1836) 160 ER 328.

upon, where the conduct carried out by the misrepresentee is consistent with the inducement, you would normally expect there to be a finding of misrepresentation.

Where the person making the representation may be able to avoid a finding of misrepresentation is by showing that the decision of the other party to enter into the contract was as a result of arriving at a decision independent of the misrepresentation. Therefore, the misrepresentation does not induce their decision making, and the statement maker escapes liability.

ESSENTIAL DEFINITION: MISREPRESENTEE

The person to whom a misrepresentation is made – the recipient of the misrepresenting statement. The person making the misrepresentation would be referred to as the misrepresentor.

ESSENTIAL DEFINITION: MISREPRESENTOR

The person who makes the misrepresentation. The person acting upon the misrepresentation would be referred to as the misrepresentee.

If the misrepresentee chooses not merely to rely on what has been represented to him, but to make further investigations of his own, the misrepresentation has not been acted upon, because he has used his own judgement in arriving at the conclusion. For example, in *Attwood v Small* there was an attempt to avoid a contract because of false statements made by the seller of a mine. The buyer had asked for information about the potential of the mine, but the seller had exaggerated this in his reply. However, the buyers also appointed an expert to conduct an independent investigation, and his conclusions had matched up with those of the seller. The court found that there could be no action for misrepresentation, due to the fact that the buyers had not relied upon what had been represented, but had obtained their own advice. Just because the expert had not discovered that the other party's statement was inaccurate did not make the sellers liable.

This case must be contrasted with that of *Redgrave v Hurd*,[22] where a solicitor selling his share in a partnership had made representations that the income was around £300 a year, and had given the buyer the opportunity to inspect the relevant documentation, in this case a bundle of papers said to represent part of the business income. Initially, the court had not allowed the buyer to claim misrepresentation, because when faced with the opportunity to inspect the papers, he had not. However, this was overturned on appeal. The principle therefore stands that even where given an opportunity to discover the truth, this does not prevent a person from relying upon the misrepresentation made.

---

22 (1881) 20 Ch D 1.

Of significance, in *Hayward v Zurich Insurance Company plc*[23] the Supreme Court held that there is no independent requirement that the defrauded party must have actually believed the representations to be true. The fact that it had doubts or suspicions may be highly relevant to the court's assessment of whether it was influenced, but it will not be determinative. The test is whether the party was 'influenced by' its opponent's representations in entering the agreement.

8.5.5 MAKING CONNECTIONS

This is where you can see a direct link between what one party has said or done and the other party's response to this. One party has to create a false impression, but that has to directly link with the other party's reliance upon their statement. So, if either of these two parts is missing, there is no misrepresentation. One party can make all the false statements he wishes, if the other party acts solely upon independent advice he has sought despite what information he has been given by the other party. In this way you can see how these two parts link together.

What this means in practice is that where it can be shown that the other party acted upon some other factor, they have not acted upon the inducement. However, even where they have been given the opportunity to do so, if they fail to do so, they are still making their decision based upon the misrepresentation made. Again, this is a situation where someone should not be saved from the careless statements they make, in a situation where they would be better off not making those statements in the first place.

8.6 AN ACTIONABLE MISREPRESENTATION

If we bring all of this together you should therefore see how this forms the definition of misrepresentation. The different elements discussed above are all important to a finding of misrepresentation and therefore the absence of one of those elements will defeat the claim for misrepresentation. Figure 8.2 may help you to bring all of this together when faced with a scenario with the various elements.

8.6.1 TYPES OF MISREPRESENTATION

Having established the key elements for a claim in misrepresentation, we can now move on to analysing the type of misrepresentation that has occurred and appreciate why we need to categorise the misrepresentation.

There are four discernible categories of misrepresentation. This has not always been the case. Prior to the 1960s only two types of misrepresentation existed at common law: fraudulent and innocent. Following the landmark case of *Hedley Byrne & Co Ltd v Heller & Partners Ltd*[24]

23 [2016] UKSC 48.
24 [1964] AC 465.

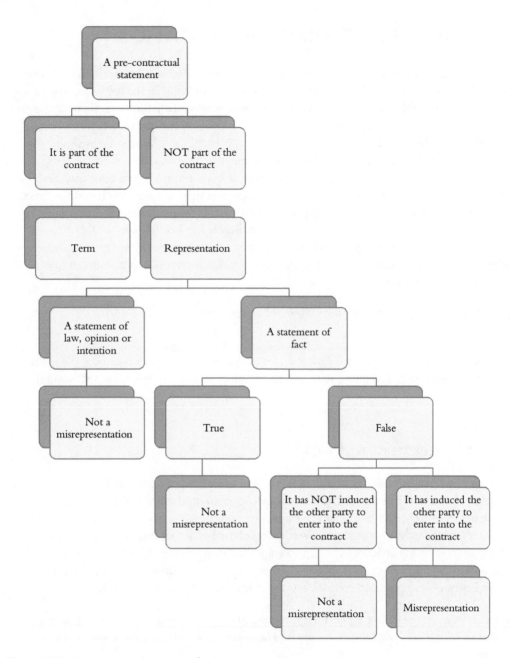

Figure 8.2 Summary – elements of misrepresentation

and the passage of the Misrepresentation Act 1967 two further important common law and statutory forms of negligent misrepresentation have evolved.

Where an action for misrepresentation is successful, the remedy advanced is contingent upon the category of misrepresentation. The category must therefore be established before the remedies can be discussed.

8.7 FRAUDULENT MISREPRESENTATION

Fraudulent misrepresentation is also referred to as the tort of deceit. The accepted definition of fraudulent misrepresentation was set out by the House of Lords in the landmark case of *Derry v Peek*[25] as a false statement 'made knowingly, or without belief in its truth, or recklessly, careless whether it be true or false'. Thus, a successful claim in the tort of deceit can only be established where an absence of an 'honest belief' is established. Where a representor can satisfy the court that he honestly believed his statement to be true, s/he will not be liable in the tort of deceit regardless of how irresponsible or nonsensical his statement may have been. In *Derry v Peek* the House of Lords emphasised that there is a clear distinction between fraud involving dishonesty and negligence that falls short of being dishonest. Carelessness is insufficient to amount to dishonesty, but the court may reach a conclusion of dishonesty if it believes the defendant has been reckless to the extent that s/he could not reasonably have believed in the truth of the statement made. So, for recklessness to amount to deceit, the fundamental ingredients are:

1) defendant's knowledge that the statement is dishonest, or
2) recklessness.

An analysis of the facts in *Derry v Peek* is useful to enable an appreciation of how the court reached its conclusion in the case itself and the development of the precedent following the judgment.

DERRY V PEEK (1889) 14 APP CAS 337

A tram company applied for an Act of Parliament to be passed permitting it to use steam power to run its trams. The subsequent Act permitted the use of steam power but subject to consent from the Board of Trade. The company then stated in its prospectus that it had the right to use steam power, being of the belief that Board of Trade approval was just a formality and would be forthcoming upon application. A company purchased shares in the tram company in reliance of the fact that steam power could be used. Later the Board of Trade refused consent and the company went into liquidation.

Held: an action of deceit against the directors of the tram company failed on the basis that the court accepted the company had honestly believed that their statement was true.

It is important to take on board that even where the representee has acted upon a false representation the representor did not believe to be true, in order to pursue a successful claim the representee must have suffered loss as a result of reliance upon the representation.

---

25 (1889) 14 App Cas 337.

If you are seeking to establish fraudulent misrepresentation, an affirmative response is necessary to one of the following propositions:

1) Did the representor know that the statement was false?
2) Did the representor act without belief in the statement?
3) Was the representor reckless or careless as to whether the statement was true?

Remember this simple equation: dishonesty + loss to claimant = fraudulent misrepresentation.

8.8 THE EMERGENCE OF NEGLIGENT MISREPRESENTATION

Until 1963 all non-fraudulent misrepresentations were classed as innocent misrepresentations, even where it was clear that the misrepresentor had been negligent in representations that had led the other party into a contractual agreement. It was the case of *Hedley Byrne & Co Ltd v Heller & Partners Ltd*[26] that introduced a significant shift in the law in this area, extending the common law tort of negligence to cover negligent misstatements where a loss is incurred. Shortly after the judgment, the enactment of the Misrepresentation Act 1967 introduced damages for negligent misrepresentation in a contractual agreement.

8.9 NEGLIGENT MISSTATEMENT AT COMMON LAW

An analysis of the facts of *Hedley Byrne & Co Ltd v Heller & Partners Ltd* is useful to see how the court reached its conclusion in the case itself and the development of the law in negligent misstatement.

HEDLEY BYRNE & CO. LTD V HELLER & PARTNERS LTD [1964] AC 645

Prior to entering into a contract, the plaintiff company sought information from the bankers of the other party to the agreement (Easipower) on their financial standing as

---

26 [1964] AC 645.

they had requested credit terms. Easipower's bankers knew the purpose of the request but failed to give accurate information and carelessly stated that the company was in good financial health.

Held: whilst the House of Lords accepted that the plaintiff was owed a duty of care by the bankers, the bankers escaped liability by relying upon a disclaimer that had accompanied the credit reference.

It is clear from the judgment in *Hedley Byrne* that a duty of care will be imposed upon the maker of a statement requiring him/her to do all that is reasonably possible to guarantee the accuracy of a statement of fact and provision of advice given in the course of contractual negotiations. The duty will arise in all instances where a 'special relationship' exists between the parties. There need not be a contractual link but a sufficient degree of proximity needs to exist for an action to be sustained.

8.9.1 DEGREE OF PROXIMITY

The question is then posed as to when a special relationship will exist. Clarity on this point was not provided in *Hedley Byrne*, although it was clear from the case that a sufficient degree of proximity between the parties would be required in order to found a successful claim. This was later reaffirmed in *Caparo Industries plc v Dickman*.[27] Degree of proximity means that a duty of care will only exist if the relationship of the claimant and the defendant is sufficiently close.

The degree of proximity will indeed exist between professional advisers and their clients, for example solicitors, accountants and barristers.[28] It also extends to commercial agreements where the representor has greater wisdom and experience than the representee and where it is reasonable for the representee to have relied upon the representor's statement. The latter is illustrated in the case of *Esso Petroleum Co Ltd v Mardon*.

ESSO PETROLEUM CO LTD V MARDON [1976] 2 ALL ER 5, [1976] 2 WLR 583

A valuer for Esso Petroleum company made a forecast about the sales capacity of a garage to a future tenant, which later turned out to be inaccurate. The valuer clearly possessed special skill and knowledge in relation to such matters, and his knowledge far exceeded that of the tenant.

Held: the Court of Appeal found a duty of care to exist. The valuer could reasonably foresee that the tenant would rely upon his statements and it was reasonable for him to do so.

27 [1990] 1 All ER 568.
28 *Rondel v Worsley* [1969] 1 AC 191.

An action in negligent misstatement is not restricted to representations that result in a contract between the representor and representee but can also apply in situations where the representation results in a contract with a third party.[29]

> **ASSESSMENT** TIP
>
> ―――――――
>
> If you are seeking to prove negligent misstatement, you must be able to establish:
>
> 1) Existence of a special relationship and a duty of care
> 2) Breach of duty of care and foreseeable loss
>
> Remember this simple equation: Special relationship + breach of duty of care where a loss is incurred = negligent misstatement.

―――――――

8.10 MISREPRESENTATION ACT 1967

The second critical development in negligent misrepresentation derived from the Misrepresentation Act in 1967. Under s. 2(1), the Misrepresentation Act introduced a statutory remedy for negligent misrepresentation, as follows:

> Where a person has entered into a contract after a misrepresentation has been made to him by another party thereto and as a result thereof he has suffered loss, then if the person making the misrepresentation would be liable to damages in respect thereof had the misrepresentation been made fraudulently, that person shall be so liable notwithstanding that the misrepresentation was not made fraudulently unless he proves that he had reasonable grounds to believe and did believe up to the time the contract was made that the facts represented were true.

One key difference between s. 2(1) misrepresentation claims and those falling under negligent misstatement is that it is not necessary to prove the existence of a special relationship between the parties. A second fundamental difference concerns the burden of proof: In negligent misstatement the representee must show the existence of a special relationship and a breach in duty of care. Conversely, under s. 2(1) claims, the burden of proof is reversed, rendering the representor liable unless he can show 'he had reasonable grounds to believe and did believe up to the time that the contract was made that the facts represented were true'. This is sometimes referred to as the 'innocence defence'.

Owing to the reversal of the burden of proof, it is likely to prove more advantageous for the claimant to take an action under s. 2(1) rather than the common law. The advantage to the

―――――――――――――――――――――

29 *Hedley Byrne & Co Ltd v Heller & Partners Ltd* [1964] AC 465.

claimant lies in the fact that all he need show is that a false statement has been made and that the false statement induced him to enter into the contract.

It is not easy for the defendant to discharge the burden of proof. It is insufficient that the representor is able to disprove negligence. The wording of s. 2(1) requires the defendant to prove that s/he had reasonable grounds for his/her belief. The onerous nature of this requirement is well illustrated in *Howard Marine & Dredging Co Ltd v Ogden & Sons (Excavations) Ltd.*

HOWARD MARINE & DREDGING CO LTD V OGDEN & SONS (EXCAVATIONS) LTD [1978] QB 574

The defendants had requested information on the capacity of certain barges that it wished to hire from the plaintiff company. The plaintiff hire company had provided the information based on figures obtained from Lloyd's Register. It later transpired that the figures in Lloyd's Register were incorrect and the correct information was contained in documents within the plaintiff's possession.

Held: the Court of Appeal determined that the hire company had not discharged the burden of showing reasonable grounds to believe that the statement regarding the capacity of the barges was true.

Another example where the defendant was unable to discharge the burden of proof can be seen in *Spice Girls Ltd v Aprilia World Service BV*,[30] where it was proven that a member of a girl band knew that she was leaving the band at the time that a contractual agreement was entered into. The agreement weighted significant importance in their identity as a band with all its members intact. Hence, they were unable to discharge the burden of proof that they had reasonable grounds for purporting to a status that they knew was inaccurate.

8.11 INNOCENT MISREPRESENTATION

An innocent misrepresentation is a false statement that is neither fraudulent nor negligent. The representor must have believed the statement to be true and must show that he had reasonable grounds for his belief. The significant difference between an innocent and a negligent or fraudulent misrepresentation is that the representee is not entitled to damages as of right.

---

30 [2002] EWCA Civ 15, [2002] EMLR 27.

APPLYING THE LAW

Ellie wished to buy a show dog and asked Sam to sell her his dog Cassey, which had won the Crufts Dog Show last year. Sam asked whether Ellie wanted to have a look at Cassey, but Ellie replied, 'She won the Crufts Dog Show last year – there can't be much wrong with her, can there? I'll give you £500 as agreed.' Sam said nothing.

When Ellie took Cassey home, she noticed that the dog was extremely restless so she took the dog to a veterinary surgeon, Curtis. Curtis advised Ellie that the dog had been suffering from a nervous disorder for several months. He prescribed a new drug, Bultex, for the dog. The side effects of Bultex were not fully known and practitioners had been advised to warn customers of this. Curtis informed Ellie that the drug may have certain side-effects, but to keep using it. After a month on Bultex, the dog still had not settled and, one evening, it became extremely aggressive and attacked Ellie.

Ellie is claiming that Sam misled her by not informing her of the illness and wants her money back. Ellie also claims that Curtis should have warned her of the side-effects of the drug, and that he should compensate her for the consequences of his failure to do so.

You are asked to provide advice to Ellie.

Where would you begin?

First of all, you would need to examine whether any of this behaviour could be categorised as a misrepresentation. There are two separate issues – keep the issues separate. You need to consider the statements made between Sam and Ellie and the conversation between Ellie and Curtis (the vet). Did you spot that there might be two grounds for misrepresentation? In both instances you would need to apply the criteria for a misrepresentation and decide whether a misrepresentation has occurred. If you decide that there has been a misrepresentation, you would then proceed to an analysis of which category the misrepresentation falls into.

Later we will be looking at remedies that will be available in the above scenario; so, just for the sake of completeness here, we should point out that in a question of this nature it would also be necessary to link the type of misrepresentation that has occurred to the remedies available and advise the claimant on what they can/cannot claim.

8.12 REMEDIES FOR MISREPRESENTATION

The range of remedies available for misrepresentation depends upon the type of misrepresentation and is regulated by a combination of equitable, common law and statute rules. Where a misrepresentation has occurred, a contract will be voidable, meaning that the misrepresentee may rescind (set aside) the contract. The representee may choose to affirm the contract; that is, exercise the right not to rescind. S/he can do this by stating an intention to affirm, or by simply continuing with the obligations under the agreement. Rescission is a remedy applicable to all types of misrepresentation. In fraudulent and negligent misrepresentation, damages may also be claimed to reflect any losses incurred.

8.12.1 RESCISSION

Rescission is available for all types of misrepresentation. The effect of rescission for misrepresentation is to render the contract void ab initio, requiring the parties be returned to their pre-contractual positions (*restitutio in integrum*). If it is impossible to return the parties to their pre-contractual state, rescission will be impossible. There are several bars to rescission (see Figure 8.3).

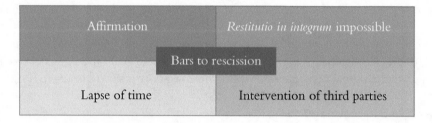

Figure 8.3 Bars to rescission

8.12.2 AFFIRMATION

Where a repudiatory breach of contract has occurred, an innocent party can either treat the contract as terminated or treat it as continuing, which is known as affirmation. Once affirmation has taken place it cannot be retracted. We already know that affirmation of a contract will prevent rescission from taking place.[31] Affirmation can be express or can be inferred from the conduct of the representee[32] and it can only occur if the representee is aware of the untruth of a particular statement.

8.12.3 *RESTITUTIO IN INTEGRUM* IMPOSSIBLE

Rescission cannot take place where restitution is impossible, in other words if the parties cannot be substantively returned to their pre-contractual positions.[33] Restitution is a remedy available in contract law that prevents a defendant gaining financially from a wrongful act. Restitution requires a defendant to forfeit gains that they have unlawfully obtained from the claimant and all that has been exchanged under the contract must be handed back. Often there will not be an issue, as a monetary exchange will accomplish this. However, if the goods have changed in composition this may not be possible. The goods may have been damaged,

31 *Long v Lloyd* [1958] 1 WLR 753.
32 *Clough v London and North Western Rly Co* (1871) LR 7 Exch 26.
33 *Erlanger v New Sombrero Phosphate Co* (1878) 3 App Cas 1218.

part consumed or altered.[34] It would not be possible to return an empty box of chocolates owing to a misrepresentation relating to their quality, if the chocolates had been consumed! In *Vigers v Pike*[35] restitution could not take place as the subject matter of the contract was a mine, which had subsequently been worked out. However, in *Salt v Stratstone Specialist Ltd (t/a Stratstone Cadillac Newcastle)*[36] the fact that a car had been registered did not prevent rescission of the contract when it was subsequently discovered that the seller had misrepresented facts about the age and history of the car.

8.12.4 LAPSE OF TIME

Where a material misrepresentation has occurred, the general rule is that rescission must take place within a reasonable time after a contract has been entered into. This principle is illustrated in *Leaf v International Galleries*[37] where the plaintiff purchased a painting following a misrepresentation that it was a genuine Constable. The plaintiff discovered the misrepresentation some five years after the sale and sought to rescind. The claim for rescission was time-barred, as the lapse of time between the contract being made and the action being taken was considered too long. This was the case even though there was no evidence to suggest that the plaintiff had affirmed the contract.

ASSESSMENT TIP

A notable exception to the rule that rescission must take place within a reasonable time is where there has been a fraudulent misrepresentation. In such circumstances the time will not start to run until the misrepresentation is discovered.

8.12.5 INTERVENTION OF THIRD PARTIES

The right to rescind will be barred where an innocent party has acquired goods in good faith and for value. The most usual occurrence is where the representee is induced into selling goods to the representor as a result of fraudulent misrepresentation. For example, A represents himself as the owner of a car which he offers to sell B. Unbeknown to B, A is a fraudster who has stolen the car. In such instances, if the representor then sells the goods on to an innocent party, C, the remedy of rescission will be barred due to the fact that the third party will have acquired good title to the goods. If the representee is able to rescind the contract before the goods have been passed on to a third party, recoverability will remain possible and, if the goods are passed to the third party *after* rescission has taken place, the representee will be able to take an action in the tort of conversion to recover the goods. Rescission was barred in the case of *Crystal Palace Football Club (2000) v Dowie*,[38] since permitting rescission would have the

---

34 *Clarke v Dickson* (1858) EB & E 148.
35 (1842) 8 Cl & Fin 562.
36 [2015] EWCA Civ 745, [2015] CTLC 206.
37 [1950] 1 All ER 693.
38 [2007] EWHC 1392 (QB).

effect of re-enacting a contract of employment, where the plaintiff had moved on and had a contract of employment with another football club.

The issue also arose in *Government of Zanzibar v British Aerospace (Lancaster House) Ltd*[39] which concerned a misrepresentation in relation to an aeroplane which had been represented as being airworthy, reliable and without defects in design and construction. At the time of the action the plane had been sold on to a third party, hence the government were not entitled to rescission or damages.

An effective revocation requires notice to be given to the other party. Problems can occur, particularly in cases of fraudulent misrepresentation, where the representor has disappeared or cannot be traced. In such instances, the notice requirement will not be strictly enforced, where every attempt has been taken to recover the goods. This situation arose in *Car and Universal Finance Co Ltd v Caldwell*,[40] where a car owner had been induced to sell it to a fraudster who then re-sold it to a finance company and made off with the proceeds. The owner was thus unable to serve notice of revocation on the fraudster. The court held that the conduct of the owner, who had notified the police and the Automobile Association, was sufficient to amount to rescission in the circumstances, since the actions had taken place prior to the car being sold to the finance company. Consequently, the original owner was able to recover his car as good title had not passed to the finance company.

8.13 DAMAGES FOR MISREPRESENTATION

Historically, damages under common law were only available for claims in fraudulent misrepresentation through the tort of deceit. Whilst a contract induced by non-fraudulent misrepresentation could be rescinded in equity, there was no legal right to damages. It is still the case that damages are not available as of right for an innocent misrepresentation; but nowadays where there has been a negligent misrepresentation it is possible to acquire damages both for negligent misstatement and under the Misrepresentation Act 1967.

8.14 DAMAGES IN LIEU OF RESCISSION

Where a misrepresentation is non-fraudulent, s. 2(2) Misrepresentation Act 1967 provides the court with a discretion to declare a contract subsisting and award damages in lieu of rescission, if it is of the opinion that it would be equitable to do so having regard to the nature of the misrepresentation and the loss that would be caused if the contract were upheld. This provision allows the courts to advance a more proportionate remedy where a

39 [2000] 1 WLR 2333, [2000] CLC 735.
40 [1961] 1 QB 525.

misrepresentation is relatively minor and where the effect of rescission would be drastic in proportion to the impact of the misrepresentation. In addition, where a party is seeking to avoid a contract that has become less financially valuable, the courts have used the discretion to prevent rescission being used by a party to escape a bad bargain.[41] In addition, in *UCB Corporate Services v Thomason*,[42] on the basis that no losses had been incurred by the claimant, the remedy of rescission was denied.

8.15 DAMAGES IN TORT OF DECEIT

Under the tort of deceit, the level of damages awarded must compensate the claimant to the extent that he is put into the position he would have been in if the misrepresentation had not been made (known as reliance loss). The leading case, detailed earlier, is *Derry v Peek*.[43]

The case of *Doyle v Olby Ironmongers Ltd*[44] offers further clarity on the remoteness of damage rule. Put simply, all that the claimant must show is that the damage flowed from the deceit. The claimant may then recover all direct loss sustained as a result of the contract that was concluded as a result of the misrepresentation, regardless of whether the loss was foreseeable. The damages will include consequential losses, such as expenses incurred.

A calculation of damages under the tort of deceit is approached by an assessment of the difference between the actual amount paid and the real value of the contract at the time the contract was made. So, for example, if you are fraudulently induced into purchasing a diamond ring that is purported to be worth £5,000 and it later transpires to be worth only £2,000, your damages would be £3,000. *Doyle v Olby* was approved, and further clarification was provided in assessing the extent of the damages, in *Smith New Court Securities Ltd v Scrimgeour Vickers (Asset Management) Ltd*[45] where the court confirmed that the misrepresentor will be responsible for all losses resulting from the transaction. This will include sales expenses.[46] Additionally, in circumstances where losses continue to accrue after the transaction date, these can be claimed if they result from the misrepresentation. In *Man Nutfahrzeuge AG v Freighliner*,[47] subsequent losses that occurred as a result of running a business where the sale had been induced by fraudulent misrepresentation were recoverable.

The question of whether loss of profits could be recovered was considered in *East v Maurer*.

41 *William Sindall plc v Cambridgeshire County Council* [1994] 1 WLR 1016, [1994] 3 All ER 932, CA.
42 [2005] 1 All ER (Comm) 601.
43 (1889) 14 App Cas 337.
44 [1969] 2 QB 158, [1969] 2 WLR 673.
45 [1997] AC 254.
46 *East v Maurer* [1991] 1 WLR 461.
47 [2005] EWHC 2347 (Comm).

EAST V MAURER [1991] 1 WLR 461

The claimant, East, purchased a hair salon from Maurer. East was induced to enter into the agreement as a result of a representation made by Maurer that he would not run a competing hair salon. After the sale was complete, Maurer started to run a hair salon in direct competition with East. East suffered a loss in profits and sued Maurer under the tort of deceit.

Held: damages for loss of profits in a claim for fraudulent misrepresentation could be awarded on a tortious basis and the court can award damages to reflect the profits that would have been earned if the misrepresentation had not been made. In this instance, the Court of Appeal made an award on the probable profit that would have been made if the claimant had bought a different 'hypothetical' hair salon at the same price as the actual salon.

Recovery of such 'hypothetical lost profit' under fraudulent misrepresentation was also approved in *Smith New Court Securities Ltd v Scrimgeour Vickers (Asset Management) Ltd*, in which Lord Steyn gave clear guidance on how the test should be applied: 'The legal measure is to compare the position of the plaintiff as it was before the fraudulent statement was made to him with his position as it became as a result of his reliance on the fraudulent statement.' The approach was again used in *Parabola Investments Ltd v Browallia Cal Ltd*,[48] where the Court of Appeal awarded a sum to reflect lost profits even where the claimant was unable to identify a specific alternative contract that he could have secured, had it not been for the misrepresentation in the disputed contract. Again in *Clef Aquitaine sarl v Laporte Materials (Barrow) Ltd*,[49] lost profits were recoverable on the basis that if the fraudulent misrepresentation had not occurred, the claimant would have entered into an alternative more favourable contract with a third party.

Thus, in summary, it is clear that elements such as lost profits and lost opportunities do indeed fall within the acceptable measure of damages for fraudulent misrepresentation; that is, all damage flowing from the agreement.[50]

8.16 DAMAGES FOR NEGLIGENT MISSTATEMENT

Damages under this head are calculated on a tortious basis and the reasonable foreseeability test will apply.[51] In contrast to fraudulent misrepresentation, the damages will be restricted to those assessed at the date of the wrong. This rule is illustrated in the case of *South Australia*

---

48 [2010] EWCA Civ 486, [2011] QB 477.

49 [2001] QB 488.

50 *Smith New Court Securities Ltd v Scrimgeour Vickers (Asset Management) Ltd* [1997] AC 254.

51 *The Wagon Mound (No. 1)* [1961] AC 388.

Asset Management Corpn v York Montague Ltd[52] where money had been lent to property developers to buy properties when the property market was prosperous. The property market later collapsed and the borrowers were unable to pay back the money that had been lent to them. They argued that they had been induced to acquire the properties as a result of negligent valuations. Whilst the negligence was upheld, the House of Lords would only permit the losses that foreseeably flowed from the negligent valuations and not the losses that arose as a result of the property collapse.

8.17 DAMAGES UNDER THE MISREPRESENTATION ACT 1967

Damages for negligent misrepresentation can be awarded under s. 2(1) of the Misrepresentation Act 1967 (see Figure 8.4).

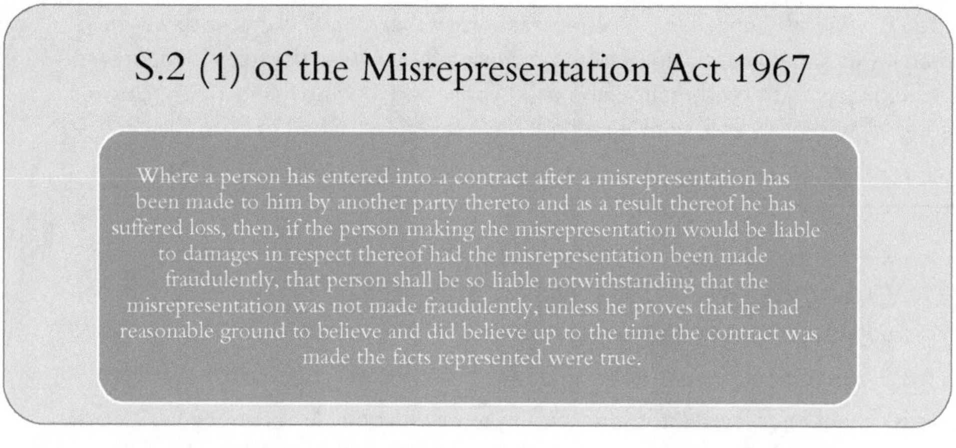

S.2 (1) of the Misrepresentation Act 1967

Where a person has entered into a contract after a misrepresentation has been made to him by another party thereto and as a result thereof he has suffered loss, then, if the person making the misrepresentation would be liable to damages in respect thereof had the misrepresentation been made fraudulently, that person shall be so liable notwithstanding that the misrepresentation was not made fraudulently, unless he proves that he had reasonable ground to believe and did believe up to the time the contract was made the facts represented were true.

Figure 8.4 Negligent Misrepresentation Act s.2(1)

The Act does not specify any particular test to be applied in assessing damages, but has been interpreted to impose liability for damages on the tortious basis. Indeed, in *Royscot Trust Ltd v Rogerson*[53] the Court of Appeal concluded that the same test of remoteness would apply in negligent misrepresentation as that approved for fraudulent misrepresentation, approved in the earlier case of *Doyle v Olby*.[54] You will recall that the damages here were assessed in the tort of deceit and were approved as including all losses flowing directly from the misrepresentation, with no limit as to foreseeability. It is important to recognise that losses for both fraudulent and negligent misrepresentation are quantified on the reliance loss basis not the expectation loss, the latter being the usual method for breach of contract.

---

52 [1996] 3 All ER 365.
53 [1991] 3 All ER 294, [1991] 2 WLR 57.
54 [1969] QB 158, [1969] 2 WLR 673.

Royscot concerned a misrepresentation made by a car dealer to a finance company with regard to the value of a car and the level of deposit made. When the purchaser of the car dishonestly sold it on to a third party, the finance company were able to recover the extra amount that they had been induced to pay as a result of the dealer's misrepresentation. The decision was based upon the 'fiction of fraud' whereby all losses flowing from a misrepresentation are recoverable, even where they are not foreseeable.

ANALYSING THE LAW

The judgment in *Royscot* effectively means that damages for honest, albeit negligent, misrepresentations are calculated in the same way as damages for fraudulent misrepresentations and all direct loss regardless of foreseeability can be claimed. A further implication of this ruling is that negligent misrepresentations under the 1967 Act are treated differently to common law negligent misstatements (*Hedley Byrne v Heller*), since damages under common law negligent misstatement must be a reasonably foreseeable consequence of the tort. The issue arose in *Yam Seng Pte Ltd v International Trade Corpn Ltd*[55] concerning a misrepresentation that a particular licence was held when it was not. Whilst acknowledging the disparity between the rules for fraudulent and negligent misrepresentation, the court confirmed that the ruling in *Royscot Trust* represented the law and, since it had not been overruled, it had to be applied.

8.18 DAMAGES FOR INNOCENT MISREPRESENTATION

Damages cannot be recovered for innocent misrepresentation. As mentioned earlier, the court can exercise its discretion and award damages in lieu of rescission under s. 2(2) of the Misrepresentation Act 1967 where rescission would be available. In *William Sindall v Cambridgeshire CC*[56] Lord Hoffmann stated that in order to exercise discretion under s. 2(2) of the Act, three factors needed to be considered to decide what is 'equitable' (see Figure 8.5).

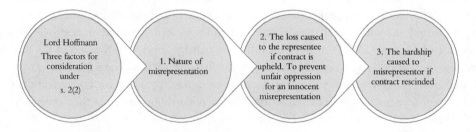

Figure 8.5 Lord Hoffmann: three factors for the exercise of discretion under s. 2(2)

55 [2013] EWHC 111 (QB), [2013] 1 CLC 662, [2013] 1 All ER (Comm) 1321.
56 [1994] 1 WLR 1016.

8.19 INDEMNITY

Whilst it is clear that damages cannot be awarded for an innocent misrepresentation, an indemnity can be granted to allow the recovery of any expenses incurred by the claimant, as a result of entering into the contract.

ASSESSMENT TIP

Do not confuse an indemnity award with an award for damages. The case of *Whittington v Seale-Hayne* is a good illustration of how the court awarded an indemnity where an innocent misrepresentation had taken place.

WHITTINGTON V SEALE-HAYNE [1900] 82 LT 49

A lease of a farm was taken on following assurances from the owner that the premises were in a sanitary condition. The buyer had leased the farm to breed poultry. Shortly after he took up occupation, the manager of the business became ill and some of the poultry died. It transpired that the water supply was contaminated.

Held: the court held that there had been an innocent misrepresentation. There was no right to damages but the court did grant an ancillary order for an indemnity to reflect the losses from wasted expenditure incurred by the poultry business owner.

APPLYING THE LAW

Let us consider a scenario whereby a leisure club agrees to rent out its swimming pool to a keep fit instructor who wishes to hold aqua aerobic classes. The instructor is mistakenly told by an employee that the pool's greatest depth is 2.8 metres. The instructor agrees a contract of hire for six months and spends a sum of £500 advertising the classes. On the evening of the first class it transpires that the pool's greatest depth is 2.3 metres. This is no good for the instructor who needs a minimum depth of 2.5 metres for health and safety reasons (and one of the participants is the local authority health and safety inspector!). All of the routines and activities had been based upon having water deeper than 2.5 metres, as the routine is based around diving in before each new activity. The instructor is unable to put on the classes and seeks to cancel the contract. Whilst the leisure club accepts the cancellation without argument, and acknowledges the breach on its behalf, it is refusing to compensate the instructor for her loss of earnings from the failed venture and for the cost of advertising and specialist equipment that had been purchased especially for the classes. It transpires that the pool depth had been incorrectly marked and the owner of the leisure club had purchased the pool having inspected it (and seen the measurement marker) and having referred to its construction plans, which stated that its maximum depth was 2.8 metres. What type of misrepresentation do you think might have occurred here?

It may be negligent misrepresentation, but if the court is convinced that the leisure club had reasonable grounds for believing that their statement regarding the depth of the pool was correct, we are left with an innocent misrepresentation for which damages are not available as of right.

In such an instance, it would be open to the court to consider an indemnity award. If the court were to do this, which costs and expenses do you think would be recoverable? The lost profit? The cost of advertising? The wasted expenditure on specialised equipment? Refer back to *Whittington v Seale-Hayne* again if you are unsure.

8.20 MITIGATION

There is a duty upon a misrepresentee to mitigate any losses incurred, to minimise the amount of the loss suffered. The test is the same as that applied in cases where a breach of contract has occurred (see later chapter on remedies for breach of contract). A claimant need not go to great extremes, but must be able to demonstrate that s/he has taken reasonable steps to mitigate any losses incurred. In *Downs v Chappell*[57] the claimant's damages were limited as he had refused two offers to purchase his business, which were higher than the price finally achieved.

8.21 CONTRIBUTORY NEGLIGENCE

Contributory negligence will be discussed in greater detail when remedies are covered in a later chapter, but it should be noted here that damages in misrepresentation can be reduced where a claimant has contributed to the harm they have suffered through their own negligence, although the defence will not be available where a fraudulent misrepresentation has occurred. This was confirmed in the case of *Standard Chartered Bank v Pakistan National Shipping Corpn (No. 2)*.[58]

---

57 [1997] 1 WLR 461.
58 [2002] UKHL 43, [2003] 1 AC 959 (HL).

8.22 EXCLUSION OF LIABILITY FOR MISREPRESENTATION

It is pertinent to link back to the earlier chapter on exclusion clauses at this point. Whilst exclusion for liability for misrepresentation was discussed, we should just remind ourselves that liability for fraudulent misrepresentation can never be excluded.[59] The Misrepresentation Act 1967, s. 3, substituted by s. 11 (1) of the Unfair Contract Terms Act 1977, does however permit a party in a business to business contract to exclude liability for a negligent misrepresentation where it can satisfy the test of reasonableness.

8.23 SUMMARY – CHARACTERISTICS AND REMEDIES

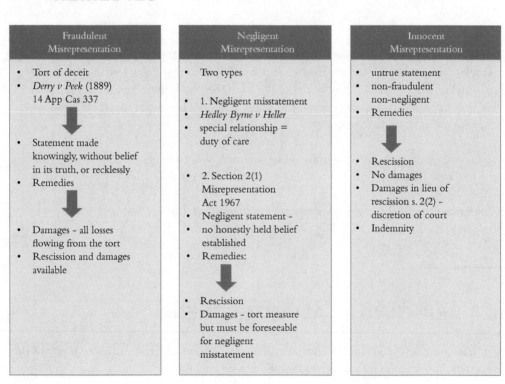

Fraudulent Misrepresentation	Negligent Misrepresentation	Innocent Misrepresentation
• Tort of deceit • *Derry v Peek* (1889) 14 App Cas 337 ⬇ • Statement made knowingly, without belief in its truth, or recklessly • Remedies ⬇ • Damages - all losses flowing from the tort • Rescission and damages available	• Two types • 1. Negligent misstatement • *Hedley Byrne v Heller* • special relationship = duty of care • 2. Section 2(1) Misrepresentation Act 1967 • Negligent statement - no honestly held belief established • Remedies: ⬇ • Rescission • Damages - tort measure but must be foreseeable for negligent misstatement	• untrue statement • non-fraudulent • non-negligent • Remedies ⬇ • Rescission • No damages • Damages in lieu of rescission s. 2(2) - discretion of court • Indemnity

Figure 8.6 Remedies

---

59 *HIH Casualty and General Insurance Co Ltd v Chase Manhattan Bank* [2003] UKHL 6, [2003] 1 All ER (Comm) 349, [2003] 2 Lloyd's Rep 61.

PUTTING IT INTO PRACTICE

APPLYING THE LAW

Imagine you are acting on behalf of a client who has entered into a contract to purchase some shares in a company as part of a share issue. Consider the effect upon the contract if any of the following has happened:

- The profits of the company are presented accurately but without comment, and in a format only understandable by qualified accountants
- Assurances are made by the directors of what they intend to spend the money raised from selling shares upon
- The company very publicly begin negotiations with a company specialising in refurbishment of business premises, creating the impression that this is what they will spend the share money on, but after the share issue decide not to go ahead with this

With regard to the above, you would need to examine whether any of this behaviour is making a misrepresentation, whether it is through what they have said (e.g. the information about the profits information) or what they have done (e.g. through the very public negotiations with the refurbishment company), in order to decide whether they are misrepresentations or not.

If you decide that a misrepresentation has occurred, what category would you place the misrepresentation within and what remedies would be available?

Guidance to answering this question can be taken from the key learning points below.

8.24 BRINGING IT ALL TOGETHER

As we have seen, it is important to take note of all elements of misrepresentation. If any of the elements are missing, the misrepresentation will not be established.

Once a misrepresentation has been established it is important to decide which category the misrepresentation falls within, as this will have an impact on the level and burden of proof necessary to establish a successful claim and the remedies available to the misrepresentee.

KEY LEARNING POINTS

Remember that you should consider the following in deciding whether there has been a misrepresentation or not:

- Is the information or impression given by the other party **false**?
- Has it come through a **statement or conduct** of the other party?
- Is it current **fact**?
- Has the other party been **induced** into entering into the contract by it?

Each of these elements must be present in order to establish that what you have is a misrepresentation.

You must then decide upon which type of misrepresentation the claim will be based:

- Fraudulent misrepresentation
- Negligent misstatement
- Negligent misrepresentation
- Innocent misrepresentation

The above may be informed by the type of remedy the claimant is seeking to secure.

Remember damages cannot be claimed under innocent misrepresentation. A claim under negligent misrepresentation is easier to establish than under fraudulent misrepresentation and the remedies are, in reality, the same.

TAKING IT FURTHER

Beale, 'Damages in lieu of Rescission for Misrepresentation' (1995) 111 LQR 60

Bigwood, 'Pre-Contractual Misrepresentation and the limits of the principle in *With v O'Flanagan*' [2005] Cambridge Law Review 94

Carter, 'Good Faith in Contracts: Is There an Implied Promise to Act Honestly?' (2016) 75 Cambridge Law Journal 608

Furmston, *Cheshire, Fifoot and Furmston's Law of Contract*, 16th edn, Oxford University Press, 2012

Hare, 'Further twists and turns in the labyrinth of statutory liability for misrepresentation' (2017) 9 JIBFL 535

Treitel, *The Law of Contract*, 14th edn, Sweet & Maxwell, 2015

9

CHAPTER 9
MISTAKE

AS YOU READ

At the end of this chapter you should be able to:

- Identify the existence of an operative mistake by the components of its definition
- Identify the type of mistake applicable in a particular set of circumstances
- Explain the effect of a finding of mistake upon an agreement
- Understand the limited circumstances where a mistake will be recognised in equity

_____

9.1 THE DOCTRINE OF MISTAKE

This chapter looks at the doctrine of mistake, a further vitiating factor in contract law. A finding of mistake can impact upon the enforceability of a contract if either or both of the parties have entered into an agreement under some form of misunderstanding. The first point to note is that a mistake will only affect the validity of a contract in very exceptional circumstances. It is not enough to simply say that you have made a mistake in entering into a transaction and now wish to rescind the contract. Nor can a contract be avoided on the grounds that you have entered into a bad bargain. Thus, if an individual agreed to buy a house from a vendor, unaware that a factory unit is set to be built to the rear of the property which will block the idyllic views, even though the vendor may be aware of this fact and the buyer is not, the buyer cannot escape from the contract on the grounds of mistake.

EXPLAINING THE LAW

The recognised grounds of mistake are limited for good reason. The law must maintain certainty and consistency in the commercial world. The attitude of the judiciary tends to favour non-interference where parties have freely entered into an agreement and have drafted their own terms. It would create great uncertainty and unfairness if the parties could later argue that they were not contractually bound because they had made a mistake. Contracts can be drafted to anticipate factors that might unfold after the contract has been agreed and, before declaring a contract is void for mistake, the courts will ensure that there is not a clause drafted into the contract to deal with any such factors. Notwithstanding the narrow approach taken, it is vital that a mechanism does exist to protect parties where an operative mistake has occurred.

KEY DEFINITION: OPERATIVE MISTAKE

A mistake in a contract that is serious enough to render the contract void and unenforceable.

KEY DEFINITION: VOID AB INITIO

Of no use, or worthless, as if the agreement never existed.

The reason for the strict approach in finding an operative mistake in contract law is that the impact can be significant. In contrast to a finding of misrepresentation, which will render a contract voidable (the contract exists and is valid until such time as the innocent party takes action to set the contract aside), where an operative mistake is found to exist at common law, the mistake will render a contract **void ab initio**. Put simply, this means that the contract will be treated as though it never existed at common law. Such an outcome can have a significant impact upon third parties, as a void agreement cannot confer any rights upon a third party. This rule is sometimes referred to by the Latin term *nemo dat quod non habet* – no-one can transfer ownership of something they do not own.

To illustrate this point, X sold goods to Y on credit under a contract. The goods are then sold on to Z but afterwards the contract between X and Y is declared void. The result will be that Y will not have obtained any title to the goods and, as such, no title will have passed to Z, who may have acted in good faith. Z will be obliged to return to goods to X. In contrast, if the contract had been voidable for misrepresentation, good title can pass to a party provided it has done so before the contract is rescinded by the original party. Using the same illustration, note the different outcome. X sold goods to Y on credit under a contract. The goods are then sold on to Z but afterwards the contract between X and Y is found to be voidable for misrepresentation. The result will be that Y will have obtained good title to the goods prior to the contract being held voidable. Following on, provided that title to the goods passed to Z before the contract was rescinded, Z will have obtained good title and is not obliged to return the goods to X.

9.2 DEFINITION AND COMPONENTS

For a mistake to be operative and result in a contract being void, a mistake must be one that exists at the time the contract is formed.[1] A mistake that is recognisable at common law will fall into one of three categories (see Figure 9.1).

---

1   *Amalgamated Investment and Property Co Ltd v John Walker & Sons Ltd* [1977] 1 WLR 164.

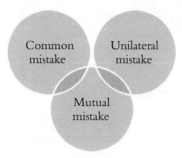

Figure 9.1 Categories of operative mistake

A common mistake will arise where both parties have made the same mistake. Both are mistaken about a primary fact that is pivotal to the contract. It could be a mistake regarding the existence of the subject matter of the contract, the quality of the subject matter of the contract, or of title to the goods. Where a mistake is found to be operative, any consent that had existed will be cancelled out. A mutual mistake will arise when the parties are at cross-purposes and a unilateral mistake occurs when only one of the parties is mistaken but the other knows of the mistake. Both a mutual and a unilateral mistake will negative any consent previously given. Let us explore these categories of mistake in more detail.

9.3 COMMON MISTAKE

As mentioned above, a common mistake will be operative where both parties have made the same mistake. The parties may have believed that a certain state of affairs existed, but which later transpired to be non-existent. If unbeknown to both of the parties a fact upon which an agreement was based ceased to exist before the agreement was made, or never existed at all at the time the agreement was made, the agreement will be void

9.3.1 MISTAKE AS TO THE EXISTENCE OF THE SUBJECT MATTER (*RES EXTINCTA*)

Where the subject matter of a contract has ceased to exist at the time the contract was agreed, a contract will be void. The common law position is supplemented by the Sale of Goods Act 1979, s. 6, which states:

a contract will be void where there is a contract for the sale of specific goods, and the goods without the knowledge of the seller have perished at the time when the contract was made.

ESSENTIAL DEFINITION: *RES EXTINCTA*

The subject matter of a contract no longer exists.

Although mistake is not mentioned in the following case, it is generally accepted that the above principle is demonstrated in *Couturier v Hastie*.

COUTURIER V HASTIE (1856) HL CAS 673

The contract concerned a cargo of corn that was understood to be in transit (by sea) to the UK when the agreement was made. Unbeknown to the parties, the corn had started to deteriorate during the journey and had been sold en route to a buyer in Tunisia.

Held: the absence of the anticipated subject matter had the effect of stripping away the content of the contract, and consequently the contract was deemed to have never been formed. Mistake was not actually mentioned in the judgement but this case tends to provide authority for the fact that where the parties are mistaken in relation to the existence of the subject matter of a contract it will be void.

Where the subject matter of a contract is found to be non-existent, it is important to determine whether or not existence of the subject matter was guaranteed by one of the parties, or whether the agreement made was merely providing a 'chance' to acquire something. If the subject matter was guaranteed, the contract will not be void if the subject matter transpires to be non-existent; the contract will be very much alive and the party that guaranteed existence will be in breach of contract. For example, in *McRae v Commonwealth Disposals Commission*,[2] it was found that the seller had guaranteed the existence of the subject matter of the contract.

MCRAE V COMMONWEALTH DISPOSALS COMMISSION (1950) 84 CLR 377, HC AUS

The Disposal Commission put out a call for tenders for the purchase of an oil tanker lying on Jourmaund Reef approximately 100 miles from the island of Samarai, near Papua New Guinea. The plaintiffs won the tender but it later transpired that the tanker did not exist and there was no place known as Jourmaund Reef. The plaintiff had gone to considerable expense in setting up a salvage expedition.

Held: the High Court of Australia awarded damages to the plaintiff. At first glance, the decision appears to go against the principles derived from *Couturier v Hastie*, which you will recall dictate that where the subject matter is non-existent at the time of the contract, it will be void. However, in this case, in placing significant weight on the construction of the contract the court found there to be an implied promise by the vendors that the tank existed. The court based its approach on its finding that

---

2   (1950) 84 CLR 377, HC Aus.

the Commission had been reckless in asserting that the tanker existed, without being able to show any reasonable grounds to substantiate its existence. Consequently, the contract was declared valid and the Commission was found in breach of contract and liable for damages.

The deliberations in this case tie in neatly with the criteria laid down by Lord Phillips in *Great Peace Shipping Ltd v Tsavliris Salvage (International) Ltd,*[3] and indeed *McRae* was discussed and endorsed. The *Great Peace* case is discussed in more detail later in this chapter.

ASSESSMENT TIP

Construction of the contract – did one side bear the risk?

When considering issues pertaining to common mistake, it is essential that you look at the construction of the contract as a whole and, if the terms of the contract appear to put the risk of a mistake on either of the parties, it is unlikely that an argument for common mistake will be upheld. Any non-delivery or non-performance will rest with the party who has borne the risk, either expressly or by implication from the actions of the parties or statements made in their negotiations.

9.4 MAKING CONNECTIONS

At this point it is worth noting the close connection of this area of law with that of **frustration of contract**, which will be considered later in the book when looking at the topic of discharge of contract. The issue as to whether there will be a finding of mistake, or whether a contract may be frustrated, will often boil down to the timing of the agreement and the position regarding the subject matter at the time the agreement is made.

ESSENTIAL DEFINITION: FRUSTRATION OF CONTRACT

A contract law doctrine that acts as a mechanism to set aside a contract where an unforeseen event renders contractual obligations impossible, or radically changes the party's main purpose for entering into the contract.

3   [2002] EWCA, Civ 1407, [2003] QB 679.

APPLYING THE LAW

If I hire the village hall on a Monday for a birthday party to take place in two weeks' time and the council official confirms the booking but, unbeknown to us both when the booking is taken, the village hall burnt down the day before I made the booking, it is likely that the contract will be void for common mistake. On the other hand, taking the same circumstances with regard to the booking, only changing the fact that the village hall burnt down the day after I made the booking, it is unlikely that the contract will be void under common law, but the doctrine of frustration will come into play. In essence, frustration can come into effect when an event occurs after a contract has been agreed, and the occurrence of the event has made the contract impossible to perform.[4] Frustration will discharge any future obligations that the parties have to each other under the agreement.

9.5 MISTAKE AS TO TITLE (*RES SUA*)

This area of mistake is less complex. A mistake in title will occur when, unbeknown to both of the parties, the buyer already owns the item that the seller is trying to sell to him. This type of transaction cannot succeed. The case of *Cooper v Phibbs* illustrates this point.

COOPER V PHIBBS (1867) LR 2 HL 149

An agreement to lease a fishery for three years was completed between Cooper and Phibbs. It subsequently transpired that Cooper, the purchaser, already owned the fishery at the time of the agreement.

The court granted rescission of the contract, but granted a lien to Phibbs in lieu of improvements made to the property. It was in a later case[5] that the case was considered to be void under the common law head of mistake as to title.

9.6 MISTAKE AS TO THE QUALITY OF THE SUBJECT MATTER

The fact that the subject matter of a contract is different in quality to that which has been agreed will not in itself be grounds for a contract to be found void. The court will not

---

4 *Taylor v Caldwell* (1863) 3 B & S 826, 122 ER 309.
5 *Bell v Lever Bros* [1932] AC 161.

protect parties to a contract from a bad bargain – the classical approach to contract law can be observed intact in this area and the principle of ***caveat emptor*** is still very much a live factor to be taken on board when considering contractual disputes.

The case of *Smith v Hughes* provides a good example of a dispute on quality.

SMITH V HUGHES (1871) LR 6QB 597

In this case, Smith showed Hughes a sample of oats and Hughes placed an order of oats as feed for his horses. The order arrived, but Hughes was not happy with the goods as he stated that the oats were new oats and he needed old oats, the latter being the only type that his horses could eat. Smith denied that any conversation had taken place with regard to the type of oats.

Held: the trial judge found in favour of Hughes, the purchaser. The case was appealed and the Court of Appeal found in favour of Smith on the basis that the mistake did not relate to the fundamental terms of the contract but to the quality of the product.

It is clear from cases such as *Smith v Hughes* that a mistake as to quality will not be operative; however, it is important to note that if the mistake is made by both parties and is such as to 'render the contract essentially and radically different from the subject matter which the parties believed to exist'[6] it will be operative and the contract will be void. An example would be a contract between two people for the sale of a painting where both parties believe it has been painted by a specific artist. The fact that a mistake has occurred in relation to the authenticity of the artist would not be sufficient to render the contract void at common law. Why not? If we look at the case of *Bell v Lever Bros*[7] Lord Atkin used the example of a painting to explain this important principle of law:

> A buys a picture from B; both A and B believe it to be the work of an old master, and a high price is paid. It turns out to be a modern copy. A would never have entered into the bargain if he had known the fact. A has no remedy, and the position is the same whether B knew the facts or not, so long as he made no representation or gave no warranty.

EXPLAINING THE LAW

The reason that the mistake would not be operative if it related to the artist is because the courts would look at the essence of the contract. Where an agreement to purchase a painting had been made, the first question that would arise would be: What is the contract for? The answer is; a painting. The next question would be:

---

6   Per Lord Steyn *Associated Japanese Bank (International) Ltd v Credit du Nord SA* [1988] 3 All ER 902.
7   [1932] AC 161.

Did the parties get a painting? The answer of course is, yes they did. But the third question would be: What about the mistake in relation to the artist? The answer would be that the mistake related to the 'quality' of the subject matter of the contract, i.e. the identity of the artist, and not the subject of the contract itself; the painting. If the facts are changed slightly, and one of the parties had guaranteed the authenticity of the artist, the conclusion would be different and a claim for mistake would probably succeed, since the very essence of the contract would be for a painting with a guarantee that it had been painted by a particular artist.

The case of *Leaf v International Galleries*[8] consisted of similar facts to the example given by Lord Atkin above in *Bell v Lever Bros*. The parties contracted for the sale and purchase of a picture that they both believed to be by Constable. The case was based on misrepresentation and mistake. The claim based on mistake was unsuccessful as the mistake related to the quality and did not render the subject matter something essentially different from that which it was believed to be. The claimant believed he was buying a painting and that is what he got. The judgment is not without criticism and this area has been the subject of debate in many later cases.

Bell v Lever Bros is generally regarded as the leading precedent in the area of mistake as to quality and the outcome of this case provides a key test on issue of mistake as to quality.

BELL V LEVER BROS [1932] AC 161

The appellants were chairmen of a subsidiary company of Lever Bros and were employed on a fixed-term contract. Following a decision to amalgamate the subsidiary with another company, the services of the appellants were no longer required but a lengthy period remained on their contracts. Lever Bros agreed to pay the appellants a sizeable amount of compensation for an early termination of contract. It later transpired that Lever Bros could have legitimately terminated the contracts without the need to pay compensation, due to irregular conduct. Lever Bros argued that the contracts were void on the basis of fundamentally mistaken belief on all sides.

Held: the House of Lords held that Lever Bros got what they bargained for, namely a severance agreement. Their mistake was with regard to the quality of the subject matter. Lord Aitken was clear that 'mistake will not affect assent unless it is the mistake of both parties, and is as to the existence of some quality which makes the thing without the quality essentially different from the thing it was believed to be'. Consequently the contract was found to be valid and the directors were entitled to their compensation.

8 [1950] 2 KB 86.

It is clear from the judgment above that in order for a contract to be set aside on the grounds of common mistake on quality of subject matter, the mistake must be fundamental. The main difficulty in successfully arguing that an operative mistake has occurred is being able to show that the mistake as to quality is sufficiently significant to render it fundamental. It is far easier to show that the non-existence of the subject matter of a contract was fundamental to an agreement than it is to show the mistake in relation to the quality of the subject matter of a contract is fundamental.

EXPLAINING THE LAW – QUALITY OF THE SUBJECT MATTER
OF A CONTRACT AND ITS POSITION RELATING TO A MISTAKE

From our analysis of the cases so far, it is clear that the courts will not entertain a claim in mistake unless the mistake is of material significance and goes to the root of the contract. The mistake must relate to 'an essential and integral part of the subject matter'.[9] It must relate to a term of the contract rather than an expectation of the quality. If a mistake merely affects the quality of a deal, it will not be upheld unless it can be shown that the mistake is sufficiently **fundamental** to render the subject matter fundamentally different to what the parties had agreed. For example, if I purchased a grandfather clock from an antique shop and I later found out it no longer kept accurate time. I wanted to buy an antique clock that was a good time-keeper but I did not at any point make my requirements known to the shopkeeper. Provided that there had not been any misrepresentation, or any guarantee given that the clock did keep good time, this contract could not be held void for mistake as the mistake would be with regard to the 'quality' of the clock rather than the fact that the item being purchased was indeed a grandfather clock.

The debate was further prolonged in the case of *Associated Japanese Bank (International) Ltd v Credit du Nord SA*.

ASSOCIATED JAPANESE BANK (INTERNATIONAL) LTD V CREDIT DU NORD SA [1988] 3 ALL ER 902

A fraudster named Jack Bennett entered into a sale and lease-back agreement for some machines with a bank. Before agreeing to the deal, the bank required a guarantor and an agreement was entered into with the defendant company. It later transpired that the machines did not exist, at which point it was discovered that Jack Bennett had disappeared with the payment from the bank. At this point the bank tried to rely on the guarantor agreement. The guarantors argued that the guarantee

---

9   Ibid per Lord Tankerton.

agreement was void on the basis that it was based on four specific machines which both parties believed to exist when the agreement was made, but in fact did not exist.

Held: Steyn J found that the contract should be void on the basis that the subject matter of the guarantee was 'essentially different from what it was reasonably believed to be' per Lord Atkins earlier judgment.[10] He stated that the subject matter of the guarantee was 'essentially different from what it was reasonably believed to be' and that 'the guarantee of obligations under a lease with non-existent machines was essentially different from a guarantee of a lease with four machines'. Steyn also made it clear that a party who seeks to rely on a mistake must show reasonable grounds for his/her belief that amounted to the mistake.

The later case of *Great Peace Shipping Ltd v Tsavliris Salvage (International) Ltd*[11] approved the judgment in *Associated Japanese Bank* and revisited the issue of when a mistake as to quality will be fundamental.

GREAT PEACE SHIPPING LTD V TSAVLIRIS SALVAGE (INTERNATIONAL) LTD [2002] 4 ALL ER 689

The ship owners of the vessel *Cape Providence* engaged the defendant salvage company to rescue their vessel, which had been damaged and was in danger of sinking in the South Indian Ocean. The defendants asked their brokers to find a ship close to Cape Providence to assist with a rescue mission. The brokers asked a reputable company to advise and were told that the *Great Peace* was the nearest ship and within 12 hours sailing distance of Cape Providence. On the basis of this information, which turned out to be inaccurate, the defendants contracted to hire the vessel for five days. However, after the hire was agreed, it transpired that the *Great Peace* was, in fact, several hundred miles from Cape Providence. Upon realising this, the defendants cancelled the hire arguing that the contract was void at common law for mistake.

Held: the question to be answered by the Court of Appeal was whether the mistake as to the distance between the vessels rendered the services to be provided by *Great Peace* as essentially different to the services that the parties had agreed. Remember the agreement was for the charter of a ship; the claimants were not asked to guarantee any distances between the ships. Following the line of precedent adopted in the earlier judgements in *Bell v Lever Bros* and *Associated Japanese Bank*, the Court of Appeal found that the mistake concerning the distance between the two vessels did

---

10 *Bell v Lever Bros* [1932] AC 161.
11 [2002] 4 All ER 689.

not render the services that were to be provided to be essentially different to those that the parties had agreed. The mistake, in their view, was not fundamental and did not relate to a 'vital element'.[12] Additionally, the mistake was that of one party only, whereas it is clear from *Bell v Lever Bros* that the mistake must be one that both parties have made.

Again in *Kyle Bay Ltd (t/a Astons Nightclub) v Underwriters*[13] the parties entered into a compromise agreement due to the fact that they had been told that their insurance did not cover certain elements of a claim that they had made. It later transpired that the correct insurance had been in place, which meant that they would have been entitled to a greater settlement, but for the compromise agreement and settlement agreement. The courts held the agreement was not void, as the wrongly assumed part of the agreement was the result of a detail and not something that went to the root of the agreement or was sufficiently fundamental to render the compromise radically or essentially different from what the parties anticipated.

9.7 MISTAKE AS TO QUALITY – THE POSITION IN EQUITY

Much debate has centred on whether a remedy for common mistake might be applied where third party interests are not affected. If a contract were voidable rather than void, it could achieve this effect. In *Solle v Butcher*[14] the court sought to distinguish *Bell v Lever Bros*, not on the determination of mistake at common law, but on the basis that *Bell* did not consider the doctrine of mistake in equity. Lord Denning introduced this concept in *Solle v Butcher*.

SOLLE V BUTCHER [1950] 1 KB 671

The agreement in this case involved a lease agreement for a seven-year period at a rent of £250 per annum. This figure was agreed on the understanding of both parties that the property was not subject to rent control under the Rent Acts. The plaintiff later found out that the property was subject to rent control and the rent payable should have been only £140 per annum. Notwithstanding this point, if the defendant had served notice, the rent could have been increased to £250 taking into account rent and improvements on the property. The plaintiff tried to recover the overpaid rent for

---

12 Ibid per Lord Phillips.
13 [2007] EWCA 57.
14 [1950] 1 KB 671.

a two-year period and sought a declaration from the court that he could remain in occupation for the remainder of the lease for a rent of £140 per annum. The defendant asked the court to set aside the lease for mistake.

Held: the Court of Appeal allowed the plaintiff to choose between surrendering the lease and paying the full amount of rent once the required notices had been served. This more or less amounted to the agreement that had been made between the parties.

In his deliberations Lord Denning referred to a doctrine of equity, by which a contract may be set aside on the basis of common mistake, including where the mistake is one as to quality. This position was applied in several decisions after this case,[15] and was recognised by Steyn J in *Associated Japanese Bank (International) Ltd v Credit du Nord*[16] as supplementing the narrow doctrine of common law mistake with a more flexible approach, and mitigating the harsh approach at common law, which to him seemed to be 'an entirely sensible and satisfactory state of the law'.[17] The difficulty that this posed was how one could draw a distinction between an instance where a mistake would be insufficiently fundamental to make the contract void at common law yet be sufficiently fundamental in equity for it to be set aside.

The need to get around this difficulty has been somewhat averted since the case of *Great Peace Shipping Ltd v Tsavliris (International) Ltd*.[18] The facts of the case were discussed earlier; however an alternative argument was put forward by the salvage company that if the contract was not void at common law it should be voidable in equity. The Court of Appeal rejected this argument and held that Lord Denning's approach in *Solle v Butcher* had not been to mitigate the common law; moreover it was to make the point that *Bell v Lever Bros* was wrongly decided. In conclusion, Lord Phillips stated that there was only one category of fundamental mistake. *Pitt v Holt*[19] also concurred that the ruling in *Great Peace* had overruled *Solle v Butcher* and the equitable doctrine of mistake.

To conclude, the denial of equity in the area of mistake does mean that scope for common mistake is extremely limited; a contract will either be void or valid and the criteria to render the contract void at common law is strict.

ASSESSMENT TIP

In *Great Peace*, Lord Phillips MR provided a useful and concise statement on the elements required for a common mistake to be upheld. If you are faced with an issue

---

15 *Grist v Bailey* [1967] Ch 532; *Magee v Pennine Insurance Co Ltd* [1969] 2 QB 507.
16 [1989] 1 WLR 255.
17 Ibid.
18 [2002] EWCA Civ 1407, [2003] QB 679.
19 [2013] UKSC 26, [2013] 2 AC 108.

on whether a contract will be void for mistake as to quality, it may be useful to apply the following criteria, drawn from Lord Phillips' statement and reproduced below to aid analysis and application in this somewhat tricky area. All of the criteria must be met for a mistake of this nature to be operative:

- There must be a common assumption as to the existence of a state of affairs
- There must be no warranty by either party that that state of affairs exists (this is very important)
- The non-existence of the state of affairs must not be attributable to the fault of either party
- The non-existence of the state of affairs must render performance of the contract impossible
- The state of affairs may be the existence, or a vital attribute, of the consideration to be provided or circumstances that must subsist if performance of the contractual adventure is to be possible

The second and third point above can be linked back to the case of *McRae v Commonwealth Disposals Commission*. In deciding whether or not a mistake can be operative, it is important that there must not be fault on either side, nor must there have been a warranty supplied by one of the parties to support their terms of contract. If either of these factors are present, there is likely to be a valid contract of which a breach will have occurred. In *McRae*, the other party had been told that a tanker existed on a named reef, and this belief had been induced by the Disposals Commission, which were at fault, as they did not know whether or not the statement was true. Additionally, where one of the parties has assumed responsibility for the risk that it may not be possible to perform the contract, it is again not possible to rely on common mistake.

Let us put some of these rules into context.

APPLYING THE LAW

Andrew entered into a contract with William for the purchase of a manuscript of a poem by Wordsworth, which they both believed to be in his handwriting. It was later discovered that, although the poem was written by Wordsworth, it had been written down by a contemporary of Wordsworth and was of little value. Advise Andrew.

- In advising Andrew, you would need to commence by stating that very few mistakes are recognised at common law.
- Move on to explain why: the reason is because the law would become uncertain if a party could withdraw from a contract because he had made a mistake.

- Now proceed with an explanation of the recognised exceptions to the rule – When will a mistake be recognised? Explain what is meant by an 'operative' mistake.
- After defining an operative mistake, drill down and analyse. Show that you can identify what type of mistake this might be. Hopefully you will have identified that the mistake here is an example of a common mistake; both parties are mistaken about the same point. You should then look at the precedent and guidance that exists in this area.
- We can see that the problem concerns the 'quality' of the subject matter of the contract. *Bell v Lever Bros* is a good starting point here. The precedent established in this case is that a mistake will not affect assent unless the mistake is fundamental and concerns the existence of some quality, which makes the thing without the quality essentially different from the thing it was believed to be.
- Support your statements by bringing in further case law. Mention the case of *Leaf v International Galleries* to emphasise the rule in operation. Explain what happened. The case involved a painting that was believed by both buyer and seller to be a Constable, but later turned out to be a copy. Explain why the court held the contract was not void for mistake. This was due to the court asking the essential question as to what was the contract for. It was of course for a painting of Salisbury Cathedral. It then turned its attention to what the parties got – they got a painting of Salisbury Cathedral. They contracted for a painting and got a painting. The painting was the subject matter of the contract and, indeed, did exist. The fact that it was not a genuine Constable was irrelevant, as it was the painting itself that was the subject of the contract, and the painting did exist.
- Compare with *Associated Japanese Bank ltd v Credit Du Nord*, which involved a guarantee in respect of some gaming machines. The machines were found not to exist, and so the guarantee was worthless. The court held that a guarantee concerning non-existent machines was essentially different from a guarantee concerning machines that both parties believe to exist. Look at *Great Peace Shipping Ltd v Tsavliris Salvage (International) Ltd*: this case provides a wealth of guidance and legal analysis in this area
- Apply the law to the problem: The circumstances in this case are analogous to those pertaining in the *Leaf v International Galleries* case. The parties had got what they bargained for – the manuscript of a poem by Wordsworth – just a bad bargain and of less value because it was not written down by him.

9.8 MUTUAL MISTAKE

A mistake will be classified as a mutual mistake when it can be shown that the parties to an agreement are at cross-purposes. For example, A thinks he is selling his Vauxhall Astra to B, whereas B thinks he is buying A's Ford Fiesta. In making a judgement in such areas, the courts adopt an objective test in an attempt to ascertain not what was in the minds of the parties, but instead the conclusion that the reasonable person would have reached, having witnessed their words and conduct. The reasonable person would need to consider whether an agreement had been made on A's terms, or on B's terms or, if unable to do so, the reasonable person may conclude that it is not possible to reach a logical conclusion. If the reasonable person would conclude that a contract had come into existence, notwithstanding the mistake, the court will uphold the contract.

In *Smith v Hughes*,[20] Blackburn J summarised the position:

> if whatever a man's real intention may be, he so conducts himself that a reasonable man would believe that he was assenting to the terms proposed by the other party, and that other party upon that belief enters into the contract with him, the man thus conducting himself would be equally bound as if he had intended to agree to the other party's terms.

The case of *Scriven Bros & Co v Hindley & Co*[21] provides a good example of a mistake that was upheld on the basis that the court could not affirm which product formed the subject of the contract.

SCRIVEN BROS & CO V HINDLEY & CO (1913) 3 KB 564

The defendants made a bid at an auction for two lots, on the understanding that both lots were hemp (a type of plant). It transpired that lot A was hemp but lot B was tow (a different product of a much lesser value than hemp). Having realised their error, the defendants refused to pay for lot B and the sellers sued for the contract price. The defendants' mistake arose from the fact that both lots contained the same shipping mark, but the defendants' manager had been shown bales of hemp as samples of the goods. The auctioneer believed that the bid was made under a mistake as to the value of the tow.

Held: it was clear that the plaintiffs intended to sell tow and the defendants intended to buy hemp. The problem lay in the fact that the plaintiffs did not know that the defendants wished only to buy hemp. Due to the ambiguity of the circumstances, the court was unable to determine the sense of the promise and the contract was held void for mistake.

Another leading case in the area of mutual mistake is *Raffles v Wichelhaus*.

---

20 (1871) LR 6 QB 597.
21 (1913) 3 KB 564.

RAFFLES V WICHELHAUS (1864) 2 H&C 906

The plaintiff agreed to sell cotton to the defendant which was 'to arrive ex Peerless from Bombay'. When the cotton arrived, the plaintiff offered to deliver but the defendants refused to accept the cotton. The defendant argued that the ship in question was believed to be the ship called the *Peerless*, which sailed from Bombay in October and that the plaintiff had not offered to deliver cotton which arrived by that ship, but instead offered to deliver cotton which arrived by another ship, also called *Peerless*, which sailed from Bombay in December.

Held: there was nothing on the face of the contract to specifically indicate which ship the parties had meant. Since there were two ships named *Peerless* travelling from Bombay and both parties brought evidence to show that the plaintiff had meant one *Peerless* and the defendant had meant the other ship with the same name, the grounds were deemed to be ambiguous to the extent that the court could find no *consensus ad idem* (meeting of the minds), and therefore no binding contract.

Let us apply the law to a set of facts.

APPLYING THE LAW

Sanjeev has entered into a contract with Vijay for the purchase of an unseen cargo of wood being transported on the *Emperor Columbus* arriving from South America. Sanjeev believes that the wood is a very sturdy Brazilian hardwood; but, in fact, the ship had merely stopped in Brazil en route from the Falkland Islands and is carrying a cargo of soft wood from the Amazon rainforest, the export of which is prohibited by the US government as a conservation measure. Vijay is aware of this, and believes that Sanjeev knows the position too. Sanjeev, a keen conservationist, would never have entered the contract had he known the true facts. Advise whether these contracts are void for mistake.

In advising the parties, you would need to commence by stating that the mistake under discussion is a potential unilateral mistake at common law. You must state the criteria for a mistake of this nature to fall as operative. The criteria is as follows:

1) One of the parties must be genuinely mistaken as to a term of the contract
2) The party would not have entered into the contract but for the mistake
3) The mistake was known, or ought reasonably have been known to the other party
4) The mistaken party must not be at fault.

You must show that you understand the law – explain that it is important that the mistake was with regard to a fundamental mistake regarding the nature of the promise made by the other party and not with regard to some quality of the subject matter.[22]

Discuss the relative likelihood of a mistake being established on this basis. Explain that recognition of this type of mistaken is very rare, and the principle of caveat emptor will often prevail in this type of situation. The aim of the court is usually to find for the existence of a binding contract, with a heavy onus on the person seeking to avoid the contract to persuade the court that there has been a fundamental mistake as to the nature of the promise and that the mistake has induced him/her into entering into the contract.

Explain and analyse the case law precedent that exists in this area. You will hopefully pick up on the fact that this scenario is based on similar principles to the case of *Smith v Hughes*, where the seller offered to sell oats which the buyer mistakenly believed to be old. The seller was not under any obligation to inform the buyer of his mistake provided that he has done nothing to encourage the buyer's belief. The passive acquiescence of the seller in the self-deception of the buyer will not entitle the buyer to avoid the contract. However, if the buyer mistakenly believes that the seller is actually offering to sell old oats and the seller is aware that the buyer has misunderstood the terms of the offer, the seller is obliged to tell the buyer about his mistake.

Let us apply the principles to the scenario: We are told that the purchase is for an unseen cargo of wood. Vijay is under impression Sanjeev knows that the cargo is soft Amazonian wood. Thus, Vijay was not aware that Sanjeev (the buyer) has misunderstood the terms of the offer and, accordingly, the contract will not be void for mistake.

9.9 UNILATERAL MISTAKE

There are two types of unilateral mistake that can render a contract void at common law:

1) Mistake as to identity
2) Mistake concerning the nature of the document.

9.9.1 MISTAKE AS TO IDENTITY

A mistake as to identity will arise when a person makes a contract with another party believing the party to be someone else, and the other person is aware of that mistake.

22 (1864) 2 H&C 906.

Cases on mistaken identity usually arise as a result of a fraud or misrepresentation of identity. A person will purport to be someone else, usually a well-known person or someone of good standing or character, to persuade another person to do business with him/her. They will then default on payment, so, for example, their cheque will bounce. The seller will then try to recover the goods from an innocent third party to whom the fraudster has sold the goods on to, due to the fact that s/he is unable to gain redress from the fraudster who has disappeared. For example, person A agrees to sell person B his car, believing him to be person C (due to the deception of person B who is usually a fraudster). Person B then passes the car to person D and disappears. The problem then arises when A seeks to recover his property from D.

In these circumstances, if the contract is void for mistake, the rogue will not have obtained a good title to the goods as the owner will not have consented to the title in the goods passing to the rogue. Having never acquired a good title, the rogue cannot pass good title to a third party. This is sometimes referred to as the principle of *nemo dat quod non habet*, which means; you cannot give something that you have not got. Consequently, because the third party has not obtained good title, s/he will be obliged to return the goods or the value of the goods to their true owner. It is worth re-iterating the point that the doctrine of mistake is not widely available for this very reason. If the contract is not void for mistake, it is likely to be voidable for misrepresentation, and it is then important to ascertain whether the owner rescinded the contract before the third party acquired the goods from the fraudster. If rescission takes place before the goods pass to the third party, the goods are recoverable; however, if the third party has already acquired title to the goods in good faith and without knowledge of the fraud, rescission will be barred due to the fact that the third party has acquired good title to the goods. You will recall having dealt with this issue and bars to rescission when we looked at misrepresentation in the preceding chapter.

The contract may be void where person A is mistaken as to the identity of person B and person B is aware of the mistake. In order for a mistake to be operative, however, it must be established that the identity of person B was of fundamental importance to person A, who is the innocent party. If this cannot be proven the contract cannot be avoided. A presumption will exist for a valid contract and it is for the person requesting the contract to be set aside under mistake (i.e. the innocent person) to rebut this presumption.

Where a unilateral mistake is being claimed, it is helpful to break the topic down into two categories (see Figure 9.2)

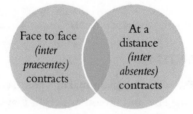

Figure 9.2 Unilateral mistake – categories

9.9.2 FACE-TO-FACE CONTRACTS

Where the parties contract in a face-to-face transaction the law raises a presumption that the parties intend to deal with the person in front of them. In circumstances where one of those persons is a fraudster, it will be for the innocent person to rebut that presumption, even if the fraudster is using an alias. On the basis that the innocent party intends to form a valid contract, the fraudster will acquire good title to the goods, but provided that the goods are not yet passed on to a third party, the innocent party may rescind at this stage for fraudulent misrepresentation.

The cases in this area largely form clear precedent for this rule; if we initially consider the case of *Phillips v Brooks*.

PHILLIPS V BROOKS LTD [1919] 2 KB 243

A rogue went into a jewellery shop and purchased some pearls and a ring, making payment by cheque. He told the proprietors that he was Sir George Bullough and provided an address in the London area. He was allowed to take the jewellery after the proprietor had checked that the name and address could be verified. Later, the cheque bounced and the rogue disappeared.

Held: the contract was not void for mistake and the plaintiff was not able to recover the ring from a third party who had purchased it from the rogue. The court found that the plaintiff had intended to contract with the person who had been present before him in the shop. The mistake was not with regards to his identity, but was a mis-judgment as to his creditworthiness which had persuaded the proprietor to allow the credit transaction.

A similar conclusion was reached in *Lewis v Averay*.

LEWIS V AVERAY [1972] 1 QB 198

The plaintiff sold his Mini Cooper to a rogue claiming to be the well-known actor Richard Greene. The rogue showed the claimant a Pinewood studio pass that had Richard Greene's name and an address on it. The plaintiff allowed him to take the car with the log book in exchange for a cheque in payment for the car. The cheque was later dishonoured. The rogue sold the car on to Mr Averay for a lesser amount, claiming to be the plaintiff. The plaintiff sought the return of the car on the grounds that the contract was void for mistake.

Held: the contract was not void for mistake. The plaintiff had been misled by the rogue into believing he was dealing with a person of good standing, but the mistake was one of the creditworthiness of the offeror; the presumption that the parties intended to deal with the person in front of them was not displaced.

Both cases share similar features. Firstly, the intention to contract with the person present had not been rebutted and, secondly, in both cases, the agreements had already been made before the method of payment and the question of identity was raised, at which point, in neither case, were the agreements halted when the purchaser offered credit. Thus, at the point when the identities of the purchasers were questioned, it was not a matter of **identity** that had arisen, but an issue relating to **creditworthiness**. It was clear that the seller was content to deal with the person with whom he was face to face in both instances.

It is upon this premise that it can be argued that the somewhat questionable outcome in *Ingram v Little*[23] can be distinguished from the general line of precedent in face-to-face contracts.

INGRAM V LITTLE [1961] 1 QB 31

Two sisters had advertised a car for sale. A rogue, going by the surname Hutchinson, negotiated a deal with them for the sale of their car. When he offered a cheque in payment, the sisters were reluctant; but, after checking the name and address he gave to them against the telephone directory, they relented and allowed him to take the car. The cheque bounced; Hutchinson disappeared and the sisters sought to recover the car from a third party to whom the car had been sold.

Held: the court held that the sisters had intended to deal with the person whom the rogue had purported to be rather than the person who had been in their presence. This appears to go against the precedent in *Phillips v Brooks Ltd* and *Lewis v Averay*, although there appears to be little difference between the facts in these cases. It is interesting to note that the third party in the instant case was a car dealer and the plaintiff sisters were two elderly ladies, and it has been suggested that this factor may have had a bearing on the judgment.

The issue was again deliberated in the case of *Shogun Finance Ltd v Hudson*.

---

23 [1961] 1 QB 31.

SHOGUN FINANCE LTD V HUDSON [2001] EWCA CIV 100, [2002] QB 834

A rogue purchased a car on **hire purchase** terms from a car dealer. As proof of ID, he produced a false driving licence in the name of Durlabh Patel. The car dealer faxed the driving licence to the claimant finance company and phoned through the details on the application form. The claimant then did a credit search on Durlabh Patel and told the dealer to let him have the car. The rogue paid 10% deposit and took the car. He then sold it on to the defendant (Hudson) and reneged on the finance agreement. The finance company brought an action against the defendant claiming to be the owner of the car as the contract was void for mistake.

Held: the contract was void for mistake. Note that the contract was between the rogue and the finance company, not the car dealer, and this contract was made *inter absentes* (the rogue was face to face with the car dealer not the finance company). The identity of the person was crucial to the contract in that it was Durlabh Patel that the credit check had been carried out on and the claimant would not have allowed the car to go without the credit check. Thus, the finance company could recover the car or damages for conversion from Hudson.

ESSENTIAL DEFINITION: HIRE PURCHASE

A technique used to provide finance for purchasers who do not have access to cash to complete a transaction. The retailer usually sells the product to the finance company and the finance company enters into a transaction with the customer on hire-purchase terms.

9.9.3 AT A DISTANCE CONTRACTS

It is generally acknowledged that it is easier to establish an identity mistake where parties negotiate at a distance (note *Shogun* above). The identity of the buyer is clearly crucial to non-face-to-face (*inter absentes*) contracts as the identity must be known in order for the goods to be correctly delivered. Where a written order is completed, the buyer must be named on the correspondence; hence it is clear that the seller will only intend to deal with that person.

The case of *Cundy v Lindsay*[24] was referred to in *Shogun*, and Lord Nicholls was of the view that both face-to-face and contracts made at a distance should be treated the same when it relates to mistake as to identity. Currently, though, this is not the case. Let us look at some cases concerning identify where the transaction was made *inter absentes*.

---

24 (1878) 3 App Cas 459.

CUNDY V LINDSAY (1878) 3 APP CAS 459

Lindsay & Co were manufacturers of linen handkerchiefs. They received correspondence from a person named Blenkarn (a rogue) who had rented premises at 37 Wood Street, but purported to be 'Blenkiron & Co', whom Lindsay & Co knew were a reputable business located at 123 Wood Street. Believing the correspondence to be from this company, Lindsay & Co delivered a consignment of handkerchiefs. Blenkarn then sold the handkerchiefs on to Cundy, who was an innocent third party. When Blenkarn failed to pay, Lindsay & Co sued Cundy for the return or value of the goods.

Held: the House of Lords had to determine whether Lindsay intended to deal explicitly with Blenkiron, or with the company that traded at 37 Wood Street. The court determined that Lindsay had intended to deal with Blenkiron and accordingly declared the contract void. Thus the goods or their value could be recovered from Cundy.

The decision in *Cundy* was a majority decision; the dissenting judges considered the distinction between distant and face-to-face contracts to be arbitrary. Lord Millet believed that the person who had been defrauded should bear the loss, as s/he would have been in a better position to discover the truth rather than the innocent party who had not played any part in the tainted agreement.

Let us consider another well-known case on identity, where the same issue had to be addressed, but where a different conclusion was reached.

KING'S NORTH METAL CO LTD V EDRIDGE, MERRETT AND CO LTD (1897) 14 TLR 98

In this case a rogue submitted an order pretending to be Hallam & Co, which was a non-existent company. King's Norton delivered the goods knowingly to Hallam & Co, which sold them on to Edridge, Merrett and Co. When the fraud was discovered, King's Norton tried to claim the goods back from Edridge, Merrett and Co.

Held: the Court of Appeal held there to be a valid contract between King's Norton and the rogue. The difference between this case and *Cundy v Lindsay* was that King's Norton had intended to sell the goods to Hallam and Co, which was the rogue using this name as an alias. There was not a choice here between the rogue and a respectable company, whereas in *Cundy v Lindsay* there had been.

ANALYSING THE LAW

It is clear with both face-to-face and non-face-to-face contracts that identity is of fundamental importance in determining whether or not a contract will stand. The offeror must consider the identity of the offeree to be fundamental to the agreement and be able to show that s/he intended to deal with no-one other than the real offeree. Interestingly in this area of mistake, it can be seen that a subjective approach is taken rather than the objective test that is generally adopted in contract law. So, the question to be asked in both face-to-face and non-face-to-face contracts is: Was the identity of the offeree a vital factor? If it was not, and the mistake related to the creditworthiness of the offeree rather than his actual identity, the contract will be upheld and the courts will not entertain a claim that the contract is void for mistake. Thus there is no real problem in justifying the different decisions in *Cundy v Lindsay* and in *Kings Norton Metal*. In *Cundy v Lindsay* there was a real company called Blenkiron & Co and in contracting with this name Lindsay & Co intended to contract with this 'real' company and not the rogue; thus the contract was correctly held voidable. Alternately in *King's Norton*, the rogue had used the fictitious name Hallam & Co and there was no-one else that King's Norton could have possibly have intended to deal with and so the contract was valid.

In face-to-face contracts, the law must presume that a person intends to deal with the person who is in front of them and making the deal. The mistake must be proven to be connected to the identity of the other party and not his/her creditworthiness. In *Ingram v Little*, identity checks were made and the courts did find in favour of the plaintiffs. However, this is generally regarded as a case with its own special circumstances. In other cases, where identity checks have been made, the court has remained of the view that the plaintiff has intended to deal with the person with whom s/he is face to face.

In *Shogun*, outlined above, the two dissenting judges were highly critical of the result in *Cundy v Lindsay*. Lord Millet and Lord Nicholls were of the opinion that there should be no distinction between contracts made *inter absentes* and contracts *inter praesentes.* and that *Cundy v Lindsay* should be overruled. However, the majority of the judges who heard the case considered it necessary to pinpoint *who* the owner intended to contract with. If the contract is made in writing, i.e. *inter absentes*, this would be the person/body named in the correspondence. If that person/body is fictitious, the person will be deemed to have intended to contract with the rogue hiding behind the alias. However, if the named person is actually in existence the intention will be deemed to have been to contract with that actual person or body. In *Shogun*, the name of the person was stated and this person did actually exist. On the basis that this was an *inter absentes* contract, Shogun Finance were deemed to have intended only to have dealt with this named person, upon whom they had made checks to verify his existence. Consequently, because the rogue was not Mr Patel, the contract was held to be void for mistake and the claimant could retrieve the car from the defendant.

APPLYING THE LAW

Simon went into Ellie's art gallery, 'Classic Elle', and expressed an interest in a painting for sale at £20,000. Simon told Ellie that he would like to buy the painting and told her that he was Sir George Restall, representing the well-known firm of Restall & Co Ltd. Ellie asked Simon for identification and he produced a cheque book with Restall & Co Ltd's name printed on it. Unbeknown to Ellie, Simon had stolen the cheque book earlier that day. Ellie allowed Simon to take the painting in return for the cheque signed by Simon on behalf of Restall & Co Ltd. The cheque has now been dishonoured and Simon has disappeared, after selling the painting to Poppy for £15,000. Ellie is seeking to recover the painting from Poppy and needs advice.

- First of all, identify what type of mistake may be at issue
- Define the rules that relate to that area of mistake
- In this instance we are looking at an issue pertaining to unilateral mistake
- Explain the law and any inconsistencies that exist
- Finally apply the law and advise Ellie

POINTS TO INCLUDE

- Explain that a unilateral mistake is where only one party to the contract has made a mistake. Stress that the other party *must be aware of the mistake.*
- There must be a fundamental mistake as to the *nature* of the promise made by the other party; a mistake in relation to the quality of the subject matter is not sufficient.
- Explain that there is a presumption for a valid and binding contract. It is for the person seeking to avoid the contract to rebut the presumption.
- The subjective test is used where one party is actually aware of the other party's mistake.

Explain that the instant case concerns **mistaken identity** and then explain the rules:

- Where the seller deals with a person who is actually present before him (*inter praesentes*), there is a presumption that the seller intends to contract with the person present.
- Mention the leading cases, i.e. *Phillips v Brookes Ltd, Lewis v Averay, Shogun* etc. A contract may be void where a party is mistaken as to the identity of the person contracted with and the other party is aware of the mistake. The question of the other party's identity must be of fundamental importance to the innocent party for the type of mistake to operate.

APPLY THE LAW

Explain that to prove unilateral mistake Ellie must prove:

1) An intention to deal with some other person
2) That the other party knew of this intention
3) That the identity was of fundamental importance
4) That reasonable steps had been taken to verify the identity.

Apply the precedent from cases in this area. The facts here are similar to *Lewis v Avery*, where the plaintiff advertised a car in a local newspaper. A rogue purporting to be R A Greene from Pinewood studios purchased the car. It transpired that he was not R A Green and his cheque bounced. The car was sold to a third party. The contract was not void for mistake as it was deemed that the plaintiff had intended to deal with the person in front of him irrespective of his identity.

Ellie will be regarded as having intended to deal with the person in front of her, which was the rogue purporting to be George Restall. Thus, the contract will not be void and Ellie will be unable to recover the painting from Poppy.

9.10 MISTAKE CONCERNING THE NATURE OF THE DOCUMENT

The main categories of mistake falling into this category are:

1) Document does not reflect the deal.
2) *Non est factum.*

9.10.1 DOCUMENT DOES NOT REFLECT THE DEAL

After the agreement has been finalised, one or both of the parties to a contract may discover that the contract they signed does not accurately reflect the deal they thought they had made. This can inevitably lead to disputes when actions are taken by the other party to enforce a term that one of the parties does not believe accurately reflects their intentions. Rectification is an equitable remedy and allows a document to be amended to reflect the common intentions of the parties. This remedy will not be awarded unless the agreement fails to reflect the agreement of both parties.[25] Rectification of a written document may be available where a transcription mistake has been made in putting an oral agreement into written form. The

---

25 *Frederick E Rose (London) Ltd v William H Pim Co Ltd* [1953] 2 QB 450, [1953] 3 WLR 497, [1953] 2 All ER 739.

courts are generally reluctant to interfere with the terms of a written document so there is a heavy burden upon the party who is contesting the agreement to show that it is not an accurate record of their intentions.

If one party is of the view that the document correctly reflects their intentions, but the other party is not of the same view, rectification cannot take place. Evidence must be provided by the party seeking rectification that the document, at the time of contracting, did not accurately reflect their intentions. In addition, there must be a discrepancy between what was agreed between the parties and what was recorded.[26] Certain things must be proven by a party seeking rectification.[27] These are summarised in Figure 9.3.

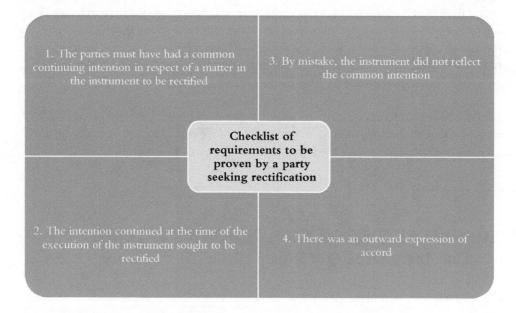

Figure 9.3 Requirements for rectification

The principles were applied in the case of *Joscelyne v Nissen.*

JOSCELYNE V NISSEN [1970] 2 QB 86

Mrs Nissen and her husband shared a house with her father, Mr Joscelyne, and his wife. Mr Joscelyne agreed to transfer his business to Mrs Nissen on the agreement that she would pay him a weekly pension and his and his wife's expenses for the household, costs such as gas, electricity and home help. At a later date they committed the

---

26 *Joscelyne v Nissen* [1970] 2 QB 86.
27 *Swainland Builders Ltd v Freehold Properties Ltd* [2002] 2 EGLR 71.

agreement to writing. One clause of the agreement stated that Mrs Nissen would discharge all costs in connection with the whole property. A further clause stated that Mr Joscelyne had the right to live in the ground floor flat free from all rent and outgoings of every kind. There was a breakdown in relations and Mr Joscelyne took court action against Mrs Nissen who then stopped paying the utility bills on the basis that these were neither rent nor outgoings.

Held: the court awarded rectification as convincing proof of intention had been provided.

9.10.2 *NON EST FACTUM*

Non est factum is a Latin phrase meaning 'it is not my deed'. It is a term used for a mistake that relates to the nature of the document signed. In some circumstances it can be used as a defence to the proposition that a person is bound by a document that they have signed.[28] If someone has relied upon another person to explain and accurately describe the contents of a document and their statements have been false or inaccurate, or a deliberate misrepresentation to trick a person into signing a document, s/he may be able to escape liability on the basis that the document does not represent their true intention, and that s/he would not have signed the document if the true situation had been known. The defence can also be used by persons who are vulnerable, such as mentally infirm or blind persons. The defence is rarely successful and the following case illustrates this. It is useful in that it sets out the modern test for *non est factum*, requiring proof that there is a fundamental or radical difference between the document actually signed and that which the signer believed it to be.

SAUNDERS V ANGLIA BUILDING SOCIETY [1970] 3 ALL ER 961

The plaintiff, Mrs Gallie, was an elderly lady who wished to give the title deeds of her property to her nephew so that he could use the property as security for a business loan. She stipulated that the agreement was on the condition that she would be permitted to live in the house for the rest of her life. Mrs Gallie was presented with a document compiled by her nephew and his business partner, which she signed without reading, as she had lost her spectacles. She believed that the document correctly recorded her wishes. It later transpired that the true extent of the agreement permitted her nephew's business partner to grant a mortgage over the property in favour of Anglia Building Society and, when the business partner defaulted on the mortgage, the building society sought to repossess the house. Mrs Gallie's executrix sought a declaration that the assignment to Lee was void by reason of *non est factum*.

---

28 *L'Estrange v Graucob* [1934] 2 KB 394.

Held: the House of Lords confirmed the decision of the Court of Appeal that the plea of *non est factum* could not be raised, the reasoning being that the transaction the widow had entered was not fundamentally different from what she intended at the time. Additionally, it was found that she had been careless in signing the document. At the very least she should have made sure that the transfer was to the person intended by her.

9.11 BRINGING IT ALL TOGETHER

Overall, it can be seen that the judicial attitude towards recognition of mistake in contract law is very restricted. The reason for this is because the finding of a mistake can have a wide impact and is often particularly detrimental to innocent third parties, who are unlikely to have had any knowledge of the events contributing to the mistake.

Finding a mistake operative at common law will result in a contract being treated as though it had never been made in the first place, i.e., void *ab initio*. Where a mistake is operative, any goods passed to a third party will have to be returned, since no title in the goods will have passed. A party to a contract cannot escape a bad bargain through a claim of mistake; the doctrine of freedom of contract is still very much alive in these circumstances and the law will not step in to rescue an imprudent person from a foolish action. Under the principle of freedom of contract, parties are free to make any (legal) agreement they so choose and the law must retain certainty by upholding these agreements. Indeed, to disallow an agreement on the whim of one of the parties due to him/her having changed their mind and claiming that a mistake has been made would result in legal unpredictability and uncertainty in the world of commerce and not provide a stable base upon which trade could be conducted effectively.

Although a strict approach towards mistake is undertaken, it is imperative that we recognise that there are some instances in which a mistake will be operative and a contract found void. A mistake as to the existence of the subject matter of a contract will render a contract void; but not a mistake as to the quality of the subject matter. A mutual mistake where the parties are at cross-purposes may also render a contract void and a unilateral mistake as to identity will sometimes render a contract void if the identity of the other party can be shown to have been of fundamental to the agreement. Rectification can be applied in some circumstances where the document does not accurately reflect the agreement and *non est factum* can also be argued in certain circumstances.

The three main areas of mistake are summarised in Figure 9.4.

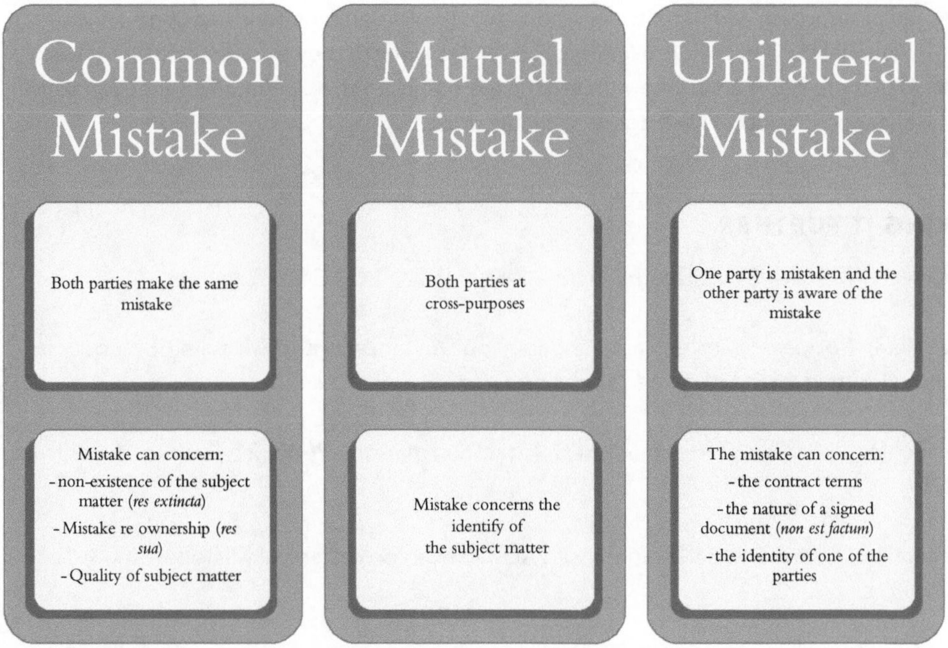

Figure 9.4 Summary

KEY LEARNING POINTS

The common law will recognise certain mistakes that are fundamental in nature. Finding a mistake will have a drastic effect upon a contract, making it void. This means that neither party will be able to claim any rights or damages under the agreement. Remember that you should consider the following in deciding whether a mistake will be operative:

- Does the mistake relate to the existence of the subject matter of the contract? If so, you must ascertain whether the subject matter was affected before or after the agreement was made. Had one of the parties guaranteed or agreed to take responsibility for the subject matter of the contract existing?
- Does the mistake relate to the quality of the subject matter of the contract? If so, it is unlikely that the mistake will be operative unless it so fundamental that it renders the subject matter radically different to that what was agreed.
- Has there been a mutual mistake? If so, and under an objective test no sense can be made of the promises, the contract will be void.
- Has there been a mistake with regard to the identity of a party? If so, was the other party aware of the mistake? If so, and identity was fundamental to the agreement, the contract may be void. The approach of the courts is a strict one due to the impact of the finding of a mistake in this category on third parties. There will always be

an assumption with face-to-face contracts that a person intends to contract with a person who is in their presence, regardless of whom they pass themselves off as.

■ Has there been a mistake with regard the nature of the document signed? In some instances the courts will agree to rectification.

TAKING IT FURTHER

Macmillan, 'Mistake as to identity clarified' (2004) 120 LQR 369–373

Macmillan, 'Rogues, Swindlers and Cheats: The Development of Mistake of Identity in English Contract Law' (2005) 64 Cambridge Law Journal 711

McLauchlan, 'Mistake of Identity and Contract Formation' (2005) 21 Journal of Contract Law 1

McLauchlan, 'The "Drastic" Remedy of Rectification for Unilateral Mistake' (2008) 124 LQR 608

McLauchlan, 'Refining Rectification' (2014) 130 LQR 83

Mcmeel, ' "Equitable" mistake repudiated: the demise of Solle v Butcher?' (2002) LMCLQ 449

Phang, 'Controversy in Common Mistake' (2003) Conveyancer and Property Lawyer 247

Smith, 'Contracts – mistake, frustration and implied terms' (1994) 110 LQR 400

Tettenborn, 'Agreements, Common Mistake and the Purpose of Contract' (2011) 27 Journal of Contract Law 91

Treitel, The Law of Contract, 13th edn, Sweet & Maxwell, 2011

CHAPTER 10
DURESS AND UNDUE INFLUENCE

10.1 INTRODUCTION

If a contract is the product of the agreement of two or more parties and a 'meeting of minds', one of the key problems with contracts is where the willingness to agree to a contract has been interfered with in some way. This is illustrated in a number of different principles discussed in this book, for example where there has been a mistake that has led to a contract or a misrepresentation by one party that has induced the other to enter into an agreement. However, it is also clearly illustrated by situations in which someone has been unduly persuaded or coerced into entering the contract, and it is such situations that are covered by **duress** and **undue influence**.

Both of the above principles represent situations in which someone has not entered into a contract as a result of their own free will; their will has been interfered with in some way, and therefore their decision to enter into an agreement has resulted from this coercion.

Proving that this has occurred can often be tricky; in some situations the pressure placed on one party by the other can be subtle and therefore this is one area where **presumptions** are used as part of the legal arguments establishing a lack of free will.

The outcome of successfully arguing that the free will of one party has been coerced is giving the coerced party the freedom to escape the contract, and therefore agreements in this area will be **voidable** at the discretion of the victim.

AS YOU READ

At the end of this chapter you should be able to:

- Understand the definitions of duress and undue influence, and recognise the situations where these principles may apply

- Understand the importance of presumptions in this area of law, where direct evidence of influence may be difficult to ascertain

- Identify the criteria that indicate that duress or undue influence has occurred

- Appreciate the development of the concept of 'constructive notice' of undue influence through judicial decisions

10.2 DURESS

The area of **duress** is aimed at agreements that have been concluded under some form of coercion. The most obvious of these are situations where physical violence or harm are threatened to the other party or his family. However, such occurrences of duress are quite rare – there have always been very few cases involving duress to the person, but this sort of duress is not as common as one where economic pressure has been threatened.

ESSENTIAL DEFINITION: DURESS

The act of making personal threats towards another party or their interests in order to coerce them into entering into an agreement against their will

---

Three key elements exist for duress to be established. Firstly, there has to be some form of pressure or threat that is exerted by one party on the other. Secondly, that pressure or threat must be illegitimate. Thirdly, that illegitimate pressure or threat must have resulted in the decision to enter into a contractual agreement. The end result is therefore that the person entered into the agreement, not through his own free will, but because he was coerced into doing so by the other party.

10.2.1 PRESSURE OR THREAT

The first thing that is required is some form of pressure or threat. The reason behind this is that there has to be some statement or action from the other party that has had an effect upon the person's decision making. Originally thought to be only those threats which are of violence towards the party themselves or their family, as mentioned above, there is now a broader understanding of duress that goes beyond this. Nevertheless, there does need to be something that is understood to be the reason behind the decision taken by the victim in this situation.

ANALYSING THE LAW

This does not mean to say that this guarantees a life free from pressure. Everyday life is full of pressure and many people will feel this in work or home life. Many decisions are made in high-pressure situations, but this does not allow us to be excused from the consequences of them. Equally, even a decision made under duress is not one made completely without choice. Even where a person is threatened with violence, they make the choice to do something because there is a decision made by them.

There may be many occasions in business where a person may be in a stressful situation. This does not mean that they have been unlawfully coerced into entering a contract, and the law of duress is about making sure that the line is drawn appropriately between what is and is not duress.

10.2.2 ILLEGITIMATE THREAT

Just as important is the illegitimacy of this threat. Threatening to carry out an action that is perfectly lawful would not be seen as forming part of duress. For example, *Williams v Bayley*[1] concerned a threat of being lawfully imprisoned. *D&C Builders v Rees*[2] illustrates an illegitimate threat that resulted in the agreement to accept less. This case was discussed in Chapter 3 with regard to consideration, but it was the threat of non-payment that was considered illegitimate by the court, such that Lord Denning prevented the application of an equitable remedy because of it.

10.2.3 EFFECT UPON DECISION TO ENTER THE CONTRACT

The third element requires there to be an effect seen as a result of the threat. If duress is about showing the will of one of the parties has been subverted in some way, there has to be a link between the decision to enter the contract and the threat made.

BARTON V ARMSTRONG [1976] AC 104, [1975] 2 ALL ER 465, [1975] 2 WLR 1050

A former chairman of a company called 'Landmark' threatened the managing director with death if he did not transfer his share of the company to Landmark for a large sum of money. However, the argument in court to strike out the transaction for duress failed, because there was some evidence that the managing director believed this to be a good deal and, although he felt apprehensive about himself and his family's safety, this did not affect his judgement and so his decision to enter into the contract was one that involved his exercise of free will. It was therefore difficult to show that the threat had affected his decision-making such that it could be thought of as duress.

Held: his decision to transfer his shares was not as a result of duress.

---

1   (1866) LR 1 HL 200.
2   [1966] 2 QB 617, [1965] 3 All ER 837, [1966] 2 WLR 288.

This is a key element in considering duress – there has to be a link between the threat and the decision made, such that the decision has been affected by the threat. As odd as it sounds, in the *Barton* case there was not the required link present. Although someone had threatened the party involved in order to ensure that he made the desired decision, that threat did not change the decision that he would have made anyway, even without that threat. See Figure 10.1.

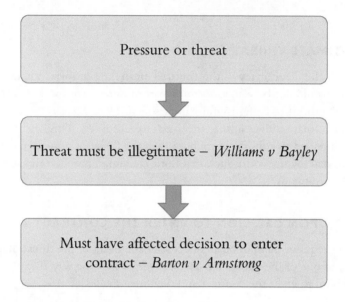

Figure 10.1 Required elements of duress

10.3 ECONOMIC DURESS

The area of more significance is that of economic duress. This was not originally considered in the context of the original doctrine of duress, but the approach of the Court of Appeal in *D&C Builders v Rees*, mentioned above, is a prime example of where the court (in this case Lord Denning) decided the case based upon the notion of **economic duress** rather than a duress based upon threats to the person.

ANALYSING THE LAW

The facts of *D&C Builders v Rees* can be found in Chapter 3. The issue of relevance here was that the creditor was faced with a choice: accept the lesser amount, or go through the (potentially lengthy) legal process of suing the other party for the whole amount. The court was of the opinion that the economic consequences that would befall him in the event of delaying payment, known to both parties, amounted to an economic threat.

The key here was that although the creditor had a choice as to what to do (he could have sued for the remaining amount owed) the practicalities of the situation left him with no realistic alternative to the choice that he took. Economically speaking, he was 'backed into a corner'. The agreement was therefore entered into by his choice, but it was the only realistic choice open to him.

ESSENTIAL DEFINITION: ECONOMIC DURESS

Economic duress can be defined as threats to financial or business interests. Typically, this will be where one party threatens breach of contract unless the other party agrees to a renegotiation. The duress is particularly effective where there are potentially disastrous consequences resulting from breach, as in the *D&C Builders* case.

This idea was taken further in *Occidental Worldwide Investment Corp v Skibs A/S Avanti*, where the idea of economic duress was further developed (although ultimately unsuccessful in this case).

OCCIDENTAL WORLDWIDE INVESTMENT CORP V SKIBS A/S AVANTI (THE SIBOEN AND THE SIBOTRE) [1976] 1 LLOYD'S REP 293

This case concerned the chartering of two ships by Occidental. They attempted to renegotiate the charter price for these ships at a time of recession, but also a time of financial hardship for them. They told the other party that if they did not reduce the charter price, they would not be able to continue with the charterparty because of their own financial position. Due to the recession, they also knew that it would be difficult for the ship owners to re-charter the ships elsewhere. This knowledge of the difficulty of re-chartering was the essence of the threat claimed by the other party – it posed a financial threat to the business of the ship owners.

The ship owners agreed to the reduction in charter price, but it later transpired that the charterers were making a considerable profit on the charter due to improvements in the financial situation generally. The ship owners gave the charterers the option to revert to the original price or terminate the agreement and, when they refused to do either, the ship owners terminated the agreement. The charterers sued for wrongful repudiation, and the ship owners argued that the agreement to reduce the price had been done under conditions of economic duress.

Held: the contract was not void for duress because, although the agreement had been made under pressure, it was not enough to amount to coercion as to amount to duress. However, in presenting his argument, Kerr J argued that there were two factors that could be used to measure whether there had been economic duress, and therefore provided some useful clarity regarding the application of a principle of economic duress. He said:

> One relevant factor would be whether the party relying on the duress made any protest at the time or shortly thereafter. Another would be to consider whether or not he treated the settlement as closing the transaction in question and binding upon him, or whether he made it clear that he regarded the position as still open.

As in his opinion the facts in this case did not meet these requirements, it was clearly not enough to argue duress, and so he found that the contract had in fact been wrongfully repudiated.

ANALYSING THE LAW

The *Occidental* case highlights problems with the doctrine of economic duress, namely that there is a fine line between the normal commercial environment, which has inherent financial risks and rewards, and a situation involving one party imposing an economic threat on the other. This case shows that the courts will not just automatically consider that a situation where financial risk exists will always be one involving duress.

The *Williams v Roffey Bros* case[3] (discussed in full in Chapter 3) could have fallen into this category as the second agreement was entered into in a situation where, if they had not done so, financial hardship in the form of a time penalty clause would have resulted. However, since this case, the doctrine of economic duress has been used as a way of preventing extorted promises from being enforced, to justify relaxing the rules on consideration. The potential this leaves for expansion of the doctrine requires that, in considering its application, we must apply it with a proper definition. In order to do so, properly developed criteria for establishing where economic duress exists need to be considered.

This can be done by considering existing case law on the issue. In *Pao On v Lau Yiu Long*[4] the court established two requirements for economic duress:

1) 'coercion of the will that vitiates consent'
2) the pressure or threat must be illegitimate.

3   [1991] 1 QB 1.
4   [1980] AC 614.

Essentially what is happening here is coercion that affects whether a person is, in reality, consenting to the agreement being made. Where it can be proved that the coercion is affecting the will of that party, there has been duress.

10.3.1 COERCION OF THE WILL THAT VITIATES CONSENT

EXPLAINING THE LAW

It is important to look at this in closer detail – are we really advocating that duress negates the will of the parties? This reasoning has been criticised by Atiyah,[5] who believed that there was no such thing as the total negating of consent, but instead the alleged victim is required to choose between the lesser of two evils. The *D&C Builders* case is a good example because, in that particular situation, the creditor had a choice. He could either accept the money and the revision to the agreement, or he could sue the other party for breach of contract. However, the difference between theory and reality is that if you look at this situation from a practical point of view, the second of these choices really was not open to him – he was in financial difficulty and so therefore did not have the time or resources necessary to pursue his claim in the courts. Therefore, there was duress present, because it required him to choose what Atiyah referred to as the lesser of two evils.

To attempt to analogise this to criminal law, duress does not require an absence of a voluntary act in that area either – see *DPP for Northern Ireland v Lynch*.[6] There is an argument that this should be applicable to contract law too, especially as duress makes a contract *voidable* and not *void*. It should really be reformulated to 'no realistic choice'. This would be more in line with the reasoning of Atiyah, and reflect the economic reality of most situations where there is duress present.

10.3.2 ILLEGITIMATE PRESSURE OR THREAT

The distinction here is fine between what is and is not illegitimate pressure. One key element of applying this doctrine is that there should be some reasonable expectation of being able to use pressure as part of the negotiating process. To remove all pressure would make for a very sterile commercial environment, and interfere with the notion that there is freedom of contract, which encourages entrepreneurship.

For example, in *Williams v Roffey Bros* the situation that arose came from an offer of more money from the main contractor. They did so unprompted by the subcontractor, except for the subcontractor's admission that they were not going to be able to meet the required

---

5   Atiyah, 'Economic Duress and the Overborne Will' (1982) 98 LQR 197.
6   [1975] AC 653.

deadline. This was a fact and not a threat. The main contractor may have felt a certain amount of pressure because of their situation – and the penalty clause that they were subject to, but this was part of the commercial risk that they took on in agreeing to the main contract and then subcontracting some of the work out.

Arguably it would have been a different matter if the suggestion had originated from the subcontractor, and could have amounted to some sort of duress, if it could have been interpreted as a threat to their business or financial interests.

Linked to this is the further consideration that, in order to establish that duress has occurred, the pressure must have had some effect. So, if the party would not have entered into the contract had the pressure not been applied, there has been some form of pressure or threat. This would not have been the case in *Barton v Armstrong*, as evidence of other reasons for entering into the contract had been put before the court.

This pressure must also be illegitimate, as we can see from the case below.

UNIVERSE TANKSHIPS INC OF MONROVIA V INTERNATIONAL TRANSPORT WORKERS FEDERATION (THE UNIVERSE SENTINEL) [1983] 1 AC 366, [1982] 2 WLR 803, [1982] 2 ALL ER 67

A trade union refused to provide tugs to tow certain ships out of harbour unless certain payments were made to its welfare fund. Without the tugs, the vessels would not have been able to sail, and this resulted in the ship being effectively 'blacked' (a term meaning that the trade union's members would not deal with it). They claimed that they were entitled to make such demands because they were protected by the Trade Union and Labour Relations Act 1974. They claimed that the money was extracted as part of a labour dispute, which was protected by the Act.

Held: The availability and eligibility of the welfare fund to employees was not connected to their terms and conditions. Therefore, the union's actions amounted to illegitimate pressure.

APPLYING THE LAW

However, it is important to distinguish between the normal 'rough and tumble' of pressures of commercial bargaining and illegitimate pressure. The law's intention is not to remove all pressure from the situation, as arguably this is still part of the negotiation process of commercial agreements. Thus, it is important to distinguish between what is legitimate and illegitimate.

For example, if Greg is looking for a supplier of cycling gear for his local cycling club, and approaches CycleBro, a company he knows is in need of orders and negotiates a discount on his order because of the size of the order and the fact that he feels he is in a good bargaining position, this is different from a situation where he knows that company is in severe financial difficulty and places an order at an extremely low price, knowing that they have no choice but to accept because of their financial position. The former might be considered to be part of commercial bargaining, but the latter would lead to an accusation of illegitimate pressure.

10.3.3 THE NEED TO PROTEST AT THE TIME OR SHORTLY AFTER

Additional to the two criteria laid out in the *Pao On* case is the need to protest about what has happened. Failure to do so will result in the inference that the person claiming duress has affirmed the agreement. This again can be linked to the fact that duress produces a voidable agreement, rather than one that is automatically void.

This point was made by Kerr J in the *Occidental* case[7] mentioned earlier in this chapter. This was a key element in deciding whether a decision had been made as a result of duress. Failure to raise an objection at the earliest available moment casts doubt upon whether there really has been duress or not.

This point was made in the following case.

NORTH OCEAN SHIPPING CO V HYUNDAI CONSTRUCTION CO (THE ATLANTIC BARON) [1979] QB 705, [1979] 3 WLR 419, [1978] 3 ALL ER 1170

This was a case involving a contract for the construction of a ship. There was a demand by the shipbuilder to breach the contract to build the ship unless 10% was added to the price of the contract. The purchaser agreed, because they needed the ship on time for a valuable charter that they were negotiating. They took delivery of the ship on time, and eight months after having done so, attempted to reclaim the extra money that they had paid. The court came to the conclusion that the extra demand did amount to economic duress, and so this would make the contract voidable. However, because they had left the matter eight months before protesting, this was held to be a constructive affirmation of the contract, and they were no longer entitled to remedies for the duress.

Held: the extra payment that had been made could not be recovered.

---

7   [1976] 1 Lloyd's Rep 293.

The key here is the need to protest at the earliest opportunity. This does not necessarily mean that they need to protest as soon as the threat has been made: in a lot of situations this would provide a problem for someone if making a protest could, for example, cause the other party to completely abandon the contract. If you find that you are only agreeing to a contract, or a variation of a contract, because of an economic threat held over you, you are unlikely to say anything at the time to object because the other party could still carry out their threat.

For example in *The Atlantic Baron*, protesting about the additional payment might have prompted the other party to delay or abandon the contract as was threatened anyway. Instead, it is important for the party affected to protest at the earliest practical point. The onus is on the victim to act to ensure that a constructive affirmation of the contract does not take place. In the *Atlantic Baron* case, it would have been sufficient for the victim to protest once he had delivery of the ship – it was the fact of the eight-month delay that had resulted in the constructive affirmation taking place.

ASSESSMENT TIP

Think about how this would go together in an assessment. As an area of law that is about establishing various criteria, it is important that all the elements we have discussed here that are needed to show duress are present. If one of them is not (e.g. if the pressure exerted upon you is not illegitimate), it may not be possible to argue that there has been duress.

Figure 10.2 Elements of economic duress

10.4 UNDUE INFLUENCE

Undue influence is another specific area of unconscionability where the courts will intervene. However, undue influence is something that stops short of duress, as rather than there being a specific threat made against the other party (as with duress), undue influence arises because of a more subtle influence that another person has over the other party. This influence arises because one person occupies a position of power over the other party and can use that position to influence the other party to enter into a contractual agreement.

ESSENTIAL DEFINITION: UNDUE INFLUENCE

This is where someone has the ability to influence one party's decision to enter into an agreement and abuses that power for their own personal gain. This is what makes the influence 'undue'.

This influence arises because of some relationship that exists between the parties that is such that one party is able to influence the decision-making of the other party. It is the abuse of this relationship to gain an unfair advantage that makes the influence undue, and again, like duress, results in a contract being voidable. The courts will intervene in such situations if it can be established that there has been *undue* influence. It is important to note at this stage that although duress is a common law principle, undue influence only exists in equity, and must therefore be subject to equitable principles.

10.4.1 THE RELATIONSHIP

The subtlety of the influence in cases is what has made the situation somewhat more complicated than with duress. The doctrine deals with situations where people are involved in personal relationships. Because of this, it is often seen as a very difficult thing to prove. The courts have therefore seen fit to divide up the different situations involved in undue influence into a number of different categories.

In *Bank of Credit and Commerce International SA v Aboody*[8] the court split undue influence into two distinct classes (see Figure 10.3).

---

8   [1990] 1 QB 923.

Class 1 undue influence

- refers to actual influence exerted by one party over the other.

Class 2 undue influence

- refers to undue influence which is presumed to have been exerted because of a relationship of trust and confidence between the parties. It is then for the party alleged to have exercised undue influence to rebut this presumption.

Figure 10.3 Classes of undue influence

ESSENTIAL DEFINITION: CLASS 1 'ACTUAL' UNDUE INFLUENCE

Class 1 undue influence is often referred to as 'actual' undue influence. This is because although, as with any type of undue influence, it concerns a relationship where one party has influence over the other, it relies upon evidence that is proof of specific incidences of undue influence having taken place. This means that, unlike Class 2, there is no need to discuss what type of relationship the parties had, because the nature of the relationship that results in the undue influence is self-evident.

This is the easiest form of undue influence to establish because, if there is proof of actual influence being exerted, this can provide a very straightforward indication that the other party's ability to consent in contract law has been compromised.

ESSENTIAL DEFINITION: CLASS 2 'PRESUMED' UNDUE INFLUENCE

Class 2 is referred to as 'presumed' undue influence. This is because the claim of undue influence is not based upon actual evidence of instances of influence, but from a presumption based upon the nature of the relationship between the two parties. This was intended to address the problem often encountered with undue influence claims, regarding the ability to prove that influence had taken place. This gives the court the ability to presume that undue influence would have taken place due to the nature of the relationship between the parties.

ANALYSING THE LAW

Why is undue influence sometimes so difficult to prove? This is mainly because the type of relationship involved is often (although not exclusively) one of a personal nature. One of the most common relationships involved in undue influence cases is that of husband and wife. What has happened in a personal relationship, often in private with only the two parties involved, is very difficult to prove, and often would involve one party's word against the other.

The role of the presumption in class 2 is therefore to provide a starting position. The court is entitled to presume that the relationship is such that, because of its nature, one party will always have the ability to influence the choice of the other. That presumption does not in itself prove that undue influence has occurred, but it then requires the other party to **rebut** that presumption.

10.5 CLASS 1: ACTUAL INFLUENCE

This area is the one most closely related to duress. Whereas in duress there must be some form of threat that induces the person to enter into the contract, class 1 undue influence concerns evidence of undue pressure applied. As the concept of undue influence is more subtle than duress, this would not be instances of threats, but would involve evidence of one party using their position to influence the decision-making of the other party. There is also no requirement for an illegitimate threat, or even a threat at all, which means that the concept of pressure in undue influence is appreciably wider than in duress.

The case of *CIBC Mortgages v Pitt*[9] was one where evidence of actual undue influence was presented in court. The case involved a husband putting pressure on his wife to agree to a £150,000 loan being taken out on the house they jointly owned in order to buy shares. The husband encountered problems with repayment of the loan after the stock market crash in the late 1980s, and the bank attempted to repossess the house in order to recover the amount of the loan. When the bank attempted repossession, the wife argued that she had only agreed to the loan because of the pressure that had been placed upon her by her husband. The undue influence in question came from a campaign of sustained pressure, rather than a particular threat. At trial, the court was satisfied that this course of conduct was such that amounted to actual evidence of undue influence. The campaign of sustained pressure overcame her initial objection to the purchase.

10.5.1 MANIFEST DISADVANTAGE

Various cases have discussed that a key element in showing actual undue influence is that the party claiming to have been pressured must demonstrate that the transaction they had entered

9   [1994] 1 AC 200, [1993] 3 WLR 802, [1993] 4 All ER 433.

into was to their 'manifest disadvantage'. The purpose behind this is therefore to show that there cannot be a rational explanation for the transaction based upon that person acting in their own interests. If you enter into a transaction that puts you at a manifest disadvantage, the only explanation could be that you are doing it because you are being pressured into doing so.

This was discussed in *BCCI v Aboody*[10] with regard to class 1 undue influence. The appeal by the wife was dismissed in this case because the court held that there must be a manifest disadvantage, and the wife was unable to demonstrate one.

However, with regard to class 1, this approach was not followed subsequently in *CIBC Mortgages v Pitt*[11] where the court felt that it was not a necessary requirement for class 1 actual undue influence. However, following the judgment of the court in *National Westminster Bank v Morgan*,[12] the court in *Pitt* argued that it was still an important part of establishing the presumption in class 2 actions for undue influence. The concept of 'manifest disadvantage' is rather difficult to define, and ultimately has led to its demise as part of undue influence. See further discussion from the case of *Royal Bank of Scotland v Etridge (No. 2)*, in the section on class 2, below.

10.6 CLASS 2: PRESUMED INFLUENCE

Because not every case involves parties who can provide actual evidence of undue influence being exerted, class 2 concentrates on the existence of a relationship that is presumed to lead to undue influence, rather than proving the influence itself. This then sets up a presumption that the other party will have to rebut if they are to show that no undue influence occurred. In this way, the focus of class 2 is more upon the relationship than the undue influence itself. In many cases it may be difficult to prove the fact of influence, but the nature of the relationship may show that such influence is self-evident.

In order to successfully demonstrate that undue influence has occurred under class 2, two things must be established:

1) there was a relationship of trust and confidence between the parties such that one party had influence over the other
2) the transaction in question cannot be explained by the relationship of the parties to one another.

The first of these is established either in class 2A or class 2B as an evidentiary issue. However, the second part of this concerns the 'undue' part of the influence. There must be something about the transaction that suggests that it has only come about due to the abuse of the position of influence by the party in a position of influence. This will be further discussed in 10.8.1 Establishing that the influence was undue.

....

10 See the judgment of Slade LJ [1990] 1 QB 923 at 948.
11 See Lord Browne-Wilkinson [1994] 1 AC 200 at 207.
12 [1985] AC 686.

10.6.1 RELATIONSHIPS OF TRUST AND CONFIDENCE

Because undue influence relies upon relationships, it became important to consider whether a particular type of relationship could come under the presumption in class 2. Therefore, the courts have distinguished between those relationships that will always fall under class 2, and those that could fall under class 2. In order to make this distinction, class 2 is further subdivided into two other categories:

- *Class 2A* covers cases where a relationship of trust and confidence will always exist. The presumption in these cases automatically arises.
- *Class 2B* covers cases where the existence of a relationship of trust and confidence is not inevitable but is proven in this specific case.

The distinction here is because, although some relationships can be stereotyped, and therefore be said to always result in one party being capable of influencing the other, not all relationships can be categorised in this way. The different relationships and their classification is further discussed below.

10.6.2 ESTABLISHING INFLUENCE

In *Barclays Bank v O'Brien*, Lord Browne-Wilkinson stated[13] that there needed to be 'a relationship of trust and confidence between the complainant and the wrongdoer of such a nature that it is fair to presume that the wrongdoer abused the relationship in procuring the complainant to enter into the impugned transaction'.

The point behind this is, as discussed above, it is often difficult to bring forward the evidence needed to establish class 1 undue influence, and therefore the courts need to be able to set up a presumption that then needs to be rebutted by the other party. The essence of Lord Browne-Wilkinson's comments above show that it is the nature of the relationship itself that establishes this. This can be either because the relationship is of a type that will always lead to this conclusion (class 2A relationships) or because the influenced party can show that the nature of *that particular* relationship is such that a presumption can be established in that particular instance (class 2B). This is where the fine distinction between the two types of class 2 relationships comes in.

What should be noted at this stage is that the presumption being established in all cases is that there is *influence*. Whether this is *undue* is a matter to be dealt with separately, a point clarified by the court in *Royal Bank of Scotland v Etridge (No. 2)*.[14] This does go against the comments from Lord Browne-Wilkinson, but this development separates out the need to show *influence* from a need to demonstrate the *undue* nature of that influence, which makes things more straightforward. *Etridge* also introduced a clearer distinction in the position of the alleged victim between the two sub-classes of class 2. We should now look at this difference.

---

13 *Barclays Bank v O'Brien* [1994] 1 AC 180 at 189.
14 [2002] 2 AC 773, [2001] 3 WLR 102.

10.7 CLASS 2A: AUTOMATIC PRESUMPTION

Certain relationships are considered to provide an automatic presumption of influence by their existence. This is because, in each of these situations, there is always a relationship of trust and confidence in existence between the parties concerned, and this relationship will always result in party A trusting party B and being capable of being influenced by them. It essentially means that these relationships are of a stereotype, with the relationship dynamic always having one dominant party, and that dominant party always being the same one. This is also the reason behind certain relationships not being capable of fitting into class 2A, as discussed later in this chapter.

> The main examples of relationships that do fit into class 2A are:
>
> ■ Doctor and patient
> ■ Solicitor and client
> ■ Parent and child[15]
> ■ Guardian and ward
> ■ Religious adviser and disciple.[16]
>
> In each of these situations, the presumption of undue influence automatically exists by the mere existence of the relationship. There is always one party that holds influence over the other, and therefore is capable of being abused.

Since the *Etridge (No. 2)* judgment, a finding of the existence of one of these relationships places the parties in a protected situation where the presumption of influence cannot be rebutted, merely the finding that the influence was undue. To allow otherwise would call into question the validity of that relationship's presence in class 2A, as they are said to be relationships that always conform to the same type.

However, there are several categories that do not give rise to this automatic presumption, but *may* fall into class 2B instead. This is because these are situations where it is possible to prove that there is a close relationship of trust and confidence, but it should not be automatically assumed from the existence of the relationship. They are:

■ Husband and wife[17]
■ Banker and customer[18]
■ Employer and employee.[19]

---

15 This excludes elderly parents and adult children: see *Avon Finance Co Ltd v Bridger* [1985] 2 All ER 281.

16 *Allcard v Skinner* (1887) 36 Ch D 145.

17 *Midland Bank plc v Shephard* [1988] 3 All ER 17.

18 See the judgment of Lord Scarman in *National Westminster Bank v Morgan* [1985] AC 686.

19 *Credit Lyonnais Bank Netherland NV v Burch* [1997] CLC 95.

The problem with recognising these relationships under class 2A is that, unlike those listed previously, it is not possible to universally stereotype these relationships. Eligibility for class 2A relies upon the relationship always being of a particular type, with one party always being identified as dominant and therefore capable of influence. In addition, the protected status afforded to those in class 2A relationships means that it must be used carefully and sparingly.

If you encounter a relationship in an assessment question that does not fall into one of the class 2A categories mentioned in the last box, even if you feel that it should be, do not fall into the trap of thinking that you can add them. There are many relationships in which it might be possible to see undue influence occurring, but unless all types of those relationships can be categorised in the same way, the relationship will always have to be dealt with through evidence of that particular relationship, otherwise known as class 2B.

10.8 CLASS 2B: RELATIONSHIPS WHERE TRUST AND CONFIDENCE HAVE TO BE PROVEN

This class contains examples of relationships where, although they fall outside the scope of class 2A, it may be proven in their particular case that the relationship of trust and confidence exists and therefore that there should be a presumption of influence. This is often referred to as evidentiary presumption, mainly because evidence of the relationship that exists in that particular instance has to show that one party held a position of influence over the other.

It is important to distinguish between evidence in a case of class 1 undue influence and class 2B undue influence, as often the distinction is confusing. In class 1 evidence of a specific instance of undue influence is being presented to the court, to demonstrate actual abuse of the relationship. Whereas in class 2B the evidence is merely to establish the existence of a relationship of trust and confidence from which a presumption of influence may be found.

The need to be mindful of this distinction is particularly relevant where judges have found there to be actual influence in situations where the party concerned is using that evidence to demonstrate a relationship where influence should be presumed (traditionally referred to as class 2B). This is arguably unhelpful in that it blurs the distinction between the two types of undue influence and has the potential to confuse claimants in this type of situation.

ANNULMENT FUNDING CO LTD V COWEY [2010] 2 P & CR DG 22

The Court of Appeal found that actual undue influence and evidence-based presumed undue influence could be considered as alternatives by the court.

This case concerned a man who was declared bankrupt, but who had a beneficial interest in a house, jointly with his partner, the amount of which more than covered the amount of debt that had led to the bankruptcy. He engaged Annulment Funding, a company that specialised in annulling the bankruptcy of its clients by loaning them the amount required to pay off their creditors in bankruptcy in the form of a bridging loan. This is a short-term loan, used until the now discharged bankrupt client can obtain a mortgage on their property to pay back Annulment Funding Ltd.

In Mr Cowey's case, the mortgage broker was unable to find a mortgage, and so Annulment Funding took action to recover the amount of the bridging loan by repossession and sale of the house that Mr Cowey and his partner jointly owned.

Mr Cowey's partner argued that the agreement she had entered into regarding the bridging loan was subject to Mr Cowey's undue influence, and argued for a presumption to be set up of undue influence that would then need to be rebutted by Annulment Funding in order for them to be able to repossess the house.

Held: there was enough evidence to establish a case of actual influence, and found on this basis. They also found that:

Even where a party argues for a finding of presumed influence on the basis of evidence, the court is at liberty to find that actual influence had taken place on the basis of that evidence.

Additionally, that as there had not been enough evidence to demonstrate actual influence, presumed undue influence could be used as an alternative.

This serves to confuse the distinction between the two types of influence, as the nature of what is being proven is different, as discussed above. Although the ability to argue either/or between the two might be explained by the fact that the evidence itself is likely to be very similar, the purpose it is being put to in actual and presumed influence is different.

Although the relationship between banker and customer does not fall within class 2A, two cases have demonstrated the ability of this relationship to fall within class 2B.

NATIONAL WESTMINSTER BANK V MORGAN [1985] AC 686

The court accepted that this relationship was capable of being one of confidence, but that, on the facts of the particular case, there was not enough to demonstrate this. Lord Scarman stated: 'the impugned transaction had not been caused by the existence or by the exercise of influence by the bank in any sense relevant to a plea of undue influence'.[20]

This approach was followed in *Lloyds Bank v Bundy*[21] although, contrary to *Morgan*, that relationship was established in the *Bundy* case. The court found that influence existed since the customer had banked at the particular branch for many years. This therefore led to a finding that the facts needed to demonstrate a relationship of trust and confidence were enough to satisfy the court that it fell under class 2B and a presumption could be established.

ANALYSING THE LAW

The most often questioned class 2B relationship is that of husband and wife. It might be considered by some that the omission of this relationship from class 2A is puzzling, as the nature of the personal and intimate relationship of marriage would logically lead one to think of a relationship of trust and confidence. By extension, one would also logically consider all marriages since the Marriage (Same Sex Couples) Act 2013, as well as cohabitees and anyone else in intimate personal relationships. This was discussed and accepted by Lord Browne-Wilkinson in *Barclays Bank v O'Brien*.[22] However, the problem with inclusion of these relationships in class 2A is that it is not possible to stereotype them as being of a particular type, and a wish to do so might be seen as being somewhat old-fashioned. It cannot be said that the wife will always defer to the husband on financial decisions, and therefore be influenced by him. As a result, there can be no automatic presumption of undue influence; but one can be shown. So it may be that in a *particular* relationship, where the wife relied on the husband to deal with all financial matters and just follows his advice, the presumption of influence may be established.

10.8.1 ESTABLISHING THAT THE INFLUENCE WAS UNDUE

The second part of what has to be shown in cases of undue influence is not only the presumption of a relationship of influence between the parties, but also that the influence was

---

20 [1985] AC 686 at 693.
21 [1975] QB 326.
22 [1994] 1 AC 180 at 198.

undue. The purpose behind this is because, as well as showing that one party had the ability to influence the other, it is important in cases of presumed undue influence to show that something has happened which can only be explained by the abuse of the influence that is held over the other party.

Historically, this has been through the use of the phrase 'manifest disadvantage'. The idea behind this is the assumption that people will always act in their own interest and therefore any action that goes against their self-interest must have come about as a result of the influence of the other party involved.

This was established as a strong evidential factor in establishing undue influence in *National Westminster Bank v Morgan*,[23] and was subsequently discussed as being a requirement, based on the *Morgan* judgment in *BCCI v Aboody*.[24] Slade LJ quoted from *Allcard v Skinner*[25] in his judgment, based on the idea discussed above regarding acting in one's own self-interest. Once you step outside of the bounds of this, you must be acting to your manifest disadvantage.

There are a number of cases demonstrating the concept of manifest disadvantage.

CIBC MORTGAGES PLC V PITT [1994] 1 AC 200, [1993] 3 WLR 802

A husband pressured his wife into taking out a £150,000 mortgage on the house in order to buy shares and speculate on the Stock Exchange.

Held: there had been actual undue influence here. However, as the husband had lied on the loan application form to the bank, they had no notice of the real purpose of the loan: they were told that the money was to buy a second property in both parties' names.

With regard to the issue of manifest disadvantage, the court at first instance was satisfied that the real purpose of the loan was to the wife's manifest disadvantage, whereas the stated purpose was not.

Further insight as to the meaning of manifest disadvantage came from the case of *Dunbar Bank plc v Nadeem*.

DUNBAR BANK PLC V NADEEM (1999) 31 HLR 402, (1999) 77 P & CR D8

The husband and wife took out a loan to purchase the lease on a property, but also to pay off the husband's debts. When the husband fell into arrears on the payments,

---

23 See Lord Scarman's judgment [1985] AC 686 at 706.
24 [1990] 1 QB 923, [1989] 2 WLR 759 per Slade LJ.
25 (1887) 36 Ch D 145.

the bank attempted to repossess, and the wife argued that the loan was the subject of undue influence. The manifest disadvantage, it was argued, was because part of the loan was to service the husband's debts.

Held: the court followed the *Aboody* case in requiring there to be a manifest disadvantage, but held that the loan was not to the wife's manifest disadvantage because she obtained a beneficial joint interest in the equity of redemption. It did not matter that part of the loan was for another purpose; she had gained from the loan and that was enough.

The test of manifest disadvantage appeared to have reached the end of the road in the case of *Barclays Bank v Coleman*.[26] This case involved a wife claiming undue influence in a situation where she had agreed to a loan secured on the matrimonial home in order to secure her husband's indebtedness. The issue of manifest disadvantage was raised in the Court of Appeal because, at first instance, the judge had held that there was no manifest disadvantage.

This case highlights difficulties with the definition of this phrase 'manifest disadvantage', and the court, bound by precedent in previous cases discussed above, defined it as being 'clear and obvious'[27] and needed to be judged at the time of the transaction. It was concluded that, in that case, the nature of the transaction and the significance of what the wife was agreeing to was a much greater risk than she could have known. On this basis, the court held that she had acted to her manifest disadvantage, although judicial discussion concerning the irrelevance of the size of the disadvantage was no more helpful in clarifying what this term actually meant.

Finally, the test of 'manifest disadvantage' was criticised in *Royal Bank of Scotland v Etridge (No. 2)*[28] when the case reached the House of Lords. The problem related to a lack of clarity regarding its meaning, and was seen as quite a high standard to meet. Lord Nicholls commented that the requirement was 'causing difficulty' and could 'give rise to misunderstanding'.[29] However he did recognise that there was a need for something as a second criterion to the requirement for presumed undue influence, because this would help to distinguish between ordinary transactions where no presumption of undue influence should arise, and those that should fall within the definition of presumed undue influence.

For this reason, he cited the need to show that the purpose of the loan is something 'which calls for an explanation'.[30] This takes a tighter line than the 'manifest disadvantage' test and allows for transactions that might be entered into because of personal feelings for the other party, in situations that on a purely individualistic analysis might not be in their own self-interest. For example, a situation where a wife agreed to a loan on the matrimonial home

26 [2001] QB 20, [2000] 3 WLR 405.
27 [2001] QB 20 at 33.
28 [2002] 2 AC 773, [2001] 3 WLR 102.
29 [2002] 2 AC 773 at 799.
30 Ibid.

in order to pay off her husband's business debts would not be considered to be something that would 'call for an explanation'. Similarly in *Portman Building Society v Dusangh*[31] parents taking out a second mortgage to support their son's business venture would also be considered to be within what family members might do to assist their offspring, however unwise or risky it might be. This provides a good example of something that may have been considered to the 'manifest disadvantage' of the parents under the old test.

ANALYSING THE LAW

Lord Nicholls in *Etridge (No. 2)* commented that transactions of a more unusual nature, for example an unusually large gift, would call for further explanation. The actions of an employee towards their employer in putting their house up as collateral security for the overdraft of the company in *Credit Lyonnais Netherland NV v Burch*, which 'would cause a bank manager to raise his eyebrows more than a little',[32] gives some insight into the meaning of something calling for an explanation.

This approach of the House of Lords in *Etridge (No. 2)* therefore discarded the idea of 'manifest disadvantage' and relied more heavily upon the judgment of *Allcard v Skinner*, where the court proposed the idea that where a gift 'is so large as not to be reasonably accounted for on the grounds of friendship, relationship, charity or other ordinary motives on which ordinary men act',[33] then it is down to the person receiving that gift to provide an explanation.

10.9 BURDEN OF PROOF

There are two issues concerning burden of proof with presumed undue influence cases. Firstly there is the issue of establishing the presumption of influence in either class 2A or class 2B; and, secondly, there is the issue of showing that the influence was 'undue'.

The burden of proof in establishing the presumption of influence lies with the party claiming undue influence. In class 2A, once that burden has been discharged, this presumption of influence is fixed and cannot be discharged. This is the consequence of the way in which the specially protected classes are now regarded in the wake of the *Etridge (No. 2)* judgment.

In class 2B, again the burden is upon the party claiming influence to establish a presumption. However, this is done through evidence of the relationship at hand, to demonstrate that trust and confidence exists. This therefore leads to a presumption, as in class 2A, that one party has influence over the other.

---

31 (2000) 80 P & CR D20.
32 *Credit Lyonnais Bank Netherland NV v Burch* [1997] CLC 95 at 107.
33 (1887) 36 Ch D 145 at 185.

APPLYING THE LAW

This is where class 2B differs. The burden is reversed, and it is then up to the other party to rebut this presumption of influence. This can be done most effectively by showing that the other party was not in fact induced, and entered into the agreement freely.

So if you were accused of unduly influencing someone's decision to enter into a contract with you, the most effective way of rebutting the presumption that you have influence over them, such that they have 'trust and confidence' in you, is to show that they made their decision independently, maybe through showing that they had independent advice.

This would therefore demonstrate that the decision made was one that was a fully informed one, based upon independent advice and not solely upon the influence of the other party.

In subsequent cases, where banks and other lenders have tried to defend themselves against the possibility of undue influence, this has often been shown by ensuring that the party concerned receives independent advice on the matter. (This was central to the decision in *Barclays Bank v O'Brien* and also the Court of Appeal judgment in *Royal Bank of Scotland v Etridge (No. 2)* – see the next section on constructive notice for further discussion.)

However, it is still up to the claimant to establish that the influence was undue, as this is now no longer considered to be part of the presumption since *Etridge (No. 2)*. In this respect, burden of proof still lies with the claimant to demonstrate that the agreement entered into goes beyond that which would normally be expected of that relationship. Inevitably this is going to be an issue based on each individual case, and one that will be satisfied by the finding that questions should be asked of the nature of the deal. This will then reverse the burden of proof to the other party, who will be expected to provide the 'further explanation' without which the court will find that the decision to enter the agreement must have been a result of *undue* influence by the other party (see Figure 10.4).

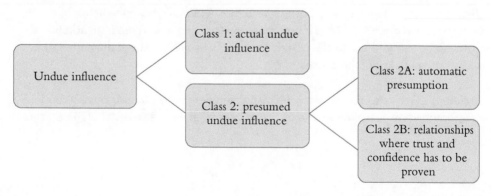

Figure 10.4 Types of undue influence

10.10 CLASSIFYING UNDUE INFLUENCE SINCE *ETRIDGE*

Courts in undue influence cases saw the class 1 and 2 distinction as being the most straightforward way of distinguishing between different types of undue influence. This was first proposed in *BCCI v Aboody* and subsequently approved of by Lord Browne-Wilkinson in his judgment in *Barclays Bank v O'Brien*.[34] However, this classification of undue influence was described by the House of Lords in *Royal Bank of Scotland v Etridge (No. 2)*[35] as unhelpful, due to the confusion that they felt it had created over the issue of presumed undue influence. A post-*Etridge* analysis of undue influence therefore tries to clarify the role of the presumption in class 2, as the point being made by the court in *Etridge* related to the difference between class 2A and class 2B.

The key difference to the pre-*Etridge* position regarding presumed undue influence is a clarification regarding what the result of the presumption is. In class 2A, this involves an automatic presumption based upon the type of relationship involved. However, what is being established through this is that there is a presumption of *influence*, but not necessarily that the influence was undue. It is still necessary to demonstrate that there was a suspicious nature to the influence such that the court could decide that the influence was undue, but the existence of influence cannot be rebutted. The defendant can only demonstrate that the influence was not abused.

In class 2B, there is again a presumption of *influence* established, but instead of being in a specially protected class, evidence of influence in that particular relationship has to be established in order to set up the presumption. This again means that the claimant also has to establish the undue nature of this influence separately but, unlike in class 2A, it is possible for the defendant to rebut the presumption of influence altogether.

ANALYSING THE LAW

The position this places those in class 2A in is therefore strengthened. Whereas before *Etridge* it might have been possible to say that setting up a presumption under class 2B places a person in the same position as those benefitting from the automatic presumption in class 2A, it is no longer possible to argue this. There is an additional protection given to those in class 2A as a result of this finding about the nature of what is rebuttable in each of the classes.

Whether this removes the need for the distinction defined by class 1, class 2A and class 2B, however, is a different matter. What we are left with as a result of the *Etridge*

---

34 [1994] 1 AC 180, [1993] 3 WLR 786.
35 [2002] 2 AC 773, [2001] 3 WLR 102.

case is a distinction between actual and presumed undue influence, and within the category of presumed undue influence, a category of protected persons, as well as those who need to establish the presumption through evidence. The elevation of those in the specially protected class is the main distinction. It is still valid to consider the classifications provided by the court in *BCCI v Aboody*.

10.11 REMEDIES FOR UNDUE INFLUENCE

As with duress, the main remedy for undue influence is to make the contract voidable at the victim's discretion. Therefore, the ability to rescind the contract is available. Similarly, as with *The Atlantic Baron* case[36] in duress, if no rescission has been applied for, this can be deemed to be constructive affirmation of the contract, and remedies will no longer be available.

ALLCARD V SKINNER (1887) 36 CH D 145

The plaintiff had joined a religious group called 'Sisters for the Poor' while under the influence of her spiritual advisor. During her time as part of this group, she had given approximately £7,000 to the religious leader. She left the group and, six years after having left, she attempted to reclaim money that she had paid.

Held: the long delay between leaving the order and claiming the money could be construed as being a constructive affirmation of the contract, and she was not entitled to recover the money.

The key here is not the end of a contractual situation, but rather the end of the influence held over a person by someone exercising undue influence. As that influence had ended at the time that the person left the 'Sisters for the Poor', this was the point at which she should have attempted to recover the money that she had paid out.

10.12 THIRD PARTY RIGHTS AND UNDUE INFLUENCE

There may be situations in which rescission is not available to the aggrieved party, and the most important example of this is where there are also third party interests involved, and any

---

36 *North Ocean Shipping v Hyundai Construction (The Atlantic Baron)* [1979] QB 705.

rescission would adversely affect them. This is effectively because it would not be possible to offer a remedy to the victim in these cases, without the third party also losing out in a situation where they are also not at fault for the undue influence that has been exerted. The problem that this creates though is the extent to which the undue influence between two parties should affect the financial position of a third party, usually the bank that had lent money under an agreement with these two parties.

The most commonly litigated example of this involves a bank or other lending institution loaning money to a husband and wife.[37] The nature of the relationship is explained in Figure 10.5.

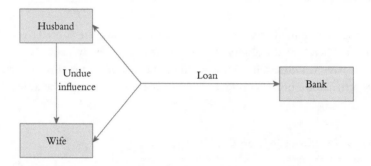

Figure 10.5 Undue influence and the connection to a third party lender

The husband and wife enter into a loan agreement, usually secured upon their matrimonial home. If the wife is able to successfully argue that this was as a result of her being unduly influenced, she is able to void the agreement with the bank. However, the consequence of this is that the bank is then unable to enforce the terms of the loan, including repossession of the house in the event of a default. This then results in the bank losing out because of the undue influence, in a situation where they have loaned the money in good faith. It can be seen that the rights of the bank and the rights of the unduly influenced party are therefore in conflict with each other.

10.12.1 THE DOCTRINE OF CONSTRUCTIVE NOTICE

The solution to this conflict came through the idea of the bank being fixed with notice of the undue influence. If the third party has actual knowledge of the undue influence, their rights are subject to the rights of the victim of the undue influence. The victim's rights take priority and, in many husband and wife cases, this therefore meant that a bank or other financial institution was prevented from taking action to recover money owed, usually by repossession of the matrimonial home.

---

37 Lord Browne-Wilkinson commented that there had been 11 such cases in the eight years prior to *Barclays Bank v O'Brien* reaching the House of Lords: [1994] 1 AC 180 at 185.

ANALYSING THE LAW

The main problem with the rights of the victim taking precedence over the rights of the lender is the likelihood of the bank having actual notice of the undue influence is very slim. As we have seen earlier in this chapter with the case of *CIBC Mortgages v Pitt*,[38] borrowers can lie on the loan application form and there is little that a lender will be able to do if the stated loan purpose is credible.

The absence of actual notice has therefore led to the development of the doctrine of constructive notice. This doctrine allows for a lender to be 'constructively' aware of the undue influence through circumstances that should have led them to make further investigations into the circumstances around the borrowers.

These cases have usually fallen under class 2B, as the husband–wife relationship does not give rise to class 2A (although the potential is there for class 1, if there is sufficient evidence to establish this class: see for example *CIBC Mortgages v Pitt*, discussed above).

BARCLAYS BANK V O'BRIEN [1994] 1 AC 180, [1993] 3 WLR 786

In this case the idea of a doctrine of constructive notice was applied. This case involved a wife who had entered into an agreement for a charge to be placed on the matrimonial home to guarantee the overdraft of the husband's company. The transaction took place at a different branch to the one that the couple usually used, and therefore the O'Brien's bank manager had left instructions for both parties to be fully appraised of the current state of the overdraft and to advise them to speak to their solicitor if they had any concerns prior to entering into the agreement. Unfortunately, the branch did not follow their instructions, and therefore the wife was unaware of the extent of the overdraft. She thought it was at £60,000 when, in reality, it was at £135,000.

When the company's overdraft reached £154,000, the bank attempted to repossess the house under the legal charge that had been placed upon it. The wife claimed that she had entered into the agreement because of the undue influence of her husband, and attempted to get the transaction set aside.

The court discussed policy considerations, with the growing number of cases involving wives, but rejected the idea of some form of special protection for wives or others in similar relationships, mainly because this might give a shortcut back to class 2A (automatic presumption of undue influence) for such parties.

38 [1994] 1 AC 200.

Held: the transaction was of such a nature that in order to avoid being fixed with **constructive notice,** the bank would have to demonstrate that certain steps had been taken by them. The first part of this relies upon the bank being 'put on inquiry' in certain circumstances. Those circumstances were:

(a) the transaction is on its face not to the financial advantage of the wife; and
(b) there is a substantial risk in transactions of that kind that, in procuring the wife to act as surety, the husband has committed a legal or equitable wrong that entitles the wife to set aside the transaction.[39]

If it were subsequently shown that there had been undue influence, the bank would have constructive knowledge of the undue influence unless they could show that they had taken reasonable steps to establish that the wife had entered into the transaction freely and knowing the facts. The court held that, as this had not happened in *O'Brien*, the bank had constructive notice of the undue influence, and could not repossess the family home.

10.12.2 AVOIDING CONSTRUCTIVE NOTICE

APPLYING THE LAW

The most important consideration for a lender that finds themselves in this situation is how to avoid being regarded as having constructive notice of the undue influence. The case law from *Barclays Bank v O'Brien* onwards has looked for effective ways of doing this. Lenders would prefer to have a transparent procedure to follow in order to ensure they avoid constructive notice, mainly because in these husband–wife transactions in particular, a finding of undue influence prevents the lender from recovering the money they have loaned by getting possession of the property the loan is secured on (usually the matrimonial home) and selling it. Arguably the best position for a lender would be to ensure that the possibility of undue influence cannot arise.

The problem here is that a lender placed on inquiry is not going to be able to just ask the wife if she has been unduly influenced. The courts therefore had to come up with some direction for the bank to follow regarding what reasonable steps needed to be taken by the bank. The reasonable steps described by Lord Browne-Wilkinson in *O'Brien* involved the bank being required to hold a private meeting with the wife (without the husband) to inform her of the extent of her liability and, where it is considered necessary, to urge her to take independent legal advice on the matter.

39 [1994] 1 AC 180 at 196.

As we can see from the requirements placed upon lenders by Lord Browne-Wilkinson's 'reasonable steps', the concept of constructive notice presents challenges for lenders because this places a burden upon the bank to discharge any presumption of notice as to the undue influence. However, recent cases have attempted to clarify what a bank would need to do to avoid constructive notice and, where possible, reduce the burden upon them. This is important because of the need to have settled and appropriate practice for the banks to apply in such situations, as the financial liability involved in being held on constructive notice can be quite high.

The problem with the requirement laid down in *O'Brien* (that the bank should advise the wife privately in an interview separate to her husband and to refer onto legal advice if necessary) was that potentially the bank could be exposing itself to more liability by providing the advice, and potentially higher liability than the constructive notice that this was intended to avoid. This subsequently led to the practice by banks to just refer all wives directly to a solicitor to get independent legal advice regardless of the circumstances, in order to ensure that they had discharged their obligations and avoided constructive notice. Usually the courts would accept a certificate obtained from the wife's solicitor stating that the wife had been suitably individually advised in order to discharge the constructive notice. In *Barclays Bank v Coleman*,[40] the court accepted confirmation that the wife had been appropriately advised by a legal executive as this still met the standard required, and often the task of advising clients on issues such as this would go to the legal executive rather than a solicitor.

Also, by focussing purely on the husband–wife relationship, this excludes consideration of a whole host of different personal relationships involving cohabitees, civil partnerships, friends, relatives, and a whole manner of other relationships between individuals that may involve undue influence being exerted on one party by the other. Therefore, the courts' acknowledgement of other relationships also being included is an important part of the doctrine: see the *O'Brien* judgment regarding this.[41]

The solution to the uncertainty and apprehension about the requirements in *O'Brien* was presented in a simplified approach in *Royal Bank of Scotland v Etridge (No. 2)*. Lord Nichols[42] attempted to clarify what was needed and from whom in discharging constructive notice. The Court of Appeal in *Etridge (No. 2)*[43] had set out numerous requirements regarding the duty on the bank and the duty on the solicitor. This moved the duty away from a need for the bank to hold meetings and dispense advice set out in *O'Brien*, and more towards the duty of the solicitor to provide the relevant advice, and was therefore more in line with the reality of post-*O'Brien* practice amongst lenders.

Further support for this came from Lord Nicholls, who stated that he did not believe that Lord Browne-Wilkinson (in the Court of Appeal version of *Etridge (No. 2)*) was suggesting

---

40 [2001] QB 20, [2000] 3 WLR 405.
41 *Barclays Bank v O'Brien* [1994] 1 AC 180 at 198.
42 [2002] 2 AC 773 at 804.
43 [1998] 4 All ER 705 at 719.

that the bank needed to know the state of the relationship of the parties involved.[44] Instead it should just be that, in a personal relationship, where one party stands as surety for the other party's debts, the bank should be considered 'on notice', and therefore know that there were steps it needed to follow to avoid constructive notice.

Lord Nicholls' judgment in the *Etridge (No. 2)* case provides guidance on the matter of avoiding constructive notice. His advice can be summarised as follows:[45]

1. Constructive notice can be avoided if the bank ensures that the steps in Figure 10.6 occur.

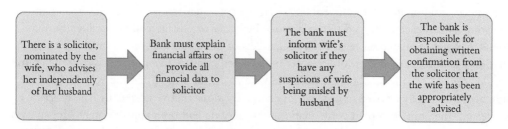

Figure 10.6 Steps to be followed in avoiding constructive notice

2. The bank merely needs to make sure that a solicitor is named by the wife, and that this solicitor is instructed to advise separately to the husband. This can be the same solicitor that her husband uses, but the wife must be given the opportunity to nominate a separate solicitor. The solicitor must advise the wife on the nature of documents and practical implications of signing them. They must also explain that the wife will be legally bound by documents once signed.
3. As the bank are in the best position to explain the financial situation, they must either do so, or pass on all the relevant financial data to allow the solicitor to properly explain the situation. The solicitor's role is then to advise and confirm in writing that this has taken place. Without the written confirmation from the solicitor, the bank should not proceed with the transaction. Even if it later transpires that the wife was subjected to undue influence, if these steps are followed then the wife will not be able to use the undue influence to argue that the transaction with the bank is unenforceable.

ANALYSING THE LAW

The effect of this ruling was to shift the burden away from the bank and towards the solicitor. This has provided relief for the bank, because it is not the bank's place to dispense legal advice, nor is it the bank's place to judge the sufficiency of any advice

---

44 [2002] 2 AC 773 at 803–804, in particular para. 46.
45 [2002] 2 AC 773 at 811–812.

given by a qualified solicitor. This therefore recognises the commercial reality of what a bank should reasonably be expected to do in the circumstances, and ensures that there are a set of transparent actions that can be taken by banks to safeguard their own interests.

EXPLAINING THE LAW

This does raise the question of why this is important. This is mainly because, without the ability to avoid constructive notice like this, banks would have to take the only other course of action available to them, which would be to stop lending money to people in personal relationships, secured on the family home or other shared property. This would have a detrimental economic effect upon (mostly) small businesses' access to finance. Banks would either

1) refuse loan applications where the collateral is the family home, or
2) lend only upon prohibitively high interest rates to reflect the level of risk and possible fallout from an undue influence claim.

It does lead to the question regarding why it was considered so important to have addressed this issue in favour of the banks in the first place. The courts in both *O'Brien* and *Etridge (No. 2)* discussed the need for a balance between the rights of an unduly influenced person, and the lender caught in a situation caused by the person exerting the undue influence.[46] A need was recognised to protect an innocent party in a situation of undue influence, but this should not be at the expense of a complete loss of rights of the lender. This was clearly for sound commercial reasons. Once this was agreed, the only thing that needed to be settled was where the balance should be struck between these two parties.

10.13 BRINGING IT ALL TOGETHER

Duress and undue influence can have a significant effect upon a contractual agreement because of the fact that it renders a contract voidable at the discretion of the victim if proved. Duress is available at common law, whereas undue influence is an equitable doctrine, to be applied at the discretion of the court where appropriate.

These two areas are considered an important part of the law of contract because of the way they affect a key aspect of contract law – that contractual agreements are made through the

---

46 See the judgment of Lord Browne-Wilkinson in *O'Brien* and the judgment of Lord Nicholls in *Etridge (No. 2)*

free will of the parties. Duress and undue influence are considered 'vitiating factors' because arguably they interfere with the ability of a person to freely and willingly enter into a contract. You should bear in mind this approach when considering the underlying theories that underpin contract law – see Chapter 1 and consider the rules regarding 'freedom of contract'.

When considering the effect of a finding of duress or undue influence, it is also important to bear in mind the impact upon parties to the contract, as well as third parties involved. The law has attempted to engage in a balancing act between the rights of a party whose will has been vitiated, and a third party who may also be innocent in the situation. Such a balance has been sought by the courts regarding undue influence and is at the heart of the discussion of cases in this chapter.

KEY LEARNING POINTS

Duress and undue influence affect the viability of a contract because it may be voidable at the discretion of the victim. Bear in mind the following points.

DURESS

- It requires some pressure or threat to be applied
- Threats must be unlawful
- Any threat has to be directed either at the other party to the agreement, or to family members or other loved ones
- Normal high-pressure business situations will not result in a finding of duress
- Duress can be found in either physical threats of violence or economic threats to business interests.

UNDUE INFLUENCE

- Relies upon relationships
- Can be proven through evidence of the undue influence that has occurred in the relationship
- Can be presumed from a particular type of relationship or from evidence of the particular relationship at hand
- Presumptions of influence based upon evidence of a relationship can be rebutted
- Presumption of the 'undue' nature of influence can be rebutted by evidence that a decision was made independently
- A party that has been unduly influenced has rights that can be limited by a third party that does not have notice of the undue influence
- Notice of undue influence can be actual or more likely constructive
- Third parties can avoid constructive notice by following the judgment of the House of Lords in *Etridge (No. 2)*.

GENERALLY

- A finding of duress or undue influence makes a contract voidable at the discretion of the innocent party
- Because of this, a contract may remain valid if it has been constructively affirmed by the innocent party.

TAKING IT FURTHER

Atiyah, 'Economic Duress and the Overborne Will' (1982) 98 LQR 197

Beatson, 'Duress as a vitiating factor in contract' (1974) 33 CLJ 97

Beatson & Burrows, *Anson's Law of Contract*, 29th edn, Oxford University Press, 2010

Devenney, 'Unconscionability and the taxonomy of undue influence' (2007) JBL 541

Mujih, 'Over ten years after Royal Bank of Scotland v Etridge (No. 2): is the law on undue influence in guarantee cases any clearer?' (2013) ICCLR 57

Peel, *Treitel on the Law of Contract*, 14th edn, Sweet & Maxwell, 2015

Thal, 'The inequality of bargaining power doctrine: the problem of defining contractual unfairness' (1988) 8 OJLS 17

11

CHAPTER 11
DISCHARGE OF CONTRACT (1)

11.1 INTRODUCTION

So far, we have considered the formation of the agreement, its content, and any vitiating factors that may affect that agreement. However contractual agreements do not last forever, and therefore we will also need to consider the point at which a contract is brought to an end. This chapter is the first of two that will consider the different ways in which a contract is discharged.

This chapter will focus upon discharge of contract by agreement, performance, and breach. Chapter 12 will focus upon the more complex situation of discharge by frustration.

The other point to bear in mind when considering discharge of contract is the consequence of that discharge. This means that alongside these two chapters, it is also important to have in mind Chapters 13 and 14 regarding remedies, particularly where the contract has been discharged by breach.

AS YOU READ

At the end of this chapter you should be able to:

- Understand how a contract is discharged by performance, agreement and breach

- Understand the necessary performance that is required in order to **discharge** a contract, compared to an incomplete or imperfect performance

- Appreciate how an agreement to discharge a contract must be supported by consideration

- Apply the law regarding breach to be able to identify both anticipatory and actual breaches of contract.

ESSENTIAL DEFINITION: DISCHARGE

The point at which a contract is discharged brings the agreement to an end. This means that the parties are no longer bound to perform obligations under the agreement; however, depending upon the way in which the contract has been discharged, they may be liable for any breaches that may have occurred.

There are four reasons for discharge of a contract (see Figure 11.1).

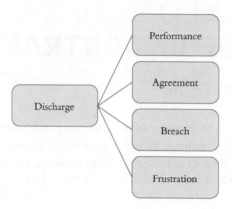

Figure 11.1 The four methods of discharge of contract

In this chapter, we will consider the first three of these: performance, agreement and breach. In Chapter 12, we will also consider a fourth type of discharge, by frustration.

In the overwhelming number of cases, a contract will be discharged by its performance. However, in a smaller number of situations, a contract can also be discharged by agreement, frustration (see Chapter 12) or breach. It should be noted at this stage that not all breaches of contract will result in a discharge of contract – this will be discussed in more detail later in the chapter.

11.2 PERFORMANCE

Most contracts are discharged by performance. In the overwhelming number of situations, a contract will be formed by the parties, and all the obligations will be performed. Once this has taken place, the contract is discharged, as there are no further duties to be performed and therefore the contract has run its course.

11.2.1 ENTIRE PERFORMANCE

This means that the contract is discharged because every obligation has been successfully performed as part of the contract. This is important because the parties will have agreed on the obligations to be performed, and they all have to be performed in order for the agreement to be discharged. This sounds on the face of it to be a very logical conclusion to arrive at – where parties have agreed to perform obligations, they have taken on a legal obligation that they must be held to.

The failure to strictly perform agreed obligations under a contract will result in a breach of contract, with the non-breaching party able to obtain a remedy for this. We will examine this issue later in the chapter.

The need for strict adherence to contractual obligations has led to this being considered 'the general rule'. It has, however, on occasion resulted in harsh outcomes, even though this in many situations appears to be the only fair way to deal with the discharge of contractual obligations.

CUTTER V POWELL (1795) 101 ER 573

Cutter was second mate on a ship sailing from Jamaica to Liverpool in the UK. He was promised 30 guineas 'provided he proceeds, continues and does his duty' until the ship reached Liverpool. The total journey time from Kingston, Jamaica to Liverpool would have been approximately eight weeks. The ship arrived at the port of Liverpool on 9 October, but Cutter had died before the arrival of the ship, on 20 September. An action was brought by his estate to recover wages equivalent to the portion of the journey that Cutter had worked on.

Held: the agreement made was for Cutter to perform his duties up to the point at which the ship arrived in Liverpool and, as he had failed to do this, the attempt by his estate to recover the money would fail.

This case is an example of the application of the general rule that all obligations must be performed strictly in order for their part of the contract to be discharged. However, it shows how this rule can sometimes result in a harsh outcome. The circumstances of the failure to completely perform under the contract are such that it was not a choice of the second mate not to continue his duties, as it was his death that prevented him from doing so.

This strict approach can also be seen in *Re An Arbitration between Moore & Co and Landauer & Co*[1] where the agreement was for the supply of canned goods in cases of 30 cans. The number of cans in each case varied, as some cases had 24 cans in them, and others had 30 cans. The overall number of cans supplied was in line with the contractual agreement. However, the Court of Appeal dismissed an appeal against the decision of the arbitrator, which stated that the other party were within their rights to reject the entire consignment based upon the discrepancy – even though it had no overall effect upon the quantity supplied. The contract had stipulated cases of 30 cans, and this is not what had been supplied.

Finally, the case of *Bolton v Mahadeva*[2] also illustrated the 'whole contract' approach of entire performance. This case involved an agreement to install a central heating system for a lump sum of £800. The central heating system was duly installed, but did not work properly, such that it did not heat the house properly, and gave off fumes. Because of this, the defendant in this case refused to pay for the installation, and the Court of Appeal decided that he was not liable for any payment.

---

1   [1921] 2 KB 519.
2   [1972] 2 All ER 1322, [1972] 1 WLR 1009.

ANALYSING THE LAW

These cases may seem to be rather harsh, but illustrate the literal interpretation applied when it comes to contractual performance. This has to be the case, purely because precision is required in order to establish that performance has been completed and the contract performed. Ambiguity would cause problems with establishing that a contract has been discharged by performance.

When considering whether a party to a contract has performed his obligations, attention must also be paid to whether the standard of performance required has also been complied with. This will affect whether the contract has been entirely performed, as often it will be important as to the quality of performance as well as merely the fact that performance has been rendered.

On this issue, the case of *Liverpool City Council v Irwin*[3] is relevant. This case was also discussed in Chapter 5. The case involved an implied duty on the council to maintain the communal areas in a block of flats. The lifts were continually breaking down, and council tenants had withheld their rent in protest at the poor state of the communal facilities. The court implied a duty into the contract, obligating the council to maintain the communal areas. The reason for many of the problems was due to vandalism carried out by persons unknown on the communal areas, and therefore the standard that the council were held to in performance of this implied duty was that of 'reasonable' performance. The House of Lords in this case concluded that, despite the continuing problems with the facilities, the council had met this reasonable standard and therefore were considered to have performed this obligation under the contract.

11.2.2 DOCTRINE OF SUBSTANTIAL PERFORMANCE

There is a great deal of potential for the above rule on performance to produce a great deal of injustice between the parties. Although it has merits in that it encourages entire performance of the contract exactly in line with the agreement, there will be occasions where it may lead to injustice.

The courts have therefore developed the doctrine of substantial performance, to cover situations where, despite the contract not being entirely performed, a party would be allowed to recover for their substantial performance of the contract. This would not allow recovery of the entire contract amount, but would result in the court calculating an amount based upon the amount of performance that has occurred.

This does require a substantial although not complete performance of the contract in order to be applicable. Where there are substantial defects that go to the heart of the contract, it is not possible to claim even a proportion of the amount payable, as discussed in *Hoenig v Isaacs*.[4] In

3   [1977] AC 239.
4   [1952] 2 All ER 176.

that case, the defendant attempted to avoid paying the complete contract price of £750 for the furnishing of a one-bedroom flat, on the grounds that there were defects and therefore entire performance had not been completed. However, the court considered that the contract had been substantially performed, and allowed for the payment of the contract price, less an appropriate deduction for the defects.

This pragmatic approach avoids the harshness of the 'entire contract' approach discussed above, but it should be noted that this applies only in situations that substantial performance has been completed, and not just any situation where there is partial performance of the contract.

> ### KEY LEARNING POINT
>
> If we consider the concept of 'substantial' performance, we can see how this would be dealt with in cases of incomplete performance. In *Cutter v Powell*, discussed above, the second mate died 19 days before the ship arrived in Liverpool, a period of more than a quarter of the expected journey time. In *Bolton v Mahadeva*, the central heating system substantially failed to do what it had been installed to do. These are not cases of substantial performance of a contract subject to some minor defects, and therefore this brings some further illumination to situations that at first glance may appear to be rather harsh.

Consider also the case of *Sumpter v Hedges*.[5] In this case, the plaintiff had entered into an agreement to build certain buildings for a total contract price of £565. He did work to the value of £333 before abandoning the contract. The building work was completed by the landowner, and the plaintiff then attempted to claim payment for the work he had done on the properties. However, the court did not allow him to recover any payment for the work he had done. We can see the underlying reasons in this case, because, as with the other two examples above, there is not a 'substantial' performance, as this was not a situation where performance was almost completed subject to minor defects – there was still considerable work to be done, as seen in the statements above about how much work had been done versus work still to be completed.

11.2.3 PART PERFORMANCE AND DIVISIBLE CONTRACTS

So far, discussion has been about 'entire' contracts. These are easy to reconcile with the need for the whole contract to be performed in order to discharge obligations and sue for the contract price. However, there are certain situations in which it is possible to claim for partial performance of a contract. This can cover a number of different situations, for example if the contract is capable of being divided into parts, or where the other party has done or said something that can be construed as being acceptance of part of the performance that should then be paid for. Alternatively, there are situations where one party attempts to perform the contract and is prevented from doing so. We will now consider all these situations.

---

5   [1898] 1 QB 673.

11.2.4 ACCEPTANCE OF PART PERFORMANCE

Where it is possible to demonstrate that the other party has entered into an agreement, either expressly or impliedly, to accept part of the performance then it is possible to sue for the payment of this part of the contract. This is different from accepting part performance in full settlement of the contract, which was discussed in regard to the sufficiency of consideration in Chapter 3. Instead, the principle here is about a *quantum meruit* payment based upon the amount of work that has been completed.

SUMPTER V HEDGES [1898] 1 QB 673

It was argued by the plaintiff that the actions of the defendant in completing the building work after the builder had abandoned the work partially finished should be construed as an acceptance of partial performance. It was on this basis that he argued that he should be entitled to the £333 for the partial completion of the building work under the contract.

The Court of Appeal disagreed, and based their reasoning upon the fact that the original judge in the case had held that the builder had abandoned the contract. Faced with this, the defendant was given no choice but to complete the buildings by other means, rather than this being an indication of their acceptance of part performance.

Held: the plaintiff's claim to part payment would be dismissed. The plaintiff had been able to recover the cost of materials used in the completion of the buildings (as these were materials left on site when the contract was abandoned) on the basis that the defendant had the choice regarding whether to use them or not. However, this did not change the court's decision regarding recovering for *work* completed by the plaintiff.

11.2.5 TENDER OF PERFORMANCE

There may be circumstances in which a party to the contract has attempted to perform obligations under the contract, but is prevented from doing so by the other party. The argument here is that as an attempt has been made to perform obligations, this should be viewed as equivalent to actual performance. It therefore requires that the tender of performance is proven, in order to truly establish that an attempt has actually been made. An example of one party tendering performance which was refused by the other party is *Startup v MacDonald*.

STARTUP V MACDONALD (1843) 134 ER 1029

This case concerned a contract for the delivery of ten tons of linseed oil which, according to the contract, was to be delivered to the other party 'within the last fourteen days of March, and paid for at the expiration of that time in cash'. Delivery took place on 31 March, which was a Saturday, at 8.30pm. The delivery was refused by the other party, who argued that it was an unreasonable time to deliver. On this basis, they also refused to pay for the attempted delivery of the goods.

The contract was silent on the issue of hour of delivery, and the plaintiffs argued that the hour of delivery gave the defendants plenty of time to receive and check the goods were in order before the end of the day (midnight).

Held: the attempted delivery had taken place within the deadline, and therefore damages for the attempted delivery should be awarded.

This approach can also be seen in *Planche v Colburn*,[6] despite a lack of actual tender of performance. The plaintiff was engaged by the defendants to write a book on costume and ancient armour, as part of a series called 'The Juvenile Library'. He was to be paid £100 for the completed manuscript. He had conducted a certain amount of preparatory work for writing this book, including a journey to inspect and draw a collection of armour, and had completed a significant amount of the work.

However, he had not tendered his manuscript to the publishers and, before he could complete it, they contacted him to inform him that, due to poor sales of earlier books in the series, the entire series had been cancelled and therefore his book would no longer be needed.

The plaintiff sued on the basis of *quantum meruit* to recover for work that he had completed in production of the book. The court agreed that, although he had not tendered the work itself, he should be entitled to £50 damages for the work completed prior to the defendants cancelling the book series.

11.3 MODIFICATION OF THE GENERAL RULE – DIVISIBLE CONTRACTS

Due to the hardship that may be caused by the general rule concerning entire contracts, judges have also allowed a contract to be divided into parts. This has the effect of mitigating the effect of treating a contract as unenforceable unless all obligations are performed.

APPLYING THE LAW

Where a contract is considered 'divisible', it means that it can be split into identifiable parts, each with obligations placed upon both parties that can be seen as a self-contained

6   (1831) 131 ER 305.

whole of itself. What this then allows the court to do is enforce the obligations separately and allow a party to sue for partial performance of the contract (although not all of it).

For example, consider a contract for the distribution of a monthly magazine to subscribers. A delivery company may have a case to argue that the contract is capable of divisibility where several months' worth of distribution had taken place; so, if the contract was breached by non-delivery of the magazine one month, payment for completed monthly performance so far would still be owed.

If we look at a case from earlier, *Cutter v Powell*, we can see what effect this would have upon a situation that might be seen as a little harsh. The second mate in this situation was not abandoning the contract but, because of his death, had only performed a certain amount of it (and it was not 'substantially performed' because he died 19 days before the end of an eight-week voyage). In this situation, had the contract been considered 'divisible', for example by dividing each day's or week's duties into an individual section, or by specifying payment as daily or weekly (rather than a lump sum at the end of the voyage) then this might have allowed his estate to claim for a certain proportion of the agreement.[7]

APPLYING THE LAW

However, this does lead us to consider what factors need to be taken into account in order to decide whether a contract is capable of being considered as 'divisible'. Consider the following factors:

1) whether the contract specifically stipulates that the contract is to be performed in its entirety before payment is due (as a 'condition precedent' in the contract)
2) in employment contracts, whether there is a stipulation for regular payment of wages, e.g. weekly or monthly
3) whether the contract price is based upon a unit price; e.g. a price per gallon or per ton
4) whether there is specific reference for payment to be made upon completion of specific tasks.[8]

An example of a contract considered 'divisible' can be seen in the case of *Ritchie v Atkinson*.

---

7   Had this matter been considered today, further protection might also be arguably provided by the provisions of the Merchant Shipping Act 1995. In particular, s. 30 deals with the payment of seamen's wages.
8   See the comments of Lord Denning MR in *Hoenig v Isaacs* [1952] 2 All ER 176 at 180.

RITCHIE V ATKINSON (1808) 10 EAST 295

This case involved the chartering of a ship, *The Adelphi*, which was required to load certain quantities of hemp and iron and then set sail from St Petersburg to London. While the ship was loading, there came news of an intended embargo on the port at St Petersburg, so *The Adelphi*, along with several other ships, loaded as much as they could within the time they thought they had left before the embargo, and set sail. Unfortunately, this meant that the ship was not fully loaded and so, when it arrived with a partial load in London, the charterers refused to pay for the goods delivered.

The court had to decide whether the contract involved a condition precedent[9] requiring the full cargo to be supplied, and therefore for the contract to be considered to be an 'entire' contract.

Held: it was not to be considered an 'entire' contract and, in the words of Bayley J, '[t]here would be a great injustice done by holding this to be a condition precedent; and none by a different construction'.[10] They therefore held that the ship owners should be paid for the cargo that they had delivered, but that the charterers were entitled to take action for the portion of the cargo that had not been delivered according to the charter agreement. This was therefore treated as a 'divisible' contract.

11.3.1 TIME OF PERFORMANCE

One final element that will affect the ability to discharge a contract by performance is that of time. In many situations, a contract will have some stipulation as to the time of performance required. In other situations, there will not be a specific reference to a time of performance, but in these instances the requirement implied into the situation will be that the contract will be performed in 'reasonable time'. In either case, if the contract is not performed on time, it raises questions about how the law is to deal with this.

The common law approach to such situations is that time is to be considered 'of the essence', and therefore a failure to perform either within a time requirement, or 'reasonable' time, will be a breach of condition. When considering this from a 'discharge by performance' perspective, this relates back to the general rule as failure to comply with a time requirement will therefore mean that the obligations in a contract will not be precisely discharged as required in this rule. It can also be considered from a 'breach' perspective, which we will do later in this chapter.

The approach of equity regarding this was, however, the opposite – equitable remedies would be applicable regardless of time stipulations, and therefore equity did not consider time to be 'of the essence'.

---

9 For more detail on conditions precedent, see Chapter 5.
10 Ibid, at 311.

APPLYING THE LAW

Consider the following factors when evaluating whether time appears to be 'of the essence' in a contract:

- Whether it has been expressly stipulated as being so by the parties in the contract
- Where one party has delayed performance beyond what would be reasonable, and has been informed by the other party that they must perform within a reasonable time or the contract will be ended
- Where there are circumstances surrounding the situation that mean that adhering to a precise agreed date is essential to the contract.

The possibility of different approaches in common law and equity changed with s. 41 of the Law of Property Act 1925, which states:

Stipulations in a contract, as to time or otherwise, which according to the rules of equity are not deemed to be or to have become of the essence of the contract, are also construed and have effect at law in accordance with the same rules.

This appears to unify the approach towards time being of the essence at common law and equity, and avoids two opposite approaches to the same situation. The effect this has upon contracts is not to remove time as an element of the contract, but instead it is like the difference between a condition and a warranty (see Chapter 5). If time is considered to be 'of the essence', a failure to comply with the time requirement would not be a precise performance of the contract, and would also be considered to be a 'repudiatory breach' (see later in this chapter). If it is not 'of the essence', it would still entitle the innocent party to sue for damages, as discussed in *Raineri v Miles*.[11] What this does mean though is that in order to work out whether time should be considered to be of the essence, it is important to consider whether one of the three possibilities mentioned above exists – in which case time will be considered to be of the essence both in common law and in equity.

A modern example of time being of the essence is in regard to agreements made under the Consumer Protection (Distance Selling) Regulations 2000.[12] This deals with consumer agreements made at a distance with the supplier. Regulation 19(1) states: 'Unless the parties agree otherwise, the supplier shall perform the contract within a maximum of 30 days beginning with the day after the day the consumer sent his order to the supplier.'

---

11 [1981] AC 1050, [1980] 2 All ER 145.
12 S.I. 2000/2334.

Although reg. 19(1) allows an agreement to contract out of this requirement, we know that this clear stipulation as to time required in this type of contract is considered to be 'of the essence' because of reg. 19(5), which states:

> A contract which has not been performed within the period of performance shall be treated as if it had not been made, save for any rights or remedies which the consumer has under it as a result of the non-performance.

This, therefore, not only places the 30-day requirement of reg. 19(1) within the category of being 'of the essence', but also any alternative arrangement that the parties may have come to in contracting out of reg. 19(1). This is therefore one area where the time stipulation will always be considered to be essential to the performance of the contract.

In summary, consider Figure 11.2:

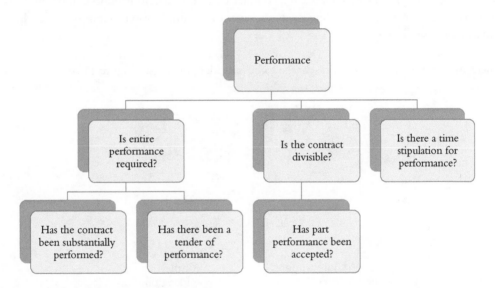

Figure 11.2 Discharge by performance

11.4 AGREEMENT

Obligations under a contract may also be discharged by the agreement of the parties. This is in keeping with the nature of a contract itself: it is an agreement to be bound by certain obligations, and therefore it can also be discharged in the same way.

In certain circumstances, contracts have formality requirements in order for them to be enforceable.[13] For example, in the case of *Morris v Baron*,[14] there was a requirement that a

13 See Chapter 4 on contract formalities for further discussion of this.
14 [1918] AC 1.

contract for the sale of goods of more than 10 shillings in value be in writing under s. 4 of the Sale of Goods Act 1893. This therefore additionally raises the issue of what is to be done where a contract with formality requirements is to be varied or discharged through an agreement. In *Morris v Baron*, the court held that this contract could be 'impliedly rescinded by a parole contract for the sale of goods', where it is clear that the intention is to discharge rather than vary the contract. Any agreement to vary a contract that is subject to the requirement of formalities also needs to be done by way of those same formalities. Essentially, what this means is that the rules for discharging a contract are more lenient than those for varying a contract, and therefore when doing either of these things it is worth bearing in mind that there may be different effects according to what is being done.

The main issue that needs to be dealt with concerns whether both parties, or just one party, still have obligations not yet performed under the contract, because any agreement to discharge obligations under a contract is a contract itself, and therefore has to comply with the usual rules of contract, including the requirement for consideration to move from each party, as discussed in Chapter 3.

There are therefore two types of discharge to be considered here (see Figure 11.3).

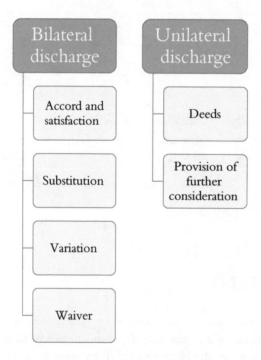

Figure 11.3 Types of discharge of contract

11.4.1 BILATERAL DISCHARGE

A situation of bilateral discharge is one where both parties still have obligations as yet unperformed under the contract. This means that they each have something 'of value' to offer in an agreement to discharge a contract. For this reason, this is therefore the most straightforward type of agreement to discharge a contract, and such agreements can take a number of forms. This is because there are a number of options available to parties wishing to discharge obligations under a contract (see Figure 11.4).

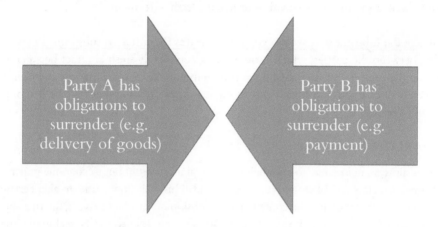

Figure 11.4 Bilateral discharge

This relates back to our discussion in Chapter 3 of consideration. A simple agreement to discharge all remaining obligations where both parties have obligations to surrender will comply with the requirement in *Dunlop v Selfridge*[15] of consideration moving from both parties. It is irrelevant whether the remaining duties are of equal value or not, as the law will not regulate the bargain itself, aside from ensuring that the law of contract is followed. See *Thomas v Thomas*[16] concerning 'peppercorn rent': the courts will not concern themselves with the market value of something, only that the requirement in consideration that something 'of value' is provided in support of the contract.

11.4.2 ACCORD AND SATISFACTION

Rescinding the agreement through accord and satisfaction results in the duties of the contract being considered discharged. As mentioned above, this has to comply with the rules of consideration, as an agreement to discharge a contract in this way also has to be supported by consideration. In bilateral discharge, this only happens where both parties have something to surrender as an obligation under the contract. The accord is the agreement to discharge, and the satisfaction is the consideration that is provided. So, if both parties agree to end the contract, and the consideration is not having to perform their obligations under that contract, this is valid: not having to perform a duty is of value to the person due to perform it, and is capable of being consideration.

....

15 [1915] AC 847.
16 (1842) 2 QB 851.

11.4.3 SUBSTITUTION

Rescission concerns situations where the parties wish to merely discharge the agreement between them, as discussed above. Provided there are obligations on both sides, a second agreement can be made to merely waive rights to enforce those obligations. Both parties are then free to walk away from the situation or make a fresh agreement.

This is where the substitution part can come in. It leaves them free to substitute a new agreement between the parties, which is treated as a completely fresh contract between them. This may be the preferred way of dealing as it therefore makes it clear that the old obligations are completely discharged, and there is no ambiguity as to anything that may be hanging over from the old agreement.

11.4.4 VARIATION

If the parties' aims are not merely to end their contractual relationship but to continue under a different agreement, it is possible to use variation instead. This will allow parties to alter certain obligations while still continuing the contractual relationship on that basis. Again, the rule applies that both parties have something 'of value' to bring to this agreement to vary, as technically the agreement to vary the original contract is a contractual agreement of itself. You should also bear in mind that unlike completely discharging the contract, if the original agreement required a particular form, the variation will also need to comply with that form to be enforceable (see discussion above regarding *Morris v Baron*). This is the major difference between merely ending the agreement and replacing it with a new one, and just making changes to the agreement. It therefore means that, depending upon the circumstances, careful thought must be paid to deciding which route to take.

11.4.5 WAIVER

One other way in which contractual terms can be altered is through waiver. This may at first appear confusing, as it is not entirely clear in some situations what the difference is between waiving rights and entering into agreements to vary the terms. Variation requires consideration and a further binding agreement, whereas waiver does not. Waiving a right is only to the benefit of one party, and so it is important not to mix up the two situations.

Waiver concerns a situation where one party has requested that certain rights under the contract are waived and, if the other party agrees, acts in reliance of this waiver. This is best illustrated by the case of *Charles Rickards v Oppenheim*.

CHARLES RICKARDS V OPPENHEIM [1950] 1 KB 616, [1950] 1 ALL ER 420

This case involved a contract to build a car body for a Rolls Royce Silver Wraith chassis that had been recently bought by the defendant. He had engaged the plaintiffs to build this because the plaintiffs had promised to build the body in 'six or seven months'. When this time had passed, without the body having been completed, the defendant agreed to wait a further three months. However, when it was still not delivered by then, the defendant informed the plaintiff that he intended to take the car abroad with him in four weeks' time and, if it was not ready by then, he would have to buy another car.

He was then informed by the plaintiff that it would not be ready for this deadline. The defendant therefore bought another car to take on holiday, and claimed back the money he had paid for the chassis, with the intention that the plaintiffs could sell on the chassis and body to someone else.

The plaintiff completed the car three months later and attempted to deliver it, but delivery was refused by the defendant.

The court concluded that the defendant had waived his right to enforce the seven-month deadline, and therefore could not insist upon precise compliance with that part of the contract. However, the later communication that required the car body to be completed within four weeks re-stated the importance of the time limit to the contract, and therefore failing to meet that deadline was treated as a breach. The waiver had only served to postpone the deadline and had not removed it permanently from the contract, so the defendant was entitled to serve notice regarding time being 'of the essence' (see discussion earlier in this chapter).

Held: the plaintiffs were in breach of the contract by failing to meet the later deadline, and therefore the defendant was entitled to reject the delivery of the car.

11.5 UNILATERAL DISCHARGE

Unilateral discharge is more problematic for the parties because it occurs in situations where only one party has obligations to perform. They therefore rely upon the other party unilaterally agreeing to allow them to discharge their obligations under the contract. The main problem this causes relates back to earlier discussion in this chapter regarding consideration. An agreement to unilaterally discharge the other party of their obligations is merely a gratuitous promise, and therefore not legally binding. Therefore, the other party could insist upon the performance of the obligation even if they had agreed to discharge it (see Figure 11.5).

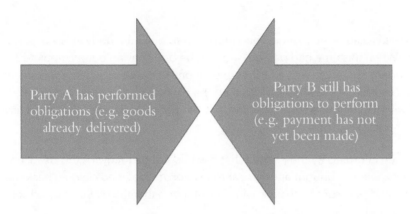

Figure 11.5 Unilateral discharge

There are, however, ways of addressing this issue where only one party has obligations to discharge.

11.5.1 DEEDS

As we have seen from discussion in Chapter 3 and Chapter 4, a contract executed in the form of a deed is exempt from the requirement of consideration flowing from both parties. This therefore means that a unilateral discharge executed by deed is enforceable. If both parties are in agreement with this arrangement, it will allow a unilateral discharge of the contract.

11.5.2 PROVISION OF FURTHER CONSIDERATION

Because a lack of consideration, usually from the party wishing to be freed from their contractual obligation, makes a unilateral discharge unenforceable, the most straightforward remedy for this is for something further of value to be provided, satisfying the consideration requirement. What that something of value is, is a matter that has been discussed in Chapter 3. Cases such as *Williams v Roffey Bros*[17] and *Pinnel's Case*[18] demonstrate that this is a broad concept and so there is a lot of scope for what could constitute consideration to support a unilateral discharge.

11.6 BREACH

Although the most common method of discharge of a contract is by performance, the one that sits almost as prominently is that of breach. Where a party breaches obligations that they have under a contract (usually by non-performance or defective performance of obligations), this *may* lead to discharge of that contract. However, it is not automatically the case.

If there are mitigating circumstances as to why obligations have not been performed, this may not be considered a breach. For example, the contract may have been frustrated by

17 [1991] 1 QB 1.
18 [1602] 5 Co Rep 117a.

outside factors instead (see Chapter 12). In those circumstances, although the contract may be discharged, it would not have been because of the breach of either of the parties.

As we shall see in Chapters 13 and 14, breach of contract has consequences for the breaching party as the other party is entitled to a remedy for the breach. But that remedy does not necessarily involve the contract being discharged. It is only the main obligations, those that go to the heart of the contract, that, once breached, result in the contract being discharged and no further obligations being due.

This is referred to as a repudiatory breach and will be discussed later in this chapter. However, there may also be breaches of contract that, although resulting in damages for the non-breaching party, do not repudiate the contract, and the remaining obligations remain due. The difference between a repudiatory and a non-repudiatory breach will often be dictated by the classification of the term that has been breached. For this, refer to Chapter 5 concerning terms. Briefly, a breach of condition will usually be considered to be repudiatory and result in discharge of the contract, but a breach of warranty will result only in damages being available to the non-breaching party.

11.6.1 WHEN IS THE CONTRACT DISCHARGED?

The moment of discharge by breach is important, mainly because it is at this point that the parties are no longer obliged to perform any further obligations under the contract. There are two types of repudiatory breach that will discharge the contract:

1) Anticipatory breach
2) Actual breach.

Whether the actions of one party amount to repudiation is important as it is only once this has been established that the possibility of an anticipatory breach can be considered. In *The Mersey Steel and Iron Co (Ltd) v Naylor, Benzon & Co*,[19] Lord Blackburn stated:[20]

> The rule of law, as I always understood it, is that where there is a contract in which there are two parties, each side having to do something, if you see that the failure to perform one part of it goes to the root of the contract, goes to the foundation of the whole, it is a good defence to say, 'I am not going on to perform my part of it when that which is the root of the whole and the substantial consideration for my performance is defeated by your misconduct.'

The withheld payment was not considered to be a condition precedent and therefore withholding the payment was not considered to be a repudiation.

A more modern example involving the singer Robbie Williams and the manager of pop group Take That is *Martin-Smith v Williams*.

---

19 (1884) 9 App Cas 434.
20 Ibid at 444.

MARTIN-SMITH V WILLIAMS [1999] ALL ER (D) 334

This case concerned circumstances surrounding the departure of the defendant, Robbie Williams, from Take That, and a dispute over whether commission was due to be paid to Take That's manager, Nigel Martin-Smith, on royalties due under the contract with the record company.

Williams had argued that Martin-Smith had failed in his duties as a manager to safeguard his interests around the time that he was negotiating his release from the record company contract so he could leave the group. This was argued to be a repudiatory breach of the management contract under which the commission payments were due.

Held: Martin-Smith's duties under the management contract were to the group as a whole and not to individual members. As he had given advice in the interests of the group, the management contract had not been repudiated.

FORCE INDIA FORMULA ONE TEAM LTD V 1 MALAYSIA RACING TEAM SDN BHD [2013] EWCA CIV 780, [2013] RPC 947

This case concerned a company that provided developmental and wind-tunnel testing services for a Formula 1 racing team. The racing team failed to make payments due under the contract, and the testing work was shut down, along with access to the computer servers where data from the testing was being held. They continued to demand payment for the work carried out under the contract, including a request for instalment payments in order to try and get the debt paid. They had also begun working for a rival F1 team under a different contract. The testing company argued that the contract with Force India had been repudiated.

Held: the suspension of work on the contract in itself did not result in a conclusion that the contract was repudiated, as continued demands for payment were being made. However, informing the other party that they had stopped work on their car and had instead switched to working on a rival team's wind-tunnel testing was a clear indication that the contract was being treated as repudiated.

11.7 ANTICIPATORY BREACH

An **anticipatory breach** will involve an attempt by one party to discharge the contract by indicating that they no longer intend to honour their obligations under the agreement. They will communicate their intention to the other party and indicate that they consider the contract to be at an end. Even though the actual obligation is not yet due to be performed, the non–breaching party can treat the contract as if it has been discharged by that breach.

ESSENTIAL DEFINITION: ANTICIPATORY BREACH

An anticipatory breach is one where one party communicates that they no longer intend to fulfil their obligations at a point before they are due. The other party is then entitled to treat the contract as breached and, if the breach is repudiatory, this can bring the contract to an end at that point.

There are several examples of this in action. In these examples, two elements are required. Firstly, there has to be the clear intention by one party not to perform obligations, and from the other party there has to be an acceptance of this.

FROST V KNIGHT (1872) LR 7 EXCH 111

The defendant had agreed to marry the plaintiff once the defendant's father had died. At this time, a promise to marry was considered to be a legally binding contract, and therefore engaged couples were legally obliged to carry out their promises.

While the defendant's father was still alive, he declared that he absolutely would not marry the plaintiff. The plaintiff therefore brought an action for breach of performance against the defendant.

In deciding whether the action brought by the plaintiff was appropriate, the court considered the fact that the time for performance was not yet due, and therefore an actual breach of the contract had not happened. Cockburn CJ stated:

> the promisee may, if he thinks proper, treat the repudiation of the other party as a wrongful putting an end to the contract, and may at once bring his action as on a breach of it; and in such action he will be entitled to such damages as would have arisen from the non-performance of the contract at the appointed time, subject, however, to abatement in respect of any circumstances which may have afforded him the means of mitigating his loss.[21]

Held: there had been an anticipatory breach, and the court awarded the plaintiff damages on the basis of treating the contract as discharged. This was so even though actual performance of the duties would have been at some unspecified time in the future (after the death of her fiancé's father). In doing this, the court applied the principle from *Hochster v De La Tour*.

---

21 (1872) LR 7 Exch 111 at 113.

HOCHSTER V DE LA TOUR (1853) 2 E & B 678

An agreement was made to employ the plaintiff as a courier. Employment was due to commence on 1 July 1852 at a wage agreed at £10 per month. However, before the commencement of the employment, the defendant refused to employ the plaintiff, and indicated that he considered the contract to be discharged at that point, releasing the plaintiff from the agreement.

The principle that was discussed concerned whether the plaintiff was obliged to wait until the first day of employment, with an actual refusal to employ the plaintiff, before he could treat the contract as discharged and sue for the breach, or whether he could sue once the other party had effectively communicated his intention not to honour the contract.

Held: the plaintiff was not obliged to wait for the moment of performance and could immediately treat the contract as ended. This meant that an action for breach of contract could also be taken before the date of performance. This is the principle that was subsequently applied to *Frost v Knight*, above.

However, it is not merely the actions of the breaching party that discharge a contract. The outcome of actions that amount to anticipatory breach (whether they be express or implied) will depend upon the reaction of the other party to that breach. As Viscount Simon LC stated in *Heyman v Darwins Ltd*:[22] 'But repudiation by one party standing alone does not terminate the contract. It takes two to end it, by repudiation, on the one side, and acceptance of the repudiation, on the other.'

KEY LEARNING POINT

This therefore puts the non-breaching party in a situation whereby they need to make a decision regarding how they are going to react to the repudiation of the contract by the other party. As we have seen, they are free to accept the repudiation. If they do so, they are able to sue at this stage for anticipatory breach. The contract is discharged upon the repudiation by the breaching party, and remedies will be calculated on this basis. In *Frost v Knight*, Cockburn CJ commented:

in assessing the damages for breach of performance, a jury will of course take into account whatever the plaintiff has done, or has the means of doing, and, as a prudent man, ought in reason to have done, whereby his loss has been, or would have been diminished.[23]

So, a non-breaching party would be able to recover, subject to whatever action is reasonable for the plaintiff to do to mitigate his losses. However, the non-breaching party also has another choice. They may choose not to accept the repudiation; as Viscount Simons

22 [1942] AC 356 at 361.
23 (1872) LR 7 Exch 111 at 115.

commented above, the discharge of the contract is reliant upon their acceptance of the repudiation. There are, however, consequences for taking such an action. If the contract is not successfully repudiated, it continues to run, and any obligations due by either party under the contract will still need to be performed.

Returning to the judgment of Cockburn CJ:

> The promisee, if he pleases, may treat the notice of intention as inoperative, and await the time when the contract is to be executed, and then hold the other party responsible for all the consequences of non-performance: but in that case he keeps the contract alive for the benefit of the other party as well as his own; he remains subject to all his own obligations and liabilities under it, and enables the other party not only to complete the contract, if so advised, notwithstanding his previous repudiation of it, but also to take advantage of any supervening circumstance which would justify him in declining to complete it.[24]

KEY LEARNING POINT

The above comment from Cockburn CJ also illustrates that not only can the contract be breached by the other party if it is allowed to run, but also it can be frustrated by an intervening act. In the event of this happening, the non-breaching party has lost out on a remedy by not accepting the repudiation, and the discharge of the contract will be resolved on principles relating to frustration instead (see Figure 11.6).

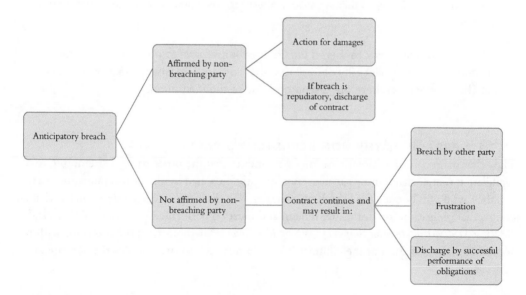

Figure 11.6 Consequences of anticipatory breach

---

24 Ibid at 112.

11.7.1 AFFIRMATION OR DISCHARGE?

The non-breaching party is faced with a choice: to affirm the contract and allow it to continue (to a possible actual breach), or to accept the repudiation of the other party and discharge the contract at the anticipatory stage. This is not a simple issue, and there is not one single answer to apply to all situations.

The main danger in allowing the contract to run is that it remains open to be affected by other factors. The main two factors that may affect a contract in such a situation are (1) frustration, or (2) breach by the non-repudiating party.

11.7.1.1 FRUSTRATION

If a contract, instead of being repudiated, is affirmed by the non-repudiating party, the contract may be frustrated by an intervening independent event,[25] as was the case in *Avery v Bowden*.

AVERY V BOWDEN (1856) 119 ER 1122

This case involved the charterparty of a ship. The plaintiff was ordered to sail to the Russian port of Odessa. Once there, it was to be ready to accept a cargo for up to 45 days, to be provided by the defendant. It was then to be brought to Great Britain.

The plaintiff presented themselves for a cargo at Odessa as required and was told to leave as it would not be possible to provide them with one. They continued to present themselves as available to take a cargo, right up to the point at which the Crimean War broke out.

Held: the outbreak of war rendered the contract impossible to perform and therefore frustrated, due to the illegality of trading with a country with which Great Britain was at war. The contract was therefore discharged due to the frustration.

11.7.1.2 BREACH BY THE NON-REPUDIATING PARTY

The other main danger with affirmation of a contract that the other party is attempting to repudiate is that, if that contract is then subsequently breached by the non-repudiating party, it is they who will be sued for breach of contract. Not discharging the contract means that all contractual obligations on both sides remain and must be performed. The case of *Fercometal SARL v MSC Mediterranean Shipping Co SA, The Simona*[26] demonstrates the problems with not accepting the repudiation of the contract if you do not stick to the terms of the agreement yourself.

---

25 See Chapter 12 for further discussion of discharge by frustration.
26 [1989] AC 788, [1988] 2 All ER 742.

FERCOMETAL SARL V MSC MEDITERRANEAN SHIPPING CO SA, THE SIMONA [1989] AC 788, [1988] 2 ALL ER 742

The owners of the ship had entered into a charterparty whereby they would make the ship available for loading the cargo on or before 9 July. If this condition was not met, the charterparty could be cancelled. On 2 July, they contacted the charterers to inform them that, because they wished to collect another cargo first, they would not be available to load until 13 July. The charterers immediately repudiated the charterparty and engaged another vessel, but the ship owners did not accept the repudiation, mainly because it was prior to the 9 July deadline.

On 5 July, the ship owners notified the charterers that the ship would be ready to load on 8 July and, upon arriving at the port, issued a notice of readiness to load. However, they were not ready, and the charterers loaded their cargo onto the other ship they had chartered instead.

Held: the ship owner's claim for wrongful repudiation was dismissed on appeal to the House of Lords on the grounds that, as they had not accepted the repudiation, all obligations (including their own) continued under the contract. The fact that they were not available for loading of the cargo on or before 9 July meant that they were in breach, and therefore the charterers could discharge the contract for their failure to meet a condition of the contract.

ANALYSING THE LAW

The issues that these cases present show the risk in allowing a contract to run. The circumstances in *Avery v Bowden* were such that it would have been plausible for the plaintiff to claim an anticipatory breach due to being informed of the impossibility of providing a cargo. If they had done this, it is the breach that would have discharged the contract, and therefore remedies would have been available on this basis. However, the frustration meant that remedies for breach were not available. In *The Simona*, if the ship owners had accepted the repudiation, they would have been able to claim wrongful repudiation of the contract and damages arising from this, because it fell before the 9 July deadline. Thus, in these situations, it is possible to see the difference in outcome between electing to discharge at anticipatory stage, or allowing the contract to continue with the aim of discharging only when actual breach occurs.

What this also means is that the repudiation of the contract, and therefore the discharge of the agreement itself, is not effective unless the innocent party acknowledges the repudiation and treats the contract as discharged. Although there are consequences for the innocent party to the contract, as we have seen above, there are also consequences for the party that has attempted to repudiate the agreement. They are also equally bound by the obligations of the contract, and therefore liable for their performance when they become due in the agreement.

11.7.1.3 CONSEQUENCES FOR PARTY ATTEMPTING TO REPUDIATE

Allowing the contract to continue means that the parties are expected to perform their obligations. Technically, this means that the contract is being treated as if the attempt at repudiation had never taken place, or indeed as if the innocent party had never even had notice of it. This approach might seem to be a little bit bizarre, because knowing that the other party no longer wants to continue with the contract will be in the contemplation of the non-breaching party when deciding what to do next. However, this has been held to be a perfectly valid response to an attempted repudiation, as was seen in the case of *White & Carter v McGregor.*

WHITE AND CARTER (COUNCILS) LTD V MCGREGOR [1962] AC 413, [1961] 3 ALL ER 1178, [1962] 2 WLR 17

This case involved a contract for advertising on council public waste bins. A company ran this scheme and funded the cost of the bins by the advertising contracts that were entered into. The dispute here was between the company selling the advertising space (the plaintiff) and a company that had entered into an agreement for advertising on the council waste bins for a period of three years (the defendant). However, on the same day that the contract was made, an attempt was made to repudiate the agreement. The plaintiff went ahead with the contract anyway, refusing to accept the attempted repudiation. They prepared the advertising plates, and performed the contract for the period of three years, advertising the defendant's business for this period of time. They then sued for the contract price.

Held: as the plaintiff had not accepted the defendant's repudiation, the contract and its obligations continued to run. Because of this, the advertisers were obligated to provide the advertising space as agreed, and the defendant was bound to pay for it.

KEY LEARNING POINT

The interesting aspect of this case is that it allowed the advertisers to behave as if they had never been informed by the other party of their intention to repudiate the contract. Rather than having any responsibility to act in accordance with the knowledge they had, they were therefore under no obligation to mitigate their losses in any way whatsoever. In fact, because they had not taken any action to perform the contract until after they had been informed of the attempted repudiation, they actually increased their losses after the other party attempted to discharge the contract. This goes against the general duty in contract law to mitigate losses under a contract. However, as we will see in Chapter 13, that duty only exists once a contract has been discharged.

The *White & Carter* case should be compared with *Clea Shipping Corpn v Bulk Oil International Ltd, The Alaskan Trader*.[27] In this situation, there was a recognition that the losses accrued by the innocent party were not unlimited.

CLEA SHIPPING CORPN V BULK OIL INTERNATIONAL LTD, THE ALASKAN TRADER [1984] 1 ALL ER 129

The Alaskan Trader involved a 24-month charter of a ship. Unfortunately, there was a serious engine breakdown one year into the charter, and it became obvious that repairs to the engines would take several months to complete. During that time, the ship would be unavailable for the charter.

Because of this, the charterers decided not to continue using the ship for the remainder of the charter and made this clear to the ship owners. They were effectively treating the contract as discharged. However, despite this, the ship owners decided to go ahead with an expensive repair, which took six months. Once the repair was complete, the ship owners maintained the ship ready to use with a full crew, and made it clear that it was ready to use. The charterers refused to use the ship.

The owners of the ship sued under breach of contract for the costs they incurred in keeping the ship in a state of readiness after the engine repair.

Held: there should come a point where equitable principles placed a limit upon what could be claimed for. The owners should have treated the contract as at an end rather than incurring additional expenses (the expensive repair, the wages of the crew that they engaged to be available to load a cargo if the charterers used the ship). Therefore, although they were allowed to claim for damages, they were prevented from claiming the hire costs they had incurred in crewing the ship after its repair. The court's view was that the ship owners had incurred these costs only with the intention of adding to what they could claim for from the other party.

Unlike *White & Carter*, the court in this instance suggested that knowledge of an attempted repudiation did mean something, and therefore should result in the innocent party limiting the damage caused by the breach to some extent. The only real additional cost that could have been reduced was in employing the crew, but nevertheless it does show that allowing the contract to continue after refusing to recognise a repudiation does not allow completely limitless claims for compensation.

This relates to part of the comment by Lord Reid in *White & Carter* justifying the decision in that case. He stated that where a party has no legitimate interest in continuing to perform

---

27 [1984] 1 All ER 129.

aside from being able to claim damages at the end, they are not justified in incurring additional expenses.[28]

The other exception discussed by Lord Reid in *White & Carter* concerns situations where the non-repudiating party can continue to perform the contract without any input from the other party. In *White & Carter*, the advertisers did not require anything else from the other party in order to perform their obligations. *Hounslow Borough Council v Twickenham Garden Developments Ltd*[29] is a good example of what happens where the contract requires some input from the other party. In such a situation, continuing to perform the contract after the other party has attempted a repudiation will be difficult due to the fact that some element of performance relies upon something they have to do as well.

In *Hounslow Borough Council v Twickenham Garden Developments*, performance of the contract was reliant upon getting access to council property. There was an attempt to continue to work under the contract after an attempted repudiation by the council; however, they relied upon being given access to council land in order to do so. Where the continued cooperation of the other party is required, it is unlikely that they are going to give this if they wish to repudiate. The only other course of action would be to sue for damages at this point.

A modern application of the principle in *White & Carter* can be found in the case of *Ministry of Sound (Ireland) Ltd v World Online Ltd*.[30] This was similar to the *Hounslow Borough Council* case as non-performance by the repudiating party prevented the other party from fully performing their obligations. However, it did apply the *White & Carter* principle that allows a party to claim for non-performance under a contract rather than just damages.

MINISTRY OF SOUND (IRELAND) LTD V WORLD ONLINE LTD [2003] EWHC 2178 (CH), [2003] 2 ALL ER (COMM) 823

This case concerned an agreement between Ministry of Sound, a series of famous nightclubs, and World Online, an internet service provider (ISP). The ISP wanted to associate itself with the popular Ministry of Sound brand, and so agreed to pay Ministry of Sound £1.6 million in eight instalments of £200,000, in exchange for which Ministry of Sound would provide services that included the distribution of software CDs containing World Online's ISP software. The CDs were to be supplied by World Online.

Part way through the agreement, World Online stopped providing the CDs, which prevented Ministry of Sound from continuing to distribute them with their products, and subsequently also stopped paying the instalments under the agreement, claiming that it had repudiated the contract.

28 [1962] AC 413 at 431.
29 [1971] Ch 233.
30 [2003] EWHC 2178 (Ch), [2003] 2 All ER (Comm) 823.

Ministry of Sound claimed for the missing instalment, claiming that World Online were still contractually obliged to continue payment under the agreement. World Online claimed that they were only liable for damages for breach. Ministry of Sound had incurred no losses as a result of the breach, as they had merely been prevented from continuing to distribute the CDs alongside their products.

Held: World Online were liable for the £200,000 instalment, but did not grant an order for specific performance of that instalment. They also suggested that part of this might be recoverable by World Online due to a partial failure of consideration.

ANALYSING THE LAW

This therefore appears at first to go against what was said in *White & Carter* about not being able to claim for performance of the contract where performance is prevented by the other party. However, in *Ministry of Sound* the court recognised that although the contract price was payable in instalments, they were not directly linked to the obligation to bundle the supplied CDs with the Ministry of Sound's products. They therefore concluded that the right to payment was not dependent upon performance, which is an unusual situation to have, because normally obligations in a contract are considered to be mutually dependent. This therefore means that this case has a narrow application, but nevertheless demonstrates the effect that the *White & Carter* case has had upon situations where one party attempts to repudiate a contract. In *Ministry of Sound*, if the repudiation had been successful, there would have been no right to damages as there was no loss, as opposed to the obligation to pay the final £200,000 instalment.

11.7.2 TAKING EFFECTIVE STEPS TO REPUDIATE

We have discussed above the act of affirming the breach and therefore repudiating the contract; however in some situations whether this has taken place is more obvious than in others. In many cases, as with the *Alaskan Trader* case above, this is about a clear communication to the other party that you no longer wish to continue. However, in other situations this is not as straightforward.

VITOL V NORELF [1996] 3 ALL ER 193

The parties had entered into a contract for the purchase of a quantity of propane, to be delivered between 1 and 7 March 1991. When the buyers found out that the cargo was not even to be loaded for shipping to them until 9 March, they contacted the sellers and indicated to them that they considered that the contract was at an end. In response to this, the sellers and the buyers each took no further steps to perform the contract, although by that stage the cargo was loaded and was on its way to the port of delivery.

The sellers sold the propane on to a third party and then sued the buyers for breach of contract, claiming the difference between the contract price and the price they had managed to sell the propane for.

Held: the seller's failing to perform any further obligations under the contract after receiving the communication from the buyer constituted an acceptance of the repudiation, and therefore the contract was at that stage discharged.

WOODAR INVESTMENT DEVELOPMENT LTD V WIMPEY CONSTRUCTION (UK) LTD [1980] 1 ALL ER 571

In this case, the court was asked to ascertain whether an attempt at repudiation of the contract for purchase of land was successful or not. The land had been sold under a contract that had a release clause in the event of a compulsory purchase order of the land being made by the government. There had been a compulsory purchase order made, but it occurred before the date of the agreement. The buyer of the land attempted to rely upon the release clause and repudiate the contract.

Held: because the buyer's attempt to bring the contract to an end was an attempt to rely upon a term of the contract, rather than a refusal to be bound by the contract, it would not be considered to be a repudiation of the contract.

Lord Wilberforce said:[31]

Repudiation is a drastic conclusion which should only be held to arise in clear cases of refusal, in a matter going to the root of the contract, to perform contractual obligations. To uphold Woodar's contentions in this case would represent an undesirable contention of the doctrine.

---

31 [1980] 1 All ER 571 at 576.

11.7.3 AFFIRMATION OF CONTRACT

If the non-breaching party wishes to affirm, even taking into account the risks discussed above, there will still be an action for damages available to them for the breach that has occurred. They are merely waiving the right to end the contract at that stage. The courts have indicated that, in deciding whether affirmation has taken place or not, the court will evaluate the behaviour of the non-breaching party in order to make a judgment as to whether they appear to be affirming the contract.[32] Where the non-breaching party continues to perform their obligations, or accepts the continued performance of the other party, this clearly indicates an affirmation that the contract should continue.

11.8 ACTUAL BREACH

Situations of actual breach are far more straightforward. If a party fails to perform obligations under a contract, this may result in the discharge of the contract. The key here is that such a breach has to be repudiatory. Any non-repudiatory breach will result in damages being available to the innocent party, but the agreement will continue and obligations due under the contract will still need to be performed.

Whether breach has occurred will depend upon the principles that have been discussed at the beginning of this chapter – the strict rule of 'entire performance' discussed in *Cutter v Powell*. The standard of performance is also important here. Some breaches result from non-performance but, where there is an attempted performance, it is important to be able to judge whether the standard of the performance offered meets the requirements of the obligation. The required standard is that of 'reasonably competent' performance. If an individual, when judged against a reasonably competent individual, fails to meet that standard, they can be said to be in breach.

An example of actual breach was shown in *Platform Funding Ltd v Bank of Scotland plc.*[33] In this case, a mortgage valuer was required to provide a valuation of a house for the purposes of getting a mortgage. Unfortunately, he valued the wrong property in the same street, and the mortgage was offered on the basis of the valuation made. The mistake was discovered at the point that the house was being repossessed, and the valuer was held to have actually breached the agreement to value the property because he fell below the standard expected of a reasonably competent member of his profession.

---

32 See *White Rosebay Shipping SA v Hong Kong Chain Glory Shipping Ltd (The Fortune Plum)* [2013] EWHC 1355, [2013] 2 All ER (Comm) 449.

33 [2008] EWHC Civ 930, [2009] QB 426.

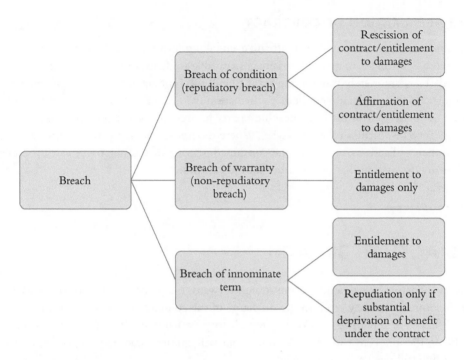

Figure 11.7 Consequences of actual breach

11.8.1 REPUDIATORY BREACH

In order to establish that a contract has been discharged by an actual breach, it is important to establish what would classify as a repudiatory breach. This takes it beyond entitlement to damages, and goes towards the ability to treat the contract as discharged at that point. The effect is the same as with acceptance of repudiation in anticipatory breach – any remaining obligations are discharged at that point.

Contractual terms have generally been divided into conditions and warranties for the purposes of classifying them in a contract. The distinction between different types of contract terms and their effect upon the contract is discussed in Chapter 5. Ordinarily, conditions have been considered to be those that go to the heart of the contract; therefore, breach thereof is considered to be repudiatory. For example, in *The Mihalis Angelos*,[34] there was a clause referred to as the 'expected readiness clause', which stipulated that the ship should be expected to be available and ready to load at Haiphong 'at around 1st July 1965'. This clause was described as being a condition of the contract, and therefore one that, if breached, would lead to a repudiatory breach. Megaw LJ commented:[35]

---

34 *Maredelanto Cia Naveira SA v Bergbau-Handel GmbH, The Mihalis Angelos* [1971] 1 QB 164, [1970] 3 All ER 125, [1970] 3 WLR 601.
35 [1971] 1 QB 164 at 205.

In my judgment, such a term in a charterparty ought to be regarded as being a condition of the contract, in the old sense of the word 'condition': that is, when it has been broken, the other party can, if he wishes, by intimation of the party in breach, elect to be released from performance of his further obligations under the contract.

However, a different approach towards the distinction between repudiatory and non-repudiatory breaches can be seen in cases that deal with terms referred to as innominate. This came from the case of *Hongkong Fir Shipping Co Ltd v Kawasaki Kisen Kaisha Ltd (The Hongkong Fir)*,[36] which established the concept of innominate terms as ones that could either be repudiatory or non-repudiatory, depending upon the circumstances of the breach itself. Diplock LJ classified repudiatory breaches as ones that 'substantially deprived the other of a benefit'. Anything that did not fall under this definition would not be considered to repudiate the contract and, although damages would be available, the other party would not be able to treat the contract as at an end.

An important point here is that a repudiatory breach is one that substantially deprives the other party of a substantial benefit of the contract. Where this occurs, it is not possible to continue with the contract because of the devastating effect that this has upon the central purpose of the agreement; so it is important that they recognise the contract as being at an end and seek remedies.[37]

11.8.2 NON-REPUDIATORY BREACH

The effect of a non-repudiatory breach is that damages are available to the non-breaching party. This is usually on a determination that the breach is a breach of warranty, as discussed in Chapter 5. An example is the case of *Bettini v Gye*,[38] where the breach was considered to be a breach of warranty because it did not 'substantially deprive the other party of a benefit'. The main object of the contract (performances by a singer) could still be carried out. For a full discussion of the type and extent of damages that would be available in such situations, refer to Chapter 13.

11.9 BRINGING IT ALL TOGETHER

How a contract is brought to an end is as important as how it is created in the first place, and this chapter has dealt with three of the four possible ways in which a contract is discharged: agreement, performance, and breach. The first two of these tend to be fairly uncontentious processes.

---

36 [1962] 2 QB 26, [1962] 2 WLR 474, [1962] 1 All ER 474.
37 See *MSC Mediterranean Shipping Co SA v Cottonex Anstalt* [2016] EWCA Civ 79.
38 (1876) 1 QBD 183.

Discharge by performance describes the end–result of the overwhelming majority of contractual agreements, but it is important to consider whether the obligations have actually been performed. In situations that require the complete performance of all obligations, the contract will not be discharged until this has occurred; however, in other situations where obligations can be separated out in the contract, it may be possible to claim part of the contract price for part performance.

Discharge by agreement is subject to the same rules regarding consideration as creating the contract in the first place. Whether it is a unilateral or bilateral discharge, the agreement to discharge must be supported by consideration (something of value) on both sides.

Finally, discharge by breach will only occur if the breach is repudiatory, i.e. something that is a breach of condition, or substantially deprives the other party of a benefit of the contract. Less significant breaches will only be subject to a claim for damages. A repudiatory breach can take place either by the failure to perform an obligation when required to by the contract, or by the other party accepting an advance notice that you intend not to perform the obligation at the required time in the future.

KEY LEARNING POINTS
....

Remember that you need to consider the following issues when considering whether a contract has been discharged:

- A contract can only be discharged by agreement, breach, frustration or performance
- Where performance discharges the contract, it must normally be a complete performance
- Where discharge takes place by agreement, it must be supported by consideration in the same way as the agreement to make the contract would be
- When discharge has taken place by breach, only a repudiatory breach will discharge the contract
- Even if the contract has not yet *actually* been breached, it can be discharged by an *anticipatory* breach
- Where an anticipatory breach has been indicated, it must be accepted by the other party in order for the contract to be repudiated at that point.

TAKING IT FURTHER

Beatson & Burrows, *Anson's Law of Contract*, 29th edn, Oxford University Press, 2010

Bojczuk, 'When is a condition not a condition?' (1987) JBL 353

Carter, 'Discharge as the basis for termination for breach of contract' (2012) 128 LQR 283

Coote, 'Breach, anticipatory breach, or the breach anticipated?' (2007) 123 LQR 503

Liu, 'Inferring future breach: towards a unifying test of anticipatory breach of contract' (2007) 66 CLJ 574

Marston, 'Contractual rights and duties after an unaccepted anticipatory repudiation' (1988) 47 CLJ 40

Peel, *Treitel on the Law of Contract*, 14th edn, Sweet & Maxwell, 2015

Treitel, 'Affirmation after repudiatory breach' (1998) 114 LQR 22

12

CHAPTER 12
DISCHARGE OF CONTRACT (2)

12.1 INTRODUCTION

This is the second chapter on discharge of contract and deals with discharge by frustration of contract.

You have already acknowledged the general rule that the obligation to completely perform a contract is strict and failure to perform in full by either of the parties will result in a breach of contract. The problem that can arise here is that, after the parties have reached an agreement, unforeseen events may occur that prevent the achievement of the contractual obligations. Thus, the entire obligations rule can produce harsh results[1] and injustice if either of the parties were prevented as a result of circumstances beyond their control from performing their obligations.

In the mid-nineteenth century the position changed significantly following the case of *Taylor v Caldwell*[2] when the doctrine of frustration evolved to mitigate the harsh results of the entire obligations rule.

The doctrine of frustration will be effective where, following the conclusion of an agreement, an event occurs that has the effect of rendering performance of the contract impossible or illegal to perform, or means that performance would result in an outcome radically different from what was contemplated in the contractual agreement. The frustrating event must not be the fault of either of the parties, nor can the doctrine be relied upon where the parties have included an express provision or *force majeure* clause in their agreement, which stipulates a contingency for the event that has occurred.

Where a contract is deemed to be discharged under the doctrine of frustration, the parties will be discharged from performance of their obligations under the contract and will not be liable for breach of contract. The Law Reform (Frustrated Contracts) Act 1943 provides directions on how advance payments, or benefits that have already been accrued, will be handled and provides recognition for any valuable benefit that has been obtained at the time of frustration.

ESSENTIAL DEFINITION: *FORCE MAJEURE* CLAUSE

A provision within a contract that allows a party to suspend or terminate the performance of its obligations when certain circumstances beyond their control arise, making performance commercially impracticable, illegal, or impossible

---

1   *Paradine v Jane* [1647] EWHC KB J5.
2   (1863) 3 B & S 826.

AS YOU READ

At the end of this chapter you should be able to:

- Identify the various components that must exist for a successful claim to frustration

- Identify and explain situations when a contract may be discharged as a result of frustration

- Understand the nature of a *force majeure* clause and explain the rationale for inserting such a clause into a contract

- Demonstrate a comprehensive knowledge and understanding of the nature and effects of frustration and apply the law to factual scenarios

12.2 DEFINITION AND COMPONENTS

So, what is meant by the term 'frustration' in contract law and when will a contract be frustrated?

Since the case of *Taylor v Caldwell*, we have experienced the advancement of the doctrine of frustration. In certain circumstances, the doctrine provides a safety net and mitigates against the harshness of the entire obligations rule, which means the whole of each contracting party's side of the bargain is an essential condition for the performance of the other. Failure to perform completely will constitute a repudiatory breach

A contract will be frustrated where performance is brought to a halt as a result of an unforeseen event that occurs and renders performance of the contract either impossible, illegal or something radically different to what was agreed by the parties when the deal was made (see Figure 12.1).

Figure 12.1 Components of a frustrated contract

As mentioned, *Taylor v Caldwell* was the first case to acknowledge that an unforeseen event could be recognised as having the effect of rendering a contract impossible to perform, and thus frustrated, rather than constituting a breach of contract:

TAYLOR V CALDWELL (1863) 3 B & S 826

An agreement was entered into for the hire of a music hall to host the performance of four concert events. Before the first concert took place, the hall was destroyed by a fire. The plaintiffs sued the defendants for breach of contract in failing to hire out the music hall to them. The defendants argued that the destruction of the music hall provided an excuse for non-performance.

Held: the courts found in favour of the defendants and found the contract to be frustrated. The court reasoned that where it can be gleaned from the outset that a contract could not be performed unless, at the time of performance, some specific feature continued to exist, the contract can be subject to an implied condition that the parties will be excused from performance if that specific feature has ceased to exist, where neither of the parties are at fault. This is often referred to as the implied term theory.

In later cases, the implied term theory has been criticised on the premise that a term cannot always be implied due to the fact that in some instances the term is not wholly obvious.[3] It was also referred to as 'unrealistic' in *Great Peace Shipping Ltd v Tsavliris Salvage (International) Ltd*,[4] wherein Lord Reid suggested that frustration depends upon looking 'at the true construction of the terms which are in the contract read in the light of the nature of the contract and of the relevant surrounding circumstances when the contract was made'.

12.3 DISTINGUISH FROM BREACH OF CONTRACT

The doctrine of frustration is often referred to as a residual doctrine. This means that it will only be effective when a contract has become impossible to perform and where the parties have not made provision in the contract to cover any such risks. If there is a provision that a contract will terminate upon a specified contingency or that the parties will not be liable where a specific type of circumstance has occurred, the doctrine of frustration cannot be relied upon and the non-performing party will be in breach of contract.

ASSESSMENT TIP

When answering a question on discharge by frustration, your answer will be enhanced by carefully analysing whether the purported frustration could instead be a discharge

---

3   *Davis Contractors Ltd v Fareham Urban District Council* [1956] AC 696.
4   [2002] EWCA Civ 1407.

by breach. You may then go on to conclude one way or another, giving reasoned advice on your application of the law. The exercise at the end of this chapter shows how to tackle a question from both perspectives

12.3.1 FRUSTRATING EVENTS

The case of *Taylor v Caldwell* involved a contract where the subject matter of the agreement had been destroyed. There are other occurrences and unforeseen events that will also render a contract void, such as the unavailability of a specific thing or person vital to a contract; the non-occurrence of a fundamental event; government intervention; delay (on some occasions), and illegality. It is important to note that the event must not be foreseen by the parties; it must not be self-induced; and a contract will not be frustrated simply because it has become more difficult or expensive to perform. Figure 12.2 provides a helpful summary of the main categories of frustrating event.

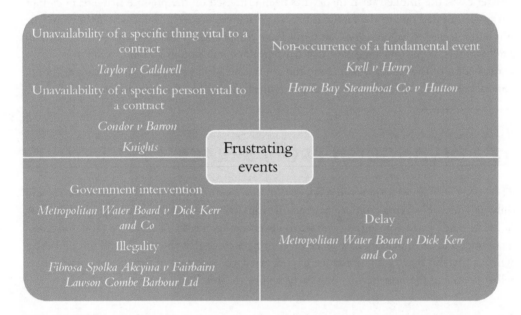

Figure 12.2 Frustrating events

ANALYSING THE LAW

Let us look at some examples of these categories in context.

What is the position where a person vital for performing a contract is not available? Let us contrast two different situations.

1) Danny has agreed to write his autobiography for a leading publisher. The book must be completed in eight months' time. Danny finished the first chapter and was taken ill. His doctor has said that he will be unable to write for at least a year. In this instance the contract would be frustrated as it is clear that Danny himself is needed to fulfil the contract; no-one else could step into his shoes to complete the book.

2) Rohzeena enters into a contract with Glam Designs, an interior design company, to have her lounge redesigned and decorated. Bella works on the room for ten days but falls ill with a chest infection. Bella is replaced by Grace who is equally qualified to do the work. Rohzeena is, however, looking for an excuse to terminate the agreement as she now feels that she cannot afford the work and she informs Glam Designs that she no longer requires their services, using the absence of Bella as an excuse. Hopefully you will have concluded that the contract will not be frustrated and, if Rohzeena prevents the company from completing their work, she will be in breach of contract. The contract has not become impossible to perform or radically different. Glam Designs can still do the work using Grace rather than Bella. The contract was between Rohzeena and Glam Designs; the identity of the person carrying out the work is not of significance to the agreement. As long as one of the employees can do the work, it will suffice as performance of Glam Design's part of the agreement.

The above examples help us to contextualise the rules that apply in this area. The position has also been clarified in various cases over the years.

12.3.2 AVAILABILITY OF A SPECIFIED PERSON

In *Morgan v Manser*[5] the unavailability of a music hall artist known as 'Cheerful Charlie Chester', who was called up for military service, resulted in frustration of the contract due to his unavailability to perform, which was beyond his control. The case of *Condor v Barron Knights*[6] also provides a good example in this category. In this instance, the drummer with a fun pop group was taken ill during a period of performances. Consequently, he was only capable of working three to four nights per week, which was hugely problematic as the group had engagements for seven nights a week. Again, the contract was frustrated, as a specific person, i.e. the drummer, was integral to the performance of the contract.

12.3.3 CANCELLATION OF AN EVENT

Let us now look at instances where an event is planned but does not go ahead. The non-occurrence of a fundamental event can frustrate a contract, but only where it can be shown that the contract is dependent on the event. It is useful to look at two key cases that arose at the beginning of the twentieth century to fully understand how the principle has evolved.

---

5   [1948] 1 KB 184.
6   [1966] 1 WLR 87.

KRELL V HENRY [1903] 2 KB 740

A room was hired by the defendant to enable him to watch the procession for the coronation of Edward VII. The purpose of the hire was clear to both parties, although this was not specifically stated in the agreement. Due to the king falling ill, the coronation was postponed and the plaintiff sought to recover the cost for the room.

Held: on the basis that it was no longer possible to achieve the main purpose of the contract, the effect of the cancellation of the coronation was found to have had the effect of discharging both parties from performance of their obligations. The contract was not just for the hire of the rooms but specifically to hire the rooms to watch the procession, a venture that was no longer possible.

Contrast the above case with *Herne Bay Steam Boat Co v Hutton*,[7] which also concerned the cancellation of King Edward VII's coronation; but note the different outcome:

HERNE BAY STEAM BOAT CO. V HUTTON [1903] 2 KB 683

This contract concerned the hire of a boat to watch the king's review of the navy, as part of the coronation celebrations, and to cruise around the fleet. Due to the king falling ill, the review was cancelled and the plaintiffs sought to recover the cost of the boat hire. The defendants argued that the contract was not frustrated as there was still a purpose to the contract as it was still possible to cruise around the fleet.

Held: the contract was not frustrated as it had not been deprived of its sole commercial purpose. The naval review was not in itself the foremost reason for the boat hire; it was just one component and it was still possible to take the boat and cruise around the fleet.

ANALYSING THE LAW

It is important to note that in order for a contract to be frustrated, it must be rendered impossible to perform or result in an outcome that is radically different to that envisaged by the parties. Clearly in *Krell*, with the very object of the contract being the procession and the positioning of the rooms, the postponement of the coronation cancelled out any value of the venture. Continuation of the contract would have resulted in something entirely different to that envisaged when the agreement was

---

7   [1903] 2 KB 683.

made. Contrarily, in *Herne Bay* part of the contract could still be performed and the outcome, whilst different, did not fall into the sphere of being entirely or 'radically' different to that anticipated by the parties.

In *Krell*, Vaughan Williams LJ used an analogy of someone hiring a cab to go to Epsom for the Derby and the race being cancelled. In his view, the race did not form the foundation of the contract with the cab driver. There was nothing of particular importance related to the actual cab hired. Any cab could have performed the task. Thus, in the event of the race being cancelled, the contract for the cab hire would not be frustrated. In contrast with *Krell*, the location of the rooms was the 'special feature' which led to their selection and the cancellation of the coronation nullified the whole purpose of the agreement.

Thus, a line can be drawn between impossible and impractical. Where it is impractical to perform a contractual agreement, it is likely that this will be sufficient to warrant a successful claim in frustration. We will return to this point later.

12.3.4 GOVERNMENT OR LEGAL INTERVENTION

Where there has been a change in the law, or an intervention by the government, it may be that a contract could physically be performed, but the parties would not be able to perform as continuance would be illegal or prohibited. The change in law or government intervention would need to have occurred after the contract had been agreed and not before in order for frustration to operate. An example of a contract frustrated as a result of government intervention occurred in *Metropolitan Water Board v Dick Kerr and Co.*

METROPOLITAN WATER BOARD V DICK KERR AND CO [1918] AC 119

A contract to construct a reservoir was agreed in 1914 with completion set to be within six years. Shortly after the outbreak of World War I, the government ordered Dick Kerr to stop work to enable its workers and equipment to be used to assist in the war. The order was to last for the duration of the war, which of course was unknown at the time. There was a clause in the contract to govern the possibility of a time extension in the event of a delay. Dick Kerr contended that the contract was frustrated due to the government intervention.

Held: the contract was frustrated. The action involved a prolonged stoppage and, if the project resumed, the outcome would be radically different to what the parties had envisaged in their agreement. The court was satisfied that the delay clause was meant to cover temporary delays only and not an event that would change the character and duration of the agreement significantly.

The position where a contract subsequently becomes illegal due to the outbreak of the war was also considered in *Fibrosa Spolka Akcyina v Fairbairn Lawson Combe Barbour Ltd.*[8] Here the agreement involved a contract for the manufacture and delivery of machinery between an English and a Polish company. Before the goods were complete, the German army invaded and occupied Poland, making it impossible for the English company to deliver the goods. The contract was frustrated as it had become impossible to perform.

12.3.5 DELAY

As noted in the *Dick Kerr* case, much will depend upon the effect of the delay on the contract and whether a provision covering delay is included in the contract. Where no provision has been made, an analysis of the impact of the delay upon the performance of the contract will be undertaken and the outcome will depend heavily upon whether performance of the contract will result in something radically different to that envisaged by the parties when the contract was created. The case of *Tatem Ltd v Gamboa*[9] concerned a delay which had been caused by the seizure of a ship during the Spanish Civil War. The effect of the delay had to be assessed in relation to its impact upon the contract:

TATEM LTD V GAMBOA [1939] 1 KB 132, [1938] 3 ALL ER 135

During the Spanish Civil War, a ship was chartered to the Spanish republican government for a 30-day period to assist in the evacuation of civilians from Spanish to French ports. The hire rate was substantially higher than that for other ships due to the nature of the mission. On 14 July the ship was detained in Bilbao until 7 September and released to the plaintiffs on 11 September. The government refused payment for the majority of the period of detention, arguing that the agreement had been frustrated as a result of the seizure of the ship

Held: the contract was frustrated. The seizure had caused substantial interruption and delay to the contract performance to the extent as to render performance significantly different to what had been agreed. The agreement did not contain a *force majeure* clause.

12.3.6 CONTRACTS THAT HAVE BECOME MORE EXPENSIVE OR MORE DIFFICULT TO PERFORM

Often it may be the case that a contract has become more difficult or more expensive to perform. It may be that the cost of materials has increased or maybe a shift in exchange rates may make a product or service more expensive to acquire. Imagine the impact upon trading agreements if one of the parties were able to pull out of a deal for this reason or were allowed to demand extra payment to make the contract financially worthwhile. It would be unfair to the other party if

---

8 [1943] AC 32.
9 [1939] 1 KB 132, [1938] 3 All ER 135.

they were unable conclude an agreement with certainty of performance and/or price. If this type of behavior were permitted, it may well become the case that the less scrupulous contractor could deliberately put in a low bid for work to secure a contract only to later increase the price. Material, labour and service costs often fluctuate, usually upwards, and there is no bar against the parties including a provision in their agreement to cover such eventualities. They may include a price variation clause to protect against such possibilities or a *force majeure* clause to cover instances where an intervening event makes a contract more difficult or expensive to perform. Such measures are acceptable and are commonplace in many contracts. However, in the absence of any such provision it is not permissible for the parties to argue that a contract has become frustrated because it is no longer convenient or financially viable to perform. The position is clearly embedded in law and the following case is the one that is usually cited to illustrate this rule.

DAVIS CONTRACTORS LTD V FAREHAM URBAN DISTRICT COUNCIL
[1956] AC 696

Davis Contractors entered into an agreement with Fareham UDC to construct a specified number of houses within an eight-month period. Throughout the project the builders experienced a number of difficulties, mainly caused by a shortage in labour and materials. It took 22 months for the houses to be completed and Davis Contractors argued that the contract had been frustrated and requested a *quantum meruit* for the work completed.

Held: the contract had become more onerous to perform but had not been frustrated. Lord Radcliffe stressed that 'it is not hardship or inconvenience or material loss itself which calls the principle of frustration into play. There must as well be such a change in the significance of the obligation that the thing undertaken would, if performed, be a different thing from that contracted for.'

ESSENTIAL DEFINITION: *QUANTUM MERUIT*

An action to recover the reasonable value of services rendered by one party to another.

Another instance where the contract became more inconvenient and expensive to perform can be seen in the case of *Tsakiroglou & Co Ltd v Noblee Thorl GmbH*,[10] which concerned an agreement for the transportation of a consignment of nuts by sea. The contract was not frustrated when the Suez Canal, which formed the transportation route, was closed to shipping. The court held that it was still possible to perform the contract; the route taken by ships through the Suez Canal had not been expressly stipulated in the contract and the fact

---

10 [1962] AC 93.

that it was more difficult or costly to perform because of a lengthy detour was insufficient to amount to frustration.

12.4 EXPLAINING THE LAW

The *Tsakiroglou* case is a good example where a special contractual provision could have been included to recognise and provide a remedy for this type of difficulty, which could have been anticipated. This was specifically picked up and remarked upon by Lord Radcliffe in the judgment itself. A *force majeure* clause seeks to settle the allocation of risks beforehand in the contract. Well-drafted *force majeure* clauses (discussed in more detail below), can provide a helpful mechanism for dealing with consequences of events of this type and the parties can themselves agree a range of remedies to resolve any issues that may arise in the performance of the contract.

12.5 RESTRICTIONS ON FRUSTRATION

Being aware of what can and cannot lead to frustration of a contract is important. It is also necessary to acquaint yourself with the types of situation that may initially appear to amount to frustration but, due to the narrow limits within frustration operates, will instead result in a breach of contract rather than frustration. The instances where a frustrating event may have occurred, but where the contract will not be frustrated, are summarised in Figure 12.3.

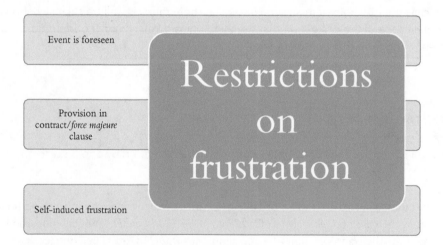

Figure 12.3 Restrictions

12.5.1 EVENT IS FORESEEN

Where either of the parties are calling for frustration of a contract, the court may take the view that the parties either did foresee, or should have foreseen, the supervening event but have not made provision for it in the contract. For example, and as mentioned earlier, in *Davis Contractors* Lord Radcliffe was of the view that the shortages that led to the difficulties in completion of the contract were occurrences that could easily have been foreseen by the parties and a clause could have been inserted into the contract to govern how such difficulties would be dealt with by the parties.

12.5.2 EVENT COVERED BY A PROVISION IN THE CONTRACT

Where an event falls outside the control of the parties but is one that is foreseen or is a type of issue that the parties would anticipate the possibility of, a clause can be included in a contract to cover such possibilities. Such clauses are known as *force majeure* clauses.

A *force majeure* clause (French for 'superior force') is a contract provision that allows a party to suspend or terminate the performance of its obligations when certain circumstances beyond their control arise, making performance commercially impracticable, illegal, or impossible. The provision may state that the contract is temporarily suspended, or that it is terminated if the event continues for a specified period of time. The events that can be the subject of a *force majeure* clause are a matter of negotiation between the parties, but examples of such events could include the outbreak of war, a fire, flood, earthquake, hurricane, explosion, power outage, act of terrorism, or a government intervention that prevents a party from performing their obligations. So if, for example, the Channel Tunnel had to be closed due to an act of terrorism, the company with a lorry stacked back in a queue, planning to transport its goods through the tunnel, would not be liable for late delivery of the goods due to a frustrating event; but where a *force majeure* clause is included in the agreement this could help the parties to allocate or apportion this type of risk.

Where there is no provision for such events in an agreement, the parties to a contract must attempt to rely on the doctrine of frustration, which, as we know, cannot be used to excuse performance unless there are exceptional circumstances.

A typical *force majeure* clause should, as a bare minimum, include the elements shown in Figure 12.4.

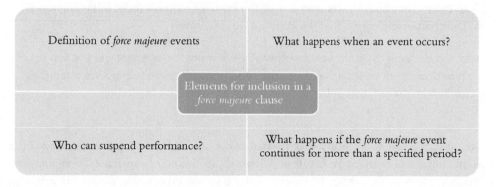

Figure 12.4 *Force majeure* clause

The advantage of using a *force majeure* clause is to bring greater certainty and flexibility to an agreement. If the clause is worded clearly, it will prevent disputes from occurring and avoid costly litigation. It also allows for events that would not usually amount to frustration to be included. So, for example, in the *Davis Contractors* case the parties could have made provision for the occurrences of shortages in labour and materials. Any *force majeure* clause will, of course, fall under the provisions of UCTA 1977 (B2B contracts) or CRA 2015 (B2C contracts) and may be subjected to the reasonableness or fairness test respectively.

12.5.3 SELF-INDUCED FRUSTRATION

Where it is clear that the event in question has amounted to frustration, it must also be established that the event was beyond the control of the parties. Where either of the parties have wholly or partially caused the event to occur, the doctrine of frustration cannot be used to excuse them from their obligations. Otherwise, a party may use the doctrine to his or her advantage by instigating the supervening event. By way of illustration, if we think back to the events in *Taylor v Caldwell*, where the music hall being destroyed by fire resulted in the contract being frustrated, but we were to subsequently learn that the fire had been started as a result of actions taken by the owner, who had employed an unqualified electrician resulting in faulty wiring that led to the fire, would the outcome differ? It is highly likely that a claim in frustration would not be granted due to the fact that the frustrating event was self-induced by the act of the owner. We would then be looking at breach of contract. This is just an example; there is no suggestion that the fire was the fault of the owner in *Taylor v Caldwell*.

The case of *Maritime Fish Ltd v Ocean Trawlers Ltd* provides a good example of self-induced frustration.

MARITIME FISH LTD V OCEAN TRAWLERS LTD [1935] AC 524

The contract involved a charter of a trawler. The parties were aware that the trawler could not be used without an otter trawl for which a licence was required. The numbers of licences were restricted – the charterers had applied for five but had only been given three. They could have used one of the licences for the trawler but elected not to. The charterers claimed that the contract was frustrated

Held: the decision to opt to license other ships and not the one that was the subject of the hire agreement was the claimant's own decision and thus could not be argued as a factor that frustrated the contract. It was in fact an act of self-frustration.

The result in this case is not really controversial as the outcome could have been avoided if a different choice had been made. Let us now look at the case of *J Lauritzen AC v Wijsmuller BV, The Super Servant Two* where the outcome may be regarded as unfair in that the defendants had little choice over a decision on how to deploy their resources.

> ### J LAURITZEN AC V WIJSMULLER BV, THE SUPER SERVANT TWO [1990] 1 LLOYD'S REP 1, CA
>
> A contract was agreed for the transportation of a drilling rig from Japan to Rotterdam. The rig was to be carried using a transportation unit, which could have been *Super Servant One* or *Super Servant Two*. The defendants had planned to use *Super Servant Two*, but the unit sank before the delivery date. In addition to the drilling rig contract, the defendants had also contracted for other work that they could only carry out using *Super Servant One*. Two weeks after the unit sank, the defendants informed the claimants that they would not be able to transport the rig and claimed frustration of contract.
>
> Held: the contract was not frustrated. The court considered this to be a case of self-induced frustration. The defendants had chosen to use their other transportation unit, *Super Servant One* for other contracts, making it unavailable for the drilling rig transportation contract.

ANALYSING THE LAW

The doctrine requires a comparison between circumstances that existed at the time the contract was made and circumstances as they exist at the time of performance. Whilst it is apparent that the defendants had little choice, the decision that they did in fact make, i.e. to use *Super Servant One* for other contracts, was the reason that performance of the contract to transport the drilling rig was impossible, not the sinking of *Super Servant Two*. The contract itself had not specified which transporter would be used. Bingham LJ stated in his judgment that if the contract had specifically stipulated that the transportation would be undertaken by *Super Servant Two*, and there had been no viable alternative, the contract may well have been frustrated. As it was, the actual contract specified that the task would be fulfilled using either *Super Servant One* or *Super Servant Two*. The outcome in this case illustrates that the doctrine of frustration is applied within very strict limits: in circumstances where a decision can be made to prevent a particular situation, even if the result is highly disadvantageous to the decision maker, it appears that frustration will not be available if that course of action would have prevented the occurrence of the 'frustrating' event.

12.6 EFFECTS OF FRUSTRATION

The contract will automatically come to an end at the time of the frustrating event, and all parties are completely released from all future obligations. Neither party is in breach of contract, nor can either of the parties sue each other in respect of the frustrating event.

12.6.1 COMMON LAW PROVISION

The position at common law originally prevented recovery of any money paid by one party to the other prior to a frustrating event. Any money due and payable before a frustrating event also had to be paid; thus it was crucial to pinpoint at exactly what point the money was payable. These rules existed when the case of *Krell v Henry* was decided. If you recall, the case concerned the hire of rooms to watch the coronation procession. The room hire charge had been agreed at £75 and a deposit of £25 was paid at the time of the booking. The cancellation of the procession occurred before the remainder of the balance of £50 was due. We are aware that the contract was frustrated, but what did the defendant get back? Under the common law rules, monies paid before a frustrating event could not be recovered, hence the £25 deposit was retained. The defendant did not, however, have to pay the £50 as it fell due to be paid after the frustrating event. The result here can be considered harsh, as the defendant was not in any way at fault; yet, as well as receiving nothing under the contract, he lost his £25 deposit. We will return to this case shortly and assess the payment under the rules that operate nowadays. *Chandler v Webster*[11] is another case that also illustrates the unfairness of the common law rules in a similar instance.

The courts recognised the inequities that occurred under the strict common law provision in the *Fibrosa* case,[12] where a more moderate approach was taken with regard to monies paid prior to a frustrating event.

FIBROSA SPOLKA AKCYINA V FAIRBAIRN LAWSON COMBE BARBOUR LTD [1943] AC 32

An English company agreed by contract in July 1939 to supply some machines to a Polish company. The machines were to be delivered in 3–4 months. £1,600 was payable up front and the balance of £3,200 payable on delivery. The Polish company paid £1,000 in July on account of the initial payment due. Early in September 1939, Germany invaded Poland and war on Germany was declared. On 23 September Orders in Council made it illegal for British companies to trade with Poland.

Held: the contract was frustrated as it was no longer possible to perform the contract because of the supervening illegality.

Fibrosa is a good example of a contract that shows the impact of a supervening event. It is also useful to look at the approach taken by the House of Lords in its assessment of what monies could/could not be recovered on the contract. The Lords stated that if there had been a total failure of consideration (meaning that no benefit had been received under the contract), it would be open to the party who had paid money over already to recover that sum and any

---

11 [1904] 1 KB 493.
12 *Fibrosa Spolka Akcyina v Fairbairn Lawson Combe Barbour Ltd* [1943] AC 32.

money due and payable before the frustrating event would not have to be paid. But, on the other hand, if a benefit had been received, any money paid was not recoverable and any sums due were still payable. In addition, any expenses incurred could not be recovered (see Figure 12.5).

Figure 12.5 Recovery of benefits

The *Fibrosa* decision heralded a welcome move forward in recovery of monies in cases where there had been a failure of consideration. However, what it did not do was:

1) address the situation where a party had incurred expenses before a frustrating event,
2) allow for any compensation where the majority of the work had been completed.

It was around this time that the legislature stepped in.

12.7 LAW REFORM (FRUSTRATED CONTRACTS) ACT 1943

In order to address the inequities of the common law, the Law Reform (Frustrated Contracts) Act 1943 was passed. The key areas it deals with are shown in Figure 12.6.

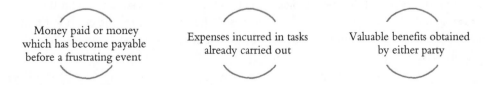

Figure 12.6 Law Reform (Frustrated Contracts) Act 1943

There are two main sections of the Act that deal with the areas shown in Figure 12.6.

Section 1(2) provides that money paid before the occurrence of a frustrating event can be recovered and money payable before the frustrating event will no longer be payable. Expenses are also covered under this head. Where an expense is incurred by the party who was owed the money before the frustrating event, it can be recovered out of the money paid and/or payable to the other party before the frustrating event occurred if the court considers it just in the circumstances. The section on expenses was welcomed as this was not dealt with in the *Fibrosa* judgment.

UP FOR DEBATE

Refer back to the case of *Krell v Henry*. How would the judgement have differed, in respect of the monies recoverable, under the Law Reform (Frustrated Contracts) Act 1943? Think in particular about the money that had been paid before the frustrating event which could not be recovered.

Expenses under s. 1(2) was the key focus of the court's deliberations in the following case.

GAMERCO SA V ICM/FAIR WARNING (AGENCY) LTD [1995] 1 WLR 1226

A concert promoter agreed to provide a concert to be held by the rock group, Guns N' Roses, at a stadium in Spain. However, the stadium was deemed unsafe and the authorities banned its use. No alternative site was available, so the concert had to be cancelled. Both parties had incurred expenses in preparation for the concert and the plaintiffs had paid the defendants $412,500 on account. The plaintiffs tried to recover the advance payment under s. 1(2) of the Law Reform (Frustrated Contracts) Act 1943, and the defendants counterclaimed for breach of contract by the plaintiffs in failing to secure the permit for the concert.

Held: the contract was frustrated essentially because the stadium was found to be unsafe, a circumstance that was beyond the control of the plaintiffs. The revocation of the permit did not in itself constitute the frustrating event; it was the ban on the use of the stadium that gave rise to the contract being frustrated. Under s. 1 of the 1943 Act, the plaintiffs were entitled to recover advance payments made to the defendants. The court did have a discretion to allow the defendants to offset their losses against this, but in all the circumstances of the present case the court felt that no deduction should be made in favour of the defendants and their counterclaim was dismissed.

Section 1(3) comes to the aid of a party who has provided something of benefit to the other party at the time that a contract becomes frustrated – commonly referred to as a 'valuable benefit'. The court may order the party who received the benefit to pay such sum as the court considers just, having regard to all the circumstances of the case. The sum must not exceed the value of the benefit. In contrast to s. 1(2), the court is not limited to the amount paid or payable before the frustrating event occurred. The court must take all circumstances into account when making an award. Any expenses incurred by the party receiving the benefit prior to the frustrating event must be taken into account and whether the frustrating event affected the benefit. Previously under common law, there was no provision for valuable benefit; thus the Act provides a further remedy and enables a just outcome to be achieved between the contracting parties in an important area of contract discharge. The following case considered an award under s. 1(3) for valuable benefit and the remit of the court in assessing such sums.

BP EXPLORATION CO (LIBYA) LTD V HUNT (NO. 2) [1979] 1 WLR 783

Hunt entered into an agreement that permitted BP to exploit oil in a field that he owned in Libya. In 1971 the Libyan government took over BP's half share. At this stage BP had already covered half its costs. Two years later, the Libyan government also took Hunt's share. BP claimed the contract was frustrated and claimed for a just sum of money to be awarded under the Law Reform (Frustrated Contracts) Act 1943.

Held: the court made an award but this was less than the amount claimed. Goff J, having calculated the value of the benefit, stated that a second step was then necessary and this was to assess what the courts regard as a just sum. The just sum was substantially lower than the valuable benefit as the contractual provisions had allocated a substantial proportion of the risks to the plaintiffs.

Thus it is fairly clear from precedent in this area that judicial discretion will play a major part in making awards under s. 1(3); the aim being to fairly compensate the claimant taking into account the circumstances of each particular case. It will first be necessary to identify and value the benefit, after which the court has discretion to fix a 'just' sum, which should not be higher than the value of the benefit. In so doing, the court will take into account factors such as apportionment of risk and expenses. Goff J stated that the principal purpose of s. 1(3) was to prevent unjust enrichment of one party at the expense of the other.

The Law Reform (Frustrated Contracts) Act 1943 applies to most contracts, but there are a few exceptions that are not covered; it will not apply to contracts for the carriage of goods by sea or a charterparty; nor will it apply to a contract of insurance.[13] Perishable goods are also excluded in certain circumstances.[14]

---

13 Law Reform (Frustrated Contracts) Act 1943, s. 2(5).
14 Law Reform (Frustrated Contracts) Act 1943, s. 2(5)(c).

12.7.1 APPLYING THE PROVISIONS OF THE LAW REFORM (FRUSTRATED CONTRACTS) ACT

Let us have a look at a scenario where frustration has occurred and see how the rules are applied:

Mary is planning a tour around Europe. She agrees to hire a super-sized motor home from Joseph for eight weeks beginning on 1 November. Mary pays a £500 deposit and will pay the balance of £3,000 on 1 November. They agreed that Joseph would install an additional toilet to accommodate Mary's disabled mother and a mini bar. Joseph had spent £800 installing the toilet and bar when a fire destroyed the motor home on 15 October.

Assuming that the contract has been frustrated, the following points need to be considered:

1) Will Mary have to pay the balance of £3,000 that was due on 1 November and can she recover her £500 deposit?
2) Can Joseph be compensated under s. 1(2) for the expenditure he has incurred? If so, what is the maximum the court can award him for expenses?
3) Has Joseph conferred a valuable benefit on Mary under s. 1(3)?

ADVICE

1) Mary will not have to pay the balance of £3,000, as frustration of the contract discharges any future obligations.
2) Section 1(2) states that any money paid before the frustrating event can be recovered. So Mary can recover her £500 deposit (subject to any award that the court makes for Joseph's expenses). Under s. 1(2) the maximum a court can award for expenses is a sum equal to the money that was paid or payable before the frustrating event. Here, the only money paid or payable before the frustrating event was the £500 deposit. Joseph could get a maximum of £500; he spent £800, so he will not be compensated in full. The court has a broad discretion when contemplating an award for expenses under s. 1(2). Its task is to do justice and it is not obliged to award retention of the maximum amount, as illustrated in *Gamerco SA v ICM/Fair Warning (Agency) Ltd*.[15] So potentially Mary can recover her £500 deposit. But if the court makes an award for Joseph's expenses, she may receive less.
3) Joseph has done some work installing the toilet and bar in the motor home. This would not constitute a valuable benefit to Mary under s. 1(3) because the frustrating event completely destroyed the work Joseph had done before Mary could benefit from it (*BP Exploration* case).

---

15 [1995] 1 WLR 1226.

12.8 THE DOCTRINE OF FRUSTRATION AND LEASES

Traditionally, the view was that a lease could not be frustrated. So, for example, in *Matthey v Curling*,[16] where the demised premises were destroyed by a fire, the tenant was not excused from performance of his obligations. This stance was defended by the argument that a lease was not simply a contract but an estate in land that could not be frustrated,[17] as a lease, being a proprietary interest (an interest that exists in land), would survive even where land cannot be used for its proposed purpose. The issue arose again in the following case.

CRICKLEWOOD PROPERTY AND INVESTMENT TRUST LTD V LEIGHTON'S INVESTMENT TRUST LTD [1945] AC 221

A 99-year lease was agreed, which included a covenant that the lessees would erect shops on the site. However, in 1939, prior to commencement of construction work, World War II broke out and, due to restrictions imposed by the government, it became impossible for the buildings to be erected. When sued for unpaid rent, the lessees claimed that the lease had been frustrated.

Held: the lease was not frustrated. Even if frustration could be permitted, in this instance the suspension of the construction work due to government action was of a temporary nature and, when taking into account the lease had more than 90 years remaining, the intervening act was found not to go to the root of the contract.

The view has shifted somewhat following the case of *National Carriers Ltd v Panalpina (Northern) Ltd*.

NATIONAL CARRIERS LTD V PANALPINA (NORTHERN) LTD [1981] AC 675

The subject of the dispute was a leasehold grant of a warehouse over a ten-year term, which commenced in January 1975. In May 1979, due to a dangerous building sited opposite the warehouse, the local authority took action to close the road, making the warehouse inaccessible. The plan was to re-open the road in 1981. The lessee argued that the lease was frustrated

Held: the House of Lords confirmed that is was possible for frustration to apply to a lease; however, in this instance, the lease was not frustrated. In total, the lessees

---

16 [1922] 2 AC 180.
17 *London and Northern Estates Co v Schlesinger* [1916] 1 KB 20.

had lost about two years' usage of the premises out of a ten-year agreement, but the closure was not deemed to be sufficiently sufficient to amount to a frustrating event as there was a period of three years remaining once access to the building was restored

EXPLAINING THE LAW

Panalpina is a useful reference, not necessarily for the facts of the case, but more so that it provides clarity in an area of previous uncertainty, that it is possible for a lease to be frustrated where the lease is for a specified purpose. Lord Wilberforce explained that there were two issues of principle to be considered:

1) Whether the fact that the lease created an estate in land was a barrier to the applicability of the doctrine.
2) Whether all risks pass to a tenant when a lease is entered into.

On the first principle, Wilberforce was not persuaded that the lease being an estate in land would be a barrier to frustration in the right circumstances. He acknowledged that events can occur that lead to the estate in land coming to an end and that there may be many instances where it was clear that the parties have a mutually contemplated purpose that could be frustrated by the occurrence of a supervening event. Neither was he convinced on the second point, that a general principle existed that all risks pass to a tenant on the creation of a lease.

12.9 APPLYING THE LAW

Now let's try applying the law to a multipart problem concerning discharge of contract.

In March 2013, Carlos went online and purchased tickets, via the Hedsworth County Drama Association (HCDA) website, for himself and his three friends, Sam, George and Tom, for the midsummer outdoor production of *Macbeth* to be held outdoors at Hedsworth Castle on 21 July. He paid £150 for the tickets.

The four friends planned to have a night out in Hedsworth after the production, and to spend the night there before going home the next day. Carlos therefore booked two apartments at the Neon Lights Aparthotel at a combined cost of £310. As required by the Aparthotel website through which he booked, Carlos paid £100 as a deposit, with the balance to be paid when the friends checked out on 22 July.

On 20 July, Carlos saw on the news that the custom-built stage at Hedsworth Castle had been set on fire the night before by vandals and many of the props had been destroyed and lay strewn over the castle grounds. Due to the level of destruction, it was now impossible for the production to go ahead as planned, so HCDA decided to cancel the one evening event. It is widely rumoured that, rather than breaking into the castle grounds, the vandals appear to have entered the grounds through an open gate, which should have been securely padlocked the evening before by Julia, a member of HCDA's staff who had been supervising the preparations.

Carlos subsequently received a telephone call from HCDA confirming the cancellation of the production and saying that, whilst they could not give a refund, the production would be held at a later date to be announced and the friends' tickets would be valid for the rearranged event.

A week later, Carlos was informed that the date for the rearranged production was 28 August, but neither Carlos nor his friends were available on that date.

The friends decided to abandon their trip to Hedsworth on 21 July, and Carlos informed the Neon Lights Aparthotel that he wished to cancel the booking. He was told by the hotel that they would not be able to relet the two apartments at such short notice and they demanded payment of the outstanding balance owed to them.

Carlos was not prepared to pay the balance and demanded that Neon Lights return the £100 deposit. He would also like to know if there is any chance of recovering the £150 paid for the tickets from HCDA.

ADVISE CARLOS

FACTS
This question requires you to weigh up whether the contracts in question have been discharged by breach or by frustration and to apply the relevant law to the facts.

DEFINE THE AREA OF LAW FROM THE FACTS PRESENTED
If an event occurs after a contract has been entered into that renders the contract either impossible to perform, or commercially pointless, this can be a frustrating event that brings the contract to an end, releasing both parties from further performance of other obligations under the contract. It is important that the supervening event is the fault of neither of the parties.

The destruction of a person or thing essential to the performance of the contract can amount to a frustrating event (*Taylor v Caldwell*).

Conversely, another circumstance that can amount to a frustrating event is the cancellation of an event that was central to the contract, as was the case in *Krell v Henry*. However, the postponement of a coronation event was not seen to be a frustrating event in the case of

Herne Bay Steamboat Company v Hutton, where a breach of contract was found rather than frustration, as only part of the purpose was to view the king reviewing the fleet (and this had been cancelled). The other purpose was to cruise around the fleet, and this could still have taken place.

ISSUES

1) Does the damage to the stage and destruction of the props amount to a frustrating event?
2) Does the cancellation of the event amount to frustration of the contract with the hotel or will Carlos's notification of cancellation be regarded as an anticipatory breach?

LAW

The *Macbeth* performance: breach or frustration?

- *Anticipatory breach*: As Carlos was informed of the cancellation by HDCA before the performance, this could amount to an anticipatory breach of contract (*Hochester v De La Tour*[18]). You will recall that an anticipatory breach occurs where one party repudiates the contract before performance is due, by indicating an intention not to perform their obligations. Following an action of this nature, the other party can accept the repudiation and choose to no longer be bound by the contract. Providing it is a repudiatory breach, i.e. the breach of a condition of the contract (which is likely to be the case here), such a breach gives rise to a choice on the part of the claimant. Carlos can either accept the repudiation, and bring a claim against HDCA straight away or wait until the due date of the performance and, when there is a further breach by HDCA (non-performance), he can then sue them (*Fercometal SARL v Mediterranean Shipping Co SA (The Simona)*[19]). If it were an anticipatory breach it would be necessary to look at the measure of damages and the remoteness rule. However these are covered in a later chapter, so will be simply mentioned for the purpose of this exercise.

- *Frustration*: If the apparently frustrating event was the fault of one of the parties, it is not a frustrating event but will amount to self-induced frustration and a breach of contract (*Maritime National Fish v Ocean Trawlers*). It appears that, although HDCA did not damage the stage and props themselves, the omission of their employee to lock the gate the night before was a contributing factor. The postponement of the performance after the contract had been entered into could therefore be seen to be a breach of contract by HDCA.

  However, if the apparently frustrating event was held to be not self-induced, the acts of the vandals might well have frustrated the contract between Carlos and friends and HDCA (as in *Krell v Henry*). In this case, the court would consider s. 1(2) of the Law Reform (Frustrated Contracts) Act 1943, which provides that the court can, at its discretion, order a party that has received an advance payment from the other party before the frustrating event to refund the advance payment. The court would, however, have to look into whether the payee has incurred expenses in preparing to perform its

18 (1853) 2 E & B 678.
19 [1989] AC 788.

obligations under the contract. If it has, the court can allow the payee to retain such a sum out of the advance payment, as represents the expenses it has incurred, up to the total of the advance payment.

Apply the law: As it is unlikely, in this context that HDCA has incurred any additional expenses solely in preparing to perform its obligations under the contract with Carlos and his friends, the court is likely to exercise its discretion to order HDCA to pay back the £150 he paid for the tickets. Whether the contract has been breached or is frustrated, Carlos and his friends are likely to be able to recover the purchase price of the tickets from HDCA.

- **Neon Lights Aparthotel v Carlos/friends**
  - *Frustration or breach?* Carlos and his friends will claim that the cancellation of the performance amounted to a frustrating event, which rendered their contract with Neon Lights pointless (*Krell v Henry*); whereas Neon Lights will argue that, like in *Herne Bay Steamboat Co v Hutton*, the contract could have gone ahead, as only part of the purpose was to go to the performance, while another part of the purpose of the contract was to go for a night out in Hedsworth, and that it would still have been possible to do this; hence cancelling the booking amounted to a breach of contract.
  - *Anticipatory breach:* as Carlos informed the hotel before the due time and date for the friends to check into the hotel had arrived, this could be held to amount to an anticipatory breach (*Hochster v De La Tour*). Proceeding to stay in the hotel as arranged, and paying for the accommodation, would be likely to be regarded as conditions of contract, and therefore any breach of those conditions would be repudiatory, entitling Neon Lights to either accept the repudiation and sue straightaway, or wait until the due date and time of the booking and, when Carlos and friends do not turn up, therefore committing an actual breach of the contract, sue for breach at this time (*Fercometal v Mediterranean Shipping*). If it were an anticipatory breach it would be necessary to look at the measure of damages and mitigation of loss rule. However these areas are covered in a later chapter, so are simply mentioned for the purpose of this exercise.
  - *Frustration:* If Carlos and friends can convince the court that this was a *Krell v Henry* situation, the contract would have been discharged by frustration rather than breach. In this case, the court would consider s. 1(2) of the Law Reform (Frustrated Contracts) Act 1943, which provides that the court can, at its discretion, order a party that has received an advance payment from the other party before the frustrating event to pay that advance payment back to the other party. The court would, however, have to look into whether the payee of that payment has incurred expenses in preparing to perform its obligations under the contract. If it has, the court can allow the payee to retain such a sum out of the advance payment as represents the expenses it has incurred, up to the total of the advance payment.

    Apply the law: If Neon Lights has incurred expenses of up to £100, the court is likely to allow it to keep an amount equal to the expenses that it incurred. If it has incurred expenses of more than £100, under s. 2(1) the court may allow Neon Lights to keep the full amount of the advance payment. It does not have discretion to order Carlos and his friends to pay more to Neon Lights to compensate it for the full amount of any expenses incurred. Conversely, if Neon Lights cannot establish that they have incurred any additional expenses, the court is likely to exercise its discretion to order Neon Lights to pay back the advance payment of £100 to Carlos and his friends. The situation appears to be much more in line with *Herne Bay Steamboat Co v Hutton* than with *Krell v Henry*, and therefore a court is likely to find Carlos and his friends liable for an anticipatory breach of contract. They are likely to have to pay the outstanding balance as compensation to Neon Lights (or potentially a lesser amount if Neon Lights has succeeded in partially mitigating its losses).

12.10 BRINGING IT ALL TOGETHER

To summarise, the doctrine of frustration will result in a contract being discharged and neither party will be in breach of contract. The obligations will be considered at the time that the contract was agreed and a determination will be made as to whether or not a supervening event will have had the effect of rendering the contract impossible to perform or produce a result that is radically different to that agreed by the parties. The doctrine operates within narrow parameters and will not be available in cases where a contract has become more difficult or expensive to perform. Nor will a contract be frustrated where an act of one of the parties has contributed to the frustrating event (self-induced frustration).

Sometimes within an agreement, it can be ascertained that one of the parties has elected to take a risk for certain factors or events or the contract may include a *force majeure* clause that will cover where the various liabilities lie in certain circumstances. In these instances, the parties will not be able to rely on the doctrine of frustration.

The Law Reform (Frustrated Contracts) Act 1943 provides instruction on how monies paid or payable and expenses will be dealt with and how any valuable benefit obtained under the contract will be addressed.

KEY LEARNING POINTS

When a contract is frustrated:

- It will be discharged automatically at the time of the frustrating event
- Both parties are released from obligations that arise after the frustrating event
- Neither party will be in breach of contract.

Remember that you should consider the following in deciding whether a contract will be frustrated:

- An event will have occurred after the contract has been formed
- The event will have made the contract impossible to perform or performance will be radically different to that envisaged by the parties

- The event will have been outside the control of the parties
- Supervening events will include areas such as unavailability of a specific thing or specific person vital to the contract; non-occurrence of an event; government intervention; illegality; delay
- Contracts that are inconvenient or more difficult/expensive to perform as a result of the supervening event will not be frustrated.

  Consider the effect of frustration:

  Law Reform (Frustrated Contracts) Act 1943 covers money paid or payable before a frustrating event, expenses incurred and any valuable benefit obtained. See also:
  - *Gamerco SA v ICM/Fair Warning (Agency) Ltd*
  - *BP Exploration Co (Libya) Ltd v Hunt.*

TAKING IT FURTHER

Clark, 'Frustration, restitution and the Law Reform (Frustrated Contracts) Act 1943' [1996] LMCLQ 170

Mayfield, 'Force of nature' (2011) 161 NLJ 773

McKendrick, 'The construction of *force majeure* clauses and self-induced frustration' [1990] LMCLQ 153

Treitel, *The Law of Contract*, 13th edn, Sweet & Maxwell, 2011

Treitel, *Frustration and Force Majeure*, 3rd edn, Sweet and Maxwell, 2014

13

CHAPTER 13
REMEDIES (1)

13.1 INTRODUCTION

This chapter is the first of two on remedies. The main objective of the first chapter is to provide an insight into the remedy of damages and to look at quantification of damages where a breach of contract has occurred. The rules governing discharge of contract by breach were discussed in an earlier chapter and it is now time to look at the remedies available where an innocent party has been the subject of a breach. The remedies available for breach of contract can be categorised into three areas:

1) common law remedy of damages
2) equitable remedies, including specific performance and injunction
3) restitution.

This chapter will primarily address the types of damages available and the heads under which damages will/will not be considered where a breach of contract has occurred. The other, non–damages, remedies will be looked at in the next chapter.

The main objective of damages in contract law is to compensate the claimant for the loss that has been suffered as a result of the defendant's breach of contract and to place the claimant in the position s/he would have been in if the contract had been performed properly.

Damages are not awarded as a punitive measure, nor will they be awarded to enforce moral obligations that may exist between the parties. The circumstances in which damages will be awarded are to cover:

1) pecuniary losses that pass the contract law test of remoteness
2) non-pecuniary losses; to compensate for intangible loss such as anxiety, distress or disappointment, which cannot be arithmetically calculated. This type of damage is not available as of right, but in certain circumstances an award can be made for disappointment suffered as a result of non-performance of a contractual obligation where elements of the claimant's well-being are central to the contract.

Parties may make provision for a specified level of compensation to be payable in the event of a breach by inclusion of a specific clause covering potential contingencies that they predict may arise in the execution of the contract. Such clauses, known as liquidated damages clauses, are enforceable as long as they do not amount to a penalty.

The claimant must show that any losses incurred were caused by the defendant's breach of contract and, in all cases, a claimant must take reasonable measures to minimise any losses sustained.

AS YOU READ

At the end of this chapter you should be able to:

- Distinguish between the measure of damages in contract and tort

- Understand the difference between expectation and reliance measures in quantification of damages

- Apply the remoteness test in an award for contractual damages

- Identify the instances in which damages can be awarded for non-pecuniary losses

- Understand the role of mitigation and contributory negligence in the calculation of a damages award

- Be able to distinguish between a liquidated damages clause and a penalty and how this impacts on enforceability of the clause

13.1.1 CONTRACT OR TORT

Damages are the main remedy where there is a claim in both contract and tort law. A contract is an agreement between parties setting out their duties and responsibilities to each other whereas tort law governs situations where one person has caused harm or injury to another. Tort law covers both intentional and unintentional acts that have harmed another person, the most common being a claim in negligence. Both contract and tort damages are usually awarded where a duty has been breached. In contract law the breach will relate to the specific express and implied duties set out in the contract, and a causal link must exist between the loss suffered and the breach of contract, whereas in tort the wrong will involve a breach of a duty of care which has caused harm or injury to another person or their property.

A contract is based upon a consensual agreement whereas a tort is never based upon consent and this factor is reflected in the way that courts award damages. In contract, the aim of damages is to restore the parties to their pre-contractual position, whereas in tort the damages are usually awarded to compensate the victim for their loss. Whilst punitive damages are sometimes awarded in tort as a way of punishing the defendant, they do not feature in an award for contractual damages (unless the claims are linked).

Contract and tort claims are usually filed separately. However, it is possible for a claim to consider both a tortious and a contractual element, where the matters are inextricably linked. Usually the tort must affect the subject matter of the contract in order for the claims to be filed simultaneously.

Table 13.1

Comparator	Contract liability	Tort liability (negligence)
Relationship between parties	Created and governed by the contract Consent of both parties	Governed by law. No contract involved Duty of care
Obligation	Contained in the terms of the contract	Defendant must meet the standard of care expected of the reasonable person
Causal link Remoteness Test	Causal link required Loss must have been foreseeable Two-limb test – loss must have been within the contemplation of the parties 1) Covers losses that are a normal result of the breach 2) Losses not in the reasonable contemplation (special losses) of the parties will only be recovered if the defendant was aware of them	Causal link required Loss must have been reasonably foreseeable – extends further than contract as extent of loss does not need to be foreseeable
Other considerations in quantification of damages	Reduction in damages where claimant fails to take reasonable steps to mitigate any loss	Damages may be reduced as a result of contributory negligence

13.2 DEFINITION AND AIM OF DAMAGES IN CONTRACT LAW

Where a breach of contract has occurred, the rule for recovery of compensation is laid down in *Robinson v Harman*.[1] To prove loss, the claimant must show that s/he would have been able to satisfy the contractual obligations if the breach had not occurred. Damages will only be awarded if the breach was a direct cause of the loss.[2] If no loss has occurred as a result of the breach, it is only possible to recover nominal damages and the court cannot award an amount in excess of the anticipated loss. Additionally, the claimant cannot recover any profits made by the defendant as a result of the breach, even where the breach can be proven to have been

1   (1848) 1 Ex 850.
2   *C and P Haulage v Middleton* [1983] 1 WLR 1461.

deliberate, as illustrated in *Surrey County Council v Bredero Homes Ltd.*[3] This case involved a breach of a land covenant by the defendant, who built properties in excess of the restriction. The court declined to transfer the benefit that the wrongdoer gained from his breach of contract to the wronged party in refusing to award the claimant a proportion of the profits that had been earned from the sale of the additional houses.

So how do the courts measure damages where a breach of contract has occurred? There are two main methods that are used in quantifying the level of damages that can be paid (see Figure 13.1).

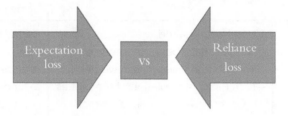

Figure 13.1 Methods of quantification of damages

13.3 EXPECTATION LOSS

The objective of the expectation measure of damages is to place the claimant in the position s/he would have been in if the contract had been performed properly.[4] A calculation of damages under this measure will protect expectations that were created when the agreement was made (see Figure 13.2).

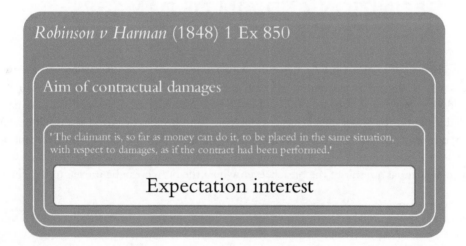

Robinson v Harman (1848) 1 Ex 850

Aim of contractual damages

'The claimant is, so far as money can do it, to be placed in the same situation, with respect to damages, as if the contract had been performed.'

Expectation interest

Figure 13.2 Expectation interest

3   [1993] 1 WLR 961.
4   *Robinson v Harman* (1848) 1 Ex 850.

The expectation interest is the value of the benefit that the claimant would have obtained if the contract had been performed as agreed. This can include loss of profits but excludes punitive damages.[5]

Where goods are defective, or a service is not carried out to standard, the court will award either the difference in value or the cost of cure. For goods this will be the difference between the actual value and the value of what the goods would have been worth if they had not been defective. For a service contract, the damages will equate to the cost of cure, i.e. cost of putting the work right. It could also include the cost of the work being carried out by a third party where this is desired and possible. Usually in cases concerning defective building work the cost of cure is appropriate.[6] However, if there appears to be a real risk of overcompensation, the usual rule will be displaced and only the difference in value will be awarded.

APPLYING THE LAW

Calculate the award in the following example.

Billy sells a Rolex watch to Maria for £3,000. It is a term of the contract that the watch is a genuine Rolex. A week later Maria has the watch valued and finds out it is a fake design worth about £20. If it had been a genuine Rolex it would have been worth £5,000.

Damages: The court is likely to award Maria £4,980. If the contract had been performed as agreed, Maria would have a Rolex watch worth £5,000. Instead she has a fake worth £20. She needs £4,980 to buy an equivalent watch.

In some instances, the court will decline an award for the cost of cure where the monetary loss is difficult to calculate, particularly where the breach results in a loss of amenity. The following case illustrates this point.

RUXLEY ELECTRONICS & CONSTRUCTIONS LTD V FORSYTH [1996] 1 AC 344

Forsyth contracted with Ruxley for the construction of a swimming pool in his garden at a cost of £17,797. Forsyth specifically requested the depth of the diving area to extend to 7 feet 6 inches. On completion, the diving area measured only 6 feet 9 inches deep. Forsyth sued for damages based upon his expectation that the diving area would be as specified in the agreement.

---

5   *Addis v Gramophone Co Ltd* [1909] AC 488.
6   *Harbutt's Plasticine Ltd v Wayne Tank and Pump Co Ltd* [1970] 1 QB 447, [1970] 2 WLR 198 CA.

Two important factors were:

1) cost of reconstruction to the specified depth would amount to £21,560 (i.e. cost of cure)
2) difference in monetary value between actual depth and what was requested was nil.

Held: the House of Lords declined to award the cost of cure but instead awarded £2,500 for loss of amenity. An award to cover the cost of reconstruction was deemed disproportionate and wasteful, since the claimant had no plans to reconstruct. The loss of amenity award was a recognition that the claimant had been deprived of his contractual benefit (the requested depth), but reflected the benefit the consumer had received (a functioning pool).

Lord Mustill highlighted the fact (*obiter*) that the consumer often demands specifications which, although not of economic value, have value to him:

the law must cater for those occasions where the value of the promise to the promise exceeds the financial enhancement of his position which full performance will secure. This excess, often referred to in the literature as the 'consumer surplus'... is usually incapable of precise valuation in terms of money, exactly because it represents a personal, subjective and non-monetary gain. Nevertheless where it exists the law should recognise it and compensate the promisee if the misperformance takes it away.

To sum up, damages for expectation loss will cover:

■ difference in value between the actual and expected performance
■ difference in cost to the contractor between actual and expected performance
■ any loss of amenity.

13.4 RELIANCE LOSS

An alternative method of assessing loss is to look at expenses incurred in reliance on the contract. The case of *Anglia Television v Reed*[7] involved a set of circumstances where it would have been difficult in advance to predict the profit that would have been made if a TV production that was cancelled had gone ahead:

---

7   [1972] 1 QB 60, CA.

ANGLIA TELEVISION V REED [1972] 1 QB 60, CA

The defendant, the actor Oliver Reed, had contracted with Anglia TV to play the lead role in a TV play. When he later refused to perform, Anglia were forced to cease production as they were unable to find a substitute to fill the role.

Held: Anglia were awarded damages for wasted expenditure on the production. The damages included items of expenditure for fees incurred for directors, management and design.

The claimant will usually elect the method under which s/he will pursue a damages claim. Damages are usually awarded under the expectation loss method, but sometimes the court will follow the reliance approach if expectation loss is difficult to predict. Expectation loss and reliance loss are mutually exclusive, thus preventing a double recovery that would lead to the perverse situation of the claimant being in a better position overall than s/he would have been if the contract had been performed. This relationship between expectation loss and reliance loss was analysed further in *OMAK Maritime Ltd*.

OMAK MARITIME LTD V MAMOLA CHALLENGER SHIPPING CO, THE MOMOLA CHALLENGER [2010] EWHC 2026, [2011] 1 LLOYD'S REP 47

Following a breach of contract, the claimant had been successful in mitigating the effects of the defendant's repudiation of the contract, which meant that the claimant's position following the breach was financially better than it would have been if the contract had been performed, by an amount in excess of the wasted expenditure. The court had to determine whether the mitigation efforts were relevant to the claim for wasted expenditure, in the same way that they would have been to a claim for loss of profits. In making its decision the High Court considered the question of whether reliance damages are simply a type of expectancy damages or whether they are distinct from each other.

Held: the court concluded that reliance damages are not based on a separate principle to the expectation loss calculation, as set out in *Harman*.

In discussing the expectation loss principle, Teare J stated the principle 'underpins the award of damages in wasted expenditure cases' and is 'not fundamentally different'.

So, in ruling that wasted expenditure damages are a 'type' of expectation damages, the court confirmed that compensation is subject to the rule that the claimant cannot be put into a better position overall than he would have been if the contract had not been breached.

A similar position arose in *C and P Haulage v Middleton*,[8] although in contrast to *OMAK* it was the terms of the contract rather than the breach that caused the loss. The case involved a claim for wasted expenditure resulting from money spent by the claimant on installation of fixtures for his garage business. Under the agreement, it was always intended that the fixtures would become part of the premises. The claim for wasted expenditure arose following the early termination of the agreement by the landlord. The court refused an award for lost expenditure for the works undertaken, as it had always been intended that the fixtures would become part of the premises overall; neither was the court prepared to make an allowance for the loss of usage of the garage as the tenant had been able to make alternative arrangements.

In wasted expenditure cases, the initial presumption will be that the expenditure would have been recouped if the contract had been performed correctly. Whilst the presumption can be rebutted, the burden of proof will lie with the defendant who is seeking to defend a wasted expenditure claim.[9]

The date for assessment of damages is usually the date of breach, but the courts have shown some flexibility where this approach would lead to an injustice or where an alternative date enables a more accurate calculation.[10]

Lord Wilberforce summarised the position in *Johnson v Agnew*:[11]

> The general principle for the assessment of damages is compensatory, i.e. that the innocent party is to be placed, so far as money can do so, in the same position as if the contract had been performed. Where the contract is one of sale, this principle normally leads to assessment of damages as at the date of the breach, a principle recognised and embodied in s 51 of the Sale of Goods Act 1893. But this is not an absolute rule; if to follow it would give rise to injustice, the court has power to fix such other date as may be appropriate in the circumstances,

In some instances, assessment of damages may not be straightforward or will be more difficult to calculate. Unless the claim is purely speculative, the courts will not decline an award. Various categories such as lost opportunity, distress and disappointment will be considered in certain circumstances.

ESSENTIAL DEFINITIONS: TYPES OF DAMAGE

Pecuniary damages: paid for losses that can be quantified in monetary terms. The actual monetary loss will dictate the amount of the award.

---

8 [1983] 1 WLR 1461.

9 *CCC Films (London) Ltd v Impact Quadrant Films Ltd* [1985] 1 QB 16.

10 *Golden Strait Corpn v Nippon Yusen Kubishika Kaisha, The Golden Victory* [2007] UKHL 12, [2007] 2 AC 353.

11 [1980] AC 367.

Non-pecuniary damages: damages that are not readily quantified or valued in monetary terms, such as compensation for anxiety, distress, disappointment and pain and suffering.

Punitive damages (exemplary): to punish or deter the defendant and others from engaging in activity similar to that upon which the legal action was founded. Punitive damages are very rare in contract cases, but can be awarded in some fraud or tort cases that overlap with contract law.

Nominal damages: awarded when no monetary loss has been incurred, but the court wants to show that the successful party was in the right. These are typically rarely awarded in contract cases, but are sometimes awarded in tort cases that overlap with a breach of contract case.

Consequential damages: to compensate the injured party for indirect damages other than contractual loss; for example, loss of business profits due to undelivered materials. The damages must pass the remoteness test.

Liquidated damages: damages that are expressly specified in the contract. These are available when damages may be difficult to anticipate and must be a fair estimate of what damages might be if there is a breach.

13.5 LOST OPPORTUNITY

The court may award damages for a lost opportunity. The case of *Chaplin v Hicks*[12] provides an illustration of an award granted under this head.

CHAPLIN V HICKS [1911] 2 KB 786

A talent contest arranged by the *Daily Express* newspaper offered a prize of work in theatrical productions over a three-year period. The top 50 contenders were invited for an audition where 12 winners were selected. The claimant was selected as one of the 50 contenders but the organisers failed to provide her with details of the audition arrangements. Since she did not take part in the auditions, it was unknown whether or not she would have been one of the 12 winners.

12 [1911] 2 KB 786.

Held: the claimant was awarded damages to compensate for having the chance to win the competition taken away from her, i.e. her loss of opportunity. Vaughan Williams LJ summarised the position as follows: 'the fact that damages cannot be assessed with certainty does not relieve the wrongdoer of the necessity of paying damages for his breach of contract'.

A further example of lost opportunity arose in *Blackpool Fylde Aero Club v Blackpool Borough Council*,[13] where the council had invited tenders from interested parties to run a concession operating pleasure flights. Blackpool Flyde correctly submitted a tender but their tender was not considered due to an administrative error made by the council. The club was successful in a claim for lost opportunity.

13.6 MENTAL DISTRESS AND DISAPPOINTMENT

Most parties will experience an element of frustration, distress and disappointment following a breach of contract. As a general rule, the courts are reluctant to award damages in contract law for injury to feelings or mental discomfort owing to actions or non-actions of one of the other partiy. Not only would calculations be based on subjective information, but evidence to support claims can be difficult to substantiate. Having said that, it is important to be aware that there are some exceptions to the rule (see Figure 13.3).

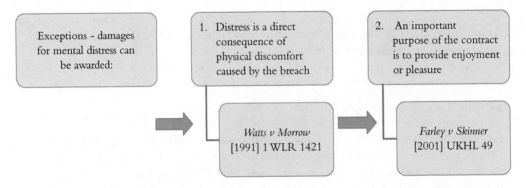

Figure 13.3 Damages for mental distress

---

13 [1990] 1 WLR 1195, CA.

13.7 CONTRACTS FOR ENTERTAINMENT AND ENJOYMENT

The case of *Jarvis v Swan's Tours*[14] concerned a claim for damages related to a poor holiday experience where the promise of 'a great time' turned out to be quite different to what was described:

JARVIS V SWAN'S TOURS [1973] 1 QB 233, CA

The claim brought by the plaintiff concerned a skiing trip that had failed to comply with the description in the holiday brochure on several grounds. He had been promised 'a great time', which did not materialise. He was provided with inadequate skis, an unsatisfactory bar service and the party that was highlighted as a feature of the holiday did not go ahead due to the lack of guests. Owing to these failures, the plaintiff had a poor experience and claimed damages for breach of contract.

Held: at first instance damages were awarded to represent the difference in value between what the plaintiff paid for and what he actually got. However, on appeal, Denning MR took the view that damages for mental distress could be recovered in contracts aimed at providing entertainment and enjoyment. He acknowledged the potential difficulties in quantifying such claims but drew an analogy with the task of calculating personal injury awards in tort law, where decisions frequently have to be made in relation to loss of amenities. Denning did not perceive the difficulty in assessing monetary damages to be a factor that should prevent an award of damages:

> People look forward to a holiday. They expect the promises to be fulfilled. When it fails, they are generally disappointed and upset. It is difficult to assess in terms of money, but it is the task of the judges to do the best they can.

Since this case, it is accepted that holiday claims are an exception to the rule that damages for breach of contract cannot be claimed for mental distress and disappointment, on the basis that the whole purpose of a holiday contract is to provide entertainment and enjoyment or mental satisfaction.

A more recent case heard by the Court of Appeal was *Milner v Carnival plc (t/a Cunard)*,[15] where the Court of Appeal set out clear guidance on the assessment of damages. The holiday in this case was a 106-day cruise on the maiden voyage of the *Queen Victoria*, priced at £59,052.20. It was the Milners' case that that was what they got, but not in the way they

---

14 [1973] 1 QB 233, CA.
15 [2010] EWCA Civ 389.

bargained for. Due to an issue with extremely noisy floorplates in their cabin, the couple
were unable to sleep. They abandoned the cruise after 28 days and, although refunded for the
remainder of the cruise, they were also successful in securing damages for the 28 days spent
on board. In making their judgment the court looked at what the correct measure of damages
for a ruined holiday should be for distress and disappointment. The recommendation of Lord
Steyn in *Farley v Skinner* (discussed later) was that awards in this area should be restrained and
modest to prevent huge amounts of litigation in this area; notwithstanding this, in *Milner*, the
judge felt that an exceptional award was warranted due to the horrendous experience that the
claimants had endured on their holiday.

A central factor in assessment of consequential damage such as inconvenience or discomfort is that
the damage must have been reasonably foreseeable as a likely outcome of any breach at the time
the contract was made. This test, which pervades all claims for damages in breach of contract, is
known as the remoteness test and will be discussed in greater detail later in this chapter.

13.8 MENTAL DISTRESS CAUSED BY PHYSICAL INCONVENIENCE AND DISCOMFORT

The courts will consider an award of damages for mental distress where physical inconvenience
has been experienced as a result of a breach of contract. In *Hobbs v L & SW Railway Co*,[16] a
railway company was required to pay damages to a family who were deposited at the wrong
station, resulting in them having to walk nearly five miles home on a rainy night. Here Sir
Alexander Cockburn CJ stated that damages for personal inconvenience were recoverable 'where
it is sufficiently serious' and Mellor J provided further guidance on this point by saying that:

> for the mere inconvenience, such as annoyance and loss of temper, or vexation, or for
> being disappointed in a particular thing that you have set your mind upon, without real
> physical inconvenience resulting, you cannot recover damages. That is purely sentimental
> and not a case where the word inconvenience as I here use it would apply.

The later case of *Watts v Morrow*[17] provides further clarity on awards for mental distress, where
the distress has been caused by physical discomfort:

WATTS V MORROW [1991] 1 WLR 1421

The case concerned a report compiled by a surveyor, who negligently failed to disclose
a number of defects in a property. The clients, who had purchased the property in
reliance on the report, remedied the defects and sued for damages.

16 (1875) LR 10 QB 111.
17 [1991] 1 WLR 1921.

> Held: the Court of Appeal awarded damages based on the difference between
> the value of the property as stated in the surveyor's report and the actual value
> of the property with defects. Damages were also awarded for 'distress and
> inconvenience', but were limited to a modest sum relating only to the physical
> discomfort experienced.

The case is helpful in that Bingham LJ provided further useful guidance on when damages should be awarded for distress and inconvenience:

> Where the very object of a contract is to provide pleasure, relaxation, peace of mind or
> freedom from molestation, damages will be awarded if the fruit of the contract is not
> provided or if the contrary result is procured instead.

Bingham LJ referred to these types of contract as an 'exceptional category' and went on to determine that a survey on a house would not fall generally within this exceptional category. However, he went on to conclude that in his view damages 'are recoverable for physical inconvenience and discomfort caused by the breach and mental suffering directly related to that inconvenience and discomfort'.

The important principle to be taken from this judgment is that, in order to obtain damages where a breach of contract has occurred and physical discomfort has resulted, the physical discomfort must have resulted from something more 'tangible' than feelings of disappointment. It must be something physically connected.

For example, you book out the ground floor of a restaurant for your 80th birthday party. You have very bad arthritis and breathing difficulties and cannot climb stairs. You arrive on the evening of your party only to find that the upstairs has been reserved for you instead due to a larger party needing the downstairs room. The stress of having to climb the stairs brings on a panic attack and you are taken away by ambulance and miss the party. Also, due to the exertion of trying to climb the stairs you are bedridden for a whole week. Clearly the physical discomfort has resulted from the restaurant's breach of contract and the physical symptoms result from the distress experienced as a result of the breach, meaning that a successful claim would be likely in this instance.

In further analysing what types of loss can be claimed under the category of physical inconvenience and discomfort, discussed above, it is helpful to review the guidance provided by Lord Scott in the case of *Farley v Skinner*,[18] where further clarity was provided on availability of damages in cases of disappointment and/or inconvenience resulting from the loss of a pleasurable amenity.

---

18 *Farley v Skinner* [2001] UKHL 49, [2002] AC 732.

FARLEY V SKINNER [2001] UKHL 49, [2002] AC 732

The plaintiff was interested in buying a property located in the Sussex countryside. In order to find out whether the property would be affected by aircraft noise from Gatwick Airport, he engaged a surveyor to undertake a survey. The plaintiff made it clear that he required a property that offered peace and tranquility. The surveyor reported it unlikely that the property would suffer significantly from aircraft noise. It later transpired that the property was badly affected by aircraft noise due to its proximity to a navigation beacon where aircraft stacked up at busy times whilst waiting to land. The plaintiff's enjoyment of the property was seriously affected at these peak times.

Held: the House of Lords held that the 'sole' object of the contract need not be to provide pleasure, enjoyment or peace of mind, but emphasised that these elements must be an *important* object of the contract.

Lord Scott stated that:

> If the cause is no more than disappointment that the contractual obligation has been broken, damages are not recoverable even if the disappointment has led to a complete mental breakdown. But, if the cause of the inconvenience or discomfort is a sensory (sight, touch, hearing, smell etc.) experience, damages can, subject to the remoteness rules, be recovered.

It is clear that since the case of *Farley v Skinner* the test for damages is now less stringent and damages are recoverable in contracts where an 'important' object of a contract is to provide pleasure, enjoyment or peace of mind, whereas previously pleasure, enjoyment or peace of mind had to be 'the very object' of the contract.[19]

The position with regard to damage recovery for mental distress can be summarised into three key rules:

Mental distress – three key rules		
1. where a predominant object of a contract is for mental satisfaction (such as holidays) damages can be awarded for mental distress	2. damages can be awarded for mental distress where physical inconvenience has been suffered as a result of a breach of contract (*Watts v Morrow*)	3. Damages can be awarded for mental distress where the breach has caused the loss of a pleasurable amenity that was an important object of the contract (*Farley v Skinner*)

Figure 13.4 Damages for mental distress

---

19 *Watts v Morrow* [1991] 1 WLR 1421.

13.9 THE REMOTENESS RULE

The remoteness test is applicable in contract law, just as it is for awards of damages in tort. The remoteness test is a legal test of causation which is used in determining the level of loss caused by a breach of contract in order to ascertain the quantum of damages. It would be unfair to hold a person in breach of contract responsible for all losses that flow from the breach and you will see that not all damage is recoverable.

APPLYING THE LAW

Due to the late delivery of a hire car, Shakira misses her plane to Glasgow, which makes her late for a conference and she acquires a speeding ticket en route. Her employer calls her later in the day and terminates her contract of employment on the basis that she was on her last final warning for being late for work events. She arrives home the next day in a very distressed state and argues with her husband who tells her that he wants a divorce.

In an extremely distressed state, Shakira takes her husband's car and drives carelessly, crashing the car into an ice cream van. The collision has left her with a broken arm and her husband's car and the van are a write-off.

The car hire company is in breach of contract for the late delivery of the car. What do you think the extent of their liability is? Will they be responsible for any or all of Shakira's losses? Think about the advice that you would give to Shakira as you work through the rules on remoteness.

Once factual causation is established, it is necessary to ascertain whether the damage can be linked to the particular breach. Damage that is regarded as too remote is not recoverable even where a factual link between the breach of contract and the loss can be established. The remoteness test can be justified on the basis that if a contract breaker were liable for all losses, however remote, the balance between the contract value and an unlimited liability is likely to be disproportionate and place an unfair burden on the party in breach of contract.

In contract law, the remoteness rule derives from the case of *Hadley v Baxendale*:

HADLEY V BAXENDALE (1854) 9 EXCH 341

The plaintiffs owned a flour mill that was forced to stop production due to the breakdown of a crankshaft that was an integral part the operating system. The defendants agreed to deliver the shaft to Greenwich but, due to a delay on their part, the shaft was delivered late. Consequently, the mill lay idle for a period of five extra days than would have been the case if the delay had not occurred.

The plaintiffs sued for loss of profits for the period of non-production.

Held: the plaintiffs were unable to recover their loss of profit because the loss did not arise naturally from the breach due to the fact that, in this profession, millers usually keep a replacement shaft to prevent their mill from lying idle in such circumstances. The defendants were not informed that the mill had no replacement shaft and so could not have anticipated the impact of their delay upon the profits of the company.

ANALYSING THE LAW

The remoteness rule formulated in *Hadley v Baxendale* is often referred to as a two-limb test which covers both direct damages and special or consequential damages (see Figure 13.5).

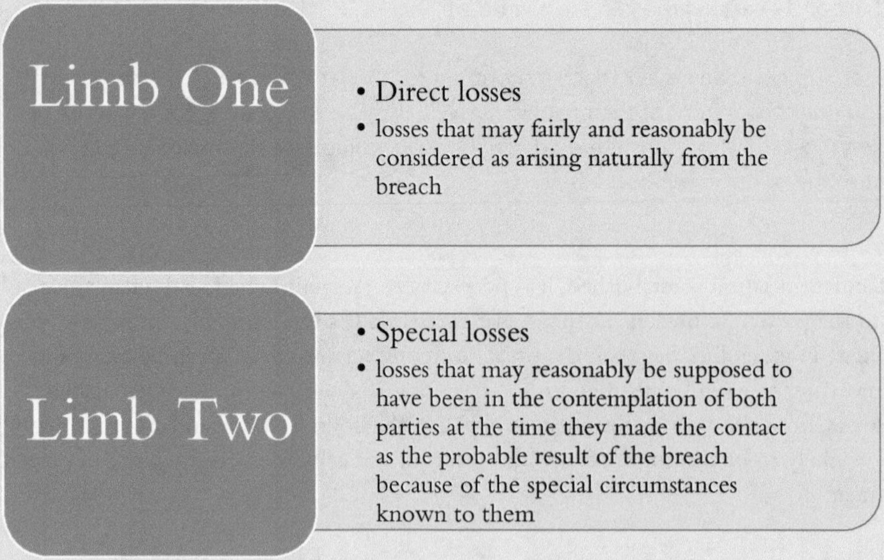

Limb One	• Direct losses • losses that may fairly and reasonably be considered as arising naturally from the breach
Limb Two	• Special losses • losses that may reasonably be supposed to have been in the contemplation of both parties at the time they made the contact as the probable result of the breach because of the special circumstances known to them

Figure 13.5 Two-limb test

To contextualise the rules: if a seller is in breach of contract for the sale of a product that is not fit for its purpose, the damages that flow naturally from the breach will be the difference between the contract price and the market price for a replacement product. These are categorised as direct losses. However if unbeknown to the seller the buyer had needed the product to manufacture something else in an agreement with a third party and the buyer has been unable to fulfil his/her promise, the seller would only be liable for further damages if he knew at the time of contracting that these damages were likely to result if the goods were not fit for their purpose. On the other hand, if a seller is in breach of contract for the sale of a product that is to be used to produce further products to be sold on to a third party, the buyer's damages are the difference between the profits he would actually earned on his actual output and the profits he would have earned if the product had been supplied as agreed.

In *Hadley v Baxendale*, if the defendants had known the mill would be idle for the period of time taken for the crankshaft repair to be completed when they agreed to transport it, the outcome of the case would most likely have been different, and the defendants would have been required to compensate for the losses, owing to the fact that the loss would have been within their contemplation.

ASSESSMENT TIP

In quantifying damages, look at all the circumstances and ask yourself whether the party in breach was aware of any unusual losses that were likely to occur in the event of a breach. If not, it is unlikely that s/he will be liable for these losses. Also check whether provision has been made in the contract to allocate or apportion any such losses.

It is also important to note that the remoteness test takes into account what was known to the defendant at the time the contract was made, not at the time of the breach.[20] This makes total sense, as it would be at the agreement stage that the parties would be able to negotiate and concur on any limitation clauses that they wished to include and the price of the contract would reflect these additions.

The rule in *Hadley v Baxendale* has been applied and developed in several later cases. In *Newman Industries v Victoria Laundry*,[21] a delay in delivering a boiler to a laundry resulted in ordinary lost profits being recoverable, as it is clear that a laundry business cannot operate without a working boiler. However, in the same case damages for lost profits on a lucrative dying contract were not recoverable as they were not deemed to have been foreseeable by the defendant, nor had the defendant been specifically alerted to this aspect of the business when the contract was formed. Asquith LJ stressed that the defendant's knowledge at the time the contract was formed is a critical factor when quantifying loss. The knowledge itself can either be imputed or actual. Imputed knowledge is largely the type of knowledge that everyone would be expected to have in the context of the agreement, whereas actual knowledge is

---

20 *Jackson v Royal Bank of Scotland plc* [2005] UKHL 3, [2005] 1 WLR 377.
21 [1949] 2 KB 528.

something wider and extends beyond general awareness of the usual type of knowledge that
can be imputed. So in this case, the ordinary lost profits from the laundry would have been
categorised as imputed knowledge, whereas knowledge of the profits that would have been
realised from the lucrative dying contract could not be imputed and would need to have been
specifically known about (i.e. actual knowledge) when the agreement was made if they were
to be recovered.

In *Koufos v C Czarnikow Ltd, The Heron II*[22] the House of Lords clarified that the remoteness
test in tort imposes a wider liability than the remoteness test in contractual claims and the
degree of foreseeability of loss required is higher in contract than in tort claims. Per Lord
Reid; there must be a 'serious possibility', a 'real danger', or a very 'substantial probability' of
the type of loss in a contract claim. The tests are summarised in Figure 13.6.

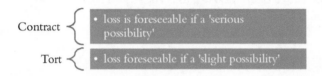

Figure 13.6 Contract v tort

The reasons that the test of foreseeability in contract is stricter than in tort law are twofold:

1) Where a contract exists, each party knows who they are dealing with and can take
    measures within the agreement to manage or apportion any unusual losses
2) In tort the parties do not know in advance who they may need to make a claim against
    and so cannot forewarn of the possibility of any unusual loss or damage. Remember, in
    tort, provided the damage is foreseeable, the defendant is liable for the full extent of the
    damage no matter whether the extent of the damage is foreseeable.

It is often the case that an act by one of the parties could be classified as both a breach in
contract and a tort often where a breach of duty to take reasonable care has occurred. The
relationship between the remoteness test in contract and tort was analysed in *Parsons (Livestock)
Ltd v Uttley Ingham & Co Ltd* and a method of calculation was agreed to arrive at what the
court considered to be a reasonable result.

PARSONS (LIVESTOCK) LTD V UTTLEY INGHAM LTD [1978] 1 QB 791

The claimants purchased a storage hopper from the defendants to guarantee
safe storage of their pig food. In installing the hopper at the claimants' farm, the
defendants forgot to unseal the ventilator at the top of the hopper, which led to the
contamination of the food. As a result, many of the pigs caught an infection and died.

22 [1969] 1 AC 350, HL.

Held: the Court of Appeal held that if the type of loss can be contemplated as a serious possibility, all loss of that type will be recoverable even though it can be argued that the extent of the loss could not have been contemplated. In this case, since some harm to the pigs could be contemplated, it did not matter that the actual death of a large number of pigs was not in the contemplation of the defendant and damages were recoverable. Scarman LJ considered it unnecessary to draw a distinction between physical damage and loss of profit. He stated that the type of consequence, loss of profit or physical injury will all be important in determining whether a loss or injury was of a type that the parties could reasonably have contemplated at the time the contract was made.

Later cases, such as *Transfield Shipping Inc v Mercator Shipping Inc. (The Achilleas)*[23] raise the potential that, in unusual cases, due to the particular commercial context and specific circumstances, it may be necessary to consider whether a party has assumed responsibility for losses of a particular kind. *Achilleas* concerned the late return of a ship that had been chartered from the claimant. The late return amounted to a breach of contract and resulted in the claimant being unable to re-charter the ship at a highly profitable rate, although it was re-chartered at a lower rate. In deciding whether damages could be recovered for the 'extra' profit that could have been achieved at the highly profitable rate, the House of Lords were unanimous in their conclusion that such loss was too remote. In his judgment, Lord Hoffmann appeared to move away from the traditional approach in *Hadley v Baxendale* and looked at whether or not the charterers could have assumed responsibility for the claimant's losses, taking into account the type of contract and its commercial background. Whilst he concluded that the charterers had not assumed this responsibility, his considerations marked a departure from the established approach followed by the other judges (see Figure 13.7).

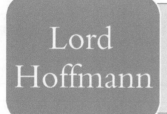

Lord Hoffmann

- 'departure from the ordinary foreseeability rule based on individual circumstances will be unusual but limitation on the extent of liability in particular types of contract arising out of general expectations in certain markets, such as banking and shipping, are likely to be more common.'

Figure 13.7 A different approach?

13.10 MITIGATION

The concept of mitigation means that the claimant must take reasonable steps to minimise the losses incurred as a consequence of the breach. If it is shown that damages could have been

23 [2008] UKHL 48, [2009] 1 AC 61, HL.

limited or avoided by taking reasonable steps, the level of damages will be limited or non-recoverable. By way of illustration, in *Brace v Calder*,[24] where the plaintiff claimed damages for wrongful dismissal when two of the partners of the company retired, it was held that he could not claim damages to cover the cost of his earnings as he had failed to take the opportunity to reduce his losses by accepting an offer of employment from the remaining partners.

ASSESSMENT TIP

It appears that the traditional approach towards remoteness of damage is still the accepted method of assessment, but it is good advice when assessing damages to ask the question whether or not a party has assumed responsibility for losses of a particular kind. In summary in terms of remoteness, see Figure 13.8.

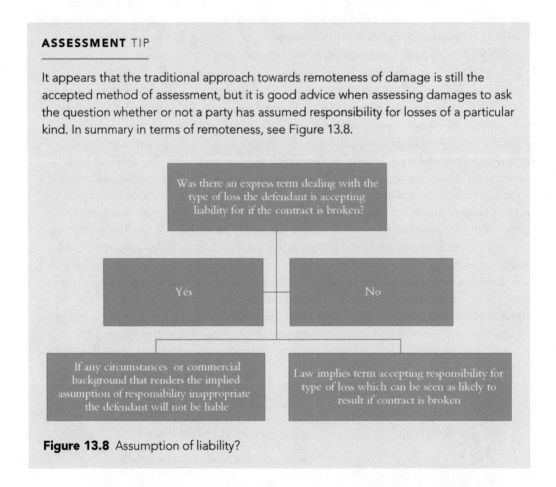

Figure 13.8 Assumption of liability?

The answer to how far the claimant is expected to go to mitigate loss lies in an assessment of what a reasonable person in the position of the claimant might have been expected to do in the ordinary course of business. There is no obligation to 'take any step which a reasonable and prudent man would not ordinarily take in the course of his business'.[25] That said, the

24 [1895] 2 QB 253.

25 Per Viscount Haldane LC in *British Westinghouse Electric and Manufacturing Co Ltd v Underground Electric Railways Co of London Ltd* [1912] AC 673.

claimant cannot sit back, do nothing and allow damages to accumulate, but nor can s/he be expected to go to extreme lengths to mitigate the loss, such as engaging in unreasonable expense or inconvenience.[26] The onus is on the defendant to prove that the claimant has not taken reasonable steps to mitigate any loss.[27]

What is reasonable will vary depending upon the subject matter of the contract. If the goods are perishable, a refusal to sell at a lower price may have an impact on damages awarded. For example, if the buyer refuses to accept an order of goods or refuses to make payment, it is incumbent on the seller to recover as much as they are able by selling the goods to a third party. The damages will be calculated in accordance with the difference between the contract price and the amount that the seller manages to achieve from a third-party sale. If the seller receives the contract price or in excess of the contract price from a third party, the claimant will receive only nominal damages. If a claimant fails to mitigate their loss, the damages awarded may be reduced by the amount that could have been recoverable if they had taken action to mitigate their loss.

13.11 CONTRIBUTORY NEGLIGENCE

Under tort law, the Law Reform (Contributory Negligence) Act 1945 dictates that where a claimant has suffered injury as a result of action that is the fault of the defendant, the claimant's damages will be reduced proportionately in line with the level to which his own negligence has contributed to his loss. Fault is defined under s. 4 of the 1945 Act as 'negligence or other act or omission which gives rise to liability in tort or would, apart from this Act, give rise to the defence of contributory negligence'.

Whether this Act will cover a breach of contract depends upon the type of obligation broken by the defendant. The position was considered in the case of *Forsikringsaktieselskapet Vesta v Butcher*,[28] where claims were categorised into three areas. The relevant category for contract claims is the third category, which provides that where a contract imposes a duty to exercise reasonable care, which would also amount to an independent tort, the Law Reform (Contributory Negligence) Act 1945 will apply and the claimant's damages can be reduced on account of his contributory negligence.

A claim for damages will be reduced by an amount that the court considers to be just and equitable having regard to the claimant's share in responsibility for the damage.

26 *Zodiac Maritime Agencies Ltd v Fortescue Metals Group Ltd* [2010] EWHC 903 (Comm).
27 *Payzu Ltd v Saunders* [1919] 2 KB 581.
28 [1986] 2 All ER 488.

ASSESSMENT TIP

Some areas are often overlooked in quantification of damages:

1) In answering a problem question on quantification of damages, mitigation is a common area that students often overlook. It is important to assess whether the claimant has taken action to mitigate any losses and, if they have not, it is likely that the damages will be reduced. Remember, if the effect of mitigation eliminates the losses altogether, only nominal damages will be awarded.
2   Another factor that must be considered in addition to mitigation of loss is the possibility of a reduction for contributory negligence, where a contractual breach has occurred and the defendant's liability in contract is the same as his liability in negligence.

13.12 LIQUIDATED DAMAGES AND PENALTY CLAUSES

As touched upon earlier, it is fairly common for the parties to make their own provisions within a contract to cover the payment of specified damages in the event of a breach of contract. Such provision will not oust the standard principle that damages are to compensate the claimant for actual loss sustained and, with this in mind, it is necessary, when seeking to rely on such a clause, to ascertain whether it falls under the category of liquidated damages or a penalty clause.

The question to be answered is whether the clause is:

1) a genuine attempt to pre-estimate losses that could arise as a result of a breach (known as liquidated damages), or
2) whether the provision can be categorised as a penalty that would conflict with the principle that damages in contract law should not be punitive.

EXPLAINING THE LAW

So where is the line drawn between what is a penalty and what is a liquidated damages clause?

In *Dunlop Pneumatic Tyre Co Ltd v New Garage & Motor Co Ltd*[29] a clause was described as a penalty 'if the sum stipulated for is extravagant and unconscionable in

---

29 [1915] AC 79.

amount in comparison with the greatest loss that could conceivably be proved to have followed from the breach'. The test of whether a clause is a penalty or a liquidated damages clause is an objective one, although the courts will have some regard to the thought processes of the parties at the time that the contract was created and the onus of proof is on the party seeking to establish that a clause amounts to a penalty to substantiate their claim.

Where a clause is proportional to the level of the breach it is likely to be enforceable as a liquidated damages clause, but the closer the clause comes to being punitive in the nature, or an unconscionable bargain, the more likely it is to be a penalty. Whilst a penalty is unenforceable, the court can award damages in the traditional way, under the usual remoteness test rule discussed earlier.

The Supreme Court also considered a penalty clause in *Cavendish Square Holding BV v Talal El Makdessi and ParkingEye Ltd v Beavis*,[30] in which Lord Mance defined a penalty clause as a provision that 'imposes a sanction for breach which is extravagant to the point where the court will in no circumstances enforce it according to its terms'.

MAKING LINKS

These cases were referred to earlier in the chapter on unfair contract terms and you may recall that, in *ParkingEye*, in assessing the parking penalty charge term for 'fairness' the court determined that a contentious term relating to a parking charge did not create a significant imbalance in the parties' rights and obligations under the contract, nor was it contrary to the requirements of good faith.

In addition to the assistance provided on the test of fairness of contractual terms, the purpose of revisiting the *ParkingEye* case here is to assess the modern-day approach of the Supreme Court to penalty clauses.

PARKINGEYE LTD V BEAVIS [2015] UKSC 67, [2015] 3 WLR 1373

You will recall that the case involved the imposition of a parking charge of £85 levied upon Mr Beavis by ParkingEye for overstaying in a retail shopping centre car park. He argued that the charge was a penalty clause and was far too high to constitute a genuine pre-estimate of the loss that ParkingEye had experienced as a result of his breach of contract.

30 [2015] UKSC 67, [2015] 3 WLR 1373.

The two issues upon which the Supreme Court had to determine were:

1) Whether a charge of £85 for exceeding a maximum car parking period was an unenforceable penalty
2) Whether a charge of £85 for exceeding a maximum car parking period was unfair under the UTCCR 1999 (the regulations preceding CRA 2015).

The law on penalty clauses as it stood allowed contracting parties to agree in advance the amount of damages that should be paid if a particular contractual obligation is subsequently breached. The provision that sets such an amount of damages is called 'a liquidated damages clause'. Nevertheless, there is a limit to the extent to which enforcement of such clauses is permitted. A penalty clause cannot be enforced, in the sense that the detriment imposed is disproportionately excessive in comparison with the legitimate interest of the innocent party in enforcing those provisions.

Held: the parking charge was enforceable. The term was not regarded as an unfair term since ParkingEye had a legitimate interest in charging overstaying motorists, which extended beyond the recovery of any loss. The company was managing car parks in the interests of the retail outlets, their customers and the public at large and had a legitimate interest in influencing the conduct of the contracting party. This interest was not satisfied by the mere right to recover damages for breach of contract. ParkingEye could not charge a sum out of all proportion to its interests, but the court did not consider the sum of £85 was to be out of all proportion.

As a result of *ParkingEye*, the general test now appears to be based upon whether the sum or remedy stipulated as a consequence of a breach of contract is exorbitant or unconscionable when regard is had to the innocent party's interest in the performance of the contract. The major shift in the interpretation of the penalty rule is the acknowledgment that the traditional test based simply on the comparison between the stipulated sum and the greatest amount of loss that could be caused by the breach will need further consideration and regard may need to be had to the wider interest of the innocent party in enforcing the claim for the specified sum.

ANALYSING THE LAW

To sum up, since the *ParkingEye* judgment, liquidated damages need no longer be solely a reflection of a genuine pre-estimate of loss but can reflect the wider commercial context of a transaction and seek to protect legitimate commercial interests on the proviso that the amount of the liquidated damages is not extravagant, exorbitant or unconscionable.

This change in approach to penalty clauses will most likely make it more difficult to challenge the enforceability of liquidated damages clauses, where arguments are put forward that the pursuit of the sum included in an agreement is to serve a wider legitimate interest.

In support of penalty clauses, it can be argued from a freedom of contract perspective that an agreement between parties, particularly within a commercial setting, should not be interfered with and the parties should be free to agree whatever terms they deem appropriate when forming their agreement. Having such clauses can also prevent the need for costly litigation when things go wrong in the performance of contractual duties. Additionally, interference by the courts in private agreements could lead to uncertainty.

Conversely, a counter-argument against a more relaxed approach to penalty clauses can be made in relation to cases where an imbalance of bargaining power exists between the parties resulting in unfairness to the weaker party. To a certain extent, statutes such as the Consumer Rights 2015 should help and operate to prevent unfairness in contractual clauses. However, the difficulty will lie in the analysis of what is and what is not unreasonable when considering what will and what will not constitute the pursuance of a legitimate interest in the performance of a contract. Where will the line be drawn between the two, and how can a consistent and fair approach be achieved?

13.13 SUMMARY

The focus of this chapter has been on the main remedy available where a breach of contract has occurred, namely damages. There are other remedies available and we will be looking at these in the next chapter.

To sum up on damages, we should remember that, as a general rule, the aim of an award for damages in contract law is to place the claimant in the same position as if the contract had been performed as agreed. Damages can be awarded to compensate for the loss of the bargain, known as expectation loss, or for wasted expenditure, referred to as reliance loss. Damages may sometimes be awarded for non–pecuniary losses such as mental distress and disappointment where a central aspect of the contract is for pleasure, enjoyment or peace of mind.

In quantifying damages following a breach of contract the areas shown in Figure 13.9 should be considered to ensure an accurate assessment of damages.

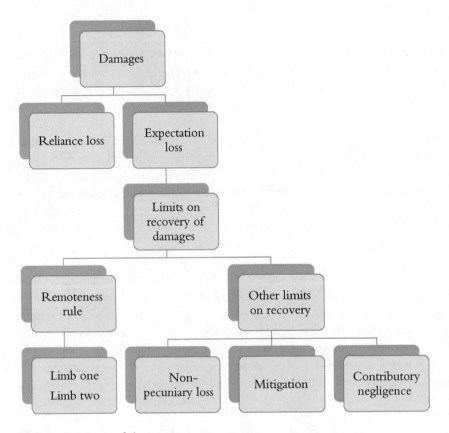

Figure 13.9 Assessment of damages

PUTTING IT INTO PRACTICE

Consider the following problem scenario, identify the issues and then explain the relevant legal rules and apply them to provide advice to the parties on what losses they can recover.

Mr Wheat, a wholesale farm produce dealer, entered into an agreement with Farmer Grain to purchase his entire crop of potatoes at 10% above the normal market price, to be delivered no later than 17 October. Unknown to Farmer Grain, Mr Wheat had already contracted to sell the potatoes on to Mr Fry, who had agreed to pay an especially high price in order to secure the whole crop. In the summer, there had been a drought and there had been widespread media reports of crop shortages. Mr Wheat considered himself to have been lucky to be able to purchase a crop of potatoes at all as the season had been so bad. Mr Fry had been very worried about his supply of potatoes as he owns a busy fish and chip shop and needs to produce large quantities of chips at cheap prices, so had jumped at the opportunity to buy the potatoes even though the price he paid was high. Mr Wheat had also promised that if he failed to deliver the potatoes by 18 October the price would drop by 20%.

Farmer Grain started harvesting the potatoes on 14 October and normally would have finished in two days, but his tractor broke down on the 15th. He rang Mr Peel the local mechanic and asked him to come out to repair it that afternoon. Mr Peel agreed but went to a music festival instead and did not turn up until two days later. As a result, Farmer Grain did not finish harvesting the crop of carrots until 28 October. Mr Fry was unable to open his fish and chip shop between 25–29 October due to the fact that his potatoes had not arrived.

Facts: From the facts presented it can be seen that Farmer Grain, Mr Wheat and Mr Fry will all sustain losses. You need to assess what losses they can claim.

Define the area of law: The area of law concerns an assessment of what type of damages can be awarded and how the damages will be quantified taking on board the rules for remoteness and any factors that might limit losses.

Issues:

- Expectation or reliance loss?
- Remoteness rule – what can/cannot be claimed
- Were any steps taken to mitigate the loss?

Law:

Explain the different methods of calculating damages

- Expectation loss
- Reliance loss

Explain the remoteness rule:

Hadley v Baxendale plus other relevant cases such as *Victoria Laundry (Windsor) Ltd v Newman Industries Ltd; Koufos v C Czarnikow Ltd, The Heron II*

State damages recoverable:

- Those arising naturally out of the breach
- Those which because of special knowledge would have been within the contemplation of the parties (Limb one; Limb two)

Based on knowledge (two types):

Limb one

- Imputed knowledge
- Actual knowledge
- Serious possibility, real danger or on the cards

Limb two

- Special knowledge, knowledge specifically communicated

The Heron II – House of Lords confirmed that higher degree of foreseeability is required in contract than in tort. Must be: a real danger; serious possibility, or the loss must be highly likely to result.

Explain the rules of mitigation

Application

Expectation loss would be relevant here as the difference in value between what the claimant actually received and what he should have received can be calculated,

Farmer Grain

If Mr Wheat repudiates the contract, Farmer Grain may wish to claim damages for loss at a price 2% above market value from Mr Peel. Was the loss foreseeable? The delay was only two days, yet the harvesting was finished at a time much later than the two-day delay. Did the two-day tractor repair create the longer harvesting delay?

If so, damages – what would have been in Mr Peel's contemplation? Normal loss of profits at market price (limb one) – was he aware of the 2% increased payment? (limb two). If not, this will be non-recoverable. If Mr Wheat is sued by Mr Fry – will Mr Peel be liable? He may not have been aware that the potatoes had been sold on at an exorbitant price. Would need to prove that he had this knowledge, to make him liable for these damages (limb two).

Mitigation – Farmer Grain would have to mitigate his losses and try to sell the potatoes elsewhere.

Mr Wheat

If time were a condition, Mr Wheat could repudiate contract and sue for damages against Farmer Grain. Normal loss would be foreseeable – i.e. contract price with

Mr Fry – but could Mr Wheat claim the 25% of his full expected profit back from Farmer Grain that he had lost due to his late delivery to Mr Fry?

Was the loss foreseeable? Did Farmer Grain have actual knowledge of the agreement? Or was this type of loss a serious possibility in this type of trade? Probably not. He may only be liable if he had been told about the agreement with Mr Fry – we are told that he was not aware of the agreement.

13.14 BRINGING IT ALL TOGETHER

Which method will be used for quantification of damages?

- Expectation loss
- Reliance loss

Both are valid methods. The reliance loss basis can be used where expectation losses are difficult to calculate.

How do we treat non-pecuniary losses?

- Loss of opportunity
- Mental distress and disappointment
- Contracts for entertainment and enjoyment

Damages can be awarded subject to certain rules.

REMOTENESS RULES

Damages for breach of contract are subject to the rules of remoteness; the test being stricter than that applied in tort claims. The test for remoteness can be said to fall within two limbs:

- Limb one: damages that would have been within the reasonable contemplation of the parties at the time that the contract is agreed.
- Limb two: enables recovery of special damages, but only those that were drawn to the attention of the other party at the time that the contract was formed.

In certain instances, damages that go beyond a strict measure of compensation can be awarded. Such non-compensatory damages include:

- nominal damages
- aggravated damages

- restitutionary damages and
- account of profits.

These will be considered in the next chapter.

MITIGATION AND CONTRIBUTORY NEGLIGENCE

In addition to the application of the remoteness rule in damage quantification, it is also necessary to assess whether reasonable steps were taken to mitigate loss by the claimant and indeed whether there is any ground for a claim of contributory negligence in limited circumstances.

PENALTY CLAUSES V LIQUIDATED DAMAGE CLAUSES

Where a contract includes a clause specifying the amount of compensation payable in the event of a breach, it is important to consider whether the clause constitutes a penalty or a liquidated damages clause. The validity of a penalty clause must fulfil certain criteria to be enforceable (see *ParkingEye* case).

TAKING IT FURTHER

Capper, 'Damages for Distress and Disappointment – The Limits of Watts v Morrow' (2000) 116 LQR 553

Capper, 'Damages for Distress and Disappointment – Problem Solved' (2002) 118 LQR 193

Coote, 'Contract Damages, Ruxley, and the Performance Interest' [1997] CLJ 537

Isaacs and Davies, 'The fine line between liquidated damages and penalties' (2008) 23 Butterworths Journal of International Banking and Financial Law 152

McKendrick and Graham, 'The sky's the limit: Contractual damages for non-pecuniary loss' [2002] LMCLQ 161

McLauchlan, 'The redundant reliance interest in contract damages' (2011) 127 LQR 23

McLauchlan, 'Repudiatory breach, prospective liability, and *The Golden Victory*' [2015] JBL 530

Robertson, 'The Basis of the Remoteness Rule in Contract' (2008) 28 LS 172

Shackleton, 'Penalties and liquidated damages law restated' (2015) 26 (10) Cons Law 14

CHAPTER 14
REMEDIES (2)

In the last chapter, we examined the monetary compensation that is available in the event of a breach of contract. This has the very specific aim of providing monetary relief for the breach of contract, mainly a calculation of damages that would cover the breach that has occurred, usually because of non-performance or other such breach. However, these are not the only remedies available to the non-breaching party. There are also remedies that can be just as valuable in resolving the breach as damages, but by providing some form of specific relief. They are often awarded in cases as a form of equitable relief, attempting to achieve what cannot be achieved through a bare calculation of compensation alone. In this chapter, we will discuss these specific remedies, and their effectiveness as a compliment or alternative to damages as a remedy for breach.

Secondly, we will also examine the use of damages that goes beyond the strict application of compensation. This can be through the use of nominal damages, or various types of restitutionary remedies as an alternative method of recovery for the non-breaching party, such as account of profits. This involves considering both partial and total failure of consideration.

The purpose behind equitable remedies is very similar to the reasons behind damages awards: it relates back to the purpose of remedies in the first place. In contract law, the objective is to put the non-breaching party in the position they would have been in if the contract had been correctly performed. Such 'specific' remedies attempt to do just that: use means other than just an award of damages to put the non-breaching party in the position they should have been in had the contract been performed correctly. There have been some attempts to introduce other types of remedies into contract law: these are also discussed towards the end of the chapter.

14.1 EQUITABLE REMEDIES

The remedies discussed here are described as '**equitable remedies**'. Damages are available as of right at common law as a result of breach of contract; however, remedies such as specific performance and injunctions are available only at the discretion of the court, and therefore the non-breaching party cannot insist upon them. This discretionary nature means that they can be applied in situations where they are deemed more appropriate, and also ensures that there is no double compensation for the same breach (e.g. application of both damages and specific performance that compensates the non-breaching party twice).

ESSENTIAL DEFINITION: EQUITABLE REMEDIES

Equitable remedies, applied at the discretion of the court, are those applied to a situation in order to promote the idea of an equitable or 'fair' solution to the case, where damages are either not available or inadequate to resolve the breach of contract that has occurred.

This discretionary nature was demonstrated in the case of *Shell (UK) Ltd v Lostock Garage Ltd*.[1] The case concerned a tie-in agreement between a petrol station (Lostock Garage) and the oil company that supplied their fuel (Shell (UK)). Shell were seeking an equitable remedy because Lostock Garage had bought fuel elsewhere in breach of their agreement as the exclusive supplier. However, Ormrod LJ refused to apply an equitable remedy to the situation, on the grounds that Shell had been subsidising other garages in the locality that were competitors of Lostock Garage. He argued that whilst this 'support scheme', which was part of a petrol price war in the UK, was still in place, Shell should be left only to the remedy of damages that they were entitled to as of right.

14.2 SPECIFIC PERFORMANCE

DEFINITION: SPECIFIC PERFORMANCE

An order of specific performance, when awarded by the court, requires one party to perform primary obligations that they owe under a contract. The other party is therefore able to gain the benefit of that performance rather than be compensated for non-performance.

As a remedy, specific performance can therefore deliver a valuable benefit to the non-breaching party in that it requires the performance of contractual obligations in situations where this is a much more appropriate solution. A party to a contract enters into such an agreement in order to gain the benefit of performance, not to receive compensation for lack of performance, so there is an underlying and obvious benefit to an order that ensures that this performance is going to take place.

An example of the application of specific performance was seen in *Beswick v Beswick*.[2] This case concerned privity of contract and, on this issue, can be seen in Chapter 15.

---

1   [1976] 1 WLR 1187.
2   [1968] AC 58, [1967] 3 WLR 932.

BESWICK V BESWICK [1968] AC 58, [1967] 3 WLR 932

This case concerned the sale of a business by a man to his nephew. As part of the deal, the nephew agreed to make payments to the uncle for his lifetime, and thereafter to his widow. The uncle died, and the nephew stopped making payments to the widow after one payment. Because of privity rules, the widow could not sue in her own right because she was not privy to the contract. She could sue as administratrix of her husband's estate, but could not claim damages in this capacity because, as administratrix, she had lost nothing.

Held: because of the unavailability of damages as a remedy in this situation, it was appropriate to apply an order of specific performance of the contract. The court therefore ordered that the payments to the widow be specifically performed as required in the agreement with the uncle.

Although this seems like a very obvious remedy to apply to all contractual situations (as the point of all contracts is logically for them to be performed) it is not universally applied, and instead reserved for situations in which it is deemed a more appropriate remedy, under the discretion of the court discussed above. For an example of this, see *Cohen v Roche*.

COHEN V ROCHE [1927] 1 KB 169

This case concerned the sale of a set of dining room chairs, bought by the claimant as part of an auction. The chairs were not described as rare, particularly valuable or unusual and, when the seller refused to deliver or allow the claimant to collect the chairs, he sued for breach of contract.

Because of the ordinary nature of the chairs, the court refused the claimant's application for specific performance of the contract, instead limiting the award to damages for breach of contract.

ASSESSMENT TIP

The practical nature of where specific performance is possible is shown in the above case. Had the goods in the contract been of a type that were unusual, or possibly difficult to replace, the argument for specific performance would have been more appropriate. This is because awarding damages would not have allowed the claimant to go elsewhere and purchase alternative chairs. Therefore, the appropriateness of specific performance is often tied to the question of damages as an appropriate remedy.

14.3 INADEQUACY OF DAMAGES

One area where specific performance can be particularly valuable is where damages are seen as inadequate to compensate the injured party for the breach that has occurred. This is usually through the circumstances in that particular case. For example, as we have seen above in *Cohen v Roche*, where the goods cannot be bought from elsewhere, it may be seen as appropriate to require specific performance instead. Another example of the circumstances leading to damages being inadequate is *Sky Petroleum Ltd v VIP Petroleum Ltd*.

SKY PETROLEUM LTD V VIP PETROLEUM LTD [1974] 1 WLR 576

This case concerned an agreement to purchase petrol and diesel from the defendants, at fixed prices and requiring certain minimum quantities to be ordered. The circumstances at the time meant that such fuel was in short supply, and therefore it would not have been possible for the claimant to enter into an alternative agreement, as the contract took place during an oil crisis in the 1970s. Despite this, the defendants terminated the contract because the claimants had exceeded the credit provisions in the contract. The claimants brought an action, requesting an injunction to prevent supplies of petrol and diesel being withheld by the defendant.

Held: an injunction in the circumstances would be the same as requiring specific performance of the contract. Ordinarily, such an order would be refused on the grounds that damages would provide a sufficient remedy. However, because of the circumstances (that the defendant was the only available supplier, and without fuel supplies the claimants would be out of business), damages would be inadequate and therefore an injunction would be granted.

The same argument could be applied to the *Beswick v Beswick* case discussed above. Damages in the circumstances there were also inadequate due to the different capacities that the widow, Mrs Beswick, occupied. In her own personal capacity, as a beneficiary of the contract but not party to it, she was not able to sue due to privity rules (and therefore was not able to claim damages). In her capacity as administratrix of her dead husband's estate, she suffered no loss. It could be said that, like in the *Sky Petroleum* case, damages would be inadequate. As a result, the application of specific performance was the only remedy that would provide a solution to the breach that had been clearly committed by the nephew.

14.4 NOT POSSIBLE TO SPECIFICALLY ENFORCE

There are circumstances where, rather than not being the desirable remedy to apply, it has been held that a breaching party cannot be required to specifically perform obligations. There are three main areas where such contracts have arisen (see Figure 14.1).

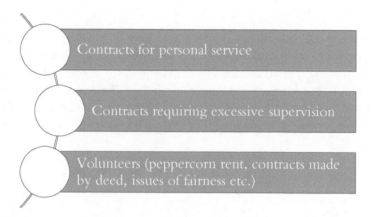

Figure 14.1 Contracts which cannot be specifically enforced

14.5 CONTRACTS FOR PERSONAL SERVICE

Problems with specific performance in contracts for personal service concern the implications of compelling an individual to perform obligations in an employment situation. If a person is compelled to perform personal services in a situation where circumstances have resulted in the breakdown of the relationship between the parties, this can be seen as an infringement of personal liberty of the person compelled to perform. There have been several examples where this has been argued.

WARNER BROTHERS V NELSON [1937] 1 KB 209

Nelson, better known as Bette Davis, was a film star who signed a contract with Warner Brothers film studio. Part of the agreement was that she would not appear in films produced by any third party without the express written permission of Warner Brothers. She breached this agreement when she entered into a contract to appear in a film for a third party.

Warner Brothers applied for an injunction to prevent Nelson from appearing in the film, and Nelson argued that this injunction was effectively an order for specific performance of the contract with Warner Brothers, as her only other choice was appearing in their films as per the contract she had with them. As the contract was one for personal service, this would effectively put her in the servitude of Warner Brothers for the duration of the agreement.

The court were required to consider whether this was a circumstance where specific performance was unavailable and, in fact, whether the injunction was effectively an order for specific performance.

Held: the nature of the restriction in the contract meant that Nelson was not prevented from engaging in any other work as a result of the restriction, but was merely prevented from working as an actress. She could engage in any other type of work and not be in breach of her contract with Warner Brothers. '[T]he effect of the contract was not to drive the defendant either to specific performance or to idleness', and therefore an injunction was available. There would, as a result, be no compulsion to perform the contract.

ANALYSING THE LAW

The key issue with cases such as these is that the effect of requiring specific performance (or in the *Nelson* case an injunction) was that the only choice that the individual had was to perform their obligations. This may seem like no bad thing; however, the result would be a form of personal servitude, which, as mentioned above, has implications for a person's liberty. The court was not saying that there would be no consequence for breaching the contract as damages would still be available. However, it was that 'no other choice' element that was missing in Nelson's circumstances, and therefore the injunction was an appropriate remedy to apply in the circumstances.

An example of where this was successfully argued came in *Page One Records v Britton*.[3] The injunction sought here was the equivalent of specific performance in a personal service contract.

PAGE ONE RECORDS V BRITTON [1968] 1 WLR 157

The 1960s pop group, The Troggs, employed the claimant as their manager under a contract for five years. During the term of the contract, they were prohibited from engaging anyone else in a managerial capacity, and none of the group were allowed to act as manager themselves. There was a breakdown in the relationship between The Troggs and their manager, and the claimant sought an injunction to prevent them from engaging any other person as their manager.

The argument put forward by the group was that an injunction preventing them from engaging another manager was the equivalent of an order for specific performance and, as this was a contract for personal service, that specific performance should not be available as a remedy.

3   [1968] 1 WLR 157.

Held: the court agreed with the above argument and denied the application for an injunction. The court's view was that the group could not continue without a manager, and therefore the injunction would require them to continue with the claimant as their manager. The fiduciary and personal relationship had broken down, and therefore it was not appropriate to compel them to keep the claimant as their manager. Damages for breach would be available, but not an injunction.

The objection to injunctions or orders of specific performance in contracts for personal service can, however, be defeated in situations whereby the employee is not placed in a situation of having to specifically perform the contract in order to avoid financial ruin. A good example of this can be found in *Evening Standard Co Ltd v Henderson.*[4] A key point of this case was the willingness of the employer to continue paying the employee throughout his lengthy notice period, and therefore he was not placed in the situation of having to work in order to survive. The employer's interest was in not losing this valuable employee to a competitor, so he continued to pay him throughout his notice period.

EVENING STANDARD CO LTD V HENDERSON [1987] ICR 588, [1987] FSR 165

An employee of the *Evening Standard* newspaper gave notice to leave his employment. The contract had a requirement that the employee not work for a direct rival of the *Evening Standard* during his notice period, and an injunction was sought to prevent him from doing this.

During the period of notice, the employee was fully paid as usual, and the employer offered him work if he wished (alternatively he could serve his notice on 'gardening leave', whereby he would be paid but not required to come to work).

The employee argued that the injunction would effectively be a restraint of trade and, under the principle discussed above regarding specific performance in contracts of personal service, an injunction could not be granted by the court.

Held: the injunction would be granted to prohibit the employee from working for their rival, because the effect of him doing this would be very difficult to quantify in terms of damages. They would also be required to comply with the following three undertakings: (1) to honour the contract of employment, (2) to permit the employee to continue working during his notice period if he so wished, and (3) to forgo any claim for damages if the employee chose not to work during the notice period but to go on 'gardening leave' instead.

---

4   [1987] ICR 588, [1987] FSR 165.

This case can be contrasted with the later case of *Provident Financial Group v Hayward*[5] which, rather than giving the employee the option of deciding whether they wished to work or not, instead involved an enforced period of 'gardening leave'. The reason behind this requirement was that the employee, who was an accountant, was privy to sensitive and confidential information that his employer was concerned would be taken by the employee to his next employment at a rival company. Enforced gardening leave therefore ensured that he was no longer able to access such information.

The court in *Hayward* upheld the trial judge's refusal to grant an injunction preventing the accountant taking up alternative employment during his gardening leave, and left the employer with only the possibility of damages (if appropriate). It is easy to see the issue of whether to enforce a restriction on taking up alternative employment during a notice period as being one of survival, as in both this case and the *Henderson* case, the employees were still being paid in full and therefore there was no danger of them starving. However, if this was the dominant consideration in *Hayward*, the court would have enforced the notice period as they did in *Henderson*. Dillon LJ commented in his judgment in the *Hayward* case:

> It is not enough just that the employee has contracted in certain terms and will not starve if the terms are enforced against him while the employer continues to pay him in full. The employee has a concern to work and to a concern to exercise his skills. That has been recognised in some circumstances concerned with artists and singers who depend on publicity, but it applies equally, I apprehend, to skilled workmen and even to chartered accountants.

KEY LEARNING POINT

It is clear therefore that the issue is one of personal freedom. If an order effectively limits that personal freedom by specific performance, it will not be permitted. If there appears to be an element of choice on the part of the individual, as we have seen in the *Nelson* case and the *Henderson* case, both discussed above, there is not the same level of limitation imposed, which removes the objection to an order that results in a contract being specifically performed.

14.6 CONTRACTS REQUIRING EXCESSIVE SUPERVISION

Where considerable supervision of performance is required, the court would not apply an order for specific performance. This is because the complexity of ensuring that the obligations are performed would make such an order unworkable. This was demonstrated in the case of *Ryan v*

---

5   [1989] 3 All ER 298.

Mutual Tontine Westminster Chambers Association,[6] where there was a term in a lease that provided for a porter to be in constant attendance at the block of flats. The man employed as porter had another job elsewhere as a chef and was therefore not present for large parts of the day whilst he performed his other job. The court in this instance refused an order of specific performance because it was not possible to constantly monitor the performance of the obligations. This would have required some way of ensuring that the porter was at work all the time.

The decision in *Ryan* was distinguished by the court in *Posner v Scott-Lewis.*[7] This case had similar facts, but the reasons for denying specific performance in *Ryan* were not evident in *Posner.*

POSNER V SCOTT-LEWIS [1987] CH 25, [1986] 3 WLR 531

This case concerned a block of flats with a resident porter. It was written into all the tenancy agreements that a resident porter would be employed by the landlord; however, the resident porter resigned and moved to a nearby block of flats. The landlord arranged for him to continue in his job as porter by returning to the block of flats to perform his duties every day. However, as the agreement was for a *resident* porter who would live in the block of flats, an action was brought against the landlord for specific performance of this obligation.

Held: an order for specific performance of the obligation for a resident porter would be granted. The tenants derived a specific benefit from a porter that lived on the premises; in particular there was peace of mind and security that they derived from this arrangement. It was distinguished from the decision in *Ryan* on the basis that it was merely the existence of a resident porter that was required by the order of specific performance, without any specific reference to their duties. In *Ryan*, the duties would need constant supervision to ensure they were performed. In this case, the existence of an employed porter that lived in the block would be easy for the court to verify without any excessive supervision required.

Difficulty in supervision can also include the problems in formulating an order for specific performance in the first place, as shown by *Cooperative Insurance Society Ltd v Argyll Stores (Holdings) Ltd.*

COOPERATIVE INSURANCE SOCIETY LTD V ARGYLL STORES (HOLDINGS) LTD [1998] 1 AC 1, [1997] 2 WLR 898

This case concerned the breach of a 'keep open' clause in the lease of a unit in a shopping centre. The defendant had closed the shop in the unit, when they had

---

6   [1893] 1 Ch 116.
7   [1987] Ch 25, [1986] 3 WLR 531.

agreed to keep it open. The claimants made an application for specific performance of the clause, requiring the defendants to continue running a business in the unit. The judge initially made an order for damages only, which was overturned by the Court of Appeal. The matter was then further appealed to the House of Lords (now the Supreme Court).

Held: the appeal court's decision to grant an order of specific performance would be overturned. There were several reasons for this. The original judge's decision was that it was inappropriate and against settled practice to grant an order of specific performance. It was also possible that forcing the defendant to continue a business in a situation where they had decided to close it on the grounds that it was no longer economically viable might be considered to be oppressive. Finally, the court considered that the definition of 'continuing a business' in the unit was vague, and an order for specific performance would therefore be virtually impossible to accurately draft and even more difficult to supervise. It is an important consideration that an order for specific performance must be accurate enough to be effectively enforced.

ANALYSING THE LAW

Two things are important from the decision in this case. The court was reluctant to order specific performance in a situation where the end result would be one of the parties being compelled to run an uneconomical business (the reason for closing the shop in the unit being that it was no longer making money). Additionally, it illustrates the fact that the judge in each case still has a discretion to grant specific performance, based upon the particular circumstances. The court in *Argyll* pointed to a 'settled practice' against granting specific performance in cases such as this, but did not form the basis for an absolute restriction due to the difficulty of supervision. This is in line with the view of Megarry J in *CH Giles & Co Ltd v Morris*,[8] who was also of the opinion that it must remain in the discretion of the judge to decide whether an order for specific performance is appropriate or not.

It is therefore important for you to consider further the practicality of supervising an order of specific performance. The discretion of the judge in the case in question is important to ensure that the theory behind the legal principle does not overtake the practicality of how that principle might apply in practice.

---

8   [1972] 1 WLR 307, [1972] 1 All ER 960.

14.7 VOLUNTEERS (PEPPERCORN RENT, CONTRACTS MADE BY DEED)

The third circumstance under which the courts will not make an order of specific performance is in relation to 'volunteers'. Again, this relates back to the discretion that the courts have in awarding equitable remedies, because the principle is that equity will not 'assist a volunteer', and equitable remedies will only be available in situations where the parties have each provided 'true consideration'. This therefore covers a number of situations whereby the parties are in a valid and legally binding contract according to the rules of consideration (see Chapter 3), but only nominal consideration or no consideration at all has been provided.

14.7.1 PEPPERCORN RENT AND NOMINAL VALUE

A party to a legally binding contract may have provided a 'peppercorn rent', i.e. a nominal sum in order to be bound by a contract. You should refer back to Chapter 3 and the case of *Thomas v Thomas*,[9] where a 'peppercorn rent' of £1 per year was provided, or *Chappel v Nestlé*,[10] where the consideration was an object perceived to be of value to the party requesting it. Although these result in a contract being *legally* binding, the court's discretion will allow it to apply equitable remedies only where they see it as being fair to do so. In these situations, they will therefore not apply specific performance.

This principle is also applicable to circumstances where no consideration has been applied, where the contract has been made by way of deed, and therefore one party has not provided consideration. In Chapter 3 we discussed the fact that a contract is legally enforceable even though one party has not provided consideration, but the same principle discussed above regarding the application of equity applies here. For example, see *Re Parkin*,[11] a case where the parties had made marriage settlements by way of deed in order to establish how their property should be disposed of. An order for specific performance was refused – as a contract by deed, there was no requirement for consideration and therefore these situations are described as being where there is 'no real consideration'.

14.7.2 DISCRETION IN APPLYING SPECIFIC PERFORMANCE

It is important to remember that orders for specific performance are at the discretion of the court and, even leaving aside the above examples of where the courts have laid down general principles regarding the inapplicability of specific performance, it is important to bear in mind some other rules of equity that will affect such an order.

---

9 (1842) 2 QB 851, 114 ER 330.
10 [1960] AC 87.
11 [1892] 3 Ch 510.

For example, one equitable maxim states that 'he who comes to equity comes with clean hands', the lack of which was evident in *Pateman v Pay*, which led the court to find that specific performance should not be available to them.

PATEMAN V PAY (1974) 232 EG 457

This case involved an agreement to give one party an option to purchase a house, in a situation where it had not been made clear by the other party that this was a legally binding agreement giving them the power to buy if they so wished. The agreement had been made on a piece of scrap paper, which gave the impression that this was not an important, legally binding matter.

Held: the purchaser had clearly been engaging in what the court referred to as 'sharp practice' and, for this reason, they refused to grant an order of specific performance of the option.

The 'clean hands' principle was also applied in *Quadrant Visual Communications Ltd v Hutchinson Telephone UK Ltd*,[12] where the court held that they had a discretion to refuse an equitable remedy when the party requesting it had not acted fairly in the transaction. They also held that this discretion could not be fettered where an attempt had been made in the contract to exclude equity in the terms of the agreement. This underlines the importance of the court's discretion not only to award specific performance where it is deemed necessary, but also to refuse it in situations where it is not deemed appropriate.

Finally, the court may also exercise its discretion in situations where the contract is too vague to allow obligations to be specifically performed. This is not that dissimilar to the principle that allowed the court in *Cooperative Insurance v Argyll*, discussed earlier in this chapter, to refuse specific performance because an order would be unnecessarily complex and difficult to draft. In *Tito v Waddell (No. 2)*[13] the contract was vague regarding what was required of certain contractual obligations, including a requirement to replant certain land. Because it was not possible to accurately state what would satisfy the obligation in the contract, it was therefore not possible to make an order of specific performance: because it was unclear what precisely would satisfy the obligation in the contract.

14.8 INJUNCTIONS

Injunctions are used generally to prevent a party from carrying out a specific activity. In the context of contract law, they are most commonly used to prevent a party from breaching a negative stipulation – an agreement in a contract *not* to do something, rather than the order of

---

12 [1993] BCLC 442, (1992) 89(3) LSG 31, (1992) 136 SJLB 32.
13 [1977] Ch 106, [1977] 2 WLR 496, [1977] 3 All ER 129.

specific performance, which compels the party in question to carry out a *positive* stipulation to carry out an obligation under the contract.

As with specific performance, they can be a useful tool to prevent a party from carrying out an act where this is more appropriate than the award of damages. The same rules apply as we have already discussed regarding specific performance, and so for example a party requesting that the court impose an injunction on the other party will have to demonstrate that damages would be inadequate to compensate the loss suffered.

ARACI V FALLON [2011] EWCA CIV 668

This case concerned an agreement by a jockey to ride a particular horse belonging to a trainer, for a period of 12 months, at races where he was required to do so. The contract also had a negative stipulation that the jockey was not to ride a rival horse during the period of the contract.

The jockey refused to ride the trainer's horse at the Derby that year, on the grounds that he had already agreed to ride the rival's horse in that race. The trainer therefore applied for an injunction preventing the jockey from riding the rival's horse.

Held: the injunction would be granted, preventing the jockey from breaching a negative stipulation in the contract. The court stated that damages for riding a rival's horse were difficult to calculate and dependent upon variables (including whether the jockey might finish ahead of this horse when riding the rival's horse).

This case illustrates an important distinction between the granting of an injunction here, and cases we discussed earlier in the chapter regarding injunctions having the same effect as specific performance because of leaving the party in question with no other option but to perform obligations under the contract. In this case, it was possible to clearly show the injunction was intended to prevent the breach of a particular negative stipulation. The requirement was that the jockey was not to ride a particular rival horse. This therefore makes it somewhat different from injunctions that leave a party with no choice but specific performance, as the requirement was not to ride a particular horse and not other horses in general.

The court in *Araci* made the point that damages would not have been an adequate or easily quantifiable remedy, a point further illustrated in *AB v CD*.[14] This case involved an argument of inadequacy of damages where such damages were capped by a term of the contract itself. The court applied a principle from *Bath and North East Somerset DC v Mowlem plc*[15] that allowed an injunction to be applied where a clause limiting liability placed a cap on the available damages.

---

14 [2014] EWCA Civ 229.
15 [2004] EWCA Civ 115, [2015] 1 WLR 785.

14.8.1 INJUNCTIONS AS NEGATIVE STIPULATIONS OF SPECIFIC PERFORMANCE

Courts have exercised caution regarding the use of injunctions where the effect of granting one leaves the party concerned with no other choice but to perform the obligations under the contract. The key cases in this area were discussed earlier in this chapter regarding the limitations on specific performance in contracts of personal service. These cases have usually involved injunctions where the objection to the injunction being granted is on the grounds that it compels a person to perform where this leads to restrictions on personal liberty.

This was the argument in *Warner Bros v Nelson*,[16] as the actress Bette Davis had argued that the injunction in question would leave her no other choice but to perform her personal obligations under the contract. However, this was not the case, as the injunction restricted only a particular type of employment, acting, and not alternative employment in general.

This was not the situation in the later case of *Page One Records v Britton*,[17] as the effect of the injunction applied for here was to force the parties to work together in a situation where the pop group needed a manager and would therefore have only had the choice to use the claimant for this purpose. The breakdown in the relationship that existed meant that this was an unworkable situation and therefore the injunction was not granted.

14.9 THE RELATIONSHIP BETWEEN DAMAGES AND EQUITABLE REMEDIES

As discussed at the start of this chapter, the purpose of remedies is to compensate the non-breaching party for losses they have incurred as a result of the breach. There are two considerations here therefore:

1) Any award made must do no more than compensate for losses – in English law there is no concept of using remedies as a punitive measure
2) Where an appropriate equitable remedy is applied, this may reduce or eliminate the need for damages, under the principle of double compensation (the principle that no-one should be compensated twice for the same loss).

In the spirit of this, it may therefore be necessary to compensate only nominally in terms of damages because an equitable remedy provides a suitable remedy itself. In some situations, only nominal damages are appropriate anyway.

MARATHON ASSET MANAGEMENT LLP V SEDDON [2017] EWHC 300

A company sued several former employees who had left in order to set up their own company. In leaving, they had taken various confidential data with them, which was a

---

16 [1937] 1 KB 209.
17 [1968] 1 WLR 157.

breach of their contract of employment, as well as being a breach of fiduciary duty and a breach of confidence. The company sued for damages as a result of the breach.

Held: nominal damages of £1 per employee were awarded on the grounds that, as no use was ever made of the information that the employees took in breach of contract, there was no loss incurred by the company that it was taken from.

Clearly, remedies are intended to be compensatory in nature. The idea that they can be used to punish the breaching party is not something that is recognised in UK law. Punitive damages have been awarded in other jurisdictions, for example in Canada where there has been shown to be an independent actionable wrong arising from the breach, and also punitive damages can be awarded in English law as a result of a tort. However, the principle of remedies as compensatory remains in English law. There have been attempts to introduce some forms of award that do not rely upon a calculation of expectation loss by the claimant, but they have had a mixed reception. For example, we will discuss account of profits later in this chapter.

14.10 RESTITUTION

An alternative way of considering damages is with the principle of **restitution**. Whereas compensatory damages (see Chapter 13) focus upon compensating the loss that has been incurred by the non-breaching party, the principle of restitution focusses on the unjust enrichment of the breaching party, and recovering that rather than compensation.

ESSENTIAL DEFINITION: RESTITUTION

Restitution in contract is the principle of recovery of money where the other party has received unjust enrichment. The amount to be recovered is based upon the value of the unjust enrichment rather than a compensatory amount for loss.

The purpose of restitution is, like the equitable remedies we have discussed in this chapter, to achieve fairness. However, restitution is focussed upon achieving this where there has been unjust enrichment between the parties, and is a way of allowing a party either to recoup that enrichment or to receive reasonable value for the performance itself.

In this way, the remedy sought here is different from traditional damages, because it is based not upon the expectation of the other party (see Chapter 13 regarding expectation loss) but instead upon the existence of a benefit that the other party has received that has not been paid for. In this way, it can result in money paid or a benefit being conferred where there is no contract in the first place. It is therefore not reliant upon the existence or enforceability of a contract, and therefore the rules discussed in earlier chapters of this book regarding the formation of a contract are not relevant here.

The most straightforward way of explaining how this works is through examples. In a commercial situation, it is possible for one of the parties to carry out some of the work that both parties accept as being necessary, prior to the contractual agreement being finalised between them. If the contract negotiations fail and there is no contractual agreement, the party that has carried out the work in good faith cannot use contract law to recover his costs because there is no contract.

This is resolved through restitution: to ensure that the party that has carried out the work, at the request of the other party, can then claim back a fair amount to cover the costs of carrying out that work in the first place.

A real-life example of work done in anticipation of a contract is *British Steel* v *Cleveland Bridge and Engineering*,[18] where work was carried out at the request of the other party before a contract was agreed. However, as negotiations failed, and the claimant was left with a situation whereby they had done work but had no means to claim compensation for it, the court ordered restitution to recover costs of completing the work.

There are several elements here that need to be satisfied in order for restitution to be an applicable remedy (see Figure 14.2).

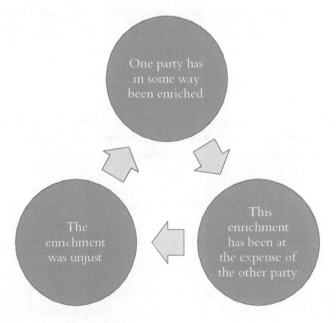

Figure 14.2 Requirements for restitution

18 [1984] 1 All ER 504.

14.10.1 TOTAL FAILURE OF CONSIDERATION

The way in which this works therefore allows a party to claim for something that the other party has gained at their expense even where there has been a total failure of consideration. Examples include where a contract has not subsequently materialised between the parties, or where that contract has been brought to an end, e.g. through frustration, or even where the contract has been ruled void, e.g. because of illegality.

The purpose of restitution is therefore to provide a means whereby an unjust enrichment can be rectified where there has been a total failure of consideration, in a situation where there is no contractual means by which that unjust enrichment can be compensated for.

A classic example of the purpose of restitution can be found in the following case.

FIBROSA SA V FAIRBURN LAWSON COMBE BRABOUR LTD [1943] AC 32

A contract was frustrated by the outbreak of war, in a situation whereby part of the contract price had been paid in advance of performance by the other party. None of the performance had taken place before the frustrating event, and therefore there was an attempt to recover the money already paid because of a total failure of consideration by the other party.

Held: they would be entitled to recover the money already paid despite the fact that the contract had already been discharged by the frustration. There was an unjust enrichment in that one party had been partly paid for contractual obligations they had not performed and, because there had been no performance by them, this was a total failure of consideration.

This therefore can create difficulties where part of the obligations have been performed. This therefore means that there has not been a total failure of consideration. It complicates matters because, if there has been partial performance in exchange for the money paid by the other party, it is necessary to begin proportioning the amount of money against the expected performance. Therefore, where there has been some performance, restitution is not available.

STOCZNIA GDANSKA SA V LATVIAN SHIPPING CO [1998] 1 WLR 574

This case concerned the design and construction of ships, for which payment was to be made in instalments. After rescission of the contract, there was an attempt made to recover instalments already paid under the contract via the principle of restitution. The argument was that as they had received no ships by that stage, there had been a total failure of consideration, and they should be entitled to their payments back.

Held: the contract was for the design and construction of ships and, although no ships had been completed and delivered by the time of the failure of the contract, there had been partial performance of the agreement and therefore restitution was not available. The court pointed out that the crucial point in assessing whether there had been total failure of consideration was not whether they had received anything, but whether any contractual obligations had been performed. As the design of the ships was part of the contractual performance, there had been a partial performance of obligations.

ANALYSING THE LAW

This may seem to be a subtle difference, regarding the distinction between performance and benefit received by the other party; however, the point being made in *Stocznia* was that restitution of the money paid was only available where the other party was unjustly enriched. This could only be said to have happened if they had received a benefit for which they had offered no performance and, although it was true that the purchasers of the ships to be built had not received anything, it could not be said that the shipbuilders had done nothing in exchange for payment.

This does also raise questions regarding what would count as performance that would prevent a finding of total failure of consideration. This is important because otherwise a party might try and offer some minor and inconsequential performance relating to the contract in order to avoid the possibility of restitution being applicable. However, a principle laid down in *Rover International Ltd v Cannon Film Sales td (No. 3)*[19] and subsequently applied in *Giedo Van der Garde BV v Force India Formula One Team Ltd*[20] was that if a benefit received was merely incidental to the performance of the contract, it would not count for the purposes of evaluating whether there had been a total failure of consideration. In *Rover*, the receipt of certain films under the contract was considered incidental to the main purpose of the contract (and therefore there was still a total failure of consideration), whereas in *Force India* the right to drive in Friday morning F1 test sessions was not, and therefore there had been partial performance and restitution was unavailable.

14.10.2 DECIDING ON THE MOST APPROPRIATE REMEDY

Based on the above discussion, there will be situations where a party to a contract will be able to claim either damages or restitution. The key issue is in deciding which is the most appropriate remedy to apply. Damages are awarded on the basis of putting the party in the position they would have been in had the contract been performed, whereas restitution is about recovery of the contract price because of a failure of consideration by the other party.

19 [1989] 1 WLR 912.
20 [2010] EWHC 2373 (QB).

This therefore means that if an assessment of expectation losses puts them in a better position, damages should be applied for; however, if the contract made was a 'bad bargain', they will gain more by applying for restitution instead.

14.10.3 PARTIAL FAILURE OF CONSIDERATION

As discussed above, total failure of consideration is essential in order to establish a case for restitution. However, there are two circumstances where it may still be possible to use restitution where failure is only partial:

1) Law Reform (Frustrated Contracts) Act 1943
2) Where partial performance is returned.

The Law Reform (Frustrated Contracts) Act 1943 is intended to assist in resolving issues caused specifically by frustration of a contract. Section 1(2) of the Act provides for the repayment of sums already paid under a frustrated contract. This applies even in situations where there has been partial performance, and therefore provides an effect equivalent to restitution in these specific circumstances.

The second circumstance is that where it is possible to return partial performance of the contract, it would then be subsequently possible to claim for restitution rather than claiming for damages. This is subject to the limitation of whether it is possible to return the consideration or not. With regard to payment of money or provision of some fairly portable commodity, this would be a straightforward situation. However, where the performance in question cannot easily be returned, this becomes significantly more difficult or even impossible, e.g. with regard to construction work.

14.10.4 *QUANTUM MERUIT*

ESSENTIAL DEFINITION: *QUANTUM MERUIT*

Quantum meruit is a Latin phrase that means 'the amount deserved'. It is a principle of calculating an award to a party based upon the amount of work in a contract that has been partially completed, and giving an award based upon the proportion of the contractual obligation that has been performed.

An award based upon *quantum meruit* is a remedy to allow a party to recover a fair amount for the proportion of work completed. It is related to restitution as it can be a way of making an appropriate award where it has been established that unjust enrichment has occurred. It is available independently of the existence of a contract and can therefore be useful where it is not possible to obtain payment through contract law.

Figure 14.3 gives examples from elsewhere in this book of where *quantum meruit* has been used in contract law.

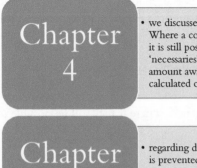

Figure 14.3 Examples of *quantum meruit*

The case of *British Steel Corpn v Cleveland Bridge and Engineering Co Ltd*[21] (discussed earlier in this chapter) is a classic example of unjust enrichment that cannot be recovered because it is not part of a binding contract. The work that was carried out was commenced before a contract was agreed between the two parties, in reliance of a contract being eventually agreed between them. When final agreement was never reached, and there was an attempt to recover for the work carried out, it was done on a *quantum meruit* basis.

However, this case is distinguished from *Regalian Properties plc v London Dockland Development Corpn*[22] due to the fact that, in the *British Steel* case, the work carried out before an agreement was reached was done at the request of the other party to the contract. However, in *Regalian Properties*, the work was done in order to persuade the other party to award them the contract, and so was not at their request. For this reason, a *quantum meruit* calculation was not awarded – they had carried out this work at their own risk.

14.11 ACCOUNT OF PROFITS

A key principle of contract law is that damages recovered as a result of breach are there to compensate the innocent party, and to place them as close to the position they would have been in had the contract been performed fully and correctly. Damages in this area are not intended to punish the breaching party, or to extract value that does not represent compensation to them for their loss. Account of profits in situations where this is not for the purposes of compensating loss would therefore go against this principle.

21 [1984] 1 All ER 504.
22 [1995] 1 WLR 212.

There has been historical resistance to the principle of making awards to remove the profit of the party in breach where it is not for the purposes of compensating loss. For example, see the following case.

SURREY COUNTY COUNCIL V BREDERO HOMES LTD [1993] 1 WLR 1361

This case concerned a covenant entered into by the defendant, a property developer. They agreed by way of a covenant not to build more than 72 homes on a plot of land, but in fact built 77. The council sued him for breach of covenant, but the main problem was in establishing damages. The council claimed the cost of altering the covenant to accommodate the extra houses; however, it was not possible for them to show that they had any losses. They were in exactly the same position that they would have been in had the contract not been breached. There was an argument that the developer had received an unjust enrichment by way of the extra profit from the additional houses but, as it did not correspond with a loss incurred by the claimants, restitution was not relevant.

Held: the court was unable to make the defendant pay part of their profits over, as this would have been punitive rather than compensatory, and this is not what damages awards in contract law are intended to do. This was also considered to be an important issue of policy; it would not be appropriate to have a general right to an account of profits rather than a claim based upon the losses of the claimant.

14.11.1 NEGOTIATION DAMAGES: THE *WROTHAM PARK* PRINCIPLE

There is one example of a different conclusion to that in *Bredero*, but that has been distinguished from *Bredero* by virtue of the fact that the action was brought by an adjacent landowner, and therefore there would have been losses relating to the interference with the neighbouring land.

WROTHAM PARK ESTATE CO LTD V PARKSIDE HOMES LTD [1974] 1 WLR 798

This case concerned a restrictive covenant that prevented the building of houses on a piece of land. The covenant was in favour of the owner of an adjacent property, who brought an action when the defendant built houses in breach of the covenant. The action brought was initially for an injunction against the building of the houses, but this was not granted.

Held: instead of an injunction, the court awarded an amount of damages that reflected what it would have cost the defendant had he negotiated a legal solution to the restrictive covenant, as the owner of the neighbouring property would have been able to charge a fee for the waiving of the restrictions in the covenant.

Despite this, the principle from *Wrotham Park* is not an easy one to argue. There was an attempt to use this principle in *Marathon Asset Management LLP v Seddon*[23] mentioned earlier in this chapter. In that case, there was an attempt by the claimants to apply for *Wrotham Park* damages, claiming £15 million as the price of the employees in question negotiating their way out of their contracts of employment. However, instead the court awarded nominal damages of £1 per employee, because there was no loss incurred by the claimant as the confidential information had not been used.

However, there has been a limited place for account of profits in contract law through the case of *Attorney General v Blake*.[24] It should, however, be pointed out that the majority of the House of Lords considered this was a principle to be used in 'exceptional circumstances'.

ATTORNEY GENERAL V BLAKE [2001] 1 AC 268

This case concerned an action against a spy by the UK government to recover profits from a book he had written about his time working for the security services. This book included information that he had agreed never to reveal in public. The problem that the Attorney General had was in establishing a loss incurred by the government as a result of Blake's breach, and this was part of the reason for attempting to claim all the profits from the book.

Held: the House of Lords concluded that an account of profits would be awarded here. It was an appropriate remedy to apply, but *only* in exceptional circumstances. Ordinarily, other remedies such as damages, specific performance and injunction would be adequate; but where these remedies are inadequate, and taking into account the circumstances, an account of profits could be used.

KEY LEARNING POINT

The decision in *Blake* has received a mixed response. It has been regarded very carefully by the courts, particularly in the commercial sphere, due to the potential problems that could be caused by an expansive approach to the application of account of profits to other cases. The House of Lords seemed to be making a big deal out of emphasising the exceptional nature of the *Blake* case, in order to try and limit its scope. However, there was very little in the way of guidance that could demonstrate what the courts actually mean by 'exceptional', particularly as Lord Nicholls in *Blake* considered that a court looking at whether to apply account of profits would need to do so having 'regard to all the circumstances'.[25] This is not considered particularly helpful.

---

23 [2017] EWHC 300.
24 [2001] 1 AC 268.
25 Ibid, at 285.

As a result, there have been different approaches towards the application of account of profits. A more generous approach has been considered in *Esso Petroleum Co Ltd v Niad Ltd*.

ESSO PETROLEUM CO LTD V NIAD LTD, UNREPORTED, 22 NOVEMBER 2001, CHANCERY DIVISION

Esso entered into an agreement with the owner of a petrol station that they supplied, whereby he agreed not to sell Esso fuel above a certain fixed price. In return, he received a discount on the price that he paid to Esso to supply the fuel. The petrol station owner received the discounted rate on fuel supplied to him, but broke the agreement not to sell above a certain price on several occasions. The fact that he had done this did not come to light until after the agreement was terminated, and so Esso sought to recover damages from the defendant. However, it was difficult to establish any losses that had been incurred by Esso as a result of the breach by the petrol station owner. They therefore attempted to recover profits achieved by him as a result of the higher prices he had sold their fuel at, relying upon *Blake* as justification for this.

Held: the court awarded an account of profits against the petrol station owner. This was based upon the court's assessment that this circumstance was exceptional, mainly because of 1) the inadequacy of damages to compensate in the circumstances, and 2) the legitimate interest that Esso had in preventing him from profiting from his breach of the discount agreement.

The generosity of this decision can be seen by considering a number of factors. Firstly, unlike *Blake*, which was a very unusual situation involving international espionage, this was a commercial agreement, and therefore much more commonplace. It therefore had the potential to expand the principle in *Blake* to a much wider range of situations. Secondly, the criteria applied also seem rather generous. There is still no proper clarity regarding what is considered 'exceptional', and the criterion of inadequacy of other remedies has the potential to catch a wider range of circumstances.

A more restrictive approach can be seen in *Experience Hendrix LLC v PPX Enterprises Inc.*[26] This case involved a dispute regarding royalties to be paid to the estate of Jimi Hendrix. There had been an agreement in 1973 whereby the defendants had negotiated the rights to certain Jimi Hendrix master recordings, subject to royalty payments. However, they had also licensed others to use other Hendrix recordings that they did not have permission to use, and therefore the estate of Hendrix was suing over the unlawful uses of those recordings.

The court in *Experience Hendrix* placed far more emphasis on the exceptional nature of the *Blake* case and the fiduciary position that Blake was in, with regard to his position regarding secret information of importance to national security. They refused to apply an account of profits in favour of Hendrix's estate, instead taking an approach similar to the *Wrotham*

---

26 [2003] EWCA Civ 323, [2003] 1 All ER (Comm) 830.

Park case, calculating an amount based on how much they would have been charged for an agreement to license the recordings in question.

ANALYSING THE LAW

What these cases therefore provide is not legal certainty. If you look at these decisions (and look further into the judgments of these cases) then you will see that the overall picture is not particularly helpful in defining in what circumstances an account of profits could be used.

You should think about what these cases do provide, and this can help you to understand the limitations of this principle. Consider further:

- What problem is this principle intended to solve?
- What important principles do these cases provide us with?
- What questions/definitions are still unanswered?
- Does this principle provide a fair solution to the problem it was intended to solve?

14.12 TIME LIMITS

When seeking remedies for breach of contract, there are important time limits to bear in mind, as laid down by the Limitation Act 1980. The standard limitation term for breach of contract is six years from the time of the 'cause of action'.[27] This usually refers to the point that the contract has been breached. Actions for breach cannot be brought once the time limit has expired; however, it is subject to a number of exceptions (see Figure 14.4).

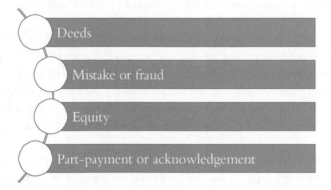

Deeds

Mistake or fraud

Equity

Part-payment or acknowledgement

Figure 14.4 Exceptions to the six-year time limit

---

27 Limitation Act 1980, s. 5.

14.12.1 DEEDS

As previously mentioned in Chapter 3, the limitation period for any contract made by way of deed is doubled to 12 years. This is seen as one of the advantages of making an agreement by deed.

14.12.2 MISTAKE OR FRAUD

Section 32 of the Limitation Act 1980 provides an exception for situations where the cause of action has been concealed by mistake or fraud. If the innocent party is unaware of the cause of action because of this, the six-year period does not start until the innocent party is aware of the problem, or a reasonable person in their circumstances would be aware of it.

14.12.3 EQUITY

Section 36 covers equitable claims, i.e. injunctions, specific performance, etc. The six-year period does not apply under what is referred to as the doctrine of 'laches'. This provides a rather vague idea that, based on the circumstances, a claimant may be able to bring an action much later than the six-year limited period. If the claimant is deemed to have taken too long to bring an action without justification for why this is the case, the equitable remedy may be refused. However, this in itself is also rather vague as it is based upon the circumstances of each individual case as to whether the court is willing to uphold a claim.

14.12.4 PART-PAYMENT OR ACKNOWLEDGEMENT

Section 30 allows the six-year period to be extended in situations where a debt is either partially paid, or the debtor acknowledges that there is a debt without dispute. This only applies to financial (liquidated) claims rather than any other form of obligation. The six-year period is re-started on the date of either the acknowledgement or the part-payment.

14.13 BRINGING IT ALL TOGETHER

Equitable remedies are an important aspect of resolving contractual breaches. They are intended to provide a fairer result, in situations where the legal remedy of damages may be inadequate or inappropriate to resolve the breach that has occurred. It is important to remember that they are at the discretion of the judge in the case concerned, and so it is important that they are convinced that it is necessary for them to be applied in order to produce an equitable result.

As we have seen in this chapter, there are remedies that can help to resolve the gaps that may be left by problems created when there is no valid contract, and this is where restitution and its related principles can provide an equitable solution when a strict adherence to the rules of contract would leave parties without a remedy.

KEY LEARNING POINTS

Equitable remedies provide for situations where:

- A person may be compelled to perform contractual obligations (specific performance)
- A person may be prevented from carrying out certain actions in breach of a contract (injunctions)
- There are limitations on when such orders can be granted to do with the discretion of the court and restrictions on personal liberty.

There are remedies available when it appears that, due to a failure of the contract, there is no right to damages:

- Restitution which recognises a right to a remedy outside the contractual relationship
- Account of profits in exceptional circumstances.

There are time limits on how long a person has to bring an action for remedies for breach of contract.

TAKING IT FURTHER

Beaatson, 'Courts, arbitrators and restitutionary liability or breach of contract' (2002) 118 LQR 377

Beatson & Burrows, *Anson's Law of Contract*, 29th edn, Oxford University Press, 2010

Carter and Tolhurst, 'Restitution for failure of consideration' (1997) 11 JCL 162

Hedley, 'Very much the wrong people: The House of Lords and publication of spy memoirs' (2000) 4 Web JCLI

Peel, *Treitel on the Law of Contract*, 14th edn, Sweet & Maxwell, 2015

Schwartz, 'The case for specific performance' (1979) 89 Yale LJ 271

15

CHAPTER 15
THIRD PARTIES
Privity and agency

15.1 INTRODUCTION

Much of what is discussed regarding the law of contract refers to rights and responsibilities of the parties to the contract. However, contracts, and the parties that enter into them, do not exist in a vacuum, and therefore the law of contract must also take into account the fact that there are external factors that affect contracts, and vice versa; that contracts will have an effect upon persons who are not parties to the contract.

This chapter aims to focus upon those issues and, in particular, where non-contractual parties can have an effect upon contracts, and be affected by those contracts. What this does is recognise the wider context within which contract law sits, and is one way that you can think about how it affects society as a whole, not just those people who enter into contractual agreements. Traditionally, contract law operated independently of those factors, and we will examine this traditional position first, through the concept of privity of contract. We will then go on to examine the circumstances where contract law has allowed exceptions to the traditional rule, specifically concerning the rights of third parties, and also the doctrine of agency.

AS YOU READ

At the end of this chapter you should be able to:

- Understand the position of third parties in contract law
- Determine the difference between those third parties with no rights or influence over a contract and those that do
- Apply the rules regarding third party rights to show those contracts where third-party rights must be taken into account
- Understand the role of agents in entering into contracts on behalf of others

---

15.2 PRIVITY OF CONTRACT

The traditional approach to contract law was seen through the doctrine of **privity of contract**. This concept therefore excluded anyone who was not a party to a contract from being able to get involved in any legal action over that contract.

ESSENTIAL DEFINITION: PRIVITY OF CONTRACT

The concept that only parties to the contract have any right to sue or be sued under that agreement. Parties to the contract are those that have entered into the agreement and therefore voluntarily promised to undertake obligations under that agreement.

This simple common law rule ensured that the only people who were in a position to bring any legal action regarding a contract were those that had entered into the agreement. Anyone not considered to be a party to the contract would have no legal standing and therefore legally would be irrelevant to any issues that might arise.

There are essentially two parts to this rule: firstly, a person may not sue unless they are privy to the contract and, secondly, a person may not be sued unless they are privy to the contract. It is the first of these two requirements that has tended to cause the most issues, predominantly because it ignores the possibility that others may be intended to benefit from a contract without being a party to it. In effect, it treats the parties to an agreement as if they are completely isolated from the rest of the world.

The exclusion demonstrated by this rule can be shown in the case of *Dunlop Pneumatic Tyre Co Ltd v Selfridge & Co Ltd*,[1] a case we first encountered in Chapter 3.

DUNLOP PNEUMATIC TYRE CO LTD V SELFRIDGE & CO LTD [1915] AC 79

This case involved a dispute between the manufacturer of tyres, and the ultimate retailer of those tyres. The dispute arose because the manufacturer had inserted a clause into their contract that required sellers to undertake not to sell those tyres below a minimum retail price.

Held: because of the rule of privity, the parties could not sue each other as they were not parties to the same contract together. Therefore, the attempt by Dunlop to enforce the minimum retail price clause was unsuccessful. They would have to rely upon the party that had entered into a direct contractual relationship with Selfridge to sue them, as they were unable to do so themselves.

The two parties involved here had not entered into a contract with each other. They were at opposite ends of a chain of contractual agreements, whereby the minimum retail price clause had been passed down from manufacturer to wholesaler, then to the retailer. Such a chain is illustrated in Figure 15.1.

---

1   [1915] AC 79.

Figure 15.1 Chain of contractual agreements as in *Dunlop v Selfridge*

As we saw in Chapter 3, there was a problem with Dunlop's ability to bring an action against Selfridge, due to the complicated contractual situation between them. In Chapter 3, we focussed upon the consideration issue, but the case also illustrated the operation of privity of contract, namely that the parties were not connected by the same contractual agreement. They were therefore not able to sue each other under the contracts they had entered into, even though those contracts were connected by a chain of agreements.

ANALYSING THE LAW

CRITICISM OF THE PRIVITY RULE

This decision might seem a little harsh in the circumstances – the parties here were not completely unconnected, but rather their relationship was an indirect one. However, the strict common law application of the doctrine of privity therefore means that they were unable to take action against one another. The privity rule follows the logic that, because a contract is an agreement, voluntarily entered into by two or more parties, it is only those parties that have any rights or obligations under that agreement. To subject any other person to any obligations would be unfair as they have not had a say in those obligations, and therefore, because of this, the same should apply to rights as well.

It is possible to see the logic behind why someone should not be subject to obligations if they have not agreed to a contract, but because of this it must also follow that the same rule be applied to rights, even though this part of the privity rule might be seen as harsh.

A modern example of the strict application of the privity rule can be seen in the case of *BBC v HarperCollins Publishers Ltd.*

BBC V HARPERCOLLINS PUBLISHERS LTD [2010] EWHC 2424 (CH)

This case concerned an action between the BBC and the publishers HarperCollins regarding an autobiography they were about to publish by the man who had been 'the Stig' on BBC's *Top Gear* between 2003 and 2010. The case mainly revolved around an issue of confidentiality; however, there was also a privity of contract issue here regarding the enforceability of confidentiality clauses in the contract involved.

Ben Collins was the man who had played the Stig, but the contract in which there was an agreement to keep the identity of the Stig secret had been between the BBC and Ben Collins' management company. The contract had been signed by Collins, but only in his capacity as director of that company.

Held: Collins was therefore not personally privy to the contract. As a result, his management company would instead be liable.

ASSESSMENT TIP

This case does require you to understand the nature of companies as legal entities. A company has 'legal personality', and so can enter into contracts in its own right, so is liable for the contracts it enters into, and its directors and shareholders have only indirect and limited involvement.

You should bear things like this in mind when dealing with situations involving companies, due to their legal position.

This case demonstrates the isolating effect of the privity rule in this situation. The case concerned the BBC's attempts to gain an injunction to prevent the publication of the autobiography because it revealed Collins as the Stig, but the court held that Collins was not bound by the confidentiality clause in the contract due to not personally being privy to the contract. The consequences for the company, however, would have been different. The BBC's main aim would have been preventing the revelation of the name of the Stig, and therefore suing Collins' management company after the unveiling of the Stig would have been of limited importance to them.

KEY LEARNING POINT

There are, however, several compelling reasons why the privity rule makes sense, and therefore why it remains part of the law today. Firstly, because a contract is based upon agreement, it ensures that only those that are part of that agreement are obligated under the contract. This is the second part of the privity rule discussed above, and this provides the strongest argument for its retention. Secondly, if the rule isolates the parties from all other persons when it comes to benefits and liabilities, it also means that variations to the contract can be made without having to factor in the effect that it has on third parties.

15.3 RELATIONSHIP TO CONSIDERATION

This rule of privity is closely linked to the requirement of consideration that was discussed at length in Chapter 3. This is because the provision of something of value (consideration) and being a party to the contract are closely linked. For an example of these two principles operating together, see the case of *Tweddle v Atkinson*.[2] This privity case also included the principle that consideration must move from the promisee, firmly linking the concept of privity of contract and the requirement for consideration.

Problems created by this rule were seen in operation in the case of *Beswick v Beswick*.

BESWICK V BESWICK [1968] AC 58, HL

A man sold his business to his nephew and, as part of the agreement, the nephew promised to pay £5 a week to his uncle's wife after the uncle died. The problem here arose because of the wife's position as a third party who had not provided any consideration in the deal, and therefore under the privity rule would not be able to sue for the £5 in the event of it not being paid.

Held: as the wife was also the administratrix of her dead husband's estate, she would have privity to sue in that capacity, but as the payments were to the wife and not to the estate, the estate had not lost anything and therefore had nothing to sue the nephew for.

This case therefore creates a 'black hole' between what the estate could sue for but had no reason to, and what the wife had reason to sue for but could not. Situations such as this show why reform of the law was subsequently called for. There was also an unsuccessful attempt at involving a third party in the case of *Woodar Investment Development Ltd v Wimpey Construction UK Ltd*.

WOODAR INVESTMENT DEVELOPMENT LTD V WIMPEY CONSTRUCTION UK LTD [1980] 1 ALL ER 571

This case involved the purchase of a piece of land for development purposes. The contract also involved a third party, as it stated that as well as the £850,000 purchase price, a further £150,000 was to be paid to a third party on completion. When the purchaser tried to repudiate the contract due to a compulsory purchase order which had been placed on the land, the seller sued for damages for themselves and also the third party.

---

2   (1861) 1 B & S 393.

Held: although the Court of Appeal allowed this (through their use of the judgment in *Jackson v Horizon Holidays Ltd³*), when the matter was appealed to the House of Lords (now the Supreme Court), the Lords allowed the appeal and therefore did not allow damages to be claimed on behalf of the third party. Although they did not overrule the *Jackson* decision, they claimed that it was confined to particular circumstances and not applicable to this case. The privity rule applied in this case correctly because of the lack of consideration supplied by the third party.

15.4 REFORM

The privity rule, particularly when it comes to conferring a benefit on a third party, has come in for some heavy judicial criticism, and therefore there has long been an appetite for its reform. This was first discussed by the Law Revision Committee in 1937.[4] However, despite clear advice from the committee that where a contract confers a benefit upon a third party this should be enforceable by that third party, nothing was done in response to this report, and judges continued to engage in the kind of judicial activism that can be seen in the cases already mentioned in this chapter. Although it might be seen as appropriate for the judiciary to be taking action to address the issues raised by privity of contract in specific cases where it produces harsh results, there were comments from judges that it was not appropriate for this to come from them.[5]

Matters in this area began to move forward again with the Law Commission issuing a consultation paper[6] in 1991, followed by a report[7] in 1996. The 1996 report also included a draft bill to be considered for enactment by Parliament. This demonstrated much clearer support for the idea of third parties having an involvement in contracts, despite the rule of privity.

ASSESSMENT TIP

The important thing to emphasise here is that the discussion on this matter relates exclusively to the ability of third parties to enforce *rights* under the contract, and therefore there was never any suggestion that contracts should be enforceable *against*

3   [1975] 3 All ER 92: see later in this chapter for discussion of this case.
4   Law Revision Committee 6th Interim Report, Cmd 5449.
5   For example, see the comments of Viscount Simmonds in *Scruttons Ltd v Midland Silicones Ltd* [1962] AC 446, who thought that changes to the law needed to come from legislation, not from case law.
6   Consultation Paper No. 121, Privity of Contract: Contracts for the Benefit of Third Parties, 1991.
7   Law Commission Report No. 242, Privity of Contract: Contracts for the Benefit of Third Parties, 1996.

third parties. This is in line with cases that had arisen prior to the reform, which had predominantly been about the ability of third parties to enforce rights.

It is therefore important to bear in mind that where considering the involvement of third parties in a contractual situation, this is a matter that does not result in liability falling on the third party.

This activity in the 1990s eventually led to an Act of Parliament enshrining the principle of third party benefits into UK law, with the Contracts (Rights of Third Parties) Act 1999.

15.5 CONTRACTS (RIGHTS OF THIRD PARTIES) ACT 1999

The effect that this Act has had upon the privity rule discussed above has been significant. It has done what several of the previously mentioned cases hinted at or tried to do, and have allowed third parties to be involved in the first part of the privity rule: the ability to enforce benefits under a contract (see Figure 15.1).

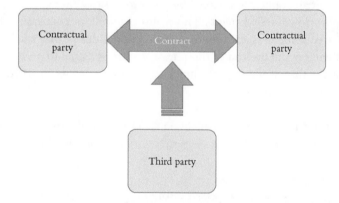

Figure 15.2 Third party enforcement of benefits under a contract

APPLYING THE LAW

Consider the effect that this Act, and third parties being given rights, has upon cases that we have looked at so far. For example, looking back at the *Beswick v Beswick* case mentioned earlier: if the 1999 Act had been in place at the time of this case, Mrs Beswick would have been able to enforce the £5 per week benefit she was entitled to under the contract without having to rely upon one of the parties doing this for her. This type of situation led to the criticisms that the rule was unfair to particular situations and therefore its inflexibility led to injustice.

15.5.1 SECTION 1: ENFORCEABILITY OF CONTRACTS BY THIRD PARTIES

Section 1(1) of the Act directly strikes out the rule under privity that prohibits third parties from enforcing contracts. It sets out two circumstances in which it is possible for a third party to enforce a right that they are entitled to under a contract:

1) where the contract expressly provides that he may or
2) a term in the contract purports to confer a benefit on him.

Rather than an all-encompassing right for third parties however, s. 1(1) focusses upon two situations that have clearly been illustrated as demonstrating injustice. The first of these allows the parties to a contract to expressly name the third party and therefore ensure that they will be able to enforce the rights that they are giving to that third party. This is surely the most straightforward part of s. 1. However, it excludes those who have not been mentioned by name in the contract. This may be because it was unclear who those parties were at the time of the agreement, or alternatively it may be because they did not exist at that time. This potential loophole was closed by the second situation in s. 1, those to whom the contract 'purports to confer a benefit'. This is also not without controversy, however, as some contractual arrangements, such as in the construction industry, may result in a chain of agreements, and therefore the breadth of this phrase has the potential to produce some rather complicated situations that would require unpicking in order to establish whether anyone has a benefit conferred upon them.

The concept of 'purporting to confer a benefit' in s. 1(1)(b) was discussed in *Dolphin & Maritime & Aviation Services Ltd v Sveriges Angfartygs Assurans Forening, The Swedish Club*.

DOLPHIN & MARITIME & AVIATION SERVICES LTD V SVERIGES ANGFARTYGS ASSURANS FORENING, THE SWEDISH CLUB [2009] EWHC 716 (COMM)

This case involved a ship that had been involved in a collision. The underwriters of the ship had agreed that money recovered to compensate for the collision was to be paid by The Swedish Club via Dolphin, who were recovery agents for the underwriters of the damaged ship. However, the matter was settled when the underwriters were paid the sum owed directly by The Swedish Club, without going through Dolphin. Had the money gone via Dolphin, they would have extracted their commission before the remainder of the money was passed on. Dolphin brought an action to recover the commission because they had not been able to deduct it from the sum paid.

Held: Dolphin were unsuccessful in their claim because they were unable to show that they were the intended beneficiaries of the agreement. The underwriters were, as the agreement was merely a means by which the money was to be paid to the underwriters. They could not argue that the contract 'purported to confer a benefit' to Dolphin, although they had lost out financially by not being able to take their commission; however, they had not handled the money either.

This case shows that there is a difference between a party gaining financially as a result of an agreement, and that agreement clearly conferring a benefit to that party directly from the nature of the contract itself.

Other issues have arisen with regard to this part of s. 1(1)(b), because of its relationship with s. 1(2). This is because s. 1(2) disapplies s. 1(1)(b) if 'on a proper construction of the contract it appears that the parties did not intend the term to be enforceable by the third party'. There are examples of where this has been the case, and it has therefore made rights unenforceable by third parties.

NISSHIN SHIPPING V CLEAVES [2003] EWHC 2602

This case involved Cleaves, who were chartering brokers. It was their role to arrange charterparties between the owners of vessels and charterers. In this role, they had arranged a number of charterparties for Nisshin Shipping Co Ltd, who owned their own ships and were intending to hire them out on charterparties to others. In the agreements, there was a clause in which Nisshin agreed to pay a 1% commission to Cleaves (through a 2% payment made that was to be split equally between Cleaves and another company, Ifchor). There was also an arbitration clause in the contract, which was to allow disputes under the contract to be arbitrated.

A problem arose when Nisshin failed to pay Cleaves the agreed commission and Cleaves therefore needed to enforce the term in the contract concerning the commission. However, as they were not parties to the contract, they had to rely upon third party rights under the Contracts (Rights of Third Parties) Act 1999. They argued that the commission clause 'purported to convey a benefit' upon Cleaves under s. 1(1)(b).

Nisshin argued that s. 1(2) prevented this because 'on a proper construction of the contract it appears that the parties did not intend the term to be enforceable by the third party'. However, this was based upon a lack of language expressly allowing Cleaves to enforce the commission clause.

Held: on a proper construction of the contract, there was clearly a benefit to Cleaves, namely the commission. Also, s. 1(2) was not applicable here because there was nothing within the contract that indicated the intention of the parties was that the commission clause should not be enforceable by Cleaves. The court held that if there is no clear intention either way within the contract, this is not enough, as s. 1(2) requires an apparent intention that it be not enforceable. Any other interpretation of the contract that was missing that intention would therefore allow the clause to be enforced by the third party. The key here is that s. 1(2) requires a deliberate exclusion of the third party from gaining a benefit under s. 1(1)(b), not merely a lack of express intention to include them. This construction of s. 1(2) therefore puts the third party in the position of being able to acquire the benefit, unless there is a clear intention revealed to exclude them from this.

This approach to s. 1(2) was confirmed in the case of *Cavanagh v Secretary of State for Work and Pensions*,[8] where union membership fees were deducted from the wages of employees of the Department for Work and Pensions at source by the employer. The court found that this was a contract between the DWP and the employee, and that the union was a third party with the ability under the 1999 Act to enforce the right to these payments. Section 1(2) was also discussed in *The Laemthong Glory (No. 2)*.

LAEMTHONG INTERNATIONAL LINES CO. LTD V ARTIS, THE LAEMTHONG GLORY (NO. 2) [2005] EWCA CIV 519, [2005] 2 ALL ER (COMM) 167, [2005] 1 LLOYD'S REP 688, [2005] ALL ER (D) 50 (MAY)

This case concerned a letter of indemnity (LOI) issued at the end of a voyage. The contract in this case was a charterparty, concerning the ship owners, the charterers, and the receivers of the goods at the destination. The receivers were required to produce the bill of lading upon receipt of the cargo, and did not have them at the time that the goods were delivered by the ship owners. Therefore, an LOI was produced, to which the charterers and receivers were party, indemnifying the charterers, as well as their servants and agents against the consequences of delivering the goods without a bill of lading being produced.

Held: the ship owners were classed as 'agents' for the purposes of the LOI and therefore covered as third parties by the indemnity. Although they were not named, under s. 1(1)(b) the LOI purported to confer a benefit upon them, and there was nothing in the LOI that would indicate that under s. 1(2) there was an intention not to include them as a third party.

8   [2016] EWHC 1136.

Section 1(2) therefore appears to cover quite a narrow set of circumstances regarding those who would be excluded from s. 1(1)(b), and case law demonstrates where judges will take a generally broad approach to defining whether there appears to be a deliberate intent to exclude certain parties.

The case of *Prudential Assurance Co Ltd v Ayres*[9] was one where the phrase 'any previous tenant' was held to include a previous tenant who had assigned the lease to the current tenant, but in assigning the lease had included a guarantee to the landlord regarding payment of rent if the current tenant failed to pay. A deed had been executed by the current tenant limiting the liability of the current individuals in the partnership that had taken out the lease, but had also included the wording mentioned above. There was nothing in the agreement to suggest that s. 1(2) could strike out any benefits purported to be conferred to the third party (the previous tenants) here, and therefore the court applied s. 1(1)(b).

Ultimately the decision of Linsay J was overturned by the Court of Appeal,[10] but only on a matter of construction, which resulted in the deed being held not to apply to the guarantee of the previous tenant. But the principle regarding the relationship between s. 1(1)(b) and s. 1(2) applies here.

Finally, s. 1(3) requires that the 'third party must be expressly identified in the contract by name, as a member of a class or as answering to a particular description but need not be in existence when the contract is entered into'.

This on the face of it appears to be restrictive in that it requires express identification of the third party to benefit, but the commercial reality that many parties will not be specifically identified by name in certain situations is dealt with by the latter parts of the subsection. A certain class or category of persons is enough to identify who generally should benefit, e.g. a particular type of subcontractor or class of individuals. However, the courts have been careful to avoid the possibility of rights in contracts being thrown open to a wide group of third parties.

For example, in the case of *Avraamides v Colwill*[11] the court was unwilling to give a benefit under a contract to persons who may have liability claims, but were in 'a large number of unidentified classes'.

AVRAAMIDES V COLWILL [2006] EWCA CIV 1533, [2007] BLR 76

The case involved the transfer of the assets and the liabilities of a company to a limited liability partnership. The agreement involved an undertaking to 'complete outstanding

---

9 [2007] EWHC 775 Ch, [2007] 3 All ER 946.
10 See *Prudential Assurance Co Ltd v Ayres* [2008] EWCA Civ 52 for the Court of Appeal judgment.
11 [2006] EWCA Civ 1533, [2007] BLR 76.

customer orders ... and to pay in the normal course of time any liabilities properly incurred by the company'. The company had refurbished a bathroom prior to transfer of the business to the partnership. The customer was dissatisfied, and attempted to hold the partnership liable, in line with the transfer agreement. As the agreement was between the original company and the partnership that took over their business, the customer was a third party and so would have to rely upon third party rights under the 1999 Act.

Held: the word 'express' under s. 1(3) did not allow third parties who may benefit from the contract to be construed or implied, but it had to be an identifiable third party, in line with the requirements of s. 1(3). The part of the contract that required the partnership to take on liabilities would benefit third parties, but it would be a large and unidentified group of third parties. This would therefore not fall under s. 1(3) and so the customer would not be able to enforce a third party right under the transfer agreement.

What s. 1 attempts to do is to balance the need to identify situations where a third party ought to have enforceable rights, in order to tackle the issues mentioned earlier in this chapter, with the need to ensure that where parties are clear and explicit regarding their language in the contract, they can exclude third parties from enforcing benefits. It is a tricky line to walk, as we have seen from the above cases.

15.5.2 SECTION 2: VARIATION AND RESCISSION

Another area that would affect third party rights is with regard to any alteration to the contract as, where third party rights are identified, they can also be affected by any variation or rescission of the contract by the parties. Section 2(1) addresses this issue:

where a third party has a right under section 1 to enforce a term of the contract, the parties to the contract may not, by agreement, rescind the contract, or vary it in such a way as to extinguish or alter his entitlement under that right, without his consent if –

(a) the third party has communicated his assent to the term to the promisor,
(b) the promisor is aware that the third party has relied on the term, or
(c) the promisor can reasonably be expected to have foreseen that the third party would rely on the term and the third party has in fact relied on it.

This avoids the possibility that any rights gained by a third party might be removed by the parties to the contract either changing or removing their rights altogether, in situations where the third party is aware of rights, has made it clear they are in agreement with those rights, or has relied upon them. A third party can show their consent by words or conduct under s. 2(2).

This has the effect of providing safeguards while not tying the hands of contracting parties completely, as the provisions in s. 2(4) and (5) allow the court to dispense with the consent of the third party in certain circumstances such as where they cannot be found, or are mentally incapable of consenting under s. 2(1)(a). Section 2(6) also allows for compensation to be paid to the third party in the event of third party consent being dispensed with.

15.5.3 SECTION 3: DEFENCES AVAILABLE TO PROMISOR

Section 3 provides situations in which a third party cannot enforce a contract. It refers to the 'promisor', who generally would be considered to be the contracting party who owes the obligation to the third party. The purpose of this section is to ensure that a contract is not absolutely enforceable by third parties in all situations but, like situations where contracting parties are suing each other, that there will be certain defences and exceptions available against a third party. These broadly split into three categories. Section 3(2) deals with 'defence[s] and set-off[s]'. Essentially a contracting party can rely upon anything that 'would have been available to him by way of defence or set-off if the proceedings had been brought by the promisee' (s. 3(2)(b)). This covers situations such as void contracts, unenforceable contracts or discharged contracts, which would not be enforceable by the other party to the contract, so should not be enforceable by a third party either. It also covers 'set-offs', which in a normal contractual situation covers where contracting parties involved in a law suit can 'set off' money owed by one party to the other, against any money they gain in suing the other party.

APPLYING THE LAW

We can see how third parties can be involved in the set-off situation in the following example.

If party A and party B are in a contract together, and party C is a third party with rights under that contract, a set-off clause could be used in the contract that would affect the amount of money that C might be able to claim.

So, if A entered into an agreement with B for refurbishment of their premises, and in the agreement the money for the refurbishment was to be paid to C, if a set-off clause exists in the contract it would allow any money that B owed to A to be set off against the money owed by A to C. This would therefore reduce the amount of money that A owed under the contract.

15.6 EXCEPTIONS TO THE ACT

The Contracts (Rights of Third Parties) Act 1999 appears to put third parties in quite a strong position in situations where they are connected with a contract, but it is important to bear in mind that the extent to which they can exert influence and control is limited. There are specific exceptions provided for in s. 6 for example. Section 6(1) excludes bills of exchange, promissory notes and other negotiable instruments from the third-party rights in s. 1. The same is also true of contracts binding on a company and its members under s. 33 of the Companies Act 2006, under s. 6(2).

There are also certain restrictions that apply to those employed or considered a 'worker'. This includes those who are home workers or agency workers, under s. 6(3)(b) and (c). This effectively means that employees' contractual terms are a matter for their employers only and not, for example, a client of the company. The client would still have the ability to enforce the contract that they have with the company, but cannot be involved in the way that the company deals with workers who may have breached one of the rights the client has under its contract with the company.

APPLYING THE LAW
────────────

This can be explained by the following example.

> Winston has paid Pro-Satellite for a satellite TV installation. They send a fitter, Derek, to carry out the installation. There is a clause in Derek's contract that prevents him from eating or smoking on the client's premises, to avoid any potential damage or hazard on the client's premises. The penalty is summary dismissal. Derek is caught smoking in Winston's house, and he causes damage from the discarded cigarettes.

> Because of s. 6(3), Winston could not insist that Derek is sacked, but is still able to claim from Pro-Satellite under the contract.

Contracts for carriage of goods are also excluded under s. 6. Whether carriage by sea, air, road or rail, the intention is that they are dealt with by the relevant transport conventions rather than by the 1999 Act. For example, rail carriage is dealt with by the Railways (Convention on International Carriage by Rail) Regulations 2005.[12]

One exception to this is with regard to an area discussed in Chapter 6 of this book regarding exclusion clauses, and also discussed later in this chapter. The effect of the Act means that those relying on exclusion clauses as agents or subcontractors, such as the *Himalaya* clauses

---

12 S.I. 2005/2092.

used in regard to stevedores loading and unloading sea cargo, can get the benefit of those clauses as third parties to the agreement.

ANALYSING THE LAW

The most significant type of exclusion comes through self-help. It is important to remember that the effect of the 1999 Act is limited in situations where the parties in drafting the agreement have the presence of mind to include express language in the contract to exclude third parties' rights. Appropriate drafting can expressly exclude the rights of third parties, and this can be by specifically referring to the parties involved (if known) or by excluding certain classes of parties from the agreement. The effect of this would be to nullify s. 1 of the Act, as the two parts of this that we discussed earlier cover those expressly provided for, or where the contract purports to give a benefit. This means that the parties to the contract still retain a great deal of control regarding the rights of third parties, if exercised at the drafting stage. An appropriately and professionally drafted contract should therefore not leave any loopholes for third party rights where the parties do not wish them to be.

Ultimately, therefore, the Act has provided a valuable solution to some problems identified in earlier case law regarding third party rights, within certain boundaries, rather than a general method of introducing the concept of third party rights. It resolves issues such as that identified in the case of *White v Jones*.[13] The court in this case identified an 'undesirable lacuna', which was caused by the beneficiary of a will not being a party to the contract with solicitors to draw that will up; the beneficiary was therefore a third party. Although the court resolved that issue by holding that a duty was owed to the widow, which could be enforced, the 1999 Act provides a more certain and straightforward solution to issues such as this regarding third parties.

15.7 CIRCUMVENTING THE DOCTRINE

Although a sound principle in theory, the above discussion shows how in practice the doctrine of privity was prone to producing injustice in particular situations. However, rather than removing the doctrine of privity altogether, there are a number of specific circumstances in which the doctrine has been circumvented. This has mainly been because, although the doctrine of privity cannot be said to be perfect, it is not so imperfect that it should be removed altogether. The main benefits of a doctrine of privity of contract have been in restricting obligations in a contract to the parties of that contract, whereas the criticisms have

---

13 [1995] 2 AC 207, [1995] 1 All ER 691.

(as we have seen above) been about restricting the benefits of the contract to contractual parties. As we will see below, the circumstances in which the doctrine has been circumvented have tended to be those where a benefit to a third party is involved.

15.7.1 AGENCY

One way in which the doctrine of privity has been circumvented is with regard to **agency**. Where a party can be said to be acting as agent for another, it is possible for the doctrine that might exclude them as a third party to be circumvented. This therefore allows agents to enter into contractual agreements on behalf of others. It allows those others to be capable of enforcing benefits under that contract; however, it also means that they can be subject to obligations as well, as agency effectively treats that third party as a party to the contract.

ESSENTIAL DEFINITION: AGENCY

Agency explains the situation whereby an agent contracts with another party on behalf of another (the principal). The agent is therefore not making an agreement with rights and obligations that he will be bound by; but the principal will be bound (see Figure 15.3).

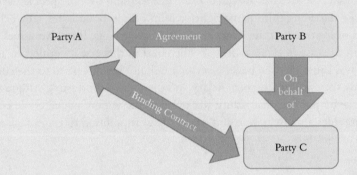

Figure 15.3 An example of an agency relationship: Party B acting as agent for Party C

This therefore goes against the general principle in the doctrine of privity, as it brings the principal into the contractual relationship when they themselves have not made the agreement. However, it does mean that it is possible to bring in another person to negotiate and agree to contracts on the principal's behalf. For example, companies, who are legal persons, cannot make agreements, but rely upon representatives, usually employees, to enter into agreements on their behalf. Authority to act as an agent will fall into one of three categories:

■ **Express authority**: where the principal has specifically requested that the agent enter into a contract on their behalf. This is the easiest to recognise.

- **Implied authority:** this is a little more difficult to recognise, but involves the agent being required to perform a task that, by implication, will involve them entering into a contract on the principal's behalf. For example, if an employee of a printing firm was instructed to complete a print order that required special materials, implied within the situation would be the need to order such materials to complete the order. The employee would be acting as agent for the printing firm in purchasing the materials needed to complete the order.
- **Apparent authority:** this is where, due to past behaviour, the agent creates the impression that they have the right to contract on behalf of the principal. It is important that this is not just as a result of the behaviour of the agent, but there has to be a good reason that leads to this impression being given. An example of this can be seen in the following case.

PHARMED MEDICARE PRIVATE LTD V UNIVAR LTD [2002] EWCA CIV 1569

This case involved an agent who had entered into an order for a product, GSP, used to alleviate the symptoms of arthritis. The principal was the company that the agent worked for and that imported this product into the UK and Ireland for re-sale. The agent had on previous occasions placed small orders for this product on behalf of the company, which were one-off orders of three metric tons or less. However, on this occasion the agent had placed an order for eight metric tons a month for 12 months. The agent was not a director of the company, and the usual order proforma required that orders be appropriately authorised. The company attempted to argue that the agent lacked the appropriate authority to contract on their behalf.

Held: he had ostensible authority to make the contract, and therefore the company was bound by the contract.

15.7.2 COLLATERAL CONTRACTS

Another method of avoiding the application of the privity doctrine is through the use of a collateral contract. This is an additional agreement with one of the parties to the contract that allows a third party to enforce certain rights in the contract. This has also been used as a way of defeating the privity rule purely because the collateral agreement allows effective third-party enforcement of part of the contract.

Scruttons Ltd v Midland Silicones Ltd[14] involved an attempt to argue that an agreement between one of the contracting parties and a third party should allow them to benefit from a clause in the contract, contrary to the rule of privity of contract.

---

14 [1962] AC 446, [1962] 1 All ER 1.

SCRUTTONS V MIDLANDS SILICONES LTD [1962] AC 446, [1962] 1 ALL ER 1

This case concerned an agreement to carry a consignment, a drum of chemicals. The contract was between the consignees and the owners of the ship that was to carry the drum. The bill of lading limited the liability of the ship owners to $500, for loss or damage to the consignment. This limitation clause included 'the ship … her owner, operator and demise charterer, and also any … person to the extent bound by this bill of lading, whether acting as carrier or bailee'.

The ship owners had a contract with stevedores, employed to load and unload cargoes from their ships at the Port of London. The contract they had with them made the stevedores liable for their own negligence, but they benefitted from the protection under the bill of lading, and therefore this would include the clause limiting liability to $500.

When the stevedores unloaded the drum from the ship, through their negligence it was damaged, and the value of the damage exceeded the $500 limit in the bill of lading. The stevedores admitted their negligence but attempted to rely upon the limitation clause. It was established that such agreements to extend limitation of liability to stevedores was common in such commercial agreements; however, this was in conflict with the doctrine of privity.

Attempts to argue that the agreement between the ship owner and the stevedores should allow the stevedores to enforce a benefit from the contract of carriage were unsuccessful.

Held: the court acknowledged that it might be possible for rights to be enforceable where the ship owners could be seen as acting as agents for the stevedores, but there had to be a clear authority to act as agents as well as some consideration provided for this collateral agreement. This was not established in this case. Lord Denning dissented from this judgment.

In his judgment, Lord Reid set out four criteria needed in order to allow the stevedores to benefit from such a limitation or exclusion clause:

1) the bill of lading must make it clear that the stevedore is to be protected by the limitation clause
2) the bill of lading makes it clear that the carrier (in this case the ship owner) is contracting not just for himself but also the stevedores
3) the carrier has authority from the stevedores to do this (although in the absence of this it may be ratified later by the stevedores)
4) any difficulties about consideration moving from the stevedores were overcome.

This decision therefore underlined the need to comply with the rule of privity, regardless of the customary approach in such commercial agreements, and that these types of contract were not exempted from the need to comply with the doctrine. However, it also allowed contracts for carriage of goods by sea to be drafted in such a way that the stevedores could be covered by the limitation clause if Lord Reid's criteria were followed. An attempt to fulfil this was seen in *The Eurymedon*.[15]

The Eurymedon involved a clause drafted to meet the requirements of Lord Reid's test, referred to as a 'Himalaya clause'. It managed to fulfil the criteria mentioned above, although the court had to find that a unilateral contract was made between the ship owners and whoever unloaded the cargo in order to satisfy the fourth criterion. It was seen as artificial, but it achieved the desired end and allowed stevedores to be covered by the contract of carriage's limitation clause. This was acceptable because it meant that the accepted commercial convention was capable of being supported at law.

More generally, the use of a collateral agreement to allow enforcement of rights when a party is not privy to a contract were seen in *Shanklin Pier Ltd v Detel Products Ltd*.

SHANKLIN PIER LTD V DETEL PRODUCTS LTD [1951] 2 KB 854, [1951] 2 ALL ER 471

This case involved a representation by manufacturers of paint that it was suitable for repainting their pier. On this basis, the pier owners engaged contractors to repaint the pier, and made it a requirement that the manufacturer's paint be used. It turned out that the paint was unsuitable, and the owners of the pier suffered a loss as a result.

The trouble here was that the paint manufacturers and the pier owners were not privy to the same contract. Their relationship was indirect, as they each had a contract with the contractors (the pier owners for the repainting of the pier, the manufacturers for supply of paint to carry out the repainting) but not with each other.

Held: the representation from the manufacturers was a warranty, and this was supported by consideration because the pier owners' requirement in their contract with the contractors to use this paint was consideration (see Chapter 3 regarding the nature of consideration). This was therefore a collateral agreement that allowed the pier owners to recover their losses from the manufacturers, as they were liable for breach of this agreement.

ANALYSING THE LAW

What we can see from the examples in this section is an attempt by the courts to make the rights of third parties enforceable in situations where a common-sense approach

---

15 *New Zealand Shipping Co Ltd v AM Satterthwaite & Co Ltd, The Eurymedon* [1975] AC 154.

would suggest that they should be enforceable. By allowing a situation where there is a collateral agreement, it means that the third party's rights can be protected. It also means that the third party can enforce the rights themselves, which may be a major issue where in other circumstances third parties rely upon the contractual party to pursue the matter on behalf of the third party.

15.8 EXCEPTIONS TO THE DOCTRINE

As well as ways of circumventing the doctrine of privity where it would normally apply, there are also exceptions where the courts have allowed decisions that fly in the face of the usual requirement of privity.

15.8.1 DAMAGES ON BEHALF OF ANOTHER

One such example is with regard to the ability to claim damages on behalf of another. It has been accepted in certain circumstances, whether it be for the purposes of convenience on behalf of a group, or because of the contract belonging to a special category of cases requiring this treatment,[16] that it should be possible for a party to the contract to take such action. One key disadvantage is that it does rather rely upon a party to the contract taking such action (as mentioned above) as there is no ability to compel them to do so by a third party.[17] An example of this was shown in *Jackson v Horizon Holidays Ltd*,[18] discussed earlier in this chapter.

JACKSON V HORIZON HOLIDAYS LTD [1975] 1 WLR 1468

This case involved a man who had booked a holiday for himself and his family, which subsequently failed to live up to their expectations. The action was brought by the plaintiff as the person who had entered into a contract for the holiday, but the amount he was claiming for was not just on his own behalf, but also on behalf of his family. Lord Denning felt that the amount awarded was in excess of the losses that the plaintiff himself incurred, but that it was justifiable on the basis that he was claiming on behalf of himself and also his family.

Held: Denning said that although the other family members were not privy to the contract, Jackson should be capable of recovering on their behalf.

16 See Lord Wilberforce's *obiter* comments in *Woodar Investment Development Ltd v Wimpey Construction (UK) Ltd* [1980] 1 WLR 277.
17 See problems with such an approach in the discussion of *Beswick v Beswick* [1968] AC 58 HL, earlier in this chapter.
18 [1975] 1 WLR 1468.

ANALYSING THE LAW

As discussed earlier in this chapter, this approach was ultimately unsuccessful in the case of *Woodar Investment Development Ltd v Wimpey Construction (UK) Ltd.*[19] Woodar was unable to recover damages on behalf of the third party to the contract. However, this case does not rule out this approach more generally, but the court, through this judgment, does appear to disapprove of this particular approach as a general rule.

Lord Wilberforce's comments in *Woodar* suggest two things. Firstly, *Jackson* should be considered to be a special type of case that needed to be treated in this way (and therefore not overruling it but confining it to situations that might result in non-pecuniary losses, like holidays or meals in restaurants, for example). It was felt that such special circumstances were not applicable in *Woodar*. Secondly it was felt that there needed to be some loss incurred by the contracting party to allow them to sue on behalf of a third party, because they would have to be pursuing a remedy for themselves *and* the third party, not just the third party. Logically, it can be seen that this makes sense with reference to the earlier discussion in this chapter of the *Beswick v Beswick* case.

More recently, the approach of the House of Lords was not as strict as that in the *Woodar* case. Although recovery on behalf of third parties was disapproved of as a general principle, it has allowed this to take place where it is clear that there is a loss by a third party that clearly arose from the contract.

Linden Gardens Trust v Lenesta Sludge Disposals[20] was a case where the court was willing to accept that third party losses could be claimed under a contract where it was foreseeable that a breach would cause damage to a third party.

This case concerned a construction contract, which was entered into between the first plaintiff ('Corporation') and the defendants ('McAlpine') for the building of flats, shops and offices. While the construction was still in progress the ownership of the property was transferred from Corporation to a third party. After the development was completed, it was discovered that the work that had been carried out was defective, leading to part of the property leaking. Remedial work to the value of £800,000 was carried out, and the corporation and the third party attempted to sue the building contractor, McAlpine, for damages to cover the repair costs.

The third party was unable to sue due to not being a party to the original construction contract, and when Corporation, who was a party to the contract, attempted to sue, they were

19 [1980] 1 WLR 277.
20 [1984] 1 AC 85, [1993] 3 WLR 408, [1993] 3 All ER 417.

only awarded nominal damages as they were not affected by the breach, due to no longer being the owners of the property.

The case was appealed to the Court of Appeal, who disagreed with the judgment, and awarded substantial damages to Corporation, the original owner of the property. The matter was appealed to the House of Lords, who agreed with the judgment of the Court of Appeal. Lord Browne-Wilkinson gave the main judgment, and said the following:

> The contract was for a large development of property which, to the knowledge of both Corporation and McAlpine, was going to be occupied, and possibly purchased, by third parties and not by Corporation itself. Therefore it could be foreseen that damage caused by a breach would cause loss to a later owner and not merely to the original contracting party, Corporation.

It was on this basis that he allowed the recovery of substantial damages by Corporation, as it was on behalf of the third party. His Lordship used a principle from contracts for carriage of goods by land, allowing the contracting party to recover on behalf of a third party, specifically because the contract prevented assignment of rights to a third party without both parties' consent. This meant that, without the principle he was applying here, there would be no other way of the third party recovering damages for their loss. Lord Browne-Wilkinson therefore commented that 'it seems to me proper' that the contracting party should be able to recover on the third party's behalf.

This principle was applied in the case of *Darlington Borough Council v Wiltshere Northern Ltd.*

DARLINGTON BOROUGH COUNCIL V WILTSHERE NORTHERN LTD [1995] 3 ALL ER 895, [1995] 1 WLR 68

This case concerned a contract between a finance company and Wiltshire Northern, to build a recreational centre on behalf of Darlington Borough Council. This was done because the council could not contract directly with Wiltshire because of government limits on spending; so instead the finance company would enter into the contract, and the council would reimburse them for the cost of construction later.

The building constructed by Wiltshere Northern was defective and needed £2 million of work to fix it. Because the finance company had no proprietary interest in the land (which was owned by the council) they had no losses, and the council was not a party to the construction contract.

Held: as a third party, they could not recover damages. The Court of Appeal applied the reasoning from the *Linden Gardens* case and allowed the council to recover. The contract was clearly for their benefit, and to prevent them from recovering damages despite being a third party would allow the builders to 'get away scot-free' without liability for a defective building.

What this principle provides is a device for third parties in situations where no liability is owed to the original contracting party, and no legal avenue for third parties, which would result in wrongdoers having no liability at all. The courts have exceptionally allowed third parties to recover in this situation as a commonsense or natural justice solution to the problem.

15.8.2 LIABILITY IN TORT

One of the better-known ways of third parties being able to recover in situations where the rule of privity excludes them is through tortious liability. *Donoghue v Stevenson*[21] provides the principle that a person can claim in tort where privity prevents them from claiming in contract. Donoghue was not a contracting party as they had not purchased the ginger beer in which the decomposing snail was found, and therefore privity of contract prevented an action. However, they were able to recover because it was shown that there was a duty of care owed to them as the consumer of the ginger beer. So, although this establishes liability for third parties, it requires the tortious principle of a duty of care to be established between the parties, which the offending party has breached.

In *Junior Books v Veitchi*[22] the court felt that a company laying a defective floor in a building should be liable even though the parties were not connected by a contract because of a duty of care arising. They felt that it was appropriate in these circumstances because the proximity of the parties was so close that they fell just short of actual privity of contract.

This has created some problems, with *Junior Books* appearing to open the way for a general principle allowing subcontractors to be sued; this therefore goes against the privity principle. This case has been confined to its facts, however; this prevents it from becoming a general principle. This is partially because of the principle against recovery of economic loss in tort.

15.9 OTHER STATUTORY EXCEPTIONS TO PRIVITY

15.9.1 INSURANCE

Generally, insurance contracts are subject to the same rules regarding privity as any other type of contract; however, there are exceptions which involve third parties when it comes to claiming. For example, s. 148(7) of the Road Traffic Act 1988 allows third parties to claim compensation against a motor insurance policy in situations where they have suffered injury or loss as a result of the actions of the driver whose insurance policy it is. Also, s. 11 of the Married Woman's Property Act 1882 allows a widow to claim against life insurance taken out by her spouse. These, however, are clear examples of where statute has provided an express right for third parties, and therefore the privity rule would not apply.

---

21 [1932] AC 562, [1932] All ER Rep 1.
22 [1983] 1 AC 520, [1982] 3 All ER 201, [1982] 3 WLR 477.

Section 56(1) of the Law of Property Act 1925 states:

A person may take an immediate or other interest in land or other property, or the benefit of any condition, right of entry, covenant or agreement over or respecting land or other property, although he may not be named as a party to the conveyance or other instrument.

The best example of this is with regard to restrictive covenants. These are devices that can restrict certain uses of property by the purchaser. They have to be registered on the land register but, if they are, they are enforceable against the purchaser and also anyone the land is subsequently sold to, regardless of privity of contract. For example, a restrictive covenant might restrict the type of use that land is put to, like requiring it be used for residential property only rather than allowing a shop or other business to be established there. A restrictive covenant can also be used to prevent commercial vehicles being parked at a residential property, as often there is a desire to preserve the residential nature of a housing estate, for example.

15.10 BRINGING IT ALL TOGETHER

The rule of privity of contract, despite the many exceptions and exclusions that have been discussed above, is still a valid principle in English law. It is important to remember that the general principle still applies; that only parties to a contract should be allowed to sue under that contract.

This very traditional view has, however, been qualified by a number of exceptions, mainly to reflect the fact that contracts do not exist in a vacuum, but instead are part of a wider context in society, and contract law is supposed to adapt to the needs of society. These exceptions and exclusions will need to be remembered and, when dealing with a particular contractual situation, you will need to evaluate whether any of them apply to that situation or whether the general rule is still relevant.

KEY LEARNING POINTS

Privity of contract means that only those party to a contract may enforce its provisions or be obliged to act according to them. However, remember the following key exceptions to this:

- There are a number of devices for circumventing the doctrine, like for example agency or collateral agreements
- The Contracts (Rights of Third Parties) Act 1999 provides certain specific situations in which third parties are entitled to rights

- There are key exceptions to the doctrine of privity, for example a party to the contract recovering on behalf of a third party, or through the application of tort law
- There are several small statutory exceptions that apply to specific circumstances.

Despite these exceptions and exclusions, the general rule of privity still stands. This is because, as a general rule, it is still seen as valid, and only inapplicable in certain situations. Had it been considered generally invalid, it would have been removed altogether rather than allowing a long list of exceptions and exclusions.

TAKING IT FURTHER

Andrews, 'Strangers to justice no longer – the reversal of the privity rule under the Contracts (Rights of Third Parties) Act 1999' (2001) 60 CLJ 353

Beatson & Burrows, *Anson's Law of Contract*, 29th edn, Oxford University Press, 2010

Macmillan, 'A birthday present for Lord Denning: The Contracts (Rights of Third Parties) Act 1999' (2000) 63 MLR 721

Peel, *Treitel on the Law of Contract*, 14th edn, Sweet & Maxwell, 2015

Stevens, 'The Contracts (Rights of Third Parties) Act 1999' (2004) 120 LQR 292

INDEX